Raising the Red Flag

Historical Materialism Book Series

The Historical Materialism Book Series is a major publishing initiative of the radical left. The capitalist crisis of the twenty-first century has been met by a resurgence of interest in critical Marxist theory. At the same time, the publishing institutions committed to Marxism have contracted markedly since the high point of the 1970s. The Historical Materialism Book Series is dedicated to addressing this situation by making available important works of Marxist theory. The aim of the series is to publish important theoretical contributions as the basis for vigorous intellectual debate and exchange on the left.

The peer-reviewed series publishes original monographs, translated texts, and reprints of classics across the bounds of academic disciplinary agendas and across the divisions of the left. The series is particularly concerned to encourage the internationalization of Marxist debate and aims to translate significant studies from beyond the English-speaking world.

For a full list of titles in the Historical Materialism Book Series available in paperback from Haymarket Books, visit: www.haymarketbooks.org/series_collections/1-historical-materialism.

Raising the Red Flag

*Marxism, Labourism, and the Roots
of British Communism, 1884–1921*

Tony Collins

Haymarket Books
Chicago, IL

First published in 2023 by Brill Academic Publishers, The Netherlands
© 2023 Koninklijke Brill NV, Leiden, The Netherlands

Published in paperback in 2024 by
Haymarket Books
P.O. Box 180165
Chicago, IL 60618
773-583-7884
www.haymarketbooks.org

ISBN: 979-8-88890-218-9

Distributed to the trade in the US through Consortium Book Sales and
Distribution (www.cbsd.com) and internationally through Ingram
Publisher Services International (www.ingramcontent.com).

This book was published with the generous support of Lannan
Foundation, Wallace Action Fund, and the Marguerite Casey Foundation.

Special discounts are available for bulk purchases by organizations and
institutions. Please call 773-583-7884 or email info@haymarketbooks.org
for more information.

Cover art and design by David Mabb. Cover art is a detail from *Painting
56, Rhythm 69, (William Morris Block Printed Pattern Book, with Hans Richter
Storyboard, developed from Richter's Rhythmus 25 and Kazimir Malevich's
film script Artistic and Scientific Film – Painting and Architectural Concerns –
Approaching the New Plastic Architectural System)*. Paint and wallpaper on
canvas (2007).

Printed in the United States.

Library of Congress Cataloging-in-Publication data is available.

Contents

List of Figures   VII
Abbreviations   IX

Introduction   1

1 Mr Hyndman versus Comrade Engels: The Birth of the Social
Democratic Federation   7
  1   The Birth of the Social Democratic Federation   12
  2   From the Socialist League to the Independent Labour Party   18

2 The Labour Party Question: Labourism, Leftism, and the Second
International   24
  1   The Russian Influence   31
  2   The Labour Party and the Second International   34

3 Britain in Crisis: Labour's Great Unrest and the Revolutionary Left   43
  1   Realignment on the Left and the British Socialist Party   46
  2   The Second International Steers towards the Labour Party   50
  3   The Rise of the Revolutionary Left   53
  4   The SLP and Revolutionary Syndicalism   57
  5   Beyond Suffragism   63

4 August 1914: British Marxists in the Face of War   69
  1   The BSP and SLP and the Test of War   73
  2   The Anti-war Left   79
  3   Revolutionary Opponents of War   85

5 The Clyde Turns Red: John Maclean and the Enemy at Home   92
  1   The War on the Home Front   96
  2   The Easter Rising and the British Left   100
  3   *Nashe Slovo*, the BSP and Revolutionary Internationalism   103
  4   The Zimmerwald Debate in Britain   108

6 'Lads Like Me Had Whacked the Bosses': The Coming of the Russian
Revolution   111
  1   Repression and Revolt   114
  2   Follow Russia! The Leeds Convention   120

3   Labourism Responds to the Russian Revolution   123
4   Bolshevism and the British Left   127

7 1919: The Question of Power   132
    1   'Are You Ready to Take Power?'   134
    2   The Police Strikes   142
    3   Leadership, the Lefts and the Left   145
    4   Racist Scourge in Europe   149
    5   Ireland's Tragedy, Labour's Disgrace   156

8 Between Labourism and Bolshevism: Towards A Communist Party   161
    1   Towards Unity ... and the Labour Party?   167
    2   The Coming of the Communist International   172
    3   Britain and the Amsterdam Bureau   177
    4   The Fate of John Maclean   183

9 'Long Live the Communist Party!' Building a British Section of the
    Communist International   190
    1   The Second Congress of the Comintern   191
    2   The Birth of the Communist Party of Great Britain   203
    3   The Unification Conference   210
    4   A Stillborn Party?   217

Conclusion   225
    1   In Praise of Learning   226

Appendix 1: Timeline   231
Appendix 2: Figures   234
Bibliography   255
Index   278

Figures

1   **Leftist Newspapers**

1   The SLP's *Socialist* (June 1915) opposes World War One.   234
2   The BSP's *Call* (15 November 1917) welcomes the October Revolution.   235
3   The *Workers' Dreadnought* (31 January 1920) features a Claude Mackay article on racism.   236
4   John Maclean's *Vanguard* (November 1915) calls for a new International.   237

2   **People**

5   Tom Mann [credit: *The Transport Worker*, August 1911]   238
6   Peter Petroff [credit: *Cotton Factory Times*, 9 November 1917]   239
7   Arthur MacManus [credit: George Grantham Bain Collection, The Library of Congress]   240
8   Eleanor Marx, Wilhelm Liebknecht (left) & Edward Aveling (right) [credit: *The Comrade*, January 1905]   241
9   Georgy Chicherin [credit: Bundesarchiv, Bild 102–12859A / CC-BY-SA 3.0, CC BY-SA 3.0 de]   242
10   Theodore Rothstein [credit: Public Domain, https://commons.wikimedia.org/w/index.php?curid=8045929]   242
11   CPGB founding central committee 1920. MacManus in front centre, flanked by Arthur Inkpin (left) and Willie Gallacher (right) [credit: *Communist Unity Convention Official Report*, 1920]   243
12   J.T. Murphy [credit: Topical Photos 1925]   243
13   John Maclean [credit: Getty Images]   244
14   Sylvia Pankhurst [credit: Getty Images]   245
15   Henry Hyndman (credit: Public Domain)   246

3   **Events**

16   SLP Offices at Renfrew Street in Glasgow [credit: *The Socialist*, November 1917]   247
17   Delegate ticket to Glasgow shop stewards' meeting with Lloyd George 1915 [credit: Clydebank District Library]   248
18   Alice Wheeldon and family on trial [credit: *Sunday Pictorial*, 4 February 1917]   248

19   London dockers' meeting addressed by unnamed woman [*Leeds Mercury*, 12 August 1911]   249

20   The ELFS's People's Army weapons training 1914 [credit: International Institute for Social History]   250

21   Melvina Walker addresses an ELFS street meeting in 1913 [credit: International Institute for Social History]   251

22   Martial law in Glasgow 1919 [credit: *Illustrated London News*, 8 February 1919]   252

23   Troops with fixed bayonets march by Liverpool strike meeting 1911 [credit: *The Sphere*, August 1911]   253

24   Women pickets at the Singer's Strike 1911 [credit: Glasgow Herald, March 1911]   254

Abbreviations

BSP	British Socialist Party, formerly the SDP and SDF
CLP	Communist Labour Party
Comintern	Communist (Third) International
CP(BSTI)	Communist Party (British Section of the Third International), the Successor to the WSF
CPGB	Communist Party of Great Britain
ECCI	Executive Committee of the Communist International
ELFS	East London Federation of Suffragettes
ILP	Independent Labour Party
ISB	International Socialist Bureau (the Second International)
ISRP	Irish Socialist Republican Party
LRC	Labour Representation Committee (forerunner of the Labour Party)
NUR	National Union of Railwaymen
PLP	Parliamentary Labour Party
SDF	Social Democratic Federation
SDP	Social Democratic Party (from 1908), formerly the SDF
SL	Socialist League
SLP	Socialist Labour Party (Britain)
SLP (US)	Socialist Labor Party (United States)
SPD	German Social Democratic Party
SPGB	Socialist Party of Great Britain
SSWCM	Shop Stewards' and Workers' Committee Movement
SWSS	South Wales Socialist Society
TUC	Trades Union Congress
TWF	Transport Workers' Federation
USC	United Socialist Council
WSF	Workers' Socialist Federation (1918), formerly the Women's Suffrage Federation (1916), formerly the ELFS
WSPU	Women's Social and Political Union

Introduction

This is a book about revolutionaries. It is about those men and women who fought to liberate working-class people from capitalism and establish a socialist society which the workers themselves would govern.

The book traces the development of Marxist politics in the British working class over the four decades from the creation of the Social Democratic Federation in 1884 to the foundation of the Communist Party of Great Britain (CPGB) in 1920. Marxism gained a foothold among workers during a time of tumultuous class struggle which saw the emergence of the modern trade union movement, the birth of the Labour Party, the devastation wrought by World War One, and an unprecedented social and political crisis throughout Britain and Ireland between 1910 and 1920.

Raising the Red Flag is necessarily also a history of the British working class during that period. It suggests the rise of a reformist Labour Party was not inevitable, and the vast number of industrial and political struggles which broke out in the years prior to 1914 were not doomed to defeat. Indeed, the book argues there was a 'long 1914', in which the 'Great Labour Unrest' of 1910 to 1914, which saw class conflict on a scale unknown since the age of Chartism in the late 1830s and early 1840s, did not end in 1914. The outbreak of war temporarily inhibited industrial conflict only for it to flare to new heights in 1919 and 1920. So, this is a book which seeks to explain not only what was, but also what could have been.

This approach stands in contrast to the mainstream trend of British labour history, which is dominated by a belief in the inexorable rise of the Labour Party and a 'British determinism' which is best exemplified by Ross McKibbin's 1984 essay 'Why Was There No Marxism in Great Britain?', which argues structural factors in British society meant it was impossible for a revolutionary tradition to emerge. Such a mechanical view leaves no room for subjective agency. Moreover, it dovetails with the dominant historiography of modern British history itself, which has presented a 'solid state' view of the working class as an essentially conservative and non-radical force.

In contrast, this book suggests, although Britain's rise as the world's dominant imperial and industrial power of the nineteenth century created powerful conservative pressures within the working class, the reluctance of the Social Democratic Federation to intervene in the rise of 'new unionism' in the 1880s and 1890s, together with its inability to capitalise on the profound shift in British politics between 1910 and 1914, were failures of the subjective factor. Other strategies could have created opportunities for at least a more favourable balance of forces for the Marxist movement.

The historiography of the revolutionary left during this period is frustratingly sparse. Henry Pelling's 1958 *The British Communist Party: A Historical Profile* touched briefly on the prehistory of the CPGB, while L.J. MacFarlane's *The British Communist Party: Its Origin and Development until 1929*, published in 1966, offered the first scholarly overview of the organisations which created the party. Other than H.W. Lee's semi-official *Social Democracy in Britain: Fifty Years of the Socialist Movement* in 1935, the first serious history of the Social Democratic Federation was Chushichi Tsuzuki's 1961 *H.M. Hyndman and British Socialism*. The Socialist League of Eleanor Marx and William Morris was extensively documented in E.P. Thompson's 1955 *William Morris: Romantic to Revolutionary*, while Yvonne Kapp's magisterial 1976 biography of Eleanor Marx detailed her key role in the nineteenth-century revolutionary movement. Little followed these works until Martin Crick's 1994 *The History of the Social Democratic Federation* and Karen Hunt's *Equivocal Feminists: The Social Democratic Federation and the Woman Question 1884–1911*.

The syndicalist movement was even more sparsely served, with only Bob Holton's *British Syndicalism 1900–1914* offering any overview of the movement, although James Hinton's definitive *The First Shop Stewards' Movement* comprehensively mapped the growth of shop-floor organisation during World War One.[1] But for the pre-communist movement as a whole, the key text remains Walter Kendall's 1969 *The Revolutionary Movement in Britain 1900–21*. Although this has a wealth of detail, the book is premised on the idea that the Communist International exerted a malign influence on the development of the British left, and artificially forced the creation of a communist party through financial subventions to its supporters. Thus, Kendall claimed, the natural development of a native revolutionary party was cut short.[2]

As will be seen, this book argues that while the Communist International did provide the British left, including the *Daily Herald*, with substantial material support, this was not a critical factor in determining the outcome of the discussions which led to the formation of the Communist Party. Moreover, Kendall's belief that the British Marxists should have been left to themselves ignores the fact that the revolutionary tendency in the British labour movement had always been decisively shaped by politics beyond Britain. It was the exiled Marx and Engels who sought to win over British trade union leaders to independent working-class politics in the First International. The left opposition in the Social Democratic Federation which created the Socialist Labour Party in 1903

---

1   Holton 1977; Hinton 1973.
2   For an alternative to Kendall, see Durham 1982.

was led by the Irishman James Connolly and based on the politics of Daniel De Leon's Socialist Labour Party in the United States. The Social Democratic Federation itself was revitalised in the 1900s by an influx of Russian and Jewish émigrés fleeing Tsarist repression and anti-Semitic pogroms. John Maclean's revolutionary opposition to World War One was heavily influenced by the left-Menshevik Peter Petrov, while the major figure in the British Socialist Party who argued for a revolutionary end to World War One and opposed racism in its leadership was George Chicherin, the future Soviet Commissar for Foreign Affairs. Given the huge nationalist pressures imposed on British Marxists by the weight of British imperialism, collaboration with foreign revolutionaries was historically one of the necessary conditions for internationalism in Britain.

After Kendall, the only substantive book on the pre-communist British revolutionary left was Raymond Challinor's 1977 monograph on the Socialist Labour Party, *The Origins of British Bolshevism*. This portrays the SLP as the British version of Lenin's Bolshevik Party, but ignores the SLP's initial support for World War One and its subsequent unity with pro-war elements in the shop stewards' movement. Like Kendall but for different reasons, Challinor also ascribes the failure of the SLP to the intervention of the Communist International. The only significant addition to the literature since Challinor has been David Burke's work on Theodore Rothstein, a man whom both Kendall and Challinor portray as a shadowy figure manipulating the British left through use of Russian money. Although Burke's political assessment of Rothstein differs from this author's, his excellent research rescues Rothstein from such misrepresentation, and rightly places him at the centre of the political debates which dominated Marxism in Britain during and after World War One.[3] The general surveys of the history of the CPGB published since the party's collapse in 1991 show little interest in nor significant new knowledge of its revolutionary forebears.[4]

The CPGB itself never seriously interrogated its pre-history. The first volume of James Klugmann's *History of the Communist Party of Great Britain*, published in 1968 following a 1956 party decision to publish its history, offered little insight into the development of the revolutionary left and offered an unexamined narrative of the process which led to the party's foundation.[5] Given that many of the participants were still alive when the book was written and that the Comintern's 1923 'English Commission' had conducted an extensive discussion on the

---

3 Burke 1997 and 2018.
4 Thompson 1992; Beckett 1995; Laybourn and Murphy 1999; Eaden and Renton 2002.
5 Materials relating to the CPGB's party history commission are in the Robin Page Arnott Papers at Hull History Centre, File DAR/6/1.

history of the groups which formed the CPGB, this was disappointing but not surprising. It was in these discussions that Rajani Palme Dutt, the CPGB's dominant intellectual since the early 1920s, had disparaged the groups that created the party as 'sects'.[6] While the party history commission deliberated the limits of its investigations – the party's central leader Harry Pollitt warned the commission's December 1956 meeting of 'the political repercussions if a detailed history were to be written' – one of its members, Brian Pearce, was already carrying out his own research into the origins of the party. Pearce left the party in the wake of Stalin's suppression of the 1956 Hungarian Revolution, became a Trotskyist, and subsequently published a number of influential articles on the history of the Marxist movement.[7]

While breaking much new ground and taking seriously the histories of the constituent parts of the CPGB, Pearce tended to view the chief problem with the CPGB's forerunners as being what he called 'the rooted sectarianism of the British Marxists'.[8] Thus the SDF's hostility towards trade union militancy, opposition to the suffragette movement, and refusal to join the Labour Party before World War One were all ascribed to 'sectarianism'. Unfortunately, 'sectarian' is a word which, like 'freedom' and 'democracy', has become devoid of meaning, and usually indicates 'someone who stands to the left of my politics with whom I disagree'. Pearce's heavy-handed use of the word forestalls a more granular understanding of the reasons for the SDF's stance on these questions and, as we shall see, underplays the very real weakness of both the CPGB and its predecessors towards the left-wing leaders of the Labour Party and trade unions.

The opening of the papers of the Communist International in the Russian State Archives in the 1990s has not inspired the production of significant new works on the early history of the CPGB. Andrew Thorpe's *The British Communist Party and Moscow 1920–43*, published in 2000, is largely an administrative account of party history which seeks to downplay the influence of the Comintern's politics on the party, while Kevin Morgan's three-volume *Bolshevism and the British Left*, an account of the British labour movement's relationship with Soviet Russia in the first decade or so after the October Revolution, pays little attention to the day-to-day political questions faced by militants at the time.

---

6 The 'English Commission' discussion of the origins of the party are in 'The Old Elements', English Commission (1923) RGASPI. F. 495. Op. 38. D. 1.

7 Pollitt quoted in Frank Jackson, 'Party History Commission' 1 August 1957; for Pearce and the History Commission, see John Gollan to Robin Page Arnott, 14 September 1956. Both documents are in the Arnott Papers, DAR/6/1, Hull History Centre.

8 Pearce 1958.

The opening of the archives did, however, result in a long-running debate between those historians who sought to defend the CPGB as an autonomous party and those who highlighted its fealty to the Stalin leadership of the Communist International. The former, dubbed the 'revisionists', sought to defend the CPGB's political practice from the late 1920s, and especially the popular front period of the 1930s. The latter focused on the CPGB's support for the twists and turns of Soviet foreign policy. Insofar as the debate impinged on the origins and birth of the CPGB, the revisionists had little sympathy for its revolutionary antecedents while their opponents veered towards Kendall's thesis that the party was the artificial creation of an alien tradition.[9]

To some extent, the small number of works produced about the pre-history of the CPGB reflects the lack of interest of contemporary academic historians in the revolutionary politics of those times.[10] But it is also the case, for Britain at least, that the opening of the Comintern archives appears to have revealed little about this period which was unknown or could not be discovered from close reading of materials already in the public domain. The work which has been produced often tends to highlight 'Moscow Gold' and the amounts of money the Comintern sent to its British supporters – facts already well-known to anyone on the British left (or in Lloyd George's government) in the early 1920s – which is an indication of its usefulness or otherwise to historians.

In contrast, *Raising the Red Flag* follows in the footsteps of recent works by historians such as Bryan Palmer in his *James P. Cannon and the Origins of the American Revolutionary Left, 1890–1928* and Jacob Zumoff in *The Communist International and US Communism, 1919–1929*, who have sought to place the revolutionary politics of the time at the centre of the study of the communist and revolutionary movements.[11] Moreover, this is a partisan book, firmly on the side of those men and women who sought to bring about the birth of a better world through workers' revolution. I make no apologies for this. All historians are politicians (and all politicians are, in their own way, historians). Their political worldviews permeate and influence their research and analyses, no matter how neutral or disinterested they may claim to be. Historians are measured by the extent to which their research draws accurately from the historical record and the degree to which their analysis offers a coherent explanation of how and why events took place when they did. There is therefore no contradiction between offering a scholarly account and taking a side.

---

9   For a flavour of the debate, see Thorpe 1998; Morgan 2002; McIlroy and Campbell 2003; Fishman 2004; and Newsinger 2006.

10   For exceptions, see the two 2020 articles of McIlroy and Campbell.

11   Palmer 2007; Zumoff 2014.

Thus, following E.P. Thompson in his *The Making of the English Working Class*, this book seeks to rescue the revolutionary men and women of the late nineteenth and early twentieth centuries from the smug dismissal of the ephemeral present. But whereas Thompson believed his subjects were ultimately the casualties of history, *Raising the Red Flag* views its protagonists as the harbingers of the future.[12]

---

12   Thompson 1968, p. 13.

Mr Hyndman versus Comrade Engels: The Birth of the Social Democratic Federation

On Wednesday, 14 August 1889 dockers unloading the ss *Lady Armstrong* cargo ship at London's West India Dock downed tools and went on strike. They were protesting against a cut in their 'plus' pay, the amount they received for unloading a ship ahead of schedule, after their employers had cut wage rates to make their ports more attractive to ship-owners during the recent downturn in trade. In response, the men demanded a rise from fivepence to sixpence per hour – 'the dockers' tanner' – and eightpence an hour overtime rate. Largely non-unionised and with little history of militancy, the strikers appeared to stand little chance of success. To win, they needed the rest of the London dockers to join them.

But their decisiveness and determination immediately struck a chord with other dock workers. They too worked for little more than starvation wages. Most suffered the ignominy of casual labour, with no permanent job and the daily humiliation of queuing each morning for the chance to be given work by gang-masters. The walk-out by the West India dockers had kindled that smouldering discontent. Members of the Amalgamated Stevedores Union also walked out and appealed 'to members of all trade unions for joint action with us, and especially those whose work is in connection with shipping – engineers and fitters, boiler makers, ships' carpenters, etc. and also the coal heavers, ballast men and lightermen'.[1] A strike committee was established to co-ordinate the action and within a few days, thanks to its highly effective organisation of 16,000 pickets, the great London waterfront, the very heart of the British imperial trading network, had been rendered silent.

Support spread quickly across the metropolis and throughout the rest of Britain. Soon messages of solidarity began to pour in from around the world. Most famously, trade unions in Australia sent £30,000, a huge amount which eliminated the threat of hunger faced by the strikers. In little more than a fortnight, 130,000 London dockworkers of all types were on strike. Such was the enthusiasm for the strike that workers unconnected with the docks also took action, including women workers at the biscuit makers, Peak, Frean & Co. The

---

1 Tillett 1931, p. 122.

possibility that solidarity action could escalate into a London-wide general strike caused the Lord Mayor of London to insist the employers came to the negotiating table. Faced with an intransigent and united workforce, the bosses conceded the strikers' main demands. On 16 September the London dockers triumphantly returned to work.[2]

It was the greatest working-class victory since the days of the Chartists. Coming shortly after the London match women's strike of 1888 and the gasworkers' strike earlier in 1889, the dockers' triumph signalled the rebirth of the British working-class movement.[3] It was the catalyst for the creation of what became known as 'new unions', general trade unions for unskilled and previously unorganised workers. Inspired by the dockers, a new spirit of self-confidence flowed through the working class, and by 1892 union membership in Britain had doubled to 1.5 million. In 1892 and 1893 Britain experienced the largest number of strikes in its history.[4]

For Friedrich Engels, the London dockers' strike was the moment 'the English proletariat, rousing itself from forty years of slumber, rejoined the moment of its class'.[5] This was the working-class movement, independent of bourgeois politicians and increasingly self-conscious of its own interests, for which he and Karl Marx had fought since the defeat of Chartism four decades earlier. Engels was intensely moved by the dockers' struggle. 'That these poor famished broken down creatures who bodily fight amongst each other every morning for admission to work', he wrote emotionally to Marx's daughter Laura Lafargue, 'should organise for resistance, turn out 40–50,000 strong, draw after them into the strike all and every trade of the East End in any way connected with shipping, hold out above a week, and terrify the wealthy and powerful dock companies – that is a revival I am proud *erlebt zu haben* [to have lived to see]'.[6]

Engels and Marx had worked for forty years to see such a revival. Their initial hopes that Chartism would be the means by which the British working class would come to power had been ended by the defeat of the 1848 revolutions across Europe, reflected in Britain by the disintegration of the Chartist movement in the 1850s. Now detached from the insurrectionary working-class movement of the 1830s and 1840s, the six democratic demands of the People's Charter became the rationale by which former left-wing Chartists allied with

---

2　For a full account of the strike, see Tsuzuki 1991, pp. 52–70.

3　See Raw 2011.

4　Board of Trade 1896.

5　'May 4 in London', *Karl Marx Frederick Engels Collected Works* [hereafter MECW] vol. 27, p. 61.

6　Engels to Laura Lafargue, 27 Aug 1889, MECW vol. 48, p. 369.

radical factions of the Liberal Party. This was also the eventual fate of Marx's former close political allies Julian Harney and Ernest Jones. They, like many others who had once proclaimed 'no more supplication to the middle classes!', now pinned their political colours to the mast of the Liberals in the hope that parliamentary pressure would deliver suffrage to the working class. As Engels later noted, the People's Charter 'actually became the political programme of the very manufacturers who had opposed it to the last'.[7]

In contrast, Marx and Engels sought to preserve Chartism's revolutionary goals. 'The only possible basis for the reconstruction of the Chartist party [is] the instinctive class hatred of the workers for the industrial bourgeoisie', wrote Engels in 1852.[8] In the early 1850s he and Marx helped edit Ernest Jones's weekly newspapers *Notes to the People* and *People's Paper*, and were active in campaigns for working-class political rights. However, their attempts to breathe life back into Chartism failed, as the political vacuum created by the defeat of the mass movement sucked the air out of its former left wing. 'All the efforts made at keeping up, of remodelling, the Chartist movement failed signally; the press organs of the working class died one by one of the apathy of the masses', said Marx sadly in 1864, 'and in point of fact never before seemed the English working class so thoroughly reconciled to a state of political nullity'.[9]

In the decades following the defeat of Chartism, Britain's global industrial manufacturing dominance expanded into the production of capital goods. The wealth produced by this expansion led to the emergence of what both Marx and Engels termed 'the aristocracy of the working class', a layer of skilled workers whose standards of living increased substantially and who were, in the words of Engels, 'on extremely good terms' with the employers, having created 'for themselves a relatively comfortable position'.[10] In 1858 Engels had suggested to Marx 'the English proletariat is actually becoming more and more bourgeois, so that the ultimate aim of this most bourgeois of all nations would appear to be the possession, alongside the bourgeoisie, of a bourgeois aristocracy and a bourgeois proletariat'.[11] The rise of craft unions, or 'new model unionism', in the 1860s was based on these higher-paid sections of the working

---

7   'England in 1845 and 1885', *MECW* vol. 26, p. 297.

8   Engels to Marx, 18 March 1852, *MECW* vol. 39, p. 68.

9   Marx, 'Inaugural Address of the International Working Men's Association' in *Documents of the First International* vol. 1, p. 283.

10   Marx first used the term in volume one of *Capital*, see *MECW* vol. 35, p. 660. The quotation is from Engels's 1885 article 'England in 1845 and in 1885', *MECW* vol. 26, pp. 298–9.

11   Engels to Marx, 7 October 1858, *MECW* vol. 38, p. 344.

class, who tended to support the Liberal Party. They were also the beneficiaries of the 1867 Reform Act, which gave the vote to householders who paid annual rent of £10 or more.

It was this 'labour aristocracy' which provided the basis for the growth of a conservative, 'non-political' leadership of the working class.[12] The leaders of the new model unions believed their role was to extract higher wages and better working conditions for their members within capitalism, not to challenge it. This meant they also sought to maintain the differentials and divisions between skilled and unskilled workers. Unlike France, where revolutionary upsurges against the ruling class punctuated the nineteenth century, or Germany, where the Social Democratic Party (SPD) offered a socialist alternative to the capitalist and monarchist parties, the leadership of the British trade unions promoted the idea that economic issues were the only concern of the working class. Insofar as they were interested in 'politics', they sought to ally with the Liberal Party, a policy which became known as 'Lib-Labism', in order to protect their interests in parliament, and financed a number of trade unionists who became Liberal MPs. The British working class therefore developed a tradition of strong workplace organisation but weak political ideology, essentially ceding political leadership to middle-class liberals and creating a culture of deference to the upper class within the labour movement. This separation between economics and politics infected even the most militant sections of the working class and, as we shall see, seriously undermined the ability of ostensible revolutionaries to offer a political challenge to the capitalist state.

This radically different post-1848 world necessitated a new tactical orientation for Marx and Engels. The core of their activity since the 1840s had been based, in the words of the *Communist Manifesto*, on three principles: 'formation of the proletariat into a class, overthrow of the bourgeois supremacy, conquest of political power by the proletariat'.[13] As the immediate prospect of revolutionary upheaval faded, they sought to foster the development of independent proletarian parties by working with trade unions and other mass labour organisations. In September 1864 Marx was one of the founding leaders of the International Workingmen's Association (IWMA), which became known to history as the First International. It began as an alliance between French and British trade unionists to organise international solidarity to stop strike breaking. The French were largely influenced by Pierre Proudhon, whose philosophy of

---

12   The debate on the labour aristocracy among British historians is extensive: key texts
        include Hobsbawm 1964; Foster 1974; Gray 1981; and Foster 2010.

13   *MECW* vol. 6, p. 498.

'mutualism' argued that the establishment of a 'People's Bank' to facilitate financial cooperation between workers would undermine and eventually replace capitalism.[14] The British element comprised long-standing trade union leaders, many of whom had been Chartists in their younger years. Marx played a central role in drawing up the International's programme, which focused on establishing the political independence of the working class. This was expressed in its fullest sense in the opening sentence of article 7a of the International's rules: 'In its struggle against the collective power of the propertied classes, the working class cannot act as a class except by constituting itself into a political party, distinct from, and opposed to all old parties formed by the propertied classes'.[15]

Marx's political activity in the late 1860s and early 1870s was dominated by the building of the International. As well as co-ordinating trade union solidarity across Europe, the International organised major campaigns for the eight-hour day, universal suffrage, the victory of the North in the American Civil War, and Polish independence.[16] Its diverse political composition inevitably led to constant factional struggles, but it wasn't until the Paris Commune of 1871, when Marx became the target of a Europe-wide witch hunt following the publication of his *Civil War in France*, that the British trade union leaders withdrew their support. Such a split had long been anticipated by Marx and Engels, the latter predicting to Marx in 1864: 'I suspect that there will very soon be a split in this new association between those who are bourgeois in their thinking and those who are proletarian the moment the issues become a little more specific'.[17]

The defeat of the Paris Commune further fractured the International and, after overcoming Mikhail Bakunin and his anarchist faction at the 1872 congress in the Hague, Marx and Engels decided to let the organisation 'recede into the background' and engage directly with the emerging working-class parties across Europe.[18] Their goal, as Engels told the International's 1871 London conference, remained nothing less than workers' revolution and that:

> whoever wants it must also want the means, political action, which prepares for it, which gives the workers the education for revolution ... But the politics which are needed are working-class politics; the workers'

---

14   Backer 1978.
15   See 'Resolution Relating to the General Rules' quoted in Engels to F.A. Sorge, 21 Sept 1872, *MECW* vol. 44, p. 433.
16   The fullest account is in Collins and Abramsky 1965, but also see Seymour 1978.
17   Engels to Marx, 7 Nov 1864, *MECW* vol. 42, p. 20.
18   Marx to Sorge, 27 Sept 1873, *MECW* vol. 44, p. 535.

party must be constituted not as the tail of some bourgeois party, but as an independent party with its own objective, its own politics.[19]

This principle was the rock upon which the British Marxist movement had to be built, but it was also one over which it would stumble many times in the future.

1 The Birth of the Social Democratic Federation

Two of the key leaders of the London dockers' strike were Tom Mann and John Burns, both of whom had been members of the self-proclaimed Marxist organisation, the Social Democratic Federation (SDF). Many other local SDF members enthusiastically threw themselves into supporting the dockers. Such was Mann's authority in the working class that after the strike ended, he was elected the first president of the Dock, Wharf, Riverside and General Labourers' Union. Yet the leadership of the SDF itself stood aside from the dockers' struggle. Its weekly newspaper, *Justice*, dismissed the strikers' victory by patronisingly saying 'petty gains are of little value' and denigrated the sacrifice of the dockers and their families by asking 'was such ridiculous mockery of success worth a month's starvation and misery?'[20] The solidarity work of SDF members was, according to its leadership, nothing but 'a lowering of the flag, a departure from active propaganda, and a waste of energy'.[21] Unsurprisingly, the SDF neither grew nor extended its influence during or after the strike.

The SDF's failure came as no surprise to Engels. It had been formed in 1881 as the Democratic Federation when Henry Hyndman, the Cambridge-educated scion of a West Indian merchant, and Conservative MP Henry Munro-Butler-Johnstone called a meeting of radical groups in London. Although Hyndman claimed he wanted to revive Chartism, the Democratic Federation was an almost entirely middle-class organisation which promoted nothing more than democratic demands.[22] Hyndman quickly became its undisputed leader and in 1883 declared himself a socialist. The following year he began publishing *Justice*, a weekly 'organ of social democracy' and at its 1884 conference the Democratic Federation changed its name to the Social Democratic Federation.

---

19 'On the Political Action of the Working Class' [handwritten text of speech to the London Conference of the First International, 21 September 1871] *MECW* vol. 22, p. 417.

20 *Justice*, 31 Aug and 21 Sept 1889. For a detailed account see Crick 1994, pp. 59–61.

21 *Justice*, 3 May 1890.

22 For the formation of the SDF, see Wilkins 1959, pp. 199–207; Crick 1994, ch. 1.

Neither Marx nor Engels were impressed by Hyndman or his organisation. Marx told his daughter Jenny that Hyndman was a 'complacent chatterbox', while Engels thought him 'hopelessly jingoistic but not stupid'.[23] Relations were fatally ruptured in 1881 when Hyndman published his manifesto, *England For All*. The book's sections on economics were taken without attribution from volume one of Marx's *Capital*, but Hyndman refused to acknowledge Marx by name. Instead, he declared he was 'indebted to the work of a great thinker and original writer, which will, I trust, shortly be made accessible to the majority of my countrymen'.[24] Hyndman justified this snub because 'Englishmen have a dread of being taught by a foreigner', an assertion Marx dismissed by recalling he had 'not found it so during the times of the [First] International, nor of Chartism'.[25] After Hyndman announced his conversion to socialism in 1883 Engels told the German Social Democratic Party leader August Bebel that Hyndman and his supporters had been

> persistently trying to look important for the past 20 years at least and with the same lack of success. All that is important is that these people have now at last been compelled publicly to proclaim our theory as their own … On no account whatever allow yourself to be bamboozled into believing that a real proletarian movement is afoot here.[26]

Despite this, Hyndman claimed his organisation was based on Marxist politics. The reality was the SDF could not be described as a Marxist organisation even in a formal sense. Hyndman's thinking owed much more to Ferdinand Lassalle, the German socialist who believed in the neutrality of the state and sought to persuade the German chancellor Otto von Bismarck to introduce universal suffrage. Lasalle was also hostile to trade unions and believed in an 'iron law of wages', the theory that wages would always be pushed down to the absolute minimum subsistence level – a view Marx dismissed as being a form of Malthusianism in his 1875 analysis of the Lasallean programme, the *Critique of the Gotha Programme*.[27] Lasalle's iron law of wages and his opposition to

---

23   Marx to Jenny Longuet, 11 April 1880, *MECW* vol. 46, p. 81; Engels to Bebel, 30 August 1883, *MECW* vol. 47, p. 54. For a contrasting view of Marx's relationship with Hyndman, see Flaherty 2020.

24   Hyndman 1881, p. vi.

25   Marx to Hyndman, 2 July 1881, *MECW* vol. 46, p. 102.

26   Engels to Bebel, 30 Aug 1883, *MECW* vol. 47, pp. 53–4.

27   For Hyndman's relationship to Lasalle, see Pierson 1973, pp. 60–74; Marx, 'Critique of the Gotha Programme', *MECW* vol. 24, pp. 75–99.

trade unions were positions also held by the SDF, while his willingness to collaborate with Bismarck was replicated by Hyndman in 1885 when he accepted £340 from the Conservative Party to run two candidates in that year's General Election in the constituencies of Hampstead and Kensington, a decision Engels regarded as an 'irreparable moral ruin'.[28]

In fact, Hyndman owed more to Thomas Carlyle than to Karl Marx. His political instincts were those of a Tory Radical; British nationalism lay at the heart of his programme. 'The Anglo-Saxon blood is still second-to-none', he proclaimed in 1884 in his *The Coming Revolution in England*.[29] It was this, rather than a desire for the working class to take control of society, that was the basis of his opposition to the established order. He believed that capitalism had wrought devastation on traditional British society and fundamentally damaged the deep-seated social harmony of his homeland. 'It will be the fault of the "governing classes", not of the people, if we have to face in this country another such period of rioting and suppressed civil war as lasted from 1835 to 1842, and partially till 1848', he explained in an article in the *Contemporary Review*. 'Let us hope that a full and timely recognition of the just demands of the people … will enable England to take that lead in the peaceful re-organisation of society for which she is fitted by the state of her economical development and the political freedom which, on the whole, her inhabitants enjoy'.[30] In other words, socialism was necessary in order to avoid working-class revolution. For Hyndman, socialism was no more than the most rational way to organise British society, and Marxism, insofar as he understood it, merely offered the most compelling analysis of capitalism. The idea that working-class people should rule society, as advocated by the revolutionary wing of the Chartists and the central political goal of Marxism, was utterly alien to him.

Nowhere was this attitude more apparent than when the working class took action in its own interests, especially by going on strike. Although many SDF members were trade unionists and its 1897 annual conference called on its members to join trade unions, its leadership essentially saw trade unions as an obstacle to the development of socialist ideas, going so far as to describe them as an 'incubus'.[31] Even as he declared himself a socialist in 1883, Hyndman wrote that trade unions were 'a hindrance to that complete organisation of the workers which alone can obtain for the workers their proper control over their own

28   Crick 1994, pp. 44–45; Engels to Bernstein, 7 Dec 1885, *MECW* vol. 47, p. 366.

29   Hyndman 1884, p. 31; On Hyndman's Tory Radicalism, see Bevir 2011, pp. 73–81.

30   Hyndman 1887, p. 136.

31   For a discussion on the SDF and the unions see Johnson 1988, pp. 244–9, and Rabinovitch 1977, p. 166.

labour'.[32] This attitude towards trade unions hardened into full-blown hostility when workers went on strike. 'When will our English workers learn that this isolated action is hopeless, and that to strike at a period of depression is merely to play the game of the capitalists?' moaned *Justice* in 1884.[33] In his book *The Historical Basis of Socialism in England* – a 'pretentious, impertinent jumble' according to Engels – Hyndman argued that it was better to elect MPs to parliament than it was to win strikes:

> the waste of Trades Union funds on strikes or petty benefits to the individuals who compose them is still more deplorable. Enormous sums have been spent or lost, directly, or indirectly, in consequence of strikes ... the return of working-class members to Parliament, as in Germany, with a definite mandate from their fellows to uphold the claims of those who produce all wealth and live in comparative misery, would have gained the unionists far more than they have secured by mere strikes.[34]

This view was widely held by other SDF leaders. When John Burns, the trade unionist who later became a Liberal cabinet minister, stood as the SDF candidate in the 1884 general election for the Nottingham West constituency he told voters that all strikes 'failed to secure their objects'.[35] Three years later he declared that the defeat of a series of strikes in Northumberland 'must prove to the dullest that isolated action by sections of the workers almost always ends in invariable failure'.[36] This was a foretaste of the SDF's dismissal of the London dockers' strike. Suspicion of working-class action remained a feature of the SDF's politics for the rest of its life. In 1898 *Justice* was still claiming that 'trade unionism, when it forms an aristocracy of labour, as in England, so far from helping on the general cause of the workers, heads that cause back'.[37] Even SDF oppositionists shared much of Hyndman's position. During the bitter 1897 engineering lock-out, a young Theodore Rothstein attacked the unions for being a 'bulwark' against socialism and a 'great conservative force'.[38]

---

32   Hyndman 1883, p. 287.
33   *Justice*, 19 Jan 1884.
34   Hyndman 1883 p. 291. Engels to Kautsky, 19 July 1884, *MECW* vol. 47, p. 165.
35   Quoted in Owen 2008, p. 192.
36   *Justice*, 3 Sept 1887.
37   *Justice*, 8 Jan 1898. This was also a position held by some in the ILP. At its 1898 conference Richard Pankhurst, husband of Emmeline and father of Sylvia, deplored 'the actions of trade unionists in resorting to strikes to obtain industrial reform', *ILP News*, April 1898, quoted in Connelly 2013, p. 34.
38   *Justice*, 18 Dec 1897.

The same article also saw Rothstein attack the working class for 'stupid self-contentment'. Blaming the working class for its own oppression was a constant theme of the SDF. It saw socialist propaganda as a form of evangelism that would convince people of the ethical superiority of socialism simply by the logic of its arguments. The failure of the intended recipients to accept these arguments often exposed an underlying contempt for the working class. As future Communist Party leader T.A. Jackson recalled, SDF members often responded to workers' indifference to their self-satisfied sermonising by deciding 'the bastards aren't worth saving'.[39]

The clearest example of this attitude can be seen in the 1914 novel *The Ragged Trousered Philanthropists* written by SDF member Robert Noonan under the pseudonym Robert Tressell. Although widely viewed as a classic of British socialist literature, the book articulates the SDF view that working-class people had only themselves to blame for their oppression. The title itself suggests that workers are 'philanthropists' because they do not understand that they are exploited by capitalism. Whereas Tressell excused 'the anti-socialist writers and the "great statesmen" who make anti-socialist speeches' because 'they do not understand socialism', he excoriated non-socialist workers as 'THE ENEMY. Those who not only quietly submitted like so many cattle to the existing state of things, but defended it, and opposed and ridiculed any suggestion to alter it. THEY WERE THE REAL OPPRESSORS [emphasis in original]'.[40] Frank Owen, the novel's working-class protagonist, is eventually saved from destitution by the charity of his fellow worker Barrington, who at the end of the book reveals himself to be secretly wealthy, a sentimental rendering of Hyndman and the SDF's belief that enlightened middle-class individuals such as themselves would come to the rescue of the working class.

On the other hand, while the SDF was quick to denounce working-class attitudes, it offered no end of advice to the ruling class about how best to preserve the British Empire. As early as 1880 Hyndman stood as an independent parliamentary candidate in Marylebone pledging to protect the 'power and dignity of England abroad' by increasing the size of the Royal Navy.[41] Belief in a strong Royal Navy would become a flagship of SDF foreign policy. Following the Jameson Raid in 1896, when British forces unsuccessfully attempted to seize control of the Transvaal in South Africa after huge gold deposits were discovered there, *Justice* called for a bigger Royal Navy because 'we are face to

---

39   Quoted in Morton and Macintyre 1979, p. 18.
40   Tressell 2005, p. 34. For a contrasting view, see Young 1985.
41   Quoted in Thompson 1955, p. 293. Similar beliefs were held in the ILP; Keir Hardie suggested building 'eight to ten cruisers' in a speech to the House of Commons on 12 Dec 1893.

face with difficulty in every corner of the globe'. This jingoistic message was
hammered home again a few weeks later: 'we don't want to be starved or to
be conquered by other powers, nor do we wish to be deprived of our colonies'.[42] In 1910 Hyndman notoriously wrote to the right-wing *Morning Post* to
demand a hugely increased budget for the Royal Navy and attack the Parliamentary Labour Party for 'pacifism' in the face of the supposed German menace.

This antipathy to Germany was also a hallmark of Hyndman's relationship
with the international socialist movement. During the preparations for the
founding of the Second International in 1889, Hyndman opposed Engels and
supported the anti-Marxist French 'Possibilists' led by Paul Brousse. The Possibilists wanted the international to adopt a reformist programme, arguing it
should promote the politics of the 'possible' rather than revolutionary solutions. Practically, this meant the Possibilists in France voted for candidates of
the bourgeois Republican Party, not dissimilar from the SDF attitude to the Conservative Party. The Possibilists also attracted the support of right-wing trade
unionists, including some from Britain such as the Lib-Lab MP Charles Fenwick.
In July 1889 the political division between the Possibilists and the Marxists resulted in two conferences being held in Paris at the same time to establish a
new international. The Possibilists met at the rue de Lancry, while the Marxists convened a mile away in the rue Rochechouart. The Marxists eventually
prevailed and the two sides came together for the Brussels conference of the
Second International in 1891.[43]

For Hyndman, the disputes in the Second International were caused by those
he referred to as 'the Germans'. 'It is useless to disguise the fact that their methods of organisation and management are essentially dictatorial and arbitrary.
Circumstances force them into this in their own country, and they seem to
be incapable of adopting any other tactics elsewhere', he wrote in his report
of the two conferences. 'It is high time that the German Social Democratic
leaders should learn that ... the hour has come for them to abandon their natural desire to dictate and lecture to social democrats of other nationalities'.[44]
In reply, SPD leader Eduard Bernstein attacked the anti-German xenophobia
of Hyndman, not least by pointing out that the SDF newspaper *Justice* had
complained that the *Sozialdemokrat*, the journal the SPD published in exile

42   *Justice*, 11 and 18 Jan, 7 March 1896.
43   See Joll 1956, pp. 31–5; Engels to Sorge, 8 June 1889, *MECW* vol. 48, p. 334; Sanders 1927,
      pp. 90–4. For William Morris and Frank Kitz's impressions of the Marxist congress, see
      Commonweal, 27 July, 3 and 10 Aug 1889.
44   Hyndman 1889, p. 34.

in London, had the temerity to be written in German! By writing in German, *Justice* argued, the SPD 'hamper the propaganda of our cause by printing their newspapers in a language which not one in ten thousand of their neighbours can understand'.[45]

As was often the case in Britain at this time, Hyndman's Germanophobia also carried the bacillus of anti-Semitism. He argued that the Anglo-South African 'Boer' War of 1899–1901 was caused by Jewish financiers manipulating British imperialism for their own business interests. 'Jew Financiers and Real Anti-Semites' and 'The Jews' War on Transvaal' were two of the headlines that accompanied his articles in *Justice* in the autumn of 1899, while the editor of *Justice*, Harry Quelch, chimed in with a piece entitled 'Jews and Jingoism'.[46] Anti-Semitic sentiments continued to appear in *Justice* throughout its existence. As late as 1914 an article about financial trusts was headlined 'Shylocks in Parliament' while an attack on anti-Semitism from the anti-Hyndmanite SDF member Joe Fineberg was criticised by another member in Leeds, home of Britain's third largest Jewish community, who complained that Fineberg 'makes no mention of the hatred the Jew has for his Christian brethren'.[47]

2   From the Socialist League to the Independent Labour Party

The depths to which Hyndman and his supporters could sink would have come as no surprise to Friedrich Engels. Writing to August Bebel in October 1884, he characterised the SDF as 'on the one hand [composed] of literati, on the other of the remnants of old sects and, thirdly, of a sentimental public'.[48] Two months later he supported a split in the SDF led by Marx's youngest daughter, Eleanor, her partner Edward Aveling, and the great British artist William Morris. The oppositionists had won a vote of censure against Hyndman and, deciding that the minuscule SDF was in its death throes, resigned. Although the victory over Hyndman seemed to suggest they could take control of the SDF, Eleanor Marx explained that 'our majority was too small to make it possible for us to really get rid of the Jingo faction [of Hyndman], and so, after due consultation with Engels, we decided to go out, and form a new organisation'.[49]

---

45   *Justice*, 16 March 1889.
46   *Justice*, 30 Sept, 7 Oct and 4 Nov 1899.
47   *Justice*, 8 Jan and 23 April 1914.
48   Engels to Bebel, 11 Oct 1884, *MECW* vol. 47, p. 198.
49   Eleanor to Laura Marx, 31 Dec 1884 in Rowbotham 1982, p. 183. The split is covered in Kapp 2018, pp. 302–6.

The newly-founded Socialist League (SL) was, declared William Morris on the front page of the first issue of its journal, *Commonweal*, 'a body advocating the principles of Revolutionary International Socialism; that is, we seek a change in the basis of Society – a change which would destroy the distinctions of classes and nationalities'.[50] Unlike the SDF, the new organisation was firmly internationalist. As Eleanor Marx wrote to Wilhelm Liebknecht, 'one of our chief points of conflict with Hyndman is that whereas we wish to make this a really international movement ... Mr. Hyndman, whenever he could do so with impunity, has endeavoured to set English workmen against "foreigners"'.[51] Yet the initial promise of the Socialist League did not bear fruit. Its leadership was not suited to the practical politics of building a revolutionary organisation. Morris was a major artist but not a political leader. Eleanor and Aveling were overworked as propagandists and organisers, and could not devote themselves to full-time work for the SL.[52] More importantly, the Socialist League also avoided political debate with Hyndman and other tendencies on the left. Rather than openly polemicising against the SDF's chauvinism and anti-trade union politics, Eleanor and Aveling, supported by Engels, believed that the SDF would quickly disappear and ignored it. But this policy – in contrast to Marx and Engels's own polemical stance against their opponents in the German and French labour movements – let Hyndman and his followers off the hook. It did nothing to differentiate the Socialist League from the SDF or other tendencies on the left.

The consequences of this non-engagement policy were quickly seen when an anarchist faction took advantage of the Socialist League's weak leadership and increasingly dictated its political direction. As early as April 1886 Eleanor Marx told her sister Laura that Morris was 'now more or less under the thumb of the anarchists'.[53] The SL was also outmanoeuvred by Hyndman, as the SDF gained considerable publicity for its campaign against unemployment. This culminated in the 'Bloody Sunday' demonstration of 13 November 1887 when police attacked demonstrators, causing fatal injuries to two of them, and then again the following week when a protest against the police violence saw passer-

---

50   *Commonweal*, February 1885, p. 1. For Engels's view of the split, see his letter to Bernstein, 29 Dec 1884 in *MECW* vol. 47, pp. 236–7. For a detailed account of the split, and of the Socialist League itself, see Thompson 1955, pp. 331–579. Thompson later changed his mind and attacked Engels and Eleanor Marx for 'sectarianism', see Thompson 1994, pp. 66–76.

51   Letter quoted in Kapp 2018, p. 302.

52   For the daily activities of the Socialist League, see Boos 1985.

53   Eleanor to Laura Marx, 23 April 1886 in Rowbotham 1982, p. 190. For British anarchism, see Quail 2014, especially chapter three which deals with the Socialist League.

by Alfred Linnell attacked and killed by police.[54] At the 1887 annual conference of the SL the anarchists formally took over its leadership, condemning it to complete irrelevancy. A year later Eleanor and Aveling led the Bloomsbury branch out of the SL to turn itself into the Bloomsbury Socialist Society.

Undeterred, Engels, Eleanor and Aveling continued their struggle for a revolutionary political programme. 'The immediate intention is to found an English labour party with an independent class programme', Engels told Friedrich Sorge in 1887. 'This would, if all went well, push both the Social Democratic Federation and the Socialist League into the background, which would be the best way of resolving the impending rows'.[55] Some of these rows were rumours about Aveling's personal financial dealings and sexual relationships which were widespread on the British left. A prolific writer and public speaker on Marxism, Aveling was also a well-known propagandist for atheism and Darwin's theory of evolution, in contrast to the Christian sympathies of much of the British left at that time. This allowed him to retain the political trust of both Engels and Eleanor Marx, but also enabled him to dissemble and obscure the moral turpitude which infected his character.[56]

Eleanor Marx in many ways became the embodiment of Engels and her father's goal of creating a working-class movement politically independent of the capitalist parties. During the upsurge of 'new union' militancy, she was an inexhaustible speaker and organiser speaking at demonstrations, strikes and conferences across Britain.[57] What was now required, she wrote in 1890, was

> an awakening of the English working-class to the fact that the immense political power in their hands must be used henceforth, not for the benefit of any middle-class political party, but to form a labour party opposed to and differing from all the old political parties; a realisation of the truth that the final emancipation of the working-class must be won by means of the seizure of political power by the workers themselves, and that in order to abolish class rule and the bourgeois state, the workers must themselves become the state.[58]

She sought to make this a reality through her work in the labour movement. Secretary of the first women's branch of the gasworkers' union, in 1890 Marx

---

54   See Kapp, 2018, pp. 444–8.
55   Engels to Sorge, 4 May 1887, *MECW* vol. 48, no. 56.
56   For Aveling's character, see Williams and Chandler 2020.
57   *Justice*, 25 July 1896.
58   Eleanor Marx 1890, p. 1097.

was elected to its national executive. She taught the gasworkers' union leader and future Labour MP Will Thorne to read and write.[59] She threw herself into organising support for every major class battle of the late 1880s and early 1890s, all while maintaining involvement in the affairs of the Second International. Her political activity during these crucial years stood in counterpoint to the disdainful abstention of Hyndman's SDF.

Politics, of course, abhors a vacuum. Where the SDF abstained, others gained. As Sydney and Beatrice Webb pointed out in their *History of Trade Unionism*, the SDF's loss of union leaders such as Tom Mann and John Burns in the 1880s and its failure to capitalise on its early advantages meant that 'revolutionary socialism ceased to grow; and the rival propaganda of constitutional action became the characteristic feature of the English socialist movement'.[60] The chief beneficiary of the SDF's refusal to involve itself in working-class struggles was the Independent Labour Party (ILP). Formed in Bradford in 1893, the ILP filled the political space that the SDF had refused to occupy. Many of its early members had previously been in the SDF. Tom Mann himself was secretary of the ILP between 1894 and 1897. John Bruce Glasier, the editor of the *ILP News*, began his political career in the SDF, as did Pete Curran, a founding member of the ILP's National Administrative Council and future Labour MP, along with Ben Turner, the first president of the National Union of Textile Workers, James O'Grady, the Bristol trade unionist and future Labour MP, and Henry Snell, another future Labour MP. In Manchester, eight of the eighteen speakers at the founding meeting of the local ILP were SDF members.[61] Even Ramsay MacDonald served a short apprenticeship in it.

The historian Martin Crick has argued that the ILP should not be seen as a direct rival to the SDF because the ILP grew in 'areas that the SDF had been unable to reach for financial and organisational reasons'.[62] But many of the areas that the SDF did not reach were in the industrial north where its hostility to strikes and trade unionism gave it little purchase on working-class militants. In contrast, the ILP had much deeper and active links to the unions and found it easier to build support in these areas. Moreover, the failure of the SDF often led to it being replaced by the ILP. For example, what became the ILP's heartland in West Yorkshire had been an SDF base in the 1880s. Leeds trade unionist Tom Maguire joined the Democratic Federation in the early 1880s and later sided with William Morris and the Socialist League, which boasted branches in Leeds

---

59   See Radice 1974.
60   Webb 1920, p. 399.
61   Reid 1981, pp. 77–8.
62   Crick 1994, p. 72.

and Bradford.[63] Maguire was one of the leaders of the great Leeds gasworkers' strike of 1890 but the inability of the SDF or the Socialist League to provide any practical leadership to the victorious gasworkers led him to throw in his lot with what became the Leeds branch of the ILP. The same was true in Bradford where 'a number of those men who were to form the backbone of the ILP' were former members of the local Socialist League branch.[64] In contrast to the SDF and the Socialist League, the ILP based itself on West Yorkshire's successful major industrial struggles such as the famous Manningham Mills strike in Bradford in 1891. The Bradford Labour Union was formed during this upsurge of militancy and provided the backbone for the formation of the ILP in the city in 1893.[65] When the ILP's Pete Curran stood in the 1897 Barnsley by-election he explicitly linked the party to 'the great struggle in the Engineering Trade, the gloomy outlook in the Textile Industry, the well-grounded discontent in the Mining Trade, with its Low Wages and Tyrannical Rules and Bye-laws'.[66] As the historian Jeff Hill noted, 'the ILP was essentially a party for the new unions'.[67]

The difference between the success of the ILP and failure of the SDF was not, as is sometimes suggested, because the membership of the ILP was more proletarian. David Young's biographical research has demonstrated that 'the SDF – in terms of age, occupation and gender – looks remarkably similar to the ILP'.[68] And, in fact, the SDF did grow in those few areas where it had a relationship with the trade unions. This was the case in Burnley, where it won support among weavers and had a member elected as vice-president of the Burnley Weavers' Association in 1895, and in Salford, where its members were active in the gasworkers' and dockers' unions.[69] The same was true in areas of London such as Hackney, as reflected by the presence of leading SDFers like Harry Quelch and Fred Knee on the London Trades Council.[70] The strength of the British Socialist Party in Glasgow in the early twentieth century can be traced back to Tom Mann's work in promoting dockers' unionisation on the Clyde in the 1880s.[71]

---

63 Thompson 1960, pp. 292–4. The ILP's ability to capitalise on the failure of the Socialist League 'especially in Yorkshire' is noted by Pelling 1965, p. 145.
64 Laybourn and Reynolds 1975, p. 320.
65 Tsuzuki 1991, pp. 96–7.
66 *Labour Leader*, 2 Oct 1897, quoted in Howell 1983, p. 13.
67 Hill 1969, p. 273. See also Pelling 1992, p. 104.
68 Young 2005, pp. 354–76. See also Crick 1991, pp. 24–40. I am grateful to Pat Saunders for her comments here.
69 Hill 1969, p. 100; Reid 1981, pp. 193–201.
70 Collins 1971, p. 66. For more on the SDF in London, see Thompson 1967; Stedman Jones, 1971, 'Postscript'.
71 Campbell 1986, pp. 23–4.

Yet it was not until its 1897 conference that the SDF decided that its members should join trade unions, thanks to a resolution proposed by Edward Aveling (who rejoined the SDF in 1895).[72] But this was not only too late to change the landscape of the labour movement; it also did little to shift the party's deep-going suspicion of working-class action.

The ILP was successful because it was universally perceived as a supporter of trade unions, strikes and workers' rights, even with its mild reformist programme, whereas the SDF's indifference to such struggles meant the potential for Marxism to become a significant force in the British working class was squandered. Although Ross McKibbin argued in 'Why Was There No Marxism in Great Britain?' that Marxism was precluded from gaining a mass following for structural reasons – such as economic, social and gender divisions in the working class, a strong pre-existing 'associational culture' and the deferential nature of British society – this deterministic view ignores the active subjective element in politics.[73] Like much writing on the history of the British labour movement, it replaces the study of politics as they were lived with the certainties of hindsight. If the SDF had been a party capable of capitalising on its early advantages and had thrown itself into the 'new union' wave of militancy from the late 1880s, there would have existed the possibility that the balance of forces in the labour movement in the 1890s could have been more favourable to Marxist politics. As Eric Hobsbawm pointed out, if the British Marxists had heeded Engels's advice to focus on the trade unions, their prospects may have been much rosier.[74] And so too, it might be added, would those of the British working class.

---

72   Rabinovitch 1977, pp. 171–7.

73   McKibbin 1990, pp. 1–41. I am grateful to Tony Barley for his comments on this and many other sections.

74   Hobsbawm 1973, p. 127.

CHAPTER 2

The Labour Party Question: Labourism, Leftism, and the Second International

A quarter of a million miners were locked out of work in July 1893 when the mine-owners announced their plans to reduce wages across Britain's coal fields. On the evening of Thursday 7 September 1893, hundreds of striking miners and their families in the small West Yorkshire pit village of Featherstone gathered to stop stockpiled coal being moved from the local Ackton Hall colliery. As the confrontation escalated, troops from the First Battalion of the South Stafford-shire Regiment were called in to disperse them. At around 9pm, after the crowd had ignored instructions to disperse, local magistrate Bernard Hartley read the Riot Act and ordered them to return home immediately. They responded by showering him with stones. Two soldiers were instructed to open fire. The demonstrators refused to be cowed and less than an hour later the troops again opened fire. This time they took deadly aim. Eight demonstrators were shot, two of whom, miners James Gibbs and James Duggan, died of their wounds shortly after.[1]

The Featherstone killings were the most violent episode in a series of major industrial confrontations that took place across Britain in the 1890s. In the spring of 1893 Hull dockers struck for seven weeks against the employers' attacks on their union, inducing such a state of anxiety in the government that the Royal Navy despatched two gunboats to the River Humber as a warning to the militant city. Between July 1897 and January 1898, the Amalgamated Society of Engineers struck and was then locked out as its members sought to resist the employers' attack on living standards and union rights. These disputes and many others were often provoked by employers to curb the growing strength of the unions, an offensive that would eventually result in the Taff Vale court case of 1901, when a House of Lords ruling effectively abolished the right to strike.[2]

In the midst of the industrial battles of the 1890s, it became clear to the more class-conscious militants that trade unionism on its own could not bring lasting change for the working class. For those workers who believed that com-promise with the capitalist class was neither desirable nor possible, Marxism

---

1 *The Guardian*, 9 Sept 1893. See also Terrett 1906; Neville 1976.
2 Saville 1960.

emerged as a pole of attraction. Partly this was a consequence of the growing interest in socialist ideas stimulated by the rise of new unionism, as seen in the formation of the ILP in 1893 and the popularity of Robert Blatchford's mass-circulation weekly *Clarion* newspaper, first published in 1891. The rising tide of class struggle raised the boats of all ostensible socialists. And, despite its abject failure to provide leadership to working-class struggles, the SDF was also a beneficiary of the increasing polarisation of British society.

Its professed Marxism seemed to offer an intellectual alternative to British reformism's deference, platitudinous religiosity and 'fog in Channel' national-ism. Promoting itself as Marxist, atheist, and seemingly internationalist due to its membership of the Second International, it was able to recruit a small layer of working-class militants whose political education had been forged in the industrial battles of the 1890s rather than in the radical middle-class milieu of the 1880s. Despite bungling its initial opportunity to become a substantial factor in the labour movement, the SDF slowly increased its membership. In 1889 it claimed to have had 1,926 members in 15 branches. By 1900 this had grown, according to its own figures, to 9,000 members in 96 branches.[3]

One such new recruit was the young James Connolly. Born in Edinburgh in 1868 to Irish parents, he was one of many young Scottish militants attracted to the SDF – or the Scottish Socialist Federation (SSF) as its supporters were known in Scotland – by its formal espousal of Marxism. He appears to have become a member around 1892 and published his first article in *Justice* in Janu-ary 1893.[4] An indication of the internationalist perspective of the SDF's Scottish recruits can be seen by the fact that one of Connolly's earliest articles for *Justice* was a report on the SSF's decision to send its own delegate to the 1893 Zurich congress of the Second International. In 1895 he became the secretary of the Edinburgh SDF and the following year he moved to Ireland and founded the Irish Socialist Republican Party (ISRP). Like other revolutionary-minded milit-ants who had been attracted to the SDF, he was soon at odds with its leadership and with his fellow Scottish leftists he sought out international co-thinkers. He was soon attracted to the Socialist Labor Party (SLP) of Daniel de Leon in the United States. In 1897 the SLP had written to the ISRP seeking to collaborate in

---

3 Figures from Tsuzuki 1961, pp. 284–5. The first figure was claimed by John Burns to be double the actual number; Tsuzuki's analysis of membership dues suggest the latter is three times the number of dues-paying members. In August 1894 Engels told Filippo Turati that one SDF member claimed a million people had passed through the SDF since its foundation, although this sounds somewhat exaggerated; see *MECW* vol. 50, p. 340. For a discussion on the survival of the SDF see Hobsbawm 1964, p. 231.

4 Nevin 2006, ch. 1.

building an Irish-American socialist organisation in the United States. The following year J.P. Doull, a blacksmith who was a member of the Edinburgh SDF, visited America and returned with copies of the SLP's *Weekly People* newspaper. Soon a regular flow of SLP literature was coming into Scotland.

For those seeking revolutionary answers, De Leon's party presented an attractive alternative to the SDF. De Leon had unequivocally opposed the Spanish-American War in 1898, was steadfastly anti-racist, and resolutely opposed all alliances with capitalist parties, in or out of government. The SLP was also committed to militant trade union action, denouncing as 'labor fakers' those trade union leaders who sought peace with the employers. In 1895 it had created the Socialist Trade and Labor Alliance as an alternative to the conservative business unionism of the American Federation of Labor, and in 1905 it helped to establish the Industrial Workers of the World (IWW), the most important syndicalist organisation in the English-speaking world. Moreover, in 1899 the SLP undertook a faction fight against the right wing of the party, which eventually broke away to link up with other right-wing socialists to form the Socialist Party of America, demonstrating the importance that De Leon attached to building an organisation of disciplined revolutionaries based on clear political principles.[5] For Connolly and other SDF leftists, the SLP provided a revolutionary alternative to Hyndman and his supporters.

Of course, there was plenty for the oppositionists to oppose. Connolly denounced Hyndman's anti-Semitism during the Boer War, which 'instead of grasping the opportunity to demonstrate the unscrupulous and bloodthirsty methods of the capitalist class, strove to divert the wrath of the advanced workers from the capitalists to the Jews' and compared *Justice* to 'the lowest of the anti-Semitic papers'.[6] In contrast, during Connolly's 1902 local election campaign in Dublin, the ISRP published an appeal to the city's Jewish workers in Yiddish.[7] That same year the coronation of Edward VII saw *Justice* simper that 'the great and growing popularity of the king is not undeserved', and hope the reign of a man they addressed as 'Sire' would 'secure for yourself a name in history which mankind will look back to with admiration and respect'.[8] The SDF leftists countered with a denunciation of the 'corpulent man who is the legal head of the capitalist state of Great Britain' and promised that 'soon we,

---

5 De Leon has yet to receive a definitive biography but see Seretan 1979; Reeves 1972. For his influence in Europe, see Stevenson 1980.

6 Connolly, 'The Socialist Labor Party of America and the London SDF', *The Socialist*, June 1903. I am grateful to Jo Woodward for comments about this section.

7 O'Riordan 1988.

8 *Justice*, 21 June 1902.

the workers, shall come to visit your palace and on the topmost turret we shall raise the red flag of the Socialist Republic'.[9]

The left wing of the SDF coalesced in opposition to the leadership's policy of compromise with the ILP. Initially, many saw the formation of the ILP as a sign of the developing socialist consciousness in the working class. A number of SDFers, Connolly included, joined the ILP after its formation in 1893, maintaining dual membership in both organisations. Engels encouraged Edward Aveling to accept a place on the ILP executive committee in the hope that the new party would offer a genuine alternative to Hyndman. Aveling chaired the committee that drafted the ILP's programme, leading Engels to comment that 'its programme is substantially the same as our own'.[10] But this optimism quickly dissipated as the ILP leadership, principally Keir Hardie and John Bruce Glasier, showed themselves to be more interested in electoral manoeuvring and pious appeals to capitalism than in class struggle. Engels viewed Hardie as 'the greatest stumbling block of all' to building a socialist party, and pointed out that he spent his time in parliament 'spouting hot air about the unemployed to no effect whatever, or else to address inanities to the Queen on the birth of some prince which, in this country, is cheap and trivial to the utmost'.[11] The distrust was mutual. The ILP refused to allow Aveling and Eleanor Marx's Bloomsbury Socialist Society to affiliate and in 1895 they both rejoined the SDF.[12]

Yet, as the ILP consolidated its reformist programme, Hyndman and the SDF leadership became increasingly flirtatious and began a campaign for 'Socialist Unity' with it. In early 1897 SDF leader Harry Quelch declared that the ILP 'is almost at one with the SDF' and began negotiating terms for a united party.[13] The discussions foundered because of the ILP leadership's hostility to the SDF's formal commitment to class struggle and, particularly galling to the Methodist-minded ILP leaders, its atheism. Hardie, who declared himself a convert *from* atheism to Christianity, objected to 'the economic side of socialism being pressed to the front' by the SDF. For him, socialism was 'brotherhood, fraternity, love thy neighbour as thyself, peace on earth, goodwill towards all

---

9   *The Socialist*, August 1902.

10 Engels to Sorge, 18 Jan 1893, *MECW* vol. 50, p. 82. Aveling was elected to the executive committee at the ILP's founding conference, see *Report of the First General Conference*, ILP, 1893, p. 10.

11 Engels to Sorge, 10 Nov 1894, *MECW* vol. 50, p. 356.

12 Kapp 2018, pp. 767–72; Pelling 1965, pp. 118 and 159. ILP National Administrative Committee minutes, 18 November 1893, in papers of the Independent Labour Party, London School of Economics, Library Archives and Special Collections, GB 97 COLL MISC 0702.

13 An excellent account of the unity process can be found in Crick 1994, pp. 88–91. The ILP leadership's attitude is debated in the *Report of the 1898 Conference of the ILP*.

men, and glory to God in the highest'. Glasier told the 1898 ILP conference that 'the SDF has failed to touch the heart of the people. Its strange disregard of the religious, moral and aesthetic sentiments of the people is an overwhelming defect'.[14] Nevertheless, in February 1900 the SDF joined with the ILP and a handful of trade union leaders to create an electoral bloc called the Labour Representation Committee (LRC).

The SDF's leftists had no time for such dalliances. Connolly attacked the SDF leadership by pointing out that since the ILP 'came into existence the SDF has never had the courage to engage in a parliamentary candidature without soliciting the help of the ILP, and playing for the votes of the Radicals [in the Liberal Party]'.[15] For the left, the ILP's reformism was another link in the chain that tied the working class to the capitalist parties, and in particular to the Liberal Party and its radical wing. This struggle for the political independence of the working class also led the SDF leftists to join the fight against 'Millerandism' in the Second International.[16] In June 1899 Alexandre Millerand, the leader of the socialist MPs in the French parliament, accepted the position of minister of commerce in the openly capitalist government of Pierre Waldeck-Rousseau, whose cabinet also included the Marquis de Galliffet, one of the military commanders responsible for the suppression of the Paris Commune and also of colonial peoples in Algeria. Hyndman and the SDF leadership supported Millerand, as did the right wing of the Second International, and the debate about participation in bourgeois governments dominated that year's congress of the International in Paris.[17]

The issue split the British delegation to the Paris congress. The main resolution criticised 'Millerandism' and reasserted 'the class struggle forbids all alliances with any fraction whatever of the capitalist class'. However, it went on to admit that 'exceptional circumstances may sometimes render coalitions necessary'. The resolution was authored by the German Social Democratic Party's Karl Kautsky and designed to placate the left while not restricting the practical politics of the right. Proposing it, Belgian socialist leader Emile Vandervelde argued that participation in government with a capitalist party 'was a ques-

---

14   Hardie and Glasier quoted in Crick 1994, p. 89. For Hardie's conversion to Christianity see Reid 1971, p. 22.

15   James Connolly, 'The Socialist Labor Party of America and the London SDF', *The Socialist*, June 1903.

16   This link was underlined in a letter from Glasgow leftist R. MacDonald to *Justice*, 24 Nov 1900.

17   For an account of the 1900 Congress, see Joll 1974, pp. 93–9. For the SDF stance on Millerand, see *Justice*, 2 Sept 1899.

tion of tactics and not of principle'.[18] George Yates, an engineer from the SDF's Leith branch and a leader of its left wing, voted against the Kautsky resolution on the basis that opposition to joining a capitalist government was definitely a question of principle and not tactics. Standing with Yates was James Connolly, whose ISRP delegates had been seated at the conference despite Hyndman objecting to their presence on the chauvinist grounds that Ireland was part of Britain and therefore only the British SDF should be allowed to attend.[19] Yates returned home from Paris convinced the fight against Millerandism and the SDF's leadership's softness towards the ILP were one and the same.

Six months later, he successfully proposed that the Scottish District Council of the SDF should withdraw from the Scottish Workers' Parliamentary Committee, the Scottish equivalent of the Labour Representation Committee. Buoyed by this victory, the leftists took the battle against Millerandism to the August 1901 SDF conference. Their motion condemning the SDF's support of Kautsky's resolution was not allowed to be debated, but a similar amendment from the Oxford branch did reach the floor of the conference. Following a speech by Quelch, who argued that the SDF would 'adopt any and every means to realise social democracy' including joining capitalist governments, the Oxford amendment was defeated by 37 votes to eight. Yates's and London bricklayer Jack Fitzgerald's motion to end negotiations with the ILP was also unsuccessful. Seeking to negate the threat from the left, Quelch proposed that the SDF should withdraw from the LRC, using the argument that in its eighteen months of existence the LRC had failed to win support from any major trade unions. The motion was carried, although many of Quelch's supporters would later regret his seemingly empty sop to the left.

At the 1902 SDF conference, the left again challenged the leadership's courtship of the ILP but were defeated by 54 votes to 22. It was by now clear that a split was looming, not least because Quelch's closing address to the conference threatened those he called a 'small knot of extremists' that they 'must either fall into line or fall out altogether'.[20] By this time the Scottish left, dubbed 'impossibilists' – a derogatory French term used to distinguish the revolutionary left from Paul Brousse's reformist 'possibilists' – was collaborating openly with De Leon's SLP. Yates had set up the International Labour Literature Depot in Glasgow to import SLP books and pamphlets, and the SLP's *Weekly People*,

---

18   The resolution and extracts from congress speeches are in *Justice*, 6 Oct 1900. For Kautsky, see Salvatori 1979, pp. 71–3.

19   Crick 1994, p. 98.

20   SDF *Conference Report 1902*, p. 25.

sold by leftists in Scotland and London, was claiming 'several hundred' British subscribers.[21] Connolly himself undertook a speaking tour of America in 1902 and worked closely with De Leon while there.

Following its 1902 conference, the London executive of the SDF voted to expel Percy Friedberg from his Finsbury Park branch after he had published a letter in De Leon's *Weekly People* which had been refused publication by *Justice* because of its criticism of the official conference report. When Friedberg's branch refused to expel him, it was expelled en bloc.[22] The Finsbury Park opposition then linked up with the Scots and provided some of the finance for the launch of *The Socialist* in August 1902, ostensibly the monthly of the SDF's Scottish District Council but in reality the paper of the party's left opposition. The internationalist aspirations of the newspaper could be seen in the fact that it was printed by Connolly's ISRP and shipped over from Dublin for distribution.

But the alliance between the London and Scottish oppositionists soon fell apart. The London group suspected the Scots had already decided to split from the SDF after the left's defeat at the 1902 conference. Moreover, in contrast to the Londoners, the Scottish leftists were well-organised, disciplined and, thanks to their links with De Leon, in possession of a clear political alternative to the SDF's programme. The alliance fell apart at the April 1903 SDF conference where, following a vote to expel George Yates, the Londoners baulked at Yates' call for the creation of a new party. Echoing the English nationalism of the SDF leadership, the Londoners declared they 'were no more ready to blindly follow would-be geniuses from Scotland than "highly educated" leaders from Queen Anne's Gate [where Hyndman lived]'.[23] Undeterred, in June 1903 the Edinburgh, Leith, Falkirk and Glasgow branches of the SDF founded the Socialist Labour Party, with new branches soon following in Bethnal Green, Southampton and Kirkcaldy. James Connolly was elected its founding chairman. In September 1904, the SLP could report to the congress of the Second International that it had 'over 200' members in 20 branches, nine of which were in Scotland.[24]

By this time, the SDF leadership had completed its purge of leftists with the expulsion of the leaders of the London opposition, who formed the Socialist Party of Great Britain in June 1904. Once out of the SDF, its leftism proved to

---

21   Tsuzuki 1956, p. 388. SLP Executive Committee minutes, 25 Aug 1904, MS 52602, British Library.

22   Correspondence on the expulsion is in Nevin 2007, pp. 160–1.

23   Quoted in Tsuzuki 1956, p. 394.

24   *The Socialist*, Sept 1904.

be a chimera. The SPGB declared its object to be 'the conquest of the powers of government, national and local, in order that this machinery [of government], including those [armed] forces, may be converted from an instrument of oppression into the agent of emancipation', and pursued a grim messianic parliamentary reformism for the next hundred years and more.[25]

1   The Russian Influence

Despite the excision of its left wing, the SDF's growth in the 1890s significantly altered its composition, although it did little to undermine the domination of the party by Hyndman and his supporters. By 1900 the party was undergoing further change due to an influx of exiled Jewish and Russian Marxists. As anti-Semitic pogroms swept across Russia in the 1880s, around 100,000 fleeing Jews arrived in London and other British cities, many bringing radical and Marxist politics with them.[26] Successive waves of Tsarist repression of political opponents also saw experienced Russian social-democratic cadres escape to Britain, just as Marx and Engels had done in the 1840s. These Russian and Jewish revolutionaries naturally sought out the local Marxist party, which happened to be the SDF, and consequently added a new dimension to the traditionally insular organisation, connecting it to the wider socialist movement and providing the basis for further opposition to Hyndman's politics.

Most prominent among those who joined the SDF was Theodore Rothstein. Born in Lithuania in 1871 to secular Jewish parents, he became a political activist as a teenager. Anxious to avoid the attentions of the Okhrana, the Tsar's secret police, he fled to England in 1891. In 1895 he and his new wife Anna Kahan, also a Russian Jewish exile, joined the SDF, where he became a leading critic of Hyndman.[27] In 1901 he topped the vote in the SDF executive elections and was a delegate to the Second International congresses of 1900, 1904 and 1907. A journalist for a number of bourgeois papers such as the *Manchester Guardian*, Rothstein was a regular contributor to the SPD's *Neue Zeit* and a London correspondent of Lenin's *Pravda*. He also became one of the main conduits between London and both wings of the Russian Social Democratic and Labour

---

25   SPGB 'Declaration of Principles' quoted in Barltrop 1975, p. 9.
26   For an overview, see Kaddish 1992. For a vibrant political portrait of London's East End, see Fishman 2004.
27   For Rothstein's biography see John Saville's introduction to Rothstein 1973, pp. v–xvii; Maisky 1962, pp. 79–87; Burke 1997. A vigorous defence of Rothstein is in Burke and Lindop 1999.

Party (RSDLP). In 1907 he helped persuade the American soap manufacturer Joseph Fels to loan £1,700 to the RSDLP in 1907.[28]

Politically, Rothstein stood firmly in Kautsky's camp in the Second International. Although after 1917 he presented himself as a lifelong supporter of Lenin, he took Kautsky's position on the Millerand question and in the subsequent dispute with the leftists who formed the SLP, Rothstein consciously took a middle position, and in 1902 voted for unity with the ILP.[29] In 1907 he opposed Lenin's strategy of developing an alliance between the Russian working class and peasantry in favour of Plekhanov's 'critical support' for the liberal Constitutional Democrat party.[30] Initially at least he also shared some of Hyndman's distrust of the organised working class, attacking trade unions in 1897 as a 'bulwark against the tide of socialism'.[31]

Rothstein first entered politics in Britain as secretary of the Leeds branch of the 'Society of Friends of Russian Freedom' which was formed in 1890 to support exiles from Tsarist repression, many of whom were among the most prominent names in Russian politics.[32] The anarchist leader Pyotr Kropotkin was perhaps the most famous Russian revolutionary who settled in England, but by the early 1900s London had become an entrepôt for the Marxists of the RSDLP.[33] Vera Zasulich made her home there, Alexandra Kollontai lived there in 1899, and Lenin, Trotsky, Plekhanov and Martov all spent time in the city in the first years of the twentieth century.[34] Within a day of his arrival in London in October 1902 the young Trotsky was taken on a sight-seeing tour by Lenin: 'Vladimir Ilych and I went for a long walk around London. From a bridge, Lenin pointed out Westminster and some other famous buildings. I don't remember the exact words he used, but what he conveyed was: "This is their famous Westminster" and "their" referred of course not to the English but to the ruling classes'.[35] Zasulich, Martov and Trotsky even shared a house in Sidmouth Street in London's King's Cross area for a short time.[36] In the early

---

28   Accounts differ as to the exact amount loaned. It was repaid to Fels widow by the 1922 Soviet trade delegation to Britain, see Rothstein 1970, pp. 27–8.

29   Burke 1997, pp. 61–70.

30   'Social Democrats and their Tactics in the Russian Duma', *Justice*, 30 March 1907.

31   *Justice*, 18 December 1897, quoted in Rabinovitch 1977, p. 195.

32   Grant 1984, chs. 1 and 2.

33   Krupskaya 1970, pp. 64–70.

34   Maisky 1962, pp. 89–93. For an overview of Russian emigres and the British Marxist movement, see Kendall 1969, pp. 77–83, and 1963, pp. 351–78.

35   Trotsky 1975, p. 147. See also Kochan 1970.

36   Rappaport 2010, p. 74. See also Henderson 2020. Issues 32 to 38 of *Iskra* were printed in London, see Rothstein 1970, p. 14.

1900s London was also briefly home to the editorial board of *Iskra*, the chief organ of the then united RSDLP, for whom Harry Quelch organised the printing of its early issues by Hyndman's Twentieth Century Press.[37] This connection was strengthened after the 1905 Russian revolution. Ivan Maisky, the exiled Menshevik who became Stalin's ambassador to Britain in the 1930s, estimated that immediately before World War One there were between four to five thousand Russian exiles in Britain. Maxim Litvinov arrived in 1908 and became the leader of the London-based Bolsheviks. Another Bolshevik leader, Alexander Shlyapnikov, worked in an engineering factory in the north London suburb of Hendon and returned again in 1915 to work as a lathe-turner at the Fiat car factory in Wembley.[38] Yet few of the leading Russian revolutionaries took any interest in the SDF or its work. 'British Marxism was not interesting', Trotsky noted bluntly about his stay in London.[39]

However, other less prominent RSDLP exiles did play active roles in the SDF. M.A. Fischer, who worked with Lenin in St. Petersburg, fled to Newcastle in 1901 with his comrade Alexander Khozetsky. Fischer worked in the engineering industry and set up a Bolshevik group in the city while he was secretary of the Newcastle SDF branch.[40] His son, Willie Fischer, was born there and followed his father into the British Socialist Party (as the SDF would become in 1911) before going to Russia after the revolution. He became a highly successful Soviet intelligence agent and found posthumous Hollywood fame when he was portrayed as Rudolf Abel in the film *Bridge of Spies*, for which the actor Mark Rylance won an Oscar.[41] Newcastle, Britain's main conduit for trade with Northern Europe, also became the home of Bolshevik novelist Yevgeny Zamyatin, the author of the 1921 dystopian novel *We*, who lived there during World War One while working as a maritime engineer.[42] The city was also a base for RSDLP smuggling operations, shipping propaganda, money and arms to the revolutionary movement in Russia.[43] Among the smugglers was a young Konni Zilliacus, the future Labour MP, who helped to transport munitions to Finland during the 1905 revolution.[44] In 1911 Alexander Sirnis, an exiled Russian living in

---

37   For Lenin's reminiscences of Quelch, see V.I. Lenin, *Collected Works* [hereafter CW], vol. 19, pp. 369–71.

38   Shlyapnikov 1982, pp. 54–9. See also Allen 2015, p. 59.

39   Trotsky 1975, p. 150. See also Krupskaya 1970, pp. 64–79 for her memories of life in London.

40   For more on Fischer, see Zelnick 1986, pp. 197–8 and 365; Saunders 2005, pp. 260–78, and 2004, pp. 625–54.

41   Arthey 2015, ch. 1.

42   'Introduction' to Zamyatin 1984, p. 10.

43   See Futtrell 1963, pp. 66–84; Lee 1935.

44   Futrell 1963, p. 69. For more on gun-running see Kendall 1963, pp. 351–78.

a Tolstoyan community in Bournemouth, joined the RSDLP in London, beginning a journey that would see him become part of the revolutionary opposition
to the BSP leadership during World War One, and one of the first translators into
English of Karl Liebknecht and Lenin. His daughter Melita Norwood would also
become a successful Soviet spy, remaining undetected for over sixty years.[45]

The RSDLP held three of its congresses in London, most notably in 1903 when
the party split into Bolsheviks and Mensheviks, but also those of 1905 and 1907.
The SDF was centrally involved in the practical preparations for the fifth RSDLP
Congress in 1907 which was held at the Brotherhood Church at the corner of
Southgate Road and Balmes Road in Hackney. Harry Quelch welcomed the delegates and none other than Ramsay MacDonald attended the congress to offer
the fraternal greetings of the ILP.[46] By the early 1910s Russian and Jewish Marxists comprised a significant proportion of the membership of the BSP's London
branches. There was even a separate Jewish branch of the SDF in London's East
End that was formed in 1901.[47] Yet, despite their international experience and
sophisticated knowledge of European Marxism, Rothstein and his supporters
sought to occupy a middle ground between Hyndman and his leftist opponents
on the major political issues in the decade before the outbreak of World War
One.

2   The Labour Party and the Second International

The most important of these issues would be the attitude taken by the SDF
towards the newly created Labour Party. The Labour Party's forerunner, the
Labour Representation Committee (LRC), was formed in 1900 in response to
the employers' offensive against the trade unions. These attacks on the unions were supported, and often initiated, by the Liberal Party, which created
widespread disquiet in the TUC leadership about its traditional 'Lib-Lab' alliance with them. This led to the 1899 TUC congress voting for a motion from
ILP activists in the Amalgamated Society of Railway Servants calling for a joint
conference with socialist and co-operative organisations to discuss independent trade union representation in parliament.[48]

---

45   Burke 2008. Alexander Sirnis's letter resigning from the BSP and joining the SLP is in the
       Socialist, Nov 1917.
46   Petroff, *The Autobiography of Peter Petroff*, ch. 8, https://www.marxists.org/archive/petroff
       /memoirs/ch08.htm, retrieved 17 August 2015.
47   Lenin spoke at one of its public meetings on his fifth visit to London in 1913, see *Justice*,
       7 March 1913.
48   For the involvement of the ILP, see Howell 1983, pp. 71–83; Marquand 1977, pp. 66–8.

This conference was held at the end of February 1900, supported by 41 small unions together with the ILP, the Fabian Society and the SDF. The TUC parliamentary committee, the forerunner of the General Council, had so little interest in the venture that it did not take a seat on the LRC executive. The conference did not create a separate party but agreed to create 'a distinct Labour group in parliament' with its own policies and discipline. The ILP conspicuously refused to allow the word 'socialism' to appear in the LRC's constitution or policy documents. It also vigorously organised to defeat the SDF's motion calling for the LRC to be 'based upon a recognition of the class war, and having for its ultimate object the socialisation of the means of production, distribution, and exchange' and within a year the SDF had abandoned the LRC.

Despite a veneer of democratic functioning, the controlling force behind the LRC was the ILP, for whom it was a device with which to garner influence among trade union leaders. Moreover, as the SDF leftists had warned, the ILP was also quick to extend a hand to the Liberals. Less than three months after its formation, the LRC was already indicating its willingness to negotiate with local Liberal or Conservative parties 'to leave an open field for the Labour candidates'. In 1903 Keir Hardie and Ramsay MacDonald, the LRC's founding secretary, reached a secret agreement with Herbert Gladstone, the Liberal Party's chief whip, whereby the LRC would show 'friendliness to the Liberals in any constituency where it had influence' in exchange for the Liberals dropping opposition to selected LRC candidates.[49] That same year, Hardie called on the rising star of the Liberal Party, David Lloyd George, to 'lead a Progressive Alliance of Radicals, Irish and Labour', an idea to which MacDonald would return in the years immediately before World War One.[50]

Far from trying to free the labour movement from the alliance with the Liberal Party, the formation of the LRC was an attempt by the ILP leadership to reconfigure the relationship with the Liberals by using the growing strength of the unions as a bargaining tool. 'Independent' trade union-supported MPs would give the union leadership a stronger negotiating position with the Liberal Party than that currently enjoyed by the small number of 'Lib-Lab' MPs who sat on the Liberal benches. Moreover, the potential of the LRC to win working-class votes from the Conservatives and thus help Liberal candidates against their Tory rivals was not lost on the leaders of the Liberal Party, who reacted to the rise of the LRC with quiet equanimity. The LRC may have separ-

---

49   Quotations from Miliband 1961, pp. 19–20. See also Pelling 1965; Thorpe 2015.
50   *Labour Leader*, 7 March 1903, quoted in Wrigley 1976, p. 22, and pp. 44–5 for MacDonald's continuing interest in the idea.

ated organisationally from the Liberals, but politically it remained committed to an alliance with them.[51]

It is quite possible that the LRC would have remained a marginal force in the labour movement were it not for the intensification of the employers' decade-long war against the trade unions. In the summer of 1900, the Railway Servants' union in South Wales went on strike against the Taff Vale Railway Company in support of a victimised member, John Ewington. When the strike ended, the company sued the union for damages. When the case came before the House of Lords in July 1901, it ruled in favour of the Taff Vale company, ordered the union to pay £23,000 to the company and £19,000 in legal costs, and decreed that henceforth unions were liable for damages if they took industrial action. This of course meant that any union could be bankrupted by an employer if it went on strike.

So, in the face of the Liberal Party's refusal to oppose what became known as the Taff Vale decision, the LRC's call for independent labour movement MPs became much more attractive to the union leaders. Within 18 months of the Taff Vale decision the LRC had grown to 127 affiliated unions with more than 850,000 members. Its programme to pressure the Liberals and recalibrate the status quo so as to neutralise anti-union legislation expressed the narrow interests of the leadership of the trade unions. The idea that the party represented the interests of the whole of the working class or was even a vehicle for working-class struggles against the ruling class was not part of its mission. Indeed, at the 1906 general election when 29 LRC MPs were elected, 24 of them won seats due to agreements with local Liberal parties. The newly elected Liberal Government, keen to retain the support of the LRC, introduced the 1906 Trade Disputes Act reversing the Taff Vale decision.

This parliamentary breakthrough for the Labour Party (to which the LRC had changed its name when its new MPs first gathered in February 1906) brought increased pressure on the SDF to rejoin it. Partly this came from within – at the 1908 SDF conference Hyndman and Dan Irving argued for joining Labour, a view that was also held by many Lancashire branches – but significant pressure also came from the leadership of the Second International. The International's 1904 Amsterdam Congress had called for the unification of all socialist organisations in each country, arguing that:

> it is necessary that in every country there exists only one Socialist party, as there exists only one proletariat. Therefore it is the imperative duty

---

51   Hinton 1983, p. 74.

of all comrades and socialist organisations to make every effort to bring about this unity on the basis of the principles established by the international congresses, a unity necessary in the interests of the proletariat before which they are responsible for all fatal consequences of a continued breach.[52]

The immediate aim of the 1904 directive was the merger of Jules Guesde's revolutionary Parti Socialiste de France with Jean Jaures' reformist Parti Socialiste Français to create the Section Francaise de l'Internationale Ouvriere (SFIO). Over the next decade the resolution also became a weapon with which to attack the Bolsheviks' refusal to compromise with the Mensheviks. But its message also applied to British supporters of the International. Pressure was exerted on the SDF to unite with the ILP and join the Labour Party. Max Beer, Eduard Bernstein's successor as the London correspondent of the SPD's daily *Vorwärts*, was perhaps the most articulate advocate of unity. Bernstein's development of revisionism – an explicit reformism based on the axiom that 'the goal is nothing, the movement is all' – was heavily influenced by his decade-long exile in England, where he developed close relationships with many leaders of the Fabian Society, including Sidney and Beatrice Webb.[53]

Beer followed in Bernstein's wake both journalistically and politically. In 1902 he criticised Hyndman for allowing 'revolutionary vocabulary' to stand in the way of the SDF joining the LRC. He deliberately provoked the SDF in 1908 by writing to the ILP's weekly *Labour Leader* in lavish praise of Keir Hardie – 'of all British Socialists none, in my judgment, has grasped the essence of modern Socialism – aye, of Marxism – better than Hardie', and accusing the recently-elected militant left-wing MP Victor Grayson of 'sentimental harangues' about the poor.[54] That same year the ILP's new monthly *Socialist Review* printed some hitherto unpublished correspondence between Marx, Engels and Friedrich Sorge criticising Hyndman and the SDF. The letters, it claimed, demonstrated that by taking the leading role in the Labour Party, the ILP was implementing the *Communist Manifesto*'s injunction that 'communists do not form a separate party opposed to the other working-class parties'.[55] Given that the ILP's attitude

---

52   Quoted in 'Resolution on unification and statements at the London conference of the International Socialist Bureau, Dec. 14, 1913' in Gankin and Fisher 1940, p. 94.

53   Bernstein 1921, ch. 10. According to Theodore Rothstein, Beer had spent time in America and supported Daniel de Leon, but once in Britain became 'attached to the Labour Party, supporting it and the tactics of its leaders through thick and thin', see 'Max Beer and the Labour Opportunists' *Justice*, 5 Dec 1908.

54   *Justice*, 26 July 1902. *Labour Leader*, 27 Nov 1908.

55   *Socialist Review*, no. 1, March 1908, pp. 24–32. The letter from Engels to Sorge of 18 January

to Marx usually veered between wilful ignorance and Little England dismissive-
ness, it seems safe to assume that the publication of the heavily edited letters
was inspired, if not initiated, by Beer and the increasingly right-wing leadership
of the Second International, for whom the Labour Party's electoral gains at the
1906 General Election had whetted its electoral appetite. Of course, what the
Socialist Review article ignored was that Marx and Engels wanted 'an English
labour party with an independent class programme', not merely organisational
separation from the Liberal Party. Nor did it mention that Engels had little time
for Hardie.[56]

A few months later, at its October 1908 executive meeting in Brussels, the
International Socialist Bureau, as the Second International was known from
1900, accepted the Labour Party into membership. The motion was proposed by
Kautsky, who argued that although Labour did not 'explicitly accept the proletarian class struggle', it should be allowed to join because 'nevertheless, it carries
it on in practice, and by its organisation, which is independent of bourgeois
parties, bases itself on the foundations, the principles of international socialism'.[57] This latter assertion was based on the fact that Labour's annual conference that year had narrowly passed an ambiguously-worded motion from
ILP leader and Labour Party chairman J.J. Stephenson declaring 'the time has
arrived when the Labour Party should have as a definite object the socialisation of the means of production, distribution, and exchange, to be controlled
by a democratic state in the interest of the entire community; and the complete
emancipation of Labour from the domination of capitalism and landlordism,
with the establishment of social and economic equality between the sexes'.[58]
As the wily Stephenson knew, the ambiguous modal verb 'should' allowed the
motion to be embraced or ignored according to individual taste. Although
Theodore Rothstein informed the readers of the SPD's theoretical journal *Neue
Zeit* that 'everyone knew that this resolution did not make the Labour Party
socialist', it was a large enough fig-leaf for Kautsky and the International to
embrace the British party without undue embarrassment.[59]

Lenin also attended the meeting and argued that the Labour Party's membership should be accepted because, as the parliamentary representative of

---

   1893 (p. 31) was edited to remove Engels's reference to Keir Hardie's 'personal ambition'
   and 'sundry ulterior aims', see *MECW* 50, pp. 81–4. The same argument was used by Keir
   Hardie in his 1910 pamphlet, *Karl Marx: The Man and His Message*, pp. 10–11.

56   Engels to Sorge, 4 May 1887, *MECW* vol. 48, p. 56.
57   Gankin and Fisher 1940, p. 67.
58   Quoted in Beer 1920, p. 333.
59   Theodore Rothstein, 'Eine Resolution und ihre Bedeutung', *Die Neue Zeit*, vol. 21 (1908),
   p. 733.

the British trade unions, it was little different from the trade unions led by bourgeois politicians which the International had previously accepted as members. However, echoing Engels, he argued that Kautsky's motion was wrong because Labour was 'not a party really independent of the Liberals, and does not pursue a fully independent class policy'. Instead, he offered an amendment to Kautsky's motion stating that the Labour Party 'represents the first step on the part of the really proletarian organisations of Britain towards a conscious class policy and towards a socialist workers' party'. Kautsky refused to accept Lenin's amendment and his unamended motion was passed with only four votes against, most oddly by Hyndman, who had voted *for* affiliation to the Labour Party at that year's SDF conference, and, more seriously, Roman Avramov, the delegate of the leftist Bulgarian Social Democratic 'Narrow' Party.[60]

Other than being organisationally separate from the Labour Party, the SDF's practical politics were not significantly different from those of the ILP. Although there was much breast-beating in the pages of *Justice* about Labour's non-aggression electoral pacts with the Liberals, Harry Quelch himself tried to arrange a no-contest deal with the Liberal Party when he stood for parliament at Southampton in 1906.[61] It had been just such an agreement with the Liberals that had enabled the SDF's Will Thorne, the former leader of the gasworkers' union, to win the West Ham South constituency for the LRC at the 1906 general elections.[62] Thorne's record as an MP was hardly that of a revolutionary firebrand seeking to rouse the masses through parliamentary agitation. He was indistinguishable from any other Labour MP (and probably most Liberals), notoriously sitting silently on the Labour benches in October 1908 when MP Victor Grayson was suspended from the House of Commons for protesting about starvation caused by unemployment – but not before calling it 'a house of murderers' and denouncing the silent Labour Party MPs such as Thorne as traitors to their class. Quelch also joined with Max Beer in condemning Grayson's 'theatrical, irresponsible, inconsequent and, worst of all, futile' protest.[63]

---

60 V.I. Lenin, 'Meeting of the International Socialist Bureau' *CW* vol. 15, pp. 233–9. The section on Britain was translated by Zelda Kahan and published as 'A Foreign View of the British Labour Party' in *Justice*, 28 Nov 1908. Rothschild 1959, pp. 58–9. See also Schlesinger 1965, pp. 448–58.

61 Crick 1994, p. 191.

62 See Radice 1974, p. 58.

63 For Thorne's parliamentary activity, see Radice 1974, pp. 58–62. For Grayson, see *Hansard*, HC Deb 16 Oct 1908, vol. 194 cc. 614–34. Quelch, 'The Future of the Labour Party' in *The Social Democrat*, vol. 12, no. 11, Nov 1908, pp. 481–7.

The admission of the Labour Party into the International renewed the debate about the SDF joining Labour. In March 1909, Karl Radek, an ally of Rosa
Luxemburg in the left wing of the German SPD, wrote an article for *Neue Zeit*
in which he criticised Max Beer for calling on the SDF to join the Labour Party.
Beer had written in *Vorwärts*, the SPD daily, 'if I had to choose between a small
and efficient socialist party and a large non-socialist, but politically and economically independent working class party, I should decide, without hesitation
in favour of the latter' and called on British Marxists to join Labour.[64] In reply,
Radek argued that the Labour Party was not politically independent but tied to
the Liberals and thus ultimately to the capitalist class. The hostility of its members to socialist ideas was not because they did not understand them or were
unaware of them, but because 'they are possessed of bourgeois ideas, and wish
to determine their policy accordingly'.

He went on to argue that the experience of the SPD in Germany had demonstrated that Marxists could not win over the mass of the working class by
'mere abstract propaganda of their principles; they must take part in the political and economic struggle of the working class for the raising of its position'. To join Labour necessarily meant compromising the practical struggle
for Marxist politics and implementing Labour's programme. The article continued:

> what is the effect of such a policy upon the Social-Democratic elements?
> The leaders become demoralised, the policy of compromise cuts away
> every solid foundation from under their feet, for such a foundation can
> only be formed by a principle; they become confused; that which was to
> be a clever trick in order to accelerate events, becomes their real point of
> view. And those of the workers who had already become Socialists sink
> back from the heights they have reached into the morass of 'Labour polit-
> ics'.[65]

Kautsky himself responded to Radek's article, believing that it was he who was
its real target. At the 1908 plenary meeting of the Second International, both
he and Victor Adler had spoken in support of the ILP's relationship with the
Labour Party and its refusal in that year's Newcastle by-election to oppose the
Liberals – a stance that put them to the right of most ILP members, who sup-

---

64   'Die Britische Arbeiterpartei und der Sozialismus', *Vorwärts*, 30 Dec 1908.
65   Karl Radek, 'Bemerkungen zur Frage der Einheit der Arbeiterklasse', *Die Neue Zeit*, 12
      March 1909, p. 872.

ported the SDF candidate.[66] The Millerandist, 'lesser-evil' underpinnings of this position would be spelt out by Adler's successor as leader of the Austrian SPD, Otto Bauer:

> the Labour Party cannot nominate candidates everywhere: if it takes away part of the Liberal votes in a constituency, without obtaining a relative majority for itself, the Conservative imperialist is elected ... The greatest precaution is therefore necessary in the nomination of candidates; otherwise the effect of the party's agitation would be that instead of the least dangerous, the most dangerous among the bourgeois opponents would be elected.[67]

In his reply to Radek, Kautsky appeared to restate Marxist orthodoxy: 'the peculiarity of England consists in the fact that the conditions there render it necessary for the Marxists to form a separate, solid organisation'.[68] Yet at the same time he blurred the political differences between the Marxists and the Labour Party by contending that they were each 'to be considered as two organs with different functions of which one is the complement of the other, and of which one can function but imperfectly without the other'.[69] In contrast to Radek's clarity about the pro-capitalist nature of the Labour Party's politics and practice, Kautsky suggested, contrary to all evidence, that it was 'a Labour Party without a programme' that could be compared to 'a tremendous ship, but the socialist organisations are the compass and rudder of this ship – without these it would be tossed hither and thither by the waves'. He concluded by stating 'the social democracy as a separate body is still indispensable for the education of the Labour Party, but this could best be done as a member of the Labour Party'.[70]

How this 'could best be done' in the Labour Party was not explained. At this time the Labour Party had no organised branch structure (in 1908 there were

---

66   McNeilly 2009, pp. 431–53. Kautsky and Adler's support for the ILP contrasted strongly with Lenin's attitude to it. Writing about the 1913 Leicester by-election when the ILP also stood aside for the Liberals, he wrote: 'Class-conscious workers in various countries quite often adopt a "tolerant" attitude toward the British ILP. This is a great mistake. The betrayal of the workers' cause in Leicester by the ILP is no accident, but the result of the entire opportunist policy of the Independent Labour Party'. CW vol. 19, p. 274.

67   Bauer, 'Imperialism and Socialism in England', published in January 1910, in Day and Gaido 2011, p. 405. For Bauer, see Czerwinska-Schupp 2017.

68   Karl Kautsky, 'Sekte oder Klassenpartei', *Die Neue Zeit*, 2 April 1909, p. 11.

69   Kautsky, 'Sekte oder Klassenpartei', p. 11.

70   Kautsky, 'Sekte oder Klassenpartei', p. 14 and p. 12.

fewer than a hundred local Labour Representation Committees in existence),
no individual members, and no control over its MPs, for whom policy was
decided largely by the leadership cabal of Ramsay MacDonald, Philip Snowden
and Arthur Henderson.[71] Rather than being a political party in the traditional
sense, it remained the same undemocratic bloc between the ILP, the Fabians
and the trade union bureaucracy that it had been when it was created in 1901.[72]
Even more importantly, at exactly the moment that Kautsky was writing these
lines, the most militant sections of the British working class were drawing precisely the opposite conclusions.

---

71   For details of branches, see Pugh 2010, p. 89. At the outbreak of World War One this had
      risen to 142.

72   For the structure of the LRC and the pre-1918 Labour Party, see McKibbin 1974, ch. 1.

Britain in Crisis: Labour's Great Unrest and the Revolutionary Left

In 1907 Victor Grayson was elected as a 'Socialist and Labour' MP for the Colne Valley in West Yorkshire, despite the Labour Party refusing to endorse him.[1] His victory, he declared, was because, unlike Labour, 'we have not trimmed our sails' and, somewhat more extravagantly, that his election was a triumph for 'pure revolutionary socialism'.[2] A month after Grayson's election, militant union leader Jim Larkin led the Belfast Dock Strike which united Catholic and Protestant workers in a bitter four-month struggle for union recognition. The British Army was called in and two Catholic workers were shot dead by troops. Although the strike was ultimately defeated, it laid the basis for the creation of the Irish Transport and General Workers Union (ITGWU).

A few weeks later, the Amalgamated Society of Railway Servants (ASRS) voted overwhelmingly for strike action for union recognition. Fearful of a repeat of the Belfast summer, the Liberal government and the railway union leaders quickly set up a conciliation board that bypassed the issue of union recognition. Outraged at this betrayal, local branches of the ASRS refused to support the secretary of the Associated Society of Locomotive Engineers and Firemen, Albert Fox, as the Labour Party parliamentary candidate in Leeds early in 1908 because of his role in derailing recognition of their union. The railworkers' intransigence set the tone for the rest of the year.

Disputes broke out in textiles, engineering and shipbuilding and the annual number of working days lost through industrial disputes quadrupled.[3] In September, simmering discontent among ILP members about the supine attitude of Labour MPs to the Liberal government broke out in open rebellion during a parliamentary by-election in Newcastle. The national ILP had instructed its candidate, J.J. Stephenson, to withdraw in order to give the Liberals a free run.

---

1 Colne Valley Labour League, Central Council minutes, 12 Jan 1907 archived at Heritage Quay, Huddersfield CVL/GV/1/1/1900. To become the candidate, Grayson defeated future ILP chair William G. Anderson. For the ILP debate on Grayson, see ILP, *Report of the 16th Annual Conference* (London: ILP, 1908) pp. 43–54.

2 Quoted in Pugh 2010, p. 70. Grayson's story is told in Clark 1985, and Groves 1975.

3 Challinor 1977, p. 63.

Outraged, local ILPers threw their support behind the SDF candidate.[4] The following month Grayson was famously thrown out of the House of Commons for protesting against unemployment, which resulted in him being denounced by the Labour Party leadership and thrown off the ILP's approved speakers' list. The title of Ben Tillett's widely-read pamphlet of that year, *Is the Parliamentary Labour Party a Failure?*, summed up the growing disenchantment felt by many working-class people. Such was the storm of discontent that at the 1909 ILP conference Hardie, MacDonald, Snowden and Glasier threatened to resign if it voted to allow local ILP branches (rather than the national Labour Party leadership) to select parliamentary candidates. In the face of the leadership's threat to behead its own party, the conference voted the proposal down. But the turmoil would not abate and a steady trickle of ILP branches broke away, disillusioned by its Labourism. One of these was the Openshaw branch in Manchester, which counted among its members Mary Pollitt and her son, future Communist Party leader Harry. In 1920 it became the Openshaw branch of the CPGB.

Discontent with the prevailing order began to spread through the working class. In 1910 over 10 million days were lost annually through strikes and lock-outs, as miners and railway workers in the north east, textile workers in Lancashire and boilermakers in the shipbuilding industry all came face-to-face with the hostility of the employers.[5] In November 30,000 miners in South Wales went on strike against the Cambrian Combine mine-owners, culminating in Winston Churchill sending cavalry and infantry to Tonypandy to restore order after the local police were overwhelmed by thousands of demonstrators.[6] 1911 was engulfed by wave after wave of strikes in the docks and on the railways. Women factory workers went on strike in London, Swansea, Leith and the Vale of Leven. Hull was flooded with Metropolitan policemen as seamen and dockers struck against the employers, supported by strikes by women workers and even schoolchildren.[7]

In Liverpool a transport workers' strike led by Tom Mann escalated into a general strike that was met by soldiers marching through the city with fixed bayonets. Gunboats were stationed in the Mersey and on 15 August John Sutcliffe, a carter, and Michael Prendergast, a docker, were shot dead by soldiers

---

4   The leadership of the Second International, including Kautsky, opposed the SDF over the Newcastle episode, see McNeilly 2009, and *Justice*, 17 Oct 1908, p. 7.

5   For background, see Pelling 1979, pp. 147–64; Halévy 1952; Sires 1955; Meacham 1972; Mates 2016; White 1982; Glasgow Labour History Workshop 1992.

6   Smith 1980.

7   Brooker 1979; Marson 1973, estimates that school strikes took place in 62 towns and cities during 1911.

from the 18th Hussars, just a small detachment of the 3,500 troops that were stationed in and around the city. Liberal cabinet minister Herbert Samuel confided to his wife that 'Liverpool is verging on a state of revolution'.[8] Four days later in Llanelli, the Worcestershire Regiment, which had been called in to stop demonstrations against scab labour, shot and killed a tin-plate worker named Jack John. Leonard Worsell, who was watching events from his back garden, was also fatally wounded by the soldiers.[9] By the middle of August, Britain was on the verge of general strike, but the wily Lloyd George, the Liberal chancellor of the exchequer, brought Ramsay MacDonald into the negotiations with the unions and a settlement was reached.

Yet this only temporarily staunched the growing self-confidence of the workers. A January 1912 ballot of miners saw the Miners' Federation of Great Britain call a nationwide strike, and a million miners walked out in support of a minimum wage. Tom Mann was jailed for sedition in May for publishing 'Don't Shoot', a statement calling on soldiers to show solidarity with strikers which was originally published in Jim Larkin's *Irish Worker*.[10] Mann was one of eight militants prosecuted for republishing the leaflet. In April the *Daily Herald* was launched as a mass circulation daily to the left of the Labour Party, sympathetic to syndicalism and openly hostile to the Labour and trade union leadership. During major strikes it sold 150,000 copies a day.[11] The following month London dockers shut down the port of London, only to be starved back after six weeks when the London County Council refused to provide free meals for docker's children during the summer holidays.[12] 1913 saw engineers and building workers locked in conflict with their employers, and in Dublin tens of thousands of workers waged a desperate struggle against an employers' lock-out designed to kill trade unionism and the Jim Larkin-led ITGWU in particular. Thousands of railway workers in Britain refused to handle goods destined for Ireland and solidarity strikes flared up across the country in support of the Dublin workers. 'The Great Labour Unrest', as it became known, demonstrated for the first time since the days of the Chartists that the working class could take the ruling class by the throat.

But its leaders failed to tighten the grip. On 9 December 1913 the TUC organised a special delegate conference to discuss solidarity action with the locked-

---

8   Taplin 1994. Davis and Noon 2014. For eyewitness accounts, see *The Transport Worker*, Aug 1911. Samuel quoted in Wrigley 1976, p. 63.

9   Hopkin 1983.

10   Fletcher 1996.

11   Richards 1997, pp. 16–21.

12   Sires 1955.

out Dublin workers. Instead, Labour's Arthur Henderson used it as an opportunity to blame the intransigence of the ITGWU leadership for the continuation of the lock out. The conference then passed a motion – proposed by erstwhile BSP executive member Ben Tillett – condemning Jim Larkin for his criticism of the TUC's failure to adequately support the Dublin workers. Instead of solidarity, the conference refused to support action to stop goods coming into British docks from Dublin.[13]

To the left-wing militants who had been at the forefront of the struggles of the preceding years this came as no surprise. Throughout the convulsions gripping British society, the Labour Party and the TUC leadership had never wavered in their commitment to the stability of the social order. In August 1911, as the railway workers' strike spread across the country, Chancellor of the Exchequer Lloyd George warned their leaders that the dispute would undermine Britain's response to the German navy's moves against French interests in Morocco, the so-called Agadir Crisis. Confronted with a test of their patriotism, the union leadership, supported by Labour's Arthur Henderson and Ramsay MacDonald, quickly reached a settlement. According to Chris Wrigley, the reality was that Lloyd George had simply concocted the supposed threat to the national interest as a negotiating gambit. It would not be the last time that the leadership of the labour movement found themselves out-manoeuvred by the Welsh Machiavelli.[14] Sometimes they even did his job for him. That same year Henderson and three other Labour MPs proposed a parliamentary bill to make strikes illegal if a union did not give thirty days' notice to the employers. J.R. Clynes, then Labour's deputy chairman, told the 1914 Labour Party conference that 'frequent strikes cause a sense of disgust'.[15] But for those militants who were fighting to replace capitalism with socialism, the Labour Party and the TUC leadership were the objects of their disgust.

1   Realignment on the Left and the British Socialist Party

For ostensible Marxists in Britain this explosion of class war and the widespread hostility to the official leaders of the labour movement presented their greatest opportunity since the 1889 London Docks Strike. But once again, the SDF failed miserably. By the time it changed its name to the Social Democratic Party in 1908 many of its members were trade unionists but the party itself still

---

13   Darlington 2016.
14   Wrigley 1976, pp. 63–5.
15   Miliband 1961, p. 38.

held a deep-seated antipathy to industrial action. During the 1912 miners' strike, Harry Quelch, a long-time member of the London Trades Council executive, told readers of the *British Socialist* that

> we social-democrats have always deprecated strikes, not because they are necessarily attended by riot and disorder, but because they entail loss and privation and want upon the strikers, and very real sacrifice, for, at best, a dubious gain. Generally they are futile, but even at the best they achieve no more than could be gained at far less cost and with greater certainty by other methods.

When it came to the regular use of the army against strikers and picket lines, Quelch saw no difference between the violence of the soldiers called on to break strikes and the anger of strikers and their families. 'We have over and over again appealed to soldiers not to allow themselves to be made use of against strikers and not to fire on their fellow-workers. But such appeals are ridiculous if at the same time we are going to encourage riot and disorder on the part of the strikers'.[16]

This neutrality extended to the relationship between trade union bureaucrats and rank and file members. Fred Knee, a London printer and a former alderman of Battersea Borough Council, even justified the privileges of full-time officials:

> having to do the work practically of lawyers, there is no help for [the trade union executive officer]; they have to live nearly up to the lawyers' level. The very additional comfort which is absolutely necessary for the product and maintenance of an efficient trade union official has the effect ... of inducing different habits of mind.

He went on to call for greater unity between officials and the rank and file: 'let us act together more solidly, leaders and rank and file, rank and file and leaders, members and officials of one union with members and official of the other union'.[17]

For those workers looking to go beyond industrial militancy, the SDF offered only parliamentary elections. 'The all-important lesson which this series of strikes should have taught the workers', Quelch explained in 1912, is 'industrial

16   'Riot and Revolution', *The British Socialist*, April 1912.
17   Fred Knee, 'The Revolt of Labour' *The Social Democrat*, 15 Nov 1910, reprinted in *Labour Monthly*, June 1950, pp. 275–9.

organisation, by all means; industrial action, certainly, in order to defend what you may have, or to win some better conditions … But a strike costs much in sacrifice and privation, whereas it costs nothing at all to vote. And if one is prepared to strike against the masters, one should, at least, be prepared to vote against them'.[18] This did not differ fundamentally from the ILP, nor indeed the Labour leadership, and put the SDF leaders far to the right of the syndicalists and industrial unionists whose militancy was now winning an audience.

Despite this, the SDF's formal commitment to Marxism once again gave it credibility among many leftward-moving militants. Between 1900 and 1911 the number of SDF branches doubled to 189, reaching a peak of 235 in 1910, with paper membership fluctuating between 12,000 and 17,000 in the latter years. In contrast, ILP membership fell sharply between 1909 and 1911, reflecting the increasing disillusionment with the Labour Party. Despite winning 42 seats at the December 1910 general election, the Labour Party remained simply a prop for Asquith's Liberal government, achieving little more, in the memorable words of George Dangerfield, than 'to wear frock coats, to attend royal garden parties, to become as time passed just a minor and far from militant act in the pantomime of Westminster'.[19]

Victor Grayson's by-election victory and his militant stance became the catalyst for the emergence of a left-wing opposition in the ILP. In 1909 Grayson and G.R.S. Taylor wrote *The Problem of Parliament*, a pamphlet attacking the Labour Party and calling for a new socialist party. This was followed in 1910 by four of the 14 members of the ILP's national council publishing *Let Us Reform the Labour Party*, known as the Green Manifesto, which placed the blame for the Labour Party's prostration before the Liberals squarely on the shoulders of MacDonald and the ILP MPs. Following the two general elections of 1910, when the Labour Party made clear that its role in parliament was to support Asquith's beleaguered Liberals, the cracks in the ILP quickly became a cleavage. A new political realignment began to take place on the left.

In some places, such as Woolwich, Openshaw, and Huddersfield, the ILP fractured as leftists broke away in opposition to the leadership's support for Labour Party policy. The Colne Valley Socialist League, for whom Victor Grayson was the MP, voted to leave the ILP by an overwhelming 481 votes to 177.[20] At its

---

18   'Socialism and the Coal Strike', *The British Socialist*, March 1912.

19   Kendall 1969, pp. 311–12 for SDF membership and p. 37 for ILP. Of those 42 seats, 38 were won through some form of pact with the Liberals. Dangerfield 2015, p. 10.

20   For Woolwich, see Thompson 1967 p. 201. For Huddersfield, Pearce 2001, p. 49. For Openshaw, Pollitt 1940, p. 32. For Colne Valley, see the minutes of the Special Council Meeting of 22 May 1910 at Heritage Quay, Huddersfield, CVL/GV/1/1/1900.

Easter 1911 conference the SDF called for socialist unity with the ILP and those Fabian Society members 'who believe in industrial and political action'. During the summer Grayson resigned from the ILP, calling for a new socialist party to be formed to the left of Labour. In September, 85 SDF branches, 41 ILP branches, 50 local socialist societies (including the Huddersfield rebels) and 32 local clubs of supporters of Robert Blatchford's weekly *Clarion* newspaper met at a conference in Salford to form the British Socialist Party. The new organisation claimed 343 branches and 40,000 members. It appeared to many that a genuine rival to the ILP was emerging.[21]

It did not. Behind the scenes, the conference was wracked by disputes between the SDF leadership and leftward-moving industrial militants about its attitude to industrial unionism. Victor Grayson was sidelined by Hyndman's experienced factionalists and quickly dropped out of politics. At the first annual conference of the BSP in May 1912, Hyndman and Quelch forced through a motion calling for the creation of a citizen army – 'to be used not only against foreign aggression but against domestic despotism' – against the objections of the left, for whom a young Willie Gallacher told the conference they 'should condemn all ideas of patriotism and all ideas of militarism, unless it took the form of shooting down those who exploited them. They must stand as internationalists, and not trouble about nationalism'. Uproar then broke out when Russell Smart, a left-wing former ILP national council member, informed the conference that the first issue of the BSP's planned newspaper had been suppressed by the party leadership because it contained an article sympathetic to syndicalism.[22] The unravelling of the BSP's constituent parts, which had begun even before the party's foundation, was quickly completed and by 1913 it had contracted back to its SDF core.

The BSP failed to make an impact on the great wave of class struggle that was engulfing Britain. The party was so far out of touch with events that Beatrice Webb, never one to let social commentary stand in the way of social snobbery, remarked in 1913 that 'syndicalism has taken the place of the old-fashioned Marxism. The angry youth, with bad complexion, frowning brow and weedy frame is now always a syndicalist'.[23] Although historians have attributed the breakup of the BSP to SDF 'sectarianism', the reality was that the BSP was a product of two ships passing in the night, as many ILP and local socialist society

---

21   BSP, *Socialist Unity Conference Report*, 1911. Crick, *The SDF*, pp. 240–1.

22   The debate on patriotism is on pp. 20–3 of the 1912 BSP *First Annual Conference Report*, 1912. See also the account of the conference in *The Times*, 27 and 28 May 1912.

23   Quoted in Darlington 2008, p. 104.

elements moved leftwards towards revolutionary politics, while its SDF component shifted rightwards towards the Labour Party.

2 The Second International Steers towards the Labour Party

Since the mid-1900s, the SDF's formal opposition to the Labour Party had become increasingly threadbare. As early as 1903 it had encouraged its branches to join their local Labour Representation Committee 'wherever there are opportunities for influencing such committees in a socialist direction' and in 1905 Lancashire branches proposed that the SDF should rejoin the national LRC, something that became an annual conference ritual for the Lancastrians.[24] The failure of the BSP to build a left-wing alternative to Labour revived the debate about 'socialist unity' with the ILP and the Fabians as a precursor to joining the Labour Party. This found significant support among those BSP members disillusioned by the inability of the party to grow. Some branches, such as in Leeds, short-circuited the discussion by simply walking away from the party. At its 1913 annual conference the BSP held a wide-ranging debate about joining the Labour Party, at which even Hyndman admitted that it had been a mistake for the SDF to leave the Labour Representation Committee in 1901.[25]

Once again, the leaders of the Second International sought to steer the BSP into the Labour Party. In preparation for the December 1913 plenary meeting of the International Socialist Bureau (ISB) to be held in London, Camille Huysmans and Emile Vandervelde, the ISB's two central leaders, called a meeting of the BSP, the ILP and the Fabians to discuss unification. Their proposal was simple. 'The BSP must join the Labour Party and the ILP must join the BSP', demanded Huysmans. When the ILP chairman Will Anderson complained about 'a small section of the BSP that is no good to any socialist party' and the BSP's Victor Fisher responded by pointing to the ILP's 'mugwumpish Liberal element', Vandervelde responded that 'unity will have the effect of rendering both extremes harmless'. The meeting ended with an agreement that the BSP would affiliate to the Labour Party and that the BSP, ILP and Fabians would create a United Socialist Council. To add insult to the BSP's self-injury, Beatrice Webb was appointed chair of the new council.[26]

---

24   Crick 1994, p. 189. *Some Dilemmas for Marxists* 1957, pp. 4–5.
25   BSP, *Annual Report* 1913, p. 15.
26   The full discussion is reprinted in *Justice*, 9 Aug 1913.

Over the next few months BSP members debated its attitude to Labour in the pages of *Justice*. Veteran SDF leader Hunter Watts set the tone by arguing that the BSP should 'get out of the prison of sectarianism' and join the Labour Party because it was 'the political expression of the working class', a phrase that would live long in the lexicon of ostensible Marxists in Britain.[27] Of the few correspondents to *Justice* opposing affiliation, only Frank Tanner criticised the conception that the Labour Party was the political expression of the working class, arguing instead that it was the political expression of the trade unions.[28] The events of the past few years demonstrated that Labour acted in the interests of the trade union bureaucrats rather than those of the working class as a whole. Tanner also perceptively noted that the clamour to join the Labour Party was not unconnected with the 'listless apathy which for the moment seems to have gripped us' following the failure to capitalise on the merger with the ILP lefts and inability to recruit militant trade unionists.[29]

On the opposite side of the debate, the most articulate proponent of joining the Labour Party was Zelda Kahan, Theodore Rothstein's sister-in-law. Kahan had led the opposition to Hyndman's infamous 1910 letter to the *Morning Post* which called for increased expenditure on the Royal Navy. For this she was attacked by Hyndman's supporters as a 'comrade alien in blood and race'.[30] The 1911 BSP conference backed this position but a plebiscite of branches later reversed the decision.[31] In February 1913 the party conference overturned the 1911 decision and pledged to implement the International's anti-war programme against 'all forms of militarism'. The wording allowed Hyndman and his supporters to vote for the resolution, and this diplomatic compromise was sealed by Hyndman and Kahan symbolically shaking hands at the end of the debate.

This rapprochement symbolised the role of Kahan and Rothstein within the BSP. They saw themselves as 'orthodox' Marxists in the tradition of Karl Kautsky. Kahan had translated Kautsky's 1909 article on the Labour Party, 'Sekte oder Klassenpartei' ('Sect or Class Party?'), from the German, and her arguments for joining Labour carried forward the logic of Kautsky's position. She believed

---

27 Watts in *Justice*, 19 July 1913. The BSP use of the phrase can be seen in the *Justice* editorial of 29 Jan 1914, 'The Labour Party: What of the Future?'.

28 Tanner's reminiscences of the SDF and BSP, albeit written over forty years later, are in Tanner 2014.

29 *Justice*, 2 April 1914.

30 Quoted in Crick 1994, p. 252.

31 *The Times*, 17 April 1911. For the full debate, see Crick 1994, pp. 232–4. Theodore Rothstein 'Die S.D.P., Hyndman und die Rüstungsfrage' *Neue Zeit*, vol. 29 (1911), pp. 179–86.

that the SDF had been mistaken to leave the LRC and that being outside of the Labour Party meant 'we often repel the most hopeful and most forward of the younger generation of the trade union members'. She continued:

> The Labour Party, with all its weakness, is an effort, however faltering, of the working class to take its destiny in its own hands, and as such should be encouraged and helped by us. And the question is, where else is there salvation? Is it seriously contended that those of the working class who are not now within the Labour Party are likely to be more revolutionary and more successful? Hardly. Or are we waiting for the Labour Party to break up and the more definitely socialist portion of it will join us? Well, anything, I suppose, may happen under the sun, but the facts hardly seem to point that way. The Labour Party will still commit many more mistakes; it will still waste much precious time in futilities; it may go through bad and good times, but it seems a force which has come to stay, and because socialism must triumph it will sooner or later become an independent socialist force. It is for us to hasten or to retard its development. Which will the party do?[32]

Rothstein himself took no part in the debate, having stepped back from party activity while working for the *Daily News*, but he had opened the door to joining the Labour Party in a 1909 article responding to Kautsky. He agreed in principle with Kautsky that the SDF should be part of the Labour Party but argued it was currently impossible because of the ILP's hostility to the SDF. But if the ILP ceased its opposition to the SDF, distanced itself from the Labour Party leadership, and declared 'its readiness to work for socialism inside the Labour Party bloc, the foundation will be created upon which the SDF could collaborate. For it would then only have the trade union leaders to fight against, and allied with the ILP it would be a match for these'.[33]

Now that the ILP had agreed to create the United Socialist Council, Rothstein's conditions had been fulfilled, and consequently his co-thinkers such as Kahan became the most determined advocates of joining the Labour Party. By the time the International issued its 'Manifesto to the Socialists of Great Britain' in January 1913, calling for 'socialist unity' and membership of the Labour Party, the Rothstein 'centre' and the Hyndmanite right were united behind it.[34] The

---

32   *Justice*, 4 Oct 1913.
33   Rothstein, 'The Crisis in the ILP', *The Social Democrat*, 15 Aug 1909, p. 378. Rothstein continued to contribute articles on foreign policy to *Neue Zeit*, however.
34   Reprinted in *Justice*, 29 Jan 1914.

agreement of the two groupings was consummated at the BSP's annual conference on 29 March 1914. The debate on the Labour Party question was led off for the executive by Dan Irving, who had long led the Lancashire branches' campaign to join Labour. Joe Fineberg, a close associate of Rothstein and Kahan, argued for joining Labour because 'it was the only way that socialism can become a force in the country'. A fellow Russian exile, the left-Menshevik Peter Petroff, spoke against joining, arguing that the International was not always right and that unity could only be based on 'co-operating together on such questions as those upon which common agreement could be arrived at'. Aside from Petroff, only two other speakers opposed the proposal. The conference decided to hold a referendum of the membership to decide the issue.[35] On 27 May the BSP executive announced that the membership had voted to join the Labour Party by 3,623 votes to 2,410, and a month later the BSP applied to join the Labour Party.[36]

3 The Rise of the Revolutionary Left

The BSP's decision to join the Labour Party led to a wave of leftist resignations from it. Branches in Derby, Farnworth, Blackley and Boston – all of which had come over from the ILP – resigned en bloc. The Dewsbury branch, the SDF's longtime flagship branch in industrial West Yorkshire, split and a significant number of members joined the Socialist Labour Party (SLP).[37] BSP executive committee members Leonard Hall and Russell Smart, former leaders of the ILP left wing, left the BSP in 1913 as the debate on joining Labour began, and Hall too linked up with the Socialist Labour Party. These were not the only gains that the SLP had made over the previous few years.

Although numbering only 80 at its founding conference in 1903, the members of the SLP did not lack for talent. They were products of the brutal industrial economy which had transformed Glasgow into one of the world's biggest cities. Taught by their everyday experience that the interests of capital and labour were irreconcilably opposed, SLPers prided themselves on their grasp of Marxist theory and were convinced that revolution rather than reform was the only way that the working class could liberate itself. In contrast to Hyndman's SDF, the SLP saw itself as a hard and uncompromisingly revolutionary party. In the words of one of its founders, the iron-moulder and future CPGB leader

35   *Justice*, 2 April 1914.
36   *Justice*, 28 May 1914.
37   Crick 1994, p. 257.

Tom Bell, its programme could be summed up as: 'against all reformism: exposure of the Labour Party and trade union officials as fakers; for socialist trade unionism; against the monarchy and exposure of the futility of Labour parliamentarism'.[38]

This clear demarcation between revolutionary and reformist politics was reflected in the way that the party was organised. Membership was viewed as a privilege which had to be earned. Members undertook a rigorous educational programme in Marxist economics, philosophy, and history, and were expected to devote their lives to party work. Like Lenin's Bolsheviks, any party member standing for election had to sign an undated letter of resignation that would be used if, once elected, they violated the party programme. Only official SLP publications could be sold by members, the editorial line of which was decided by the SLP's national executive. Unlike the BSP and the ILP, the SLP drew a sharp line between the working class and the leaders of the trade unions and Labour Party, whom they dubbed, following Daniel De Leon, 'Labour fakers'. Consequently, trade union officials were initially banned from joining the party. Not only that, but branches were barred from holding joint meetings with local trades councils, and members forbidden to speak 'under the auspices of a trade union' at public meetings.[39]

Nevertheless, the SLP sought to put its propaganda in front of the widest audience. One of its main activities was the production and distribution of high-quality Marxist pamphlets and books. Starting as the distributor of De Leon's writings, the SLP by 1910 was the leading publisher of Marxist literature in Britain, a not insignificant achievement for a small organisation. It purchased a printing press in 1906 and in August 1907 alone it printed 25,000 leaflets, 3,806 pamphlets, and 3,060 copies of that month's edition of *The Socialist*. These publishing activities placed a tremendous strain on the party's meagre resources, and in autumn 1907 a 'serious financial crisis' led to it decided to establish a commercial printing business.[40] Its subsequent political influence and commercial success also owed not a little to it becoming the British distributor of books published by the Chicago socialist publisher Charles H. Kerr & Co, allowing it to distribute cheap editions of various works by Marx and Engels.

However, despite its uncompromising belief in the need for working-class revolution, the SLP was not, as Raymond Challinor argued in *The Origins of Brit-*

---

38   Bell 1941, p. 42. The classic account of the SLP is Challinor 1977.
39   SLP Executive Committee minutes, 10 Feb 1907.
40   SLP Executive Committee minutes, 8 and 29 Sept 1907.

ish Bolshevism, the British analogue of Lenin's Bolshevik Party. Although the SLP saw itself as a disciplined, centralised organisation it did not employ full-time party organisers, placing huge burdens on its members who carried out the equivalent of full-time organisational roles for the party in their spare time while also holding down industrial jobs.[41] Moreover, it did not see the need for open political struggle against opposing tendencies within the labour movement. Once the split with the SDF had taken place, the SLP drew no public balance sheet of its struggle, nor, apart from occasional comment and invective, did it polemicise against the SDF's politics. When the London SLP branch sought to debate the Socialist Party of Great Britain in the autumn of 1905, the national executive forbade it, telling the branch that it should adopt 'the attitude taken by the SLP to all other political bodies; viz, one of hostility'. When the Londoners refused to change their attitude, their branch was expelled. Later that year, the executive also refused to debate the SPGB about an article on the SLP published in its *Socialist Standard*.[42]

Most importantly, the SLP did not share the Bolshevik conception of the party as 'a tribune of the people', as Lenin described it in *What is to be Done?*[43] The SLP's work in the trade unions focused on workplace issues. So, for example, the question of British imperialism's role in Ireland, a crucial issue in the SLP stronghold of Glasgow, was never part of its work among militant trade unionists. Nor did its overt opposition to anti-Semitism and all forms of racism become part of its day-to-day work in the trade unions. This contradiction between its often exemplary propaganda and the narrow focus of its trade union interventions would be highlighted in the starkest possible way during World War One.

The industrial struggle was the focus of the SLP's work. The majority of its members were industrial workers and active trade unionists. Its guide in this work was the experience of De Leon's SLP in the United States. Frustrated by the right-wing 'business unionism' of the American Federation of Labor and driven out of the once militant Knights of Labor, the American SLP had attempted to set up its own industrial trade unions under the banner of the 'Socialist Trade and Labor Alliance'. The STLA did not become a mass organisation but its reputation for militancy and distrust of union leaders allowed it to play a central role in the creation of the Industrial Workers of the World (IWW) in 1905. The IWW led a significant number of successful strikes, based on its programme of 'One

---

41 For this, see especially Foster 1985.

42 SLP Executive Committee minutes, 29 Oct 1905, 4 Feb and 19 Aug 1906.

43 Lenin, *CW* vol. 5, p. 423.

Big Union', which was underpinned by the belief, expressed in the preamble to its constitution, that 'the working class and the employing class have nothing in common. There can be no peace so long as hunger and want are found among millions of the working people and the few, who make up the employing class, have all the good things of life'.

The British SLP greeted the formation of the IWW by pledging itself to 'work incessantly for the formation of the British wing of that movement in place of the British (so-called) trade unions based as these are on capitalist principles'.[44] It created the Advocates of Industrial Unionism (AIU) with a programme uncompromisingly based on the class struggle:

> The Industrial Unionist stands firmly on the bed-rock of the class struggle, and declares, that so long as the means of production are in the hands of a numerically small class, the workers will be forced to sell their labour-power to them for a bare subsistence wage. Consequently, between these two classes a struggle must go on until the toilers come together on the political as well as on the industrial field and take over for themselves that which, being the result of their labour, justly belongs to them.[45]

Although it initially sought to create new industrial unions, the British SLP shifted towards advocating industrial unionism from within the existing trade unions. The AIU underwent a split in May 1908 when syndicalist supporters of 'non-political' industrial unionism, led by E.J.B. Allen, sought to break the link with the SLP and all political parties, mirroring a similar split in the USA. Nevertheless, by the middle of 1909 the AIU had thirty-nine branches and a membership several orders of magnitude greater than that of the SLP, and it felt sufficiently confident to rename itself the 'Industrial Workers of Great Britain' (IWGB).[46]

The IWGB sank roots in the Clydeside working class, most notably at two motor-manufacturing factories in Alexandria and Scotscoun, and at the massive Singer Sewing Machine factory in Clydebank. SLP members began working at Singers in 1906 and the success of their propaganda meant that when a factory branch of the IWGB was formed in 1910 it had 150 members in a workforce of 10,000. The ferment that was beginning to shake British industry inspired Singer's workers to take action against the factory's draconian management,

---

44   SLP Executive Committee minutes, 17 Sept 1905 and 21 Jan 1906.
45   Thomas Bell, 'British Advocates of Industrial Unionism', *The Socialist*, May 1908.
46   Kendall 1969, p. 71. For an overview of syndicalism and industrial unionism in this period, see Pribićević 1959.

and the IWGB's organisation of shop committees in every department thrust it into the leadership of the workforce. On 11 March 1911 a woman worker was sacked for allegedly not working hard enough. In no time 37 of the factory's 41 departments were out on strike in support of the victimised woman. The leadership of the strike fell entirely to the IWGB, which by this time had 1,500 members in the factory. Inexperienced and lacking the resources to maintain the strikers, the IWGB found itself outmanoeuvred by Singer's management and eventually the strike folded. Almost all of the SLP members working in the factory were sacked. In itself, the strike was a failure. Yet it raised the profile of the SLP immeasurably and foreshadowed the class battles that were to shake wartime Glasgow.

4   The SLP and Revolutionary Syndicalism

Despite its formal antipathy to syndicalism, the SLP became identified with the growing appeal of syndicalism during the 1910–14 period.[47] The most important of the British syndicalists was Tom Mann, the leader of the 1889 dockers' strike, who moved leftwards and resigned from the SDF in 1911, explaining that:

> I find myself not in agreement with the party on the important matter of parliamentary action. ... the real reason why the trade unionist movement of this country is in such a deplorable state of inefficiency is to be found in the fictitious importance which the workers have been encouraged to attach to parliamentary action. ... I declare in favour of direct industrial organisation; not as a means, but as THE means whereby the workers can ultimately overthrow the capitalist system and become the actual controllers of their own industrial and social destiny.[48]

The rejection of parliament as a vehicle for working-class liberation by Mann and other British syndicalists, such as Jack Tanner, was heavily influenced by French syndicalism. Mann had been to France where he had worked with syndicalist (and future communist) leaders Alfred Rosmer and Pierre Monatte, and became a regular contributor to their journal *La Vie Ouvriere*. Tanner too had

---

47   For a general survey of pre-World War One syndicalism, see Holton 1976.
48   Quoted in Frank Bohn, 'Tom Mann, Industrial Unionism and Social Democracy', in *The Social Democrat*, 15 Sept 1911. Mann rejoined the SDF on his return from Australia in 1910.

visited France to learn from the French revolutionary syndicalists.[49] Rosmer and his comrades based themselves on the belief that the working class could wield its power through mass strikes and ultimately through a general strike that would bring down capitalism. If this was so, wondered Mann and his co-thinkers, why was there a need for a political party when workers could simply cut out the middle-man and seize power through their unions? 'The syndic-alists are non-parliamentarian, anti-militarist, and fervently and determinedly anti-capitalist; they are always and everywhere in favour of DIRECT ACTION', explained Mann in 1911. 'Direct action by industrial organisation on lines that makes industrial solidarity possible and practical, that is their method. They are out to make the social revolution by means of the general strike'.[50] In the first issue of his *The Industrial Syndicalist* newspaper he declared frankly that 'a working class movement that is not revolutionary in character is not of the slightest use to the working class'.[51]

The SLP's answer to the syndicalists was that a party was necessary to win a parliamentary majority which would then support the workers as they took over industry, whereupon parliament would hand over state power to the industrial unions. Even as late as 1919 *The Socialist* was calling for the 'trans-fer of all governing power from the parliamentary legislative institution to the federal congress of people's administrative councils'. William Paul explained the relationship between parliamentary (which the SLP characterised as polit-ical) action and industrial action as being 'the revolutionary value of political action lies in its being *the* instrument fashioned to *destroy* capitalism. Just as industrial unionism is necessary to *construct* socialism'.[52] Shorn of its industrial militancy, this was not very different from the SDF or the SPGB, who believed in the manner of *The Ragged Trousered Philanthropists* that the working class would come to socialism by being educated about its benefits and thus vote for socialists in parliamentary elections. The Bolshevik conception of the working class being won to socialism through the party campaigning for its revolu-tionary programme across industrial and social struggles, a perspective gained through its experience in the Russian labour movement, did not exist in Bri-tain.

Even so, the SLP's hard revolutionary reputation and the quality of its many publications gave its ideas and those of Daniel De Leon a far wider audience

---

49   Bantman 2014.

50   *Transport Worker*, Sept 1911.

51   *The Industrial Syndicalist*, no. 1, July 1910.

52   'A Manifesto. A Plea for the Reconsideration of Socialist Tactics and Strategy', *The Socialist*, 2 Jan 1919; Paul 1918, especially p. 20.

than was achieved by *The Socialist*, helping it play a significant role in the political education of the new generation of industrial militants emerging in the years immediately before World War One.[53] This was illustrated by the rebellion of 1909 at Ruskin College, which had been founded in Oxford in 1899 to provide degree-level education for working-class men. Left-wing students led by South Wales miner Noah Ablett led a student strike against the college's right-wing curriculum which resulted in the creation of the explicitly Marxist 'Plebs League' to promote adult education based on Marxist principles.[54] The league took its name from De Leon's pamphlet *Two Pages from Roman History*, another SLP publication.[55] In 1909 the Plebs League founded a rival to Ruskin, the Central Labour College, committed to 'independent working-class education' to counter the capitalist indoctrination of public and private universities and schools.[56]

The influence of the Plebs League grew rapidly and branches were established in many towns and cities, focusing on the teaching of Marxist economics and social science. Most significantly, its influence grew among the younger leadership of the strike wave that threw Britain into turmoil before World War One.[57] On the railways and in the mines, the unofficial and in some cases official leadership of local strikes was often in the hands of militants who had been educated, directly or indirectly, by the Plebs League and SLP literature. The SLP consequently grew rapidly. In 1912 it had 28 branches across Britain and had broken out of its Scottish industrial heartland.

The syndicalist currents inspired by the SLP's publications became even more influential. In November 1910 Tom Mann founded the Industrial Syndicalist Education League at a conference in Manchester attended by 200 delegates representing 60,000 workers. Its mission, according to E.J.B. Allen, was to create an industrial unionist organisation which would be

> the embryo of a working-class republic. Our national unions, local unions, and other bodies will be the administrative machinery of an Industrial Commonwealth. ... We shall unite all the workers in any one industry, and

---

53   This was acknowledged by the Left-Wing faction of the ILP as late as 1920; see 'The Propaganda of the ILP' in *The International*, 25 Sept 1920.

54   For Ablett, see Turnbull 2017 and Egan 1986.

55   Challinor 1977, pp. 116–17.

56   For more on the Ruskin dispute, see Goldman 1995, pp. 174–80; Lewis 1976; MacIntyre 1980, pp. 72–85; Rose 2001, pp. 258–65.

57   For more on the working-class education movement, see Miles 1984; Tsuzuki 1983; Millar undated.

unite all industries. We will build a 'state within a state', a workers' democracy in opposition to the capitalists' oligarchy.[58]

In the South Wales' coalfields, the bitter Cambrian Combine strike of 1910–11 led
to the creation of the Unofficial Reform Committee led by Ablett, W.H. Main-
waring and George Dolling, all of whom had been leftward-moving members of
the ILP but shared much of the programme of Mann and Allen. They would in
1911 become the founding core of the Rhondda Socialist Society (which would
become the South Wales Socialist Society and participate in the founding of
the Communist Party) and were instrumental in the founding in August of the
Rhondda Socialist, a newspaper whose masthead proclaimed itself 'the BOMB
of the Rhondda workers'. The following year the Unofficial Reform Committee published the most famous British declaration of industrial unionism, *The
Miners' Next Step*.[59]

The pamphlet rendered the principles of the IWW into the political vernacu-
lar of the Welsh miners. It called for the formation of one industrial union
for all mine workers and demanded that 'the old policy of identity of interest
between employers and ourselves be abolished, and a policy of open hostility installed'. It called for complete union democracy and a 'constitution giving
free and rapid control by the rank and file acting in such a way that conditions
will be unified throughout the coalfield; so that pressure at one point would
automatically affect all others and thus readily command united action and
resistance'. Characterising the call for nationalisation of the mines as reformist, the pamphlet instead called for 'industrial democracy', by which it meant
'every industry thoroughly organised, in the first place, to fight, to gain control
of, and then to administer, that industry'.[60] A 'central production board' would
co-ordinate the different industries, leaving each group of workers to decide
how to fulfil its tasks.

It was probably the most sophisticated expression of revolutionary syndicalism seen in Britain. But although deeply critical of the existing leadership of
the trade unions, *The Miners' Next Step* stated that 'the remedy is not new leaders'. Ablett and his comrades, like Mann and Allen, believed that workplace
democracy would overcome reformist politics and thus reduce leadership to
a technical question, by which functions such as negotiating with employers
would be replaced with appropriate expertise when necessary. 'We came to the

---

58   Conference report in *The Industrial Syndicalist*, no. 6, Dec 1910. Allen's 'Working-Class
      Socialism' in *The Industrial Syndicalist*, no. 5, Nov 1910.
59   Egan 1978.
60   All quotes from *The Miners' Next Step* 1912.

conclusion that what was needed in the workmen's organisations was more direct control of the "leaders" by the rank and file', outlined A.J. Cook, the future
miners' leader who was then a militant young supporter of the reform committee. 'We decided that the "leaders" were only responsible for the conduct of
negotiations, and that the terms of an agreement must be left to the rank and
file, who must be given complete control of the results of collective bargaining.
The workmen, we said, must be the "bosses", the "leaders" were to be servants'.[61]

This was a programme that might win a strike but not one that could con-
quer state power for the working class. As was seen throughout the 1910–14
period, sheer industrial militancy even on a national scale was not enough to
bring victory, as even the most united and steadfast strikes were repeatedly
defeated from within by the Labour Party and trade union leaders' desire
to compromise. Despite its criticisms of the syndicalists, the SLP essentially
shared their position on questions of leadership. Its denunciation of the
'Labour fakers' leading the movement was essentially a sociological analysis,
suggesting that without the privileges of full-time officialdom the leadership of
the trade unions would be more militant and responsive to the needs of their
members. The reality was that industrial struggle could only bring lasting benefits if it was part of a generalised struggle against capitalism, which meant the
existing leaders of the labour movement had to be replaced by those committed to the overthrow of the capitalist state.

Some syndicalists saw the solution to the question of the state as being the
acquisition of arms by the working class. After a police riot in Sheffield during
the 1911 rail strike, the prominent Sheffield socialist and rail worker A.E. Chandler argued that 'working men and trade unionists should organise and drill
themselves in case of emergency'.[62] The formation of the Irish Citizen Army
in Dublin in November 1913 by James Connolly, Jim Larkin and Jack White was
a practical implementation of this sentiment. Tom Mann's monthly *The Syndicalist* carried advertisements for the King Air Rifle under the slogans 'For Young
and Old Syndicalists' and 'Learn to Shoot Straight', and debated whether trade
unions should buy guns. It thought not, but only because it was likely that conscription would soon be introduced and put firearms in the hands of all workers
for free. 'When you have a country, you will fight for it', it advised its readers in
response to a recruitment leaflet issued by the Territorial Army. 'But while that
country is theirs you are going to fight them for it. Tell them also that if milit-

---

61   'A.J. Cook Tells His Own Story', *Tit-Bits*, 15 May 1926. Ironically this was published the week
      after the TUC leadership called off the General Strike.
62   Quoted in Burke 1983, p. 93.

ary service "will be got compulsorily" and they put a rifle into your hands, you will use it as an "instrument of redemption".[63] Although it remained the view of a small minority at this time, in the aftermath of World War One this would become a great fear of the government.

Despite their weaknesses, the SLP and the syndicalists were committed to the conquest of power by the working class. This was the crucial dividing line between the revolutionary left and all wings of the BSP leadership. For the leaders of the BSP, socialism was something that would help the workers, an equitable solution to an ethical question. For the revolutionaries, socialism was a society that would be ruled by the working class itself, a reaffirmation of Marx's famous opening statement of the provisional rules of the First International that 'the emancipation of the working classes must be conquered by the working classes themselves'.[64] This meant that the revolutionaries were also convinced that this could not happen through parliament. According to Will Hay, one of the authors of *The Miners' Next Step*, parliament was

> an institution [which] can never afford the pathway along which a subject class shall travel to freedom. It can only obscure the issues, blunt the instincts of the working class, and throw a veil over the class struggle, by making the worker lose his identity as a worker.[65]

This stance also differentiated the revolutionaries from all other tendencies on the British left, from the SPGB to Theodore Rothstein to Henry Hyndman, who all believed that obtaining a parliamentary majority was the prerequisite for socialism, whatever they understood that to be. This parliamentary worldview determined the BSP's eventual decision to join the Labour Party, as well as being behind the Second International's enthusiasm for Labour. Conversely, it was the understanding that working-class power could not be exercised through parliament that underpinned the opposition to Labourism expressed by the SLP, Tom Mann and the rest of the militant left. As Trotsky noted about pre-World War One France, 'revolutionary syndicalism, despite its denial of the party, was essentially nothing but an anti-parliamentary party of the working class'.[66]

---

63   For gun advertisements see *The Syndicalist*, Feb and July 1912. For the debate on guns, see Feb and Dec 1912 editions.
64   Marx, 'Provisional Rules of the Association', *MECW* vol. 20, p. 14.
65   'The Working Class and Political Action', *Rhondda Socialist*, 28 Sept 1912.
66   Trotsky 1974a, vol. 2, p. 34. For a reassessment of the relation between syndicalism and the Great Labour Unrest, see O'Connor 2014.

5   Beyond Suffragism

The year 1913 also saw the emergence of one other significant element of the leftward movement in the British working class: Sylvia Pankhurst's East London Federation of Suffragettes break with the Women's Social and Political Union (WSPU), led by her mother Emmeline and sister Christabel. The Pankhurst family had played a central role in the Central Manchester branch of the ILP but in 1903, frustrated by what she saw as its failure to support women's suffrage, Emmeline and Christabel created the WSPU. At first the WSPU functioned largely as a single-issue campaign in the labour movement, but in 1906 it refused to vote for the ILP candidate, the militant Scottish miners' leader Robert Smillie, in the Cockermouth parliamentary by-election. The following year the Pankhursts resigned from the ILP and became hostile to the labour movement.[67]

The WSPU's campaign of civil disobedience was met by a brutal police response from Asquith's Liberal government, and from 1909 many suffragettes who had been imprisoned went on hunger strike in protest. The prison authorities responded with force-feeding, a form of torture whereby a rubber tube was forced down a woman's throat via the mouth or nose and liquid food poured down into her stomach. Although the ILP MP George Lansbury resigned his parliamentary seat in protest at force feeding in 1912, others in the ILP were not sympathetic, John Bruce Glasier declaring that 'I hardly see what the prison officials are to do with these women'.[68] In 1913 Asquith introduced the Prisoners (Temporary Discharge for Ill Health) Act, which allowed women on hunger strike to be released from gaol until they had recovered from force-feeding. They were then immediately re-arrested to undergo the torture once more. Known as the 'Cat and Mouse Act' this vicious piece of legislation received the votes of fifteen Labour Party MPs, over a third of its parliamentary party.

The WSPU's campaign for votes for women focused on winning equality under the existing franchise laws. However, at this time, only men who were property owners or renting homes for an annual rent of £10 or more could vote in parliamentary elections. This meant that between 40 and 45 per cent of men were also excluded from the franchise alongside women.[69] Equality under the existing law would bring the vote only to a minority of women, while still leaving around half the adult population disenfranchised. In contrast, the Marxist movement stood for universal suffrage for all adult women

---

67   Ugolini 2002.
68   Bruce Glasier diary entry for 28 Sept 1909, quoted in Ugolini 2002, p. 156.
69   For an extensive discussion of this issue, see Matthew, McKibbin and Kay 1976.

and men. At the Second International's 1910 International Conference of Socialist Women, chaired by the German SPD's Clara Zetkin, the debate on the suffrage question saw the delegates from the Fabian Society and the Women's
Labour League – Millicent Murby, Charlotte Despard, and future Labour MP
Marion Phillips – support the WSPU position of limited suffrage for middle-
class women. Opposed by Dora Montefiore from the SDF, Alexandra Kollontai,
and many other speakers, Murby, Despard and Phillips were the only delegates
to vote against the conference resolution stating 'the socialist women's movement of all countries repudiates the limited woman's suffrage as a falsification
of and an insult to the principle of the political equality of the female sex'.[70]

The fight for women's liberation had always been a formal part of the SDF's
politics. Eleanor Marx was one of three women who were elected to its first
executive committee, and in 1886 it published her and Aveling's pamphlet
The Woman Question.[71] In the 1890s the rise of the 'New Woman' movement,
which questioned the social and sexual mores of the era, also saw the accretion to the SDF of a number of women attracted to its apparently Marxist
programme for human liberation. Perhaps most notable was Edith Lanchester,
whose decision to defy bourgeois convention and live in an unmarried relationship with working-class SDF member James Sullivan led to her upper-class
parents having her declared clinically insane and committed to a psychiatric
asylum. The SDF waged a militant and ultimately successful campaign for her
release.[72] But, as in everything else, the SDF was also deeply flawed on women's
rights. Belfort Bax, its leading theoretician, was a zealous opponent of women's
rights. In 1908 his book *The Legal Subjection of Men* argued that women were
the oppressors of men and he became one of the founding members of the
Anti-Suffrage League, an organisation dedicated to opposing women's rights.[73]

Despite this ingrained chauvinism, in 1903 SDF executive member Dora
Montefiore set up Women's Socialist Circles, and in 1907 she played the central
role in establishing a British section of the International Socialist Women's Bureau, which in April 1909 organised meetings for Alexandra Kollontai and Clara
Zetkin in London.[74] Nevertheless, the SDF's active support for women's liberation was marginal at best and, with the exception of Eleanor Marx, it appears
that women members rarely wrote about or were involved in issues not concerning the family, children or health. The SLP had even less to say. Although

---

70   *Justice*, 3 Sept 1910. For the minority view, see *Labour Leader*, 9 Sept 1910.
71   The definite account is Hunt 1996.
72   Rubenstein 1986, pp. 58–62.
73   Cowley 1992, pp. 84–9.
74   *Justice*, 24 April and 27 Nov 1909.

it distributed Daniel de Leon's 1903 translation of August Bebel's book *Women and Socialism* and the anarchist Lily Gair Wilkinson's 1910 pamphlet *Women's Freedom*, the SLP had no perspectives for women outside of the factory. 'Let them organise in the workshop', was how *The Socialist* editor John S. Clarke responded to Jane Matheson in a debate on women's rights in January 1914.[75] In contrast, it was the Russian leftist Peter Petroff who attacked the BSP leadership at the party's 1914 annual conference for its reluctance to defend the incarcerated Suffragettes, calling for them to be declared political prisoners and arguing that the BSP should start its own campaign for universal suffrage.[76] Tom Mann's *The Syndicalist* and his monthly *Transport Worker* also defended militant suffragettes, admiring their methods while suggesting they direct their fire against capitalism.[77]

But by this time, the WSPU was moving increasingly in what Sylvia Pankhurst described as 'aristocratic Conservative circles' and oriented itself towards middle-class women. It not only opposed strikes but called on the government to outlaw them.[78] In contrast, Sylvia continued to campaign for working-class women and in October 1912 established the East London Federation of the WSPU in the heart of London's docklands.[79] She had been at the forefront of the suffragettes' militant actions, being arrested numerous times and tortured by force-feeding when on hunger strike. Between June 1913 and June 1914 alone she was arrested 10 times and went on hunger and thirst strike each time.[80] Hugely courageous and resolute, she was also one of the first suffragettes to undertake a thirst strike and later began a sleep strike against the Liberal government's refusal to treat the suffragettes as political prisoners. During 1913 and 1914 she was jailed eight times under the Cat and Mouse Act.[81]

In contrast to the anti-working-class stance of the WSPU, the East London Federation actively supported strikes and won the endorsement of local dockers' union branches. In November 1913 Sylvia spoke at a mass rally at the Royal Albert Hall alongside James Connolly and several other trade union and radical speakers to demand the release of the imprisoned Jim Larkin and support for the Dublin strikers. 'Behind every poor man is an even poorer woman', she

---

75 *The Socialist*, Jan 1914.
76 BSP *Annual Report 1913*, p. 22.
77 *The Syndicalist*, Dec 1913. *Transport Worker*, Dec 1911.
78 Pankhurst 1977, p. 366.
79 See the account of the formation of the ELF of the WSPU on the front page of the first issue of *The Woman's Dreadnought* [hereafter *TWD*], 8 March, 1914.
80 Shepherd 2002, p. 131.
81 See, among others, Winslow 1996; Davis 1999; Connolly 2013.

told the audience. That same month the East London Federation of Suffragettes launched its 'People's Army', an embryonic paramilitary organisation inspired by James Connolly's Irish Citizen Army. The People's Army trained its members in the use of firearms 'so that men and women may join to fight for freedom, and in order that they may learn to cope with the repressive methods of the government servants'.[82] Each member had to sign a pledge stating that 'I will be a friend to all and a brother to every member of the People's Army. I am a sincere believer in a Vote for every Woman and every Man'. Under the slogan of 'Votes for Women and Freedom For All', the People's Army drilled under arms in East London's Victoria Park and took the frontline in defending the Federation's demonstrations from police violence. 'The only way to meet the brutality of the government is by armed resistance', its recruitment leaflet stated, echoing the sentiments of the revolutionary syndicalists.[83]

The creation of the People's Army was too much for Christabel Pankhurst, who by this time was now the WSPU's central leader. Sylvia, still recovering from the ravages of the Cat and Mouse Act, was summoned to an audience with her sister at the Parisian apartment of the Princess Polignac, Christabel's place of exile. She informed Sylvia that 'a working women's movement was of no value: working women were the weakest portion of the sex: how could it be otherwise? Their lives were too hard, their education too meagre to equip them for the contest. Surely it is a mistake to use the weakest for the struggle! We want picked women, the very strongest and most intelligent!'[84]

On 6 February 1914, the WSPU announced its expulsion of Sylvia Pankhurst and the East London Federation. As *The Times* surmised, the cause of the breach was that Sylvia 'has believed in conducting the campaign as a class movement, and to that end she has organised the "People's Army", which included both men and women'.[85] Four weeks later, the East London Federation launched its own newspaper, *The Woman's Dreadnought*, which declared that the Federation was 'a militant non-party organisation of working women. ... Working women – sweated women, wage slaves, overworked mothers toiling in little homes – these, of all created beings, stand in the greatest need of this [the vote], the power to help themselves'.[86]

---

82   *TWD*, 8 March 1914, p. 2.
83   'Join the People's Army' leaflet, Sylvia Pankhurst Papers, Reel 24, File 201.
84   Pankhurst 1977, p. 517. See also Winslow 1996, p. 66.
85   *The Times*, 9 Feb. 1914. This is corroborated in the *Daily Sketch*, 7 Feb 1914.
86   *TWD*, Special Advance Number, 8 March 1914, p. 2. The severing of ties to the WSPU led
       to the ELF renaming itself the East London Federation of Suffragettes on 27 Jan 1914; see
       TWD, 2 Jan 1914, p. 42.

Although not Marxist in any sense, Pankhurst's organisation was moving to the left under the impact of government repression and the great wave of working-class struggle. The Ulster Unionist revolt against Home Rule and the creation of the armed Ulster Volunteer Force in 1913 led by Sir Edward Carson had also undermined many taboos about armed struggle and the supposedly pacific nature of the British state. In May 1914 the *Dreadnought*'s front page carried the banner headline 'Coercion!!! Government Forces Us to Arm, To Fight For Liberty', under which it stated 'When women preach revolution to women, and women, and men too, respond to their call, those who really trust the heart and mind of our people will alert to the fact that there is grave and earnest reason for revolt. ... Great demonstrations of popular indignation are now needed and we must go to all our meetings armed!'[87] Although there was undoubtedly a degree of bravado about such rhetoric, Sylvia Pankhurst and her supporters in the East London Federation had proved that they were prepared to fight bodily for their principles. Now they were searching for a way forward beyond suffragette militancy and parliamentary reformism.

It was not only those in the labour movement who were searching for solutions to the seemingly perpetual crisis of British society. On 17 July 1914, the Chancellor of the Exchequer, David Lloyd George, delivered his annual speech at London's Mansion House in the heart of the City of London. Designed to inform the assembled bankers, financiers and industrialists of the government's economic perspectives, he gave them a 'solemn warning' about:

> the undoubted menace of great industrial trouble. In a few months, in a few weeks, the arrangements made with a view to securing peace in some of the most important industrial enterprises in this country, enterprises upon which the very life of the community depends, are expiring. There are certain demands being put forward. Labour has an effective combination [the Triple Alliance of miners, railwaymen and transport workers' unions had been created earlier that year] which is without parallel in its magnitude. All the transport trades and the miners are organised and federated to aid each other in their demands. ... The prospect of an equitable settlement of these dangerous disputes is complicated and darkened undoubtedly by the situation in Ireland. Should there be civil strife in the land – and Heaven avert it – in the course of the next few weeks, when the industrial trouble to which I have referred is maturing,

---

87   *TWD*, 16 May 1914, p. 1.

the situation will be the gravest which any Government of this country has had to deal for centuries.[88]

Britain was once again poised on the brink of major industrial battles, and the government feared the power that the Triple Alliance represented. Even by the time that Lloyd George delivered his warning, the number of days already lost to strike action that year was approaching the 9.8 million lost during the whole of 1913.[89] The ruling class was deeply split over the future of Ireland and the Home Rule crisis spiralled into the open mutiny of elite Cavalry officers at the Curragh in County Kildare. And, if that were not enough, many upper-class families were seeing their Suffragette wives and daughters take violent action against what they saw as symbols of male power. As many working-class militants hoped, perhaps the sun was finally beginning to set on the British Empire.

In the face of such domestic menaces, it was not surprising that Lloyd George airily waved away worries about the assassination of Austria's Archduke Franz Ferdinand in Sarajevo on 28 June. 'There are always clouds in the international sky. You never get a perfectly blue sky in foreign affairs', he mused. Yet, even as he was speaking, the intricate fabric of diplomacy woven over the past thirty years to keep inter-imperialist rivalries in check was being stretched to breaking point. The two bullets fired by Gavrilo Princip on 28 June not only put paid to the heir to the Austrian throne, but also postponed the social and political reckoning that threatened the rulers of Britain and its Empire. As dockers' leader and future Labour Foreign Minister Ernest Bevin later recalled: 'if the war had not broken out, [we] would have, I believe, seen one of the greatest industrial revolts the world would have ever seen'.[90]

---

88   *The Times*, 18 July 1914.

89   Thatcher 1971, p. 396. The eventual totals were 9,878,000 in 1914 and 9,804,000 in 1913.

90   Bevin giving evidence to the 1920 Shaw Inquiry into the 'Conditions of Men Engaged in Dock and Waterside Labour', quoted in Runciman 1972, p. 67.

August 1914: British Marxists in the Face of War

Barely 48 hours before the British government declared war on Germany, 5,000 trade unionists and socialists marched through intermittent rain to Trafalgar Square from London's East End to oppose the coming slaughter. Led by the red banner of the National Transport Workers' Federation, they were met by 15,000 other protestors who overflowed into Whitehall and down the Strand. Singing the *Internationale* and the *Red Flag*, the protestors cheered George Lansbury's demand that the leaders of the Triple Alliance take action against the war. As the rain continued, the crowd repelled an attack on the speakers' platform from militarist provocateurs, and then voted for a resolution expressing their 'deepest detestation of the international war that seems to be on the point of breaking out' and urging 'the workers to unite to prevent their respective governments from engaging in war'.[1]

The London demonstration was one of a number of rapidly organised anti-war rallies held across Britain that day. In Huddersfield, two rallies took place, one in the afternoon and another in the evening, organised by the BSP, the ILP and the local Trades Council. A resolution from the local Paddock Socialist Club denounced 'the murderous gang of war-mongers responsible for the present crisis'.[2] Birmingham's Bull Ring saw 3,000 protesters declare that 'the workers have no interest in quarrels between capitalists' and that they would stand by workers of other countries. The following night in Portsmouth protestors rallied under the slogans 'War against War' and 'Whoever wins, the workers lose'. Even as late as the Tuesday night when war was declared, local trade unionists marched against the war through London's docklands.[3] 'No impartial observer can escape the conviction that the British people have very little stomach for this war', observed Frank Rose of the Amalgamated Society of Engineers in his 'Workers' Notebook' column for the *Manchester Evening News*.[4]

The day before the declaration of war Keir Hardie and Arthur Henderson issued the 'Manifesto of the British Section of the International Social-

---

1 *Daily Herald*, 3 August 1914 and *Justice*, 6 Aug 1914.
2 Pearce 2001, p. 65.
3 Pearce 2001, p. 65. *Daily Herald*, 3 Aug 1914. *Portsmouth Evening News*, 3 Aug 1914. *Daily Herald*, 5 Aug 1914.
4 *Manchester Evening News*, 5 Aug 1914.

ist Bureau', which ended with the rousing rallying cry of 'Down with class rule. Down with the rule of brute force. Down with war. Up with the peaceful rule of the people'.[5] They were following the lead of the Second International and its parties across Europe. At its 1907 Stuttgart congress, the International had passed its famous resolution opposing war and militarism, significantly amended by Lenin and Rosa Luxemburg, which concluded:

> If a war threatens to break out, it is the duty of the working classes and their parliamentary representatives in the countries involved, supported by the coordinating activity of the International Socialist Bureau, to exert every effort in order to prevent the outbreak of war by the means they consider most effective, which naturally vary according to the sharpening of the class struggle and the sharpening of the general political situation. In case war should break out anyway, it is their duty to intervene in favour of its speedy termination and with all their powers to utilise the economic and political crisis created by the war to rouse the masses and thereby to hasten the downfall of capitalist class rule.[6]

Although this resolution formally re-asserted the International's opposition to militarism and imperialist war, the congress debate revealed deep fissures between a 'social-patriotic' right led by the German SPD's Georg von Vollmar, a centre led by August Bebel, who drafted the original resolution before it was amended, and revolutionary left including Lenin and Luxemburg. In 1910 the International's Copenhagen congress reaffirmed the Stuttgart resolution, as did its extraordinary congress at Basel in 1912.[7] On paper, the vast majority of the parties of the Second International were formally committed to oppose the impending European war when it eventually broke out. Yet as soon as war was declared, the parliamentary representatives of almost every section of the Second International either supported or refused to vote against the war budgets of their 'own' ruling class. The only exceptions were the Russian Bolsheviks, the Serbian social democrats Dragiša Lapčević and Triša Kaclerović, the German SPD's Karl Liebknecht in December 1914 and the Bulgarian 'Narrow' socialists in October 1915.[8]

---

5   Reprinted in full in *Justice*, 6 Dec 1914.
6   Reprinted in Riddell 1984, p. 35.
7   Wood-Simons 1910, p. 10. The 1912 discussion is reported in L.B. Kamenev's 'On the Basel Congress' in Riddell 1984, pp. 90–1. For a British perspective, see Morris 2018.
8   Riddell 1984, pp. 125–7. Bulgaria did not enter the war until October 1915, see Rothschild 1959, pp. 65–7.

In Britain, much of the anti-war sentiment evaporated in the heat of jingoistic militarism. A 'gigantic' labour movement demonstration against the war planned for the following weekend in Manchester never materialised, and public displays of opposition to the war almost completely dried up, not least due to the violent activities of patriotic mobs that attacked meetings and demonstrations even before the start of the war.[9] On the industrial front, days lost through strike action in the last four months of 1914 fell to 161,437, a mere 1.6 per cent of the total lost in the previous eight months of the year.[10] But war fever in Britain was not as suffocating as it was portrayed in the contemporary press or by some modern historians. The war was undoubtedly popular in certain sections of the industrial working class. By mid-1915 around 25 per cent of miners had enlisted, although the opportunity to escape life underground may have been as much a motivator as patriotic duty. Conversely, recruitment in textile-producing areas was noticeably low. On the whole, it was the white collar and professional middle classes who enlisted earlier and more enthusiastically, most notably in the 'Pal's Battalions' that were specially created to encourage mass enlistment via work and other social networks.[11]

Working-class hesitancy was also noticed by the *Economist*, which in early September complained: 'few attempts have been made to enlighten us as to the attitudes of the working classes; but it has been freely stated that in the north of England there is still a good deal of apathy'.[12] As evidence, it pointed to the continuance of professional football – which by this time had become, alongside the pub, the most significant form of working-class male leisure – in defiance of demands that it should stop being played while the war was on. The even more proletarian sport of rugby league saw professional players go on strike in November against wage cuts imposed due to war-time conditions. In order to overcome working-class suspicion, Leeds businessman W.G. Doyle called for a 'sustained educational and recruiting campaign systematically organised and carried out ... in plain, homely, temperate language' to persuade 'working men' to enlist.[13] Nor was this working-class reluctance confined to the north. Recruiting drives at soccer matches in Cardiff and at Arsenal in London saw a grand total of seven spectators rally to the colours.[14] In some sections of the working

---

9   *Manchester Evening News*, 3 Aug 1914. For the attitudes of the pro-war wing of the labour movement, see Swift 2017.
10 Thatcher 1971, p. 396.
11 Winter 1988, pp. 115–21; Simkins 2005. For a recent nuanced view, see Pennell 2012.
12 'The Working-Class and Recruitment', *The Economist*, 5 Sept 1914.
13 *Yorkshire Post*, 2 Sept 1914.
14 Collins 2006, pp. 10–13; Veitch 1985, p. 373. Lenin hailed the informal football matches

class, the outbreak of war was accompanied by suspicion, distrust and a refusal to let it interfere with their own interests.

Consequently, socialists to the left of the Labour Party did not find themselves completely isolated by the militarist fervour. The ILP, a dependable weathervane of liberal opinion within the labour movement, came out in opposition to the war from a pacifist standpoint. The ILP's most prominent leader, Ramsay MacDonald, opposed the war because he believed that secret diplomatic accords with France had dragged Britain into an unnecessary conflict. Even Philip Snowden, never knowingly mistaken for a left-wing militant, was an opponent of the war. MacDonald resigned as leader of the parliamentary Labour Party on 7 August, in part because he hoped to link up with Liberal critics of the war he mistakenly believed would resign from their party.[15] He was replaced by Arthur Henderson, whose manifesto commitment to peace lasted precisely one day, who would join Asquith's cabinet in May 1915.[16] The parliamentary Labour Party itself rushed to support the war effort, declaring both an electoral truce and, alongside the trade union leaders, an industrial truce at the end of August.

The ILP viewed opposition to the war as an ethical matter of individual conscience. It did not see it as an opportunity to advance working-class interests. 'We were not revolutionary socialists', said Fenner Brockway, the editor of the ILP's *Labour Leader*, 'We were democratic pacifists'.[17] The ILP's support for social peace at home meant that in practical terms it did little to oppose the war effort, as Keir Hardie made clear in a speech to his Merthyr constituency shortly after the war began: 'a nation at war must be united especially when its existence is at stake. ... With the boom of the enemy's guns within earshot the lads who have gone forth by sea and land to fight their country's battles must not be disheartened by any discordant note at home'. Three months later, he reiterated his stance: 'I have never said or written anything to dissuade our young men from enlisting; I know too well all that there is at stake'.[18] Nevertheless, the ILP's openly pacifist statements and the individual bravery of many of

---

between British and German troops during the 'Christmas Truce' of 1914 in 'The Slogan of Civil War Illustrated', *CW* vol. 21, pp. 181–2.

15   For Liberal Party anti-war feeling, see *The Economist*, 8 Aug and 9 Sept 1914. John Burns, John Morley and Charles Trevelyan did resign from the Liberal government in opposition to the war.

16   Fenner Brockway suggests that MacDonald had hoped to link up with other Liberal opponents of the government's policy such as Lloyd George but wrongly assumed that they too would resign. See Brockway 1942, pp. 56–9.

17   Brockway 1942, p. 55.

18   *Pioneer* [Merthyr], 15 Aug and 27 Nov 1914.

its members – significant numbers of whom became conscientious objectors after conscription was introduced in 1916 – meant it was seen by the press and public opinion as the only significant political party which was a clear opponent of the war.

1   The BSP and SLP and the Test of War

The same could not be said for the ostensible Marxists of the British Socialist Party. Given Hyndman's previous positions, no-one was in the least surprised to read in the 6 August edition of *Justice* the official BSP statement pronouncing that 'in view of the declaration of war upon Germany, neutrality is now out of the question'.[19] The following week an editorial from Hyndman made explicit the BSP's support for the war. 'Everyone must eagerly desire the final defeat of Germany', he declared, pledging to support 'in any way the efforts of the government to win a speedy victory by vigorous action on land and on sea'. He attacked 'parliamentary pacifists' who had opposed his calls to build up the Royal Navy and bemoaned the fate of 'that much ill-used and plucky little nation' Belgium, whose ruling class had, over the previous thirty years, annihilated 10 million people in the Congo in its pursuit of super-profits from rubber plantations.[20]

As well as echoing government propaganda, the BSP also supported its military recruitment campaign. On 15 September *Justice* published a statement encouraging BSP members to speak at recruitment rallies. 'Recognising that the national freedom and independence of this country are threatened by Prussian militarism, the Party naturally desires the prosecution of the war to a speedy and successful issue', it stated. 'Every able-bodied citizen, high and low, rich as well as poor, should be trained and armed for the purposes of home defence'. The statement was signed by all eight members of the BSP executive, including oppositionist Edwin Fairchild and the future founding secretary of the Communist Party, Albert Inkpin. In contrast, the ILP publicly refused to participate in recruitment rallies or stand alongside 'militarists and enemies of labour'.[21]

The Socialist Labour Party, the BSP's major opponent to its left, also failed the test of August 1914. That month's issue of its newspaper *The Socialist* denounced

---

19   The Lenin story is in Trotsky 1975, p. 244. Trotsky at the Zimmerwald conference in Riddell 1984, p. 293.

20   *Justice*, 13 Aug 1914. For the Congo, see Hochschild 1999.

21   *Justice*, 17 Sept 1914. ILP National Administrative Council statement in the *Pioneer*, 5 Sept 1914.

the ILP and the Labour Party, arguing that 'had they years ago adopted the principles and revolutionary fervour of the Old International, they would have been
in the position of either preventing this war or taking advantage of it to give
the final push to the already tottering system of capitalism'.[22] Yet it said nothing about opposition to the war which had just started. The reason was the SLP
had a significant number of members who did not oppose the war, led by the
editor of *The Socialist*, John Muir. Echoing the 'poor little Belgium' rhetoric of
the British press, Muir claimed that opposition to the war was pointless:

> having failed to take effective steps to prevent the war, the Continental
> socialists had to support their respective governments or sacrifice them-
> selves uselessly. ... Neither could any British socialist, with blood in his
> veins and brains in his head, stand idly by and see his country ravaged by
> war, as Belgium has been ravaged, without lifting a hand in its defence.[23]

Muir even praised the Hyndmanites: 'they have not burked the question of how
to deal with the present situation. The task to them, as to all sensible men, is
to defeat the aims of German militarism first, and to talk of the fate of small
nations afterwards'. By December *The Socialist* was giving back-handed support to the government's recruitment drive. 'Socialists are as much interested
as other members of the community in resisting invasion, and should be prepared to take their share of the work of safeguarding the country from invasion.
The more socialists in arms the better it will be for the success of the Stop the
War movement', wrote Muir in a front-page article.[24] An editorial titled 'Shall
I Fight?' had no equivocation in beating the drum for the British war effort.
'Women are habitually the victims at such times', said Muir, repeating a common theme of the invasion panic promoted by the Fleet Street press. The article
shamefully concluded:

> the safety of Britain is dependent on successful recruiting, and if it fails
> invasion becomes imminent. ... German workers, as things stand at the
> present, are doing their utmost to get at Britain, and the British workers

---

22   *The Socialist*, Aug 1914. According to future Labour MP David Kirkwood, who was an SLP
      member at the outbreak of war, the Glasgow branch didn't discuss the war until September
      when his motion to oppose the war defeated Muir's supporting it. Kirkwood then resigned
      and joined the ILP. Kirkwood 1935, p. 86.
23   'Socialists and the War', *The Socialist*, Nov 1914. Challinor 1977, p. 124, claims wrongly that
      'the SLP never wavered from its stand of proletarian internationalism'.
24   *The Socialist*, Dec 1914, p. 25 and p. 28.

are desirous of getting at Germany. ... It is a case of kill or be killed. It is horrible, but it is true.[25]

Both the BSP and the SLP had abandoned the anti-war banner to the pacifist ILP. 'Since the outbreak of the carnage, pride of place in exposing secret diplomacy, militarism and war, must be given to the ILP', admitted Philip Frankford, a Yorkshire SLP member who had been one of the first to write opposing the war in *The Socialist*. 'The attitude of this party in refusing to become recruiting sergeants is worthy of high praise', he continued, implicitly attacking his own organisation.[26]

Frankford also noted that there was rising internal opposition within the BSP and SLP to their pro-war positions. In the BSP, disquiet about its policy spilled onto the pages of *Justice* from late September. Joe Fineberg, one of Theodore Rothstein and Zelda Kahan's closest allies, wrote opposing the BSP's position, Val McEntee accused the party of inviting 'our fellow workers to take part in the butchery' and branches in London and Glasgow announced their opposition to the leadership's line. Albert Inkpin replied on behalf of the executive by stating cynically 'it was never their intention ... to advocate recruiting', ignoring the text of the September BSP statement which instructed 'representatives who are invited to take part in the general recruiting campaign to accept such invitations'.[27] The following week Inkpin was defended by Ernie Cant, who would also become a senior member of the CPGB. It was Percy Glading of North West Ham BSP, a future CPGB leader who would be jailed for spying for the Soviet Union in 1938, who provided a clear statement of opposition to the BSP's support for army recruitment:

> we do not believe in recruiting under any circumstances. Recruiting is the business of the capitalist class, and we believe in letting them do their own dirty work. Our business is to make class-conscious socialists and we do not forget it in times of peace or panic. Marx's statement, 'Workers of the World Unite' has more value to us than it appears to have for a great many of our comrades.[28]

---

25   *The Socialist*, Dec 1914.

26   *The Worker* [Huddersfield], 30 Jan 1914. See also his article 'War Against Civilisation', *The Socialist*, Sept 1914.

27   Fineberg in *Justice*, 8 Oct 1914. McEntee and Inkpin in *Justice*, 29 Oct 1914. McEntee became a Labour MP in 1922 and member of the House of Lords in 1951. Inkpin's disingenuousness was pointed out by R.C. Fletcher Wood in *Justice*, 12 Nov 1914.

28   *Justice*, 5 Nov 1914.

In contrast, it was not until that December that any explicit opposition to its pro-war line appeared in the SLP's *Socialist*. The SLP's Tom Bell had denounced the war at a Glasgow peace demonstration on 9 August – 'wars were based on force, the force behind the gun [was] in the possession of capitalism. It was up to the workers to get control of that gun, and make war no longer possible' he reportedly told the crowd – but this was from a Glasgow BSP platform organised by supporters of John Maclean.[29] No other anti-war statements from Bell's fellow SLP leaders appear to have been made during this period.

The SLP appears to have suffered a collective nervous breakdown following the outbreak of war and seems to have barely functioned. In November, Muir admitted 'I have not been able to find out what support either side [of the war debate] has, and consequently I cannot say definitely what the official attitude of the party is'. The next month an anti-war oppositionist from Sheffield condemned the lack of an official party statement as 'a deplorable fact which is intensified by the deplorable attempts being made to formulate one'.[30] Bell's later claim in his autobiography that he and Arthur MacManus – one of the SLP's key figures in the 1911 Singer Sewing Machine strike – led the opposition to the SLP's capitulation is unsupported by any statement in *The Socialist* under either name during this period.[31] Sylvia Pankhurst later claimed that MacManus supported the war during its first eight months.[32] It was only in December that anything resembling a revolutionary position on the war appeared. Wigan councillor and long-time SLP leader in Lancashire W.R. 'Dick' Stoker pointed out 'from a worker's point of view England is always wrong, Germany is always wrong, France is always wrong. Because this nationalist ideal of "my country" is ultimately bound up with capitalist ideals, it should be the duty of all socialists to ridicule and smash these ideals'. He ended by saying that if Muir's position was also that of the party 'the sooner the SLP ceases to exist, the better for the working class'.[33] Given that Stoker's warehouse business played a significant role in financing the SLP, this was not necessarily empty rhetoric. The following month Kathryn Hassan wrote from Dublin to denounce Muir's attempts to whip up fears of invasion through the spectre of mass rape by German invaders:

---

29   *Forward* [Glasgow], 15 Aug 1914. See also Bell 1944, p. 27.
30   *The Socialist*, Nov 1914, p. 18 and Dec 1914, p. 29.
31   Bell 1941, p. 102.
32   Pankhurst 1932, p. 281. However, this accusation may have been inspired by their mutual dislike.
33   *The Socialist*, Dec 1914, p. 29.

no socialist men will find any support amongst us when they attempt to find excuses for militarist training under the shield of our protection. Working women know that as a class, war and its invading hosts holds no terror that does not already exist within the grind of the wage system. As a sex they know that in the industrial field, daily if not hourly, some woman puts up a fight for her moral integrity with all the odds of the capitalist class and its paid administrators against her.[34]

It was not until March 1915 that *The Socialist* published an official SLP statement opposing the war. Even then, it was not a party position but a resolution passed by the Glasgow branch which called on 'the workers of all countries to 'DOWN ARMS!' You have not been consulted; why, then, should you fight? You own NO Country; what, then, are you fighting for? Your liberty after the war will be the same as before the war – the liberty of a WAGE SLAVE to work for a master. You have no security of living so long as capitalism exists. Capitalism is your enemy'.[35] By this time Muir appears to have resigned from the party and the SLP now presented itself as an outright opponent of the war.[36] By July 1915 the front page of *The Socialist* was declaring that 'The Enemy Is Within Your Gates' in an echo of Karl Liebknecht's slogan 'The Main Enemy is at Home'.

However, the SLP did not capsize simply because of the wave of chauvinist hysteria sweeping Britain. As was seen in the previous chapter, its practical programme subordinated political questions to the 'real business' of industrial militancy. For many in the party, the war was a diversion from its regular routine. 'So far as war conditions will allow we shall in the coming months concern ourselves with the more pressing needs of the workers, and continue our educative work', said *The Socialist* in September 1914. As John Muir's subsequent role in the Clydeside strikes showed, it was perfectly possible to be a workplace militant and support the war effort. This also seems to have been the initial view of Tom Mann, who admitted in August 1915 that 'I am really of the opinion that it [the war] ought and must be fought out'.[37] As the French syndicalist Confédération Générale du Travail demonstrated when it joined the *Union Sacrée* to support the French war effort in August 1914, there was

---

34   *The Socialist*, Jan 1915, p. 37.

35   *The Socialist*, March 1915.

36   It is not clear when exactly Muir resigned as editor. The final editorial under his initial 'M' was in the February issue. *The Socialist* implied he was still an SLP member in its May 1916 issue, p. 60.

37   Mann letter to R.S. Ross in *Justice*, 12 Aug 1915. See also Thorpe 2001.

no inherent contradiction between syndicalism and social patriotism.[38] The SLP seemingly drew no lessons from its political collapse in 1914. Reports of its April 1915 conference said nothing about internal debates or Muir's resignation.[39] When it was attacked by the SPGB in 1917 for initially supporting the war, the SLP denied the authors of the pro-war articles in *The Socialist* were SLP members, a defence as absurd as it was cynical, until it was forced to admit that its stance in 1914 was a 'grievous error'.[40] Moreover, it continued to reflect the anti-German chauvinism of war-time by referring to the courts and the police as 'British Huns'.[41]

The nationalism underpinning the politics of some SLP leaders was seen in the party's response to the 'Allied socialist' conference organised in London by the Second International in February 1915 for parties from nations fighting Germany. Chaired by Keir Hardie, the gathering included supporters of the war, pacifists such as Ramsay MacDonald, and two cabinet ministers actually engaged in prosecuting the war, Emile Vandervelde of Belgium and Marcel Sembat of France, plus the ILP's Arthur Henderson, who would shortly join the British cabinet. The tone was set by the French Socialist Party's Edouard Vaillant, who told the meeting that France 'will not draw back until Prussian militarism had received its death blow'. The conference ended with a pious declaration that 'the victory of the Allies must be a victory of the people's rights, of the unity, independence, and autonomy of the nations in a peaceful federation of the United States of Europe and the world'.[42]

One prominent social democrat who was not invited was Maxim Litvinov, who since 1912 had been the London-based Bolshevik representative on the International Socialist Bureau. Discovering he had been excluded, he wrangled an invitation the night before the conference started and went with the aim of presenting a revolutionary alternative to war and class collaboration. Pointedly addressing the delegates as 'citizens' rather than 'comrades', Litvinov demanded the socialist ministers in Belgium and France should leave their governments and that their parties break the war-time *bloc national*, 'under cover of which the bourgeoisie celebrates its orgies of chauvinism'. When he denounced

---

38   Darlington 2012.

39   *The Socialist* published accounts of the conference in its May and June 1915 issues.

40   *The Socialist*, Aug 1917, p. 88 and Nov 1917, p. 16.

41   References to 'British Huns' were made in *The Socialist* in June 1915, p. 65, Sept 1915, p. 92, and Nov 1915, p. 108.

42   Walling 2015, pp. 424–5. A report of the meeting is in the *Labour Leader*, 18 Feb 1915, and the *Daily Herald*, 20 Feb 1915, which also reported that Jules Guesde, the other French socialist minister, did not attend due to illness.

the parties of the old international for 'treason against the proletarian cause' he was interrupted by Hardie.[43] Undeterred, he continued to attack the social patriots until Hardie refused to allow him to finish, at which point he distributed his statement which concluded:

> the Russian workers hold out their hands of comradeship to socialists who are acting like Karl Liebknecht, like the socialists of Serbia and Italy, like the British comrades of the ILP and a number of members of the BSP, and like our arrested comrades of the RSDLP. That is the path we invite you to go, the path to socialism. Down with the chauvinism which is destroying the workers' cause! Long live international socialism![44]

He then gathered up his papers and left. Yet although *The Socialist* published his speech in full, its major comment on the conference was to complain that Litvinov did not mention the SLP.

2   The Anti-war Left

Standing somewhere between the ILP and the ostensibly Marxist organisations was Sylvia Pankhurst's East London Federation of Suffragettes. Unlike the BSP and the SLP, when the ELFS committee met on 6 August it came out in opposition to the war. Pankhurst and East End docker's wife Melvina Walker spoke against it, while Norah Smyth, whose money bankrolled much of the ELFS activity, argued in favour of the war effort. Even so, Pankhurst herself was pessimistic about publicly raising the issue. 'We could not say much against the war at present as so many people have relations in [the army] that they will not listen yet', she told the meeting. Three options were discussed: '1. to go on as if nothing had happened. 2. to try and make things better for those suffering through this war. 3. to make capital out of the situation'.[45] Option two was chosen, and so the ELFS directed its energies to campaigning for a five point

43   Gankin and Fisher 1940, p. 278.

44   The full speech was reprinted in *The Socialist*, May 1915, and an extract in the *Daily Herald*, 27 Feb 1915. Litvinov's account of the meeting is in Pope 1943, pp. 103–8. His report and Lenin's assessment are in Lenin's 'The London Conference' and 'On the London Conference' in *CW* vol. 21, pp. 132–4 and 178–80.

45   East London Federation of Suffragettes, committee meeting 6 Aug 1914; Sylvia Pankhurst Papers, Reel 24, File 201. In Pankhurst 1932, she says that the ELFS's Norah Smyth and Jessie Payne initially wanted to support the war.

programme calling for government control of the food supply (there were wide-spread fears that the war would lead to starvation due to a German blockade); jobs for all men and women at trade union rates with equal pay; a rent and debt freeze; working women's representation on food and employment committees; and votes for women so that 'they may help in minimising, as far as possible, the horrors of war'.[46]

This was very markedly different to the jingoism of Pankhurst's former colleagues in the WSPU, which abandoned its suffrage campaign at the declaration of war, changed the name of its *Suffragette* newspaper to *Britannia* (subtitled 'for King, for Country, for Freedom'), and sent Emmeline and Christabel Pankhurst on tour to denounce the 'German Peril' and shame men into enlisting. In 1915 Pankhurst senior called for martial law to be declared to aid the war effort and in 1917 she visited Russia to warn Kerensky's Provisional Government against making peace with Germany.[47] The ELFS opposed such jingoism and sought to address food shortages and unemployment in working-class communities caused by the war. Nevertheless, the ELFS did not produce any explicitly anti-war propaganda at this time, so its five demands amounted to little more than a campaign for a more democratically run war effort. In early August Sylvia Pankhurst wrote to Prime Minister Asquith asking him to meet a delegation of East London women to discuss the ELFS's demands, a continuation of pre-war suffragette tactics and a reflection of Pankhurst's self-important belief in her ability to persuade the powerful.

The ELFS's desire to downplay its opposition to the war and continue with grassroots campaigning resembled the SLP's desire to continue with the 'normality' of industrial struggle. But unlike the SLP in 1914, the ELFS's militant impulses often broke through its desire 'not to say too much' about the war. Melvina Walker wrote in a front-page article for the *Woman's Dreadnought* that:

> British transport workers – trade union men – are called upon to shoot down German transport workers, and it is not so very long ago, in the time of our industrial war – I mean the great Dock Strike – when we were fighting the large ship owners, we received with joy the news that these same men had sent us £5,000 to help in our fight ... Our duty at this time is to impress upon all that the working class do not want war.[48]

---

46   *TWD*, 15 Aug 1914.
47   See Vellacott, 2007. For martial law, see *The Worker* [Huddersfield], 29 May 1915.
48   *TWD*, 15 Aug 1914.

However, the only solution offered by Walker's article was the wish that 'had all women the power of the vote, we feel sure that there would be no war', a belief belied by the activities of Sylvia's family members. The ELFS organised meetings to 'keep the votes for women flag flying' in opposition to the WSPU's abandonment of the cause, and lobbied parliament for female suffrage, price regulation and jobs.[49] The ELFS's main campaign in the first weeks of the war was to call for a rent strike if its demands for food and jobs were not met. Although this never materialised in East London, it did foreshadow the Glasgow rent strike of 1915 against landlord exploitation and evictions.

The ELFS's politics were an eclectic melange of ILP-style pacifism, activist community organising, and the type of charitable social work that had been a feature of liberal concern for the East End since the mid-nineteenth century. The *Woman's Dreadnought* featured articles about campaigns against the war across Europe – at the end of 1914, it reprinted sections from both Karl Liebknecht's Reichstag speech against war credits and Lenin's 'The War and Russian Social Democracy' – while the Federation kept up a continuous cycle of meetings and demonstrations calling for various measures to alleviate the war-time suffering of working-class women and their families.[50] At the same time, it opened 'cost-price restaurants' in its East London heartlands of Bow, Poplar and Bromley ('two-course meals 2d ... Soup 1d, a pint with a piece of bread'), four mother and baby centres, and its own shoe and toy factory at its Bow headquarters ('skilled work for a living wage') which at one point employed 59 people, a venture largely financed by Norah Smyth.[51]

Alongside this work, the ELFS increasingly saw itself as part of the left-wing of the labour movement, campaigning against conscription and extending its strong links with local trade unions. In November 1915 Pankhurst announced that the ELSF would no longer use the slogan 'Votes for Women':

Fight for freedom for all humanity – they [lovers of freedom] make no distinction of sex. Surely it is time that the British Suffrage movement should come together to reorganise its programme and write on its banners, 'Human Suffrage – a vote for every man and woman of full age!'[52]

Three months later at its annual conference, the ELFS changed its name to the Women's Suffrage Federation, calling for universal suffrage 'based neither on

49   *TWD*, 22 Aug 1914 and 30 Jan 1915.
50   *TWD*, 26 Dec 1914.
51   See *TWD*, 2 Jan and 22 May 1915; Pankhurst 1932, p. 43.
52   Editorial in *TWD*, 18 Nov 1915.

sex nor property, but on the principle of humanity'.[53] Although the war was not mentioned in any of the announcements of the name change, the 8 April 1916 issue of the *Woman's Dreadnought* carried an editorial by Pankhurst declaring that 'every day the war continues, the bounds of tyranny are extended. When will we end the war?'

This was a long way from revolutionary opposition to war, but wasn't too dissimilar to the anti-war opponents of Hyndman in the BSP. In February 1915, the BSP organised regional conferences to discuss the war, which led to the anti-war opposition gaining a 5–4 majority on the BSP executive.[54] The intense pressure of the war was fracturing the mutual dependency that had held together the Hyndmanites and their opponents before 1914. It was also demonstrating that, without its Marxist phraseology, the opposition had much in common with the ILP's pacifist politics. Its tenor could be gauged by Edwin Fairchild's concern, echoing Keir Hardie, that 'all action should be rigorously avoided [that could] endanger national defence' and Joe Fineberg's belief that 'it would certainly be a disaster for Europe if Germany were victorious'.[55] Even at its most left-wing, the Fairchild/Fineberg position was for a diplomatic end to the war. 'The government must be told, in a manner that permits no misunderstanding, that the time for opening peace negotiations is now', argued *The Call* in an editorial headed 'Negotiate for Peace Now' in May 1916, and in early 1917 the party joined the 'Peace Negotiations Committee' formed by the Union of Democratic Control to promote a diplomatic end to the war.[56]

In September 1915 the Fairchild/Fineberg opposition won a 5–3 majority to support the Zimmerwald conference, which that month brought together anti-war European socialists of all stripes in Switzerland. But even the mild pacifism of the opposition, which began publishing its own newspaper *The Call* in February 1916, was now too much for the Hyndmanites. At the BSP's April 1916 conference, Hyndman and his supporters walked out, taking around 20 branches with them to form the National Socialist Party. Somewhat relieved, the new BSP majority voted to condemn the Labour Party's entry into the government and somewhat half-heartedly endorsed the Zimmerwald manifesto, calling for the 're-establishment' of the Second International and a 'united socialist campaign'

---

53   *TWD*, 4 March 1916, although the new name was reported as the Workers' Suffrage League. *TWD* changed its name to *The Workers' Dreadnought* on 7 July 1917.

54   The confusing details are well documented in Crick 1994, pp. 268–9.

55   Fairchild in *Justice*, 28 Oct 1915. Fineberg at the 1916 BSP conference quoted in Kissin 1988, p. 205.

56   *The Call*, 18 May 1916.

for peace negotiations.[57] Shorn of its extreme chauvinists, the BSP could now take its place on the right edge of the centre of the Second International.

Almost alone among the delegates to the BSP's conference, it was Wigan miner Albert Ward who outlined something approximating a revolutionary position when he told the conference that 'the working class has no country ... they have no concern in the present conflict worth the shedding of a single drop of blood'.[58] To many in the British socialist movement, such intransigent opposition to war was a matter of individual conscience, and the introduction of military conscription in February 1916 posed this question in the most starkly personal manner. The Western Front's insatiable thirst for human life led Asquith's government to introduce conscription and call up men aged between 18 and 40 years old. But almost 20,000 men, many of them socialists but also pacifists, Christians, and Irish nationalists, refused to go into the armed forces and declared themselves to be conscientious objectors.[59] At that point, they came face-to-face with the brutal reality of British democracy.

In February 1917, the *Woman's Dreadnought* reported that 3,487 conscientious objectors had been taken into military custody since the introduction of conscription.[60] There they endured forced labour, psychological terror, and physical torture. Thirty-four were sent to France and sentenced to death by the military authorities, although none were eventually executed. A typical example of the treatment a conscientious objector could expect was that endured by Jack Gray. Following his refusal to serve, he had been sent forcibly to a regiment in East Yorkshire where he was 'thrown into a pond eight times. He was stripped naked, dragged across a field, and after being immersed in a pond in which drainings and other foul matter ran, he was put into a sack'.[61] For many, such torture so affected their health it led directly to their deaths or to their suffering from its effects for the rest of their lives. Despite their gruesome treatment, the *Workers' Dreadnought* reported in September 1917 that only 191 of

57   Crick 1994, p. 277. Kendall 1969, pp. 102–3. A full report of the conference is in *The Worker* [Huddersfield], 19 April 1916. No British delegates attended Zimmerwald. Fairchild and the ILP's Bruce Glasier were both denied passports by the government, see the *Daily Herald*, 16 Oct 1915.

58   Quoted in Kendall 1969, pp. 102.

59   No systematic records were kept but Pearce 2001 suggests between 18,000 and 19,000, p. 173. For an exhaustive review of the extensive literature on Conscientious Objectors in World War One, see Cyril Pearce, review of *Writing about Britain's 1914–18 War Resisters – Literature Review* (review no. 1779) DOI: 10.14296/RiH/2014/1779. Date accessed: 27 Dec 2018.

60   *TWD*, 3 Feb 1917.

61   *Labour Leader*, 21 June 1917.

4,584 conscientious objectors had succumbed to their torturers and renounced their opposition to military service.[62]

These courageous and honourable men took their stand against the slaughter of World War One in the traditional political framework of the British socialist movement. To them, opposition to war was, like their socialist beliefs, a moral choice. Despite the heroic bravery of the conscientious objectors, the political futility of individual protest was underlined in September 1917 when British, Australian and New Zealand soldiers mutinied at Étaples in northern France. Whereas in Russia and Germany, revolutionaries in the army and navy were able to give leadership to rebellious soldiers and sailors, when the opportunity came in the British army, dozens of anti-war BSP members were in prison or on the run from the authorities and unable to influence events.[63] This differed from the policy of the Bolsheviks, for whom, as Trotsky explained:

> the first question posed by the European catastrophe was whether socialists could take upon themselves the 'defense of the fatherland'. It was not a question of whether the individual socialist should carry out his duties as a soldier. There was nothing else he could do. Desertion was never a revolutionary policy. The question was whether a socialist party should support the war politically.[64]

Few in the British movement understood this perspective. One of the few who did was Harry MacShane, a young supporter of John Maclean, who enlisted with the Royal Engineers in 1914 to spread revolutionary propaganda among working-class soldiers. Lacking any plan or strategy, he unsurprisingly found those who had volunteered in the first months of the war to be drunk on patriotic fervour and completely unreceptive. After nine months he deserted and made his way home to take part in the class war unfolding in Glasgow.[65]

Protests against the treatment of conscientious objectors became a major campaign in the socialist press. Most active was the *Workers' Dreadnought*, which regularly featured personal accounts of torture and the deaths that resul-

---

62   *Workers' Dreadnought*, 22 Sept 1917.
63   Crick 1994, p. 278. At one point, four BSP executive members were in prison at the same time. The concentration of SLP members in engineering meant that most of its members were engaged in munitions work and exempt from military conscription.
64   Trotsky 1968, vol. 1, p. 244.
65   MacShane 1978, p. 69.

ted from such treatment. The WSF even organised a picket of Pentonville Prison in June 1917 calling for the release of anti-war prisoners.[66] Out of the public eye, leftists also built underground networks to help conscientious objectors on the run from the authorities. This came to public attention in March 1917 when Derby SLP supporter Alice Wheeldon, her two daughters, and son-in-law appeared in court charged with plotting to assassinate Lloyd George and Arthur Henderson with poison darts. They had been targeted by the secret services because they regularly provided practical assistance to war resisters. The absurdity of the charges made no difference and Wheeldon was sentenced to 10 years' penal servitude, while her son-in-law got seven years and her youngest daughter five.

This show trial was so important to the government the case was prosecuted by the Attorney-General himself, the notorious right-wing Tory F.E. Smith, who a few weeks later would successfully see Irish nationalist Sir Roger Casement sent to the gallows for treason. Emmeline Pankhurst also appeared in court to testify the suffragettes had nothing to do with the plot and 'would take great risks themselves to protect [Lloyd George] from danger'. In prison Wheeldon went on hunger strike but was eventually released on licence after the end of the war. Weakened by her prison ordeal, she died during the influenza pandemic two months after her release aged just 53.[67] In reality, the Wheeldons had been framed by William Rickard, an agent provocateur working for the Ministry of Munitions' Labour Intelligence Division, which had been created as part of the government's crackdown on Clydeside in February 1916. Rickard and his handler Herbert Booth also tried to entrap socialists in Salford and Coventry.[68] Once again, the vindictive nature of the British state caused its opponents to bear a heavy cost.

3   Revolutionary Opponents of War

The only two voices of consistent revolutionary opposition to the war from its start were those of James Connolly and John Maclean, another product of the political hothouse that was industrial Glasgow in the 1900s. Connolly returned

---

66   *Workers' Dreadnought*, 8 June 1917.

67   For the trial and Pankhurst, see *Derby Daily Telegraph*, 12 March 1917 and *The Worker* [Huddersfield], 17 March 1917. Alice Wheeldon's obituary is in *The Socialist*, 27 February 1917. Wheeldon's daughter Harriet married Arthur MacManus. See also Rippon 2009; Rowbotham 1986.

68   Hiley 1986.

to Ireland from America in July 1910 and had been appointed as the Ulster secretary of the Irish Transport and General Workers Union the following year.
He emerged as a central leader of the Dublin lock-out of 1913 following Jim
Larkin's jailing and was responsible for organising the Irish Citizen Army to
protect strikers and their families from the violence of strikebreakers and the
police. When war was declared Connolly had no hesitation in highlighting the
relationship of class war to imperialist war:

> Should the working class of Europe, rather than slaughter each other for
> the benefit of kings and financiers, proceed tomorrow to erect barricades
> all over Europe, to break up bridges and destroy the transport service that
> war might be abolished, we should be perfectly justified in following such
> a glorious example and contributing our aid to the final dethronement of
> the vulture classes that rule and rob the world. ...

> Let us not shrink from the consequences. This may mean more than a
> transport strike, it may mean armed battling in the streets to keep in this
> country the food for our people. But whatever it may mean it must not
> be shrunk from. It is the immediately feasible policy of the working-class
> democracy, the answer to all the weaklings who in this crisis of our coun-
> try's history stand helpless and bewildered crying for guidance, when they
> are not hastening to betray her. Starting thus, Ireland may yet set the
> torch to a European conflagration that will not burn out until the last
> throne and the last capitalist bond and debenture will be shrivelled on
> the funeral pyre of the last war lord.[69]

Connolly's opposition to the war was also underpinned by his struggle for Irish
freedom, and this too left no room to compromise his opposition to the war.
'We ought to clear our minds of all the political cant which would tell us that
we have either "natural enemies" or "natural allies" in any of the powers now
warring', he argued, a few days after the declaration of war. 'When it is said that
we ought to unite to protect our shores against the "foreign enemy" I confess
to be unable to follow that line of reasoning, as I know of no foreign enemy of
this country except the British Government and know that it is not the British
Government that is meant'.[70] Opposition to the British war effort eventually led
him to tilt politically towards Germany: 'We do not wish to be ruled by either

---

69   *The Irish Worker*, 8 Aug 1914.
70   *The Irish Worker*, 8 Aug 1914.

empire, but we certainly believe that the first named [Germany] contains in germ more of the possibilities of freedom and civilisation than the latter [Britain]'.[71]

But by the end of 1914 Connolly had shifted his focus from the Marxist movement to building an alliance with the nationalists of the Irish Volunteers who had rejected John Redmond's call to Irish nationalists to support the British war effort. This led to a split with Irish Citizen Army secretary Sean O'Casey, the railworker and future playwright, who accused Connolly of having 'stepped from the narrow byway of Irish socialism on to the broad and crowded highway of Irish nationalism'.[72] Seeking to take advantage of the adage 'England's difficulty is Ireland's opportunity', Connolly's working-class opposition to capitalism was now subsumed by his desire to turn the imperialist war into a war for Irish independence, which would lead to the Easter Rising in 1916.

In Scotland, John Maclean took his revolutionary opposition to the war directly to his native Glasgow working-class. In September 1914 he wrote 'The War and its Outcome', the first public document to oppose the BSP's pro-war line, attacking long-time party leader Belfort Bax's exhortation to 'hate the present Prussian military and bureaucratic State-system'. In it, Maclean explained that 'our first business is to hate the British capitalist system that, with "business as usual", means the continued robbery of the workers' and went on to say:

> It is our business as socialists to develop a 'class patriotism', refusing to murder one another for a sordid world capitalism. The absurdity of the present situation is surely apparent when we see British socialists going out to murder German socialists with the object of crushing Kaiserism and Prussian militarism. The only real enemy to Kaiserism and Prussian militarism, I assert against the world, was and is German Social-Democracy. Let the propertied class go out, old and young alike, and defend their blessed property. When they have been disposed of, we of the working class will have something to defend, and we shall do it.[73]

At the 9 August Glasgow peace demonstration, organised by leftists in the local BSP and ILP, 5,000 people heard Maclean's comrade James MacDougall say that

---

71   'The German or the British Empire' in *Workers' Republic*, 18 March 1916. See also 'The War Upon the German Nation', *The Irish Worker*, 29 Aug 1914.

72   O'Casey 1980, p. 52. I am grateful to Patrick Sliney for his comments on this and many other sections.

73   John Maclean, 'The War and Its Outcome', *Justice*, 17 Sept 1914.

'the working class did not want war. The war was a capitalistic war and would benefit the profiteers only'.[74]

Maclean was the Scottish correspondent of *Justice*, and had written its weekly column on Scotland since 1912. Born in 1879, his grandparents had been victims of the Highland Clearances. His widowed mother encouraged him to stay on at school beyond the normal working-class leaving age of 12 and he became a pupil-teacher at Polmadie School in Glasgow before qualifying fully as a teacher aged 18. By 1903 he had joined the Glasgow SDF and quickly rose to prominence in the wake of the SLP split, which seriously depleted the SDF's strength in Scotland. His energy and teaching expertise made him a popular lecturer on Marxist economics, attracting 400 people to his 1915 lecture series, as well as a contributor to numerous journals and newspapers.[75]

In contrast to his later politics, throughout most of the 1900s Maclean appears to have been an orthodox SDFer, stressing abstract socialist propaganda and largely following the lead of Hyndman. He supported Hyndman's call for SDF affiliation to the Labour Party in 1907 and the following year proposed a Hyndmanite motion to the SDF's Scottish Council which read: 'in view of the possibility of an attack on Britain by the German Empire, we demand that citizens be trained in the use of arms and have each a rifle and ammunition ready for use at a moment's notice'.[76] However, in July 1907 he and Victor Grayson undertook a speaking tour of Belfast during the dockers' strike. There they saw the militancy and unity of Catholic and Protestant workers which had been forged through the struggle against the employers. This led Maclean to abandon the Hyndmanites' traditional distrust of industrial action, and by the time he assessed the lessons of the SLP-led Singer's strike in 1911 he was arguing 'all social democrats are industrial unionists. We differ from others in that we insist that real industrial organisation must arise out of the fusion and federation of already existing trade unions. ... We rightly insist that economic organisation is subject to ... a party representing the interests of the workers as a whole'.[77]

Maclean's political evolution was not only a response to rising militancy. In 1908 he had met Peter Petroff, a veteran of the Russian Social Democratic Labour Party who escaped from exile in Siberia in 1907 and found his way to

---

74   *Forward* [Glasgow], 15 Aug 1914.
75   Ripley and McHugh 1989, pp. 17–18; Milton 1973; and James MacDougall's 1918 article on Maclean in *The Call*, 13 June 1918.
76   *Justice*, 3 Oct 1908.
77   *Justice*, 15 April 1911.

Glasgow.[78] Born in 1884, Petroff had been active in the 1905 revolution, organ-ising a revolutionary cell in the Tsarist army and taking part in an armed rising in Voronezh in south-eastern Russia. He was a left-wing supporter of Julius Martov's wing of the Mensheviks but understood the importance of political organisation and the need for the party to actively intervene in the working class rather than passively promoting abstract propaganda for socialism in the manner of the BSP. In 1913 he moved a motion arguing that 'the proper function of the BSP is to lead the working class in its economic and political struggle' and that it should 'organise the trade union members of the BSP for systematic work and socialist propaganda inside the trade unions'.[79] Petroff's position had a sig-nificant impact on Maclean's thinking and in December 1910 the Scot wrote: 'if our principles are true then we shall win. Facts prove them to be true, and yet we are not winning. Some obstacle intervenes, and I think it is insufficient organisation'.[80]

By this time Petroff had moved to London and was active in the Kentish Town branch of the party. This was a branch with a high concentration of Rus-sian exiles, including future Soviet ministers Maxim Litvinov and George Chi-cherin, and Petroff established himself as a leftist critic not only of Hyndman but also of the Rothstein/Fineberg centre group. At the 1913 BSP conference, where he sat as an official representative of the RSDLP, he opposed the Hynd-man leadership's motion to make support for government spending on arma-ments merely a matter of personal conscience.[81] He also took to the conference floor to criticise the BSP's belief that socialism was a matter of individual educa-tion, arguing that it was necessary to have 'a programme to put before the work-ers. It was useless to wait for the majority to become socialists before anything was done. They would not become socialists unless something was done'.[82] The following year he was one of the few leftist voices raised in opposition to the rightist and centrist factions call for the BSP to join the Labour Party.[83] He and

---

78 For Petroff's biography, see Rogers and Smith 1984, pp. 224–30; McHugh 2000, pp. 25–32; Morgan 2013b. John Maclean's wrote a biographical article about his close comrade in *Cotton Factory Times*, 9 Nov 1917. Petroff's own unpublished autobiography is in the Inter-national Institute of Social History, Amsterdam at ARCH04330.

79 *British Socialist Party Annual Report 1913*, pp. 19. See also Smyth and Rodgers 1984, p. 102.

80 *SDP News*, Dec 1910. See also his articles 'Some Comparison of Methods of Organisation' in *SDP News* July and Aug 1911.

81 *British Socialist Party Annual Report 1913*, p. 17.

82 *British Socialist Party Annual Report 1913*, p. 15.

83 *British Socialist Party Annual Report 1914*, p. 15. To demonstrate the perils of autobiography, Petroff later claimed that he supported the BSP joining the Labour Party. See Morgan 2013b, p. 35.

Maclean also led the call for *Justice* to be taken out of the hands of Hyndman's private company and placed under the control of the BSP.[84] Although MacLean was very much his own man, the influence of Petroff's politics was a crucial factor in the Glaswegian's journey from Hyndmanite to revolutionary Marxist.

When war was declared, Maclean and Petroff immediately and unequivocally opposed it. Maclean won a majority of the Glasgow BSP to his anti-war stance and organised an energetic campaign of street and factory-gate meetings to denounce the war. In London, Petroff stood for a vacant seat on the BSP executive on the same anti-war programme and, although he was defeated by Joe Fineberg, polled the same number of votes as arch-Hyndmanite Victor Fisher.[85] In September 1915 Maclean launched the *Vanguard*, a monthly newspaper. He was supported by James MacDougall, a young Glasgow BSP activist, and Petroff, who moved from London to become the Glasgow BSP organiser. Billing itself as the 'Organ of the BSP – Scottish Branches', the *Vanguard* was anti-war, pro-class struggle and, uniquely on the British left, internationalist. So, at the height of British war-time chauvinism from August 1914 to Russia's February revolution in 1917, Maclean stood almost alone as a revolutionary voice in the British labour movement. James MacDougall later described the scene at one of his meetings in Bath Street in the heart of Glasgow:

> Up the street, standing on a table in the midst of a dense crowd of the proletariat, stood John Maclean exhorting men in explicit terms under no circumstances to join the army! The war, he told them, was not an accident. It was the continuation of the peace competition for trade and for markets already carried on between the powers before hostilities broke out. ... The men they were asked to shoot were their brothers, with the same difficulty on Saturdays to find a rent for their miserable dwellings, who had to suffer the same insults and impertinence from their gaffers and foremen. ... What did it matter if they looked a little different and spoke a different language? The Scottish miners when on strike had often received financial help from the German miners. The international solidarity of the working-class was not only the highest moral sentiment that existed in the world, it had already found expression in many ways. He told them that the main thing for them to know was that their real enemy was the employers, and that as long as turning lathes, ploughs, coal-cutter, looms, ships – all the tools of wealth production – were possessed by a

---

84   *Justice*, 2 April 1914.
85   *British Socialist Party Annual Report 1914*, p. 18.

small class of privileged people, then so long would they be slaves. To get free from this slavery was their real concern, and that victory could only be won with assistance of his brother in other lands, for socialism could not triumph in one country alone. The victory of socialism must be world-wide.[86]

The war was the acid test for self-proclaimed revolutionaries. Many had embraced patriotism. But for Maclean the fire of war had tempered his revolutionary steel. Previously known as a brilliant working-class educator who could render economic theory into the everyday language of the factory floor, the war transformed Maclean into a fearless mass leader. More than just an inspiring orator, Maclean was defiant, unapologetic and revolutionary, the embodiment of a working class that knew its strength and its interests.

Such a man could not escape the notice of the British state.

---

86 Recounted in Milton 1973, p. 83.

The Clyde Turns Red: John Maclean and the Enemy at Home

John Maclean was arrested by two policemen at an outdoor meeting in Glasgow's Shawlands district on Thursday 2 September 1915. He was charged with using language liable to cause a breach of the peace after a drunken mob had attempted to stop him speaking at one of his regular open-air platforms. His crime was to call the war 'this murder business'.[1]

Maclean had become the most prominent victim of an intensifying wave of government repression designed to intimidate anyone who stood in the way of the British war effort. In May, the SLP's William Holliday was sentenced to three months' hard labour after making an anti-war speech in Birmingham's Bull Ring market. He later died in prison.[2] A few weeks later, Sheffield ILP anti-war campaigner Alphonso Samms was jailed for two months after discussing the war with wounded soldiers at a local military hospital.[3] This suppression of free speech was enabled by the Defence of the Realm Act, which had been rushed through parliament just four days after the declaration of war to give the government the power 'to prevent the spread of false reports or reports likely to cause disaffection to His Majesty' by imposing military justice on the civilian population.[4]

The Act was part of the Asquith government's broader assault on working-class rights as it ramped up armament production. In May, Lloyd George had been appointed Minister of Munitions and set out to boost industrial output while suppressing factory-floor opposition. He had already masterminded the 'Treasury Agreement' between the government and the trade union leaders in March, which suspended all pre-war agreements between employers and workers, outlawed strikes, and allowed skilled workers to be replaced by the unskilled, a practice known as 'dilution'. Only the leaders of the miners' and engineers' unions did not sign the agreement.

In July, the screws were tightened further when the Munitions of War Act was passed, which converted the Treasury Agreement into law and banned

---

1 Maclean's account of his arrest is in the *Vanguard*, Oct 1915.
2 *The Socialist*, June and July 1915. Holliday's death was reported in the June 1916 issue.
3 Moore 1960, p. 7.
4 *The London Gazette*, 1 Sept 1914, p. 6968.

munitions workers from changing jobs without their employers' permission, forcing compulsory arbitration tribunals on the unions, and re-defining dockers and textile workers as munitions workers. Nicknamed the 'Industrial Slavery Act' by militant workers, within days a shop steward was arrested under the act at Glasgow's Parkhead engineering works for 'slacking'. At the same time, Lloyd George declared illegal the strike of 200,000 miners in South Wales, although when faced with strikers who refused to be intimidated, he backed down and conceded virtually all of their demands. In August, 26 workers at Glasgow's Fairfield Shipwrights were arrested after a strike in defence of two men sacked for not working hard enough, and by mid-summer, the Glasgow ILP's *Forward* could identify 40 local trade unionists who had been convicted under the Munitions Act.[5]

The employers were determined to use the war to roll back the advances that the working class had made before the war.[6] The outbreak of war did not end class conflict but temporarily suppressed it. One year on from his Mansion House speech warning of the gravest industrial unrest for a century, Lloyd George now believed he had the power to prevent such conflict from ever arising again. To the militant and increasingly self-confident Scottish working class, he signalled his intent by appointing Sir William Weir, the managing director of Glasgow's huge G. & J. Weir engineering works, as the Scottish Director of Munitions.

Glasgow was a city where war-time social peace barely existed. In May 1915, angered by huge rises in rents enforced by landlords seeking to profit from the influx of labour into local factories, tenants in the industrial district of Govan had organised a rent strike. Led by women in and around the ILP, most notably Mary Barbour, Mary Laird and Helen Crawfurd, and actively supported by John Maclean as secretary of the Scottish Labour Housing Association, thousands of tenants refused to pay rent increases and organised to prevent the eviction of those of could not or would not pay. On 17 November, when around 30,000 households were involved in the strike, 18 men appeared in court for non-payment of rent. With a crowd of 10,000 demonstrating outside of the court, including workers from Govan, Partick and Whiteinch shipyards, each defendant told the court that if the rent rises were not reversed, every munition worker in the city would strike. Faced with such implacability, the court was suspended while the presiding sheriff sought guidance from the government. After allegedly conferring with Lloyd George on the telephone, the charges

5 *Forward* [Glasgow], 14 Aug 1915.
6 See Wrigley 1976, pp. 92–4.

were dropped. Eight days later, the government introduced the Rent Restriction bill into parliament which froze rents at their July 1914 level.[7]

But by now, Glasgow was wracked by open class conflict. In October, three of the striking Fairfield shipwrights refused to pay their £10 fine and were sent to jail. Govan Trades Council demanded their immediate release, 'failing which we cease work'.[8] Equally eager to prevent the situation from boiling over, the government and trade union officials reached a secret agreement whereby the jailed men's fines would be paid and they would be released. As the agreement was being finalised, Robert Bridges, a supporter of John Maclean and a shop steward at Weir's engineering works, was charged with 'molesting' a worker by asking to see his union card. Bridges appeared in court supported by 200 workmates who let it be known that Weir's workers would strike if he was jailed. The charges were dropped. A little over three weeks later Maclean himself appeared in court following his arrest in September. Charged with 'uttering statements calculated to prejudice recruiting', he was convicted and sent to prison after refusing to pay the fine. Miners from South Lanark struck on the day of his trial and demonstrated in Glasgow for his release. On 29 November an anti-conscription rally organised by the Maclean-led Free Speech Committee scheduled for the City Hall was banned by the council. When thousands attended a city centre rally in defiance of the ban, all 10 platform speakers were arrested.

As Christmas approached, industrial conflict reached such a pitch that Lloyd George felt compelled to visit the city to use his personal charisma to persuade Glasgow engineering shop stewards to accept the government's 'dilution' scheme, whereby unskilled and semi-skilled workers would do the work of skilled engineers. More strategically, he also hoped to co-opt the leadership of the shop floor movement and isolate the left. ILPer David Kirkwood, the convenor of the shop stewards at Parkhead Forge, met with him and offered to speed up production if the workers were consulted on management decisions, but when Lloyd George visited Weir's factory, the Maclean-influenced stewards flatly refused to meet him.[9] On Christmas Day he and Labour Party leader Arthur Henderson attended a city-wide meeting of shop stewards at Glasgow's St Andrew's Hall but were shouted down by widespread heckling and the singing of the *Red Flag*. When John Muir, the former pro-war SLP leader who was now chair of the Clyde Workers' Committee stood up to address the meet-

7 Hinton 1973, pp. 125–7. *TWD*, 16 Oct 1915. *Vanguard*, Dec 1915.
8 Hinton 1973, p. 116.
9 Milton 1973, p. 114.

ing, as he claimed he had been promised that he could, Henderson refused to let him speak and the meeting ended in uproar.[10]

Finding his oratory unable to coax the shop stewards, Lloyd George responded to his humiliation with force. In January, the government unveiled its plans to introduce military conscription to send more men to the Western Front. The intensification of the war effort and the imposition of dilution in Glasgow factories meant a ratcheting-up of state repression. The government drew up plans to arrest militants if strikes broke out, freeze union funds, and bring in the army, while the Ministry of Munitions set up a Labour Intelligence Division to spy on militants.[11] Over the next three months, the government banned John Maclean's *Vanguard*, the Clyde Workers' Committee *Worker*, the ILP-supporting *Forward*, and raided the SLP's printing works and smashed the presses.[12] Peter Petroff, who had come to Glasgow late in 1915 to support Maclean's work, was arrested and subsequently interned in Edinburgh Castle.[13] Maclean was arrested again, and a day later, on 7 February, Muir, Willie Gallacher and Walter Bell were arrested for publishing the *Worker*. Strikes broke out across Glasgow's engineering works in protest against the arrests.

On 17 March, Parkhead Forge workers struck in support of David Kirkwood, who had been forced to resign as the convenor when management refused to allow him to speak to women workers.[14] Five strikers were arrested under the Munitions Act. A week later in the early hours of 25 March, five leading shop stewards, including Kirkwood and the SLP's Arthur MacManus, were taken into police custody under the Defence of the Realm Act and deported from Glasgow, shortly followed by three more shop stewards from Weir's.[15] After Glasgow Trades Council's protest rally against the repression, Maclean's deputy James MacDougall and the ILP's James Maxton were also arrested for calling for strike

---

10   *Forward* [Glasgow], 1 Jan 1915. This issue was suppressed by the government for refusing to print the censor's official report of the meeting and publishing its own account. The meeting is also described in Kirkwood 1935, pp. 111–12.

11   Wrigley 1976, pp. 158–9; Hiley 1986, pp. 399–403. It was future Labour cabinet minister Christopher Addison, the parliamentary secretary to the Ministry of Munitions, who gave the order to put the spying operation on a national footing, see Hiley 1986, p. 402.

12   Brotherstone 1969. As Brotherstone notes, the architect of the ban on workers' newspapers was the future 'father of the Welfare State', William Beveridge, then the Assistant General Secretary at the Ministry of Munitions.

13   McHugh 2000, pp. 25–32; Smyth and Rodgers 1984. pp. 100–16.

14   For more on this and the support of women workers for Kirkwood and other militant leaders, see Baillie 2002, pp. 128–41; Hamilton 1925, p. 154. Maclean's *Vanguard* called for equal wages for women (*Vanguard*, Nov 1915) and for engineering unions to support a victimised school headmistress (*Vanguard*, Dec 1915).

15   Hinton 1973, p. 156.

action to free the jailed men. In early April, the government delivered its *coup de grace* by jailing Muir and Gallacher for a year and condemning Maclean to three years' penal servitude. The most militant labour movement in Britain had been decapitated.

1   The War on the Home Front

This was the most sustained government attack on the labour movement since the Chartist era, and the hammer of repression was aimed principally at the Clyde Workers' Committee (CWC). The CWC had been set up in October 1915, superseding the Central Labour Withholding Committee which was established in February following strikes at Weir's, where Maclean supporters were strong, and at the Albion Motor Works, where the BSP's Willie Gallacher was the leading shop steward. The CWC quickly became the organising body for the shop stewards' movement, with Gallacher as its chair and ex-SLP leader John Muir its leading strategist, while the ILP's Kirkwood and the SLP's Mac-Manus also played leading roles.[16] Essentially it was a bloc between the Glasgow ILP, of which John Wheatley (the founder of the Catholic Socialist Society and future Labour Minister of Housing) was the moving force behind the scenes, and the SLP, for whom opposition to the war was not something it believed should threaten its alliance with the ILP or with the pro-war John Muir.[17]

Although John Maclean was a schoolteacher and not a factory worker, he wielded considerable influence among those on the left of the CWC, especially for his revolutionary opposition to the war and his call to link the war to the industrial conflict. As Glasgow's struggles demonstrated, and the government insisted, the war was being waged as much in the factories as it was in the trenches. But this was not the view of Gallacher and Muir. As we have seen, Muir had supported the war effort as editor of the SLP's *Socialist*, while Gallacher does not appear to have made any statement against the war during this period. Both of them fought against attempts to discuss the war in the CWC. None of the surviving three of the four issues of the CWC's *Worker* newspa-

---

16   It is not clear when Muir left the SLP; in its May 1916 issue, the *Socialist* named him on the 'SLP Roll of Honour' following his jailing. McShane in his autobiography implies that Muir was still in the SLP in November 1915; MacShane 1978, 78. Muir became MP for Glasgow Maryhill in 1922.

17   MacShane 1978, p. 78. Wheatley recruited Kirkwood to the ILP from the SLP in 1914 due to the latter's refusal to oppose the war.

per mention opposition to the war. In its January 1916 issue, Gallacher argued that workers' control of production was the best way to raise productivity: 'if the highest point in efficiency is to be reached, then the policy of the Clyde Workers' Committee must be put into operation. Not only is it a sound and well-thought out scheme of industrial organisation, but it is the only scheme before the country'.[18] According to Harry MacShane, Maclean openly criticised Gallacher for not mentioning the war at a public speech in late 1915: 'how could any man calling himself a socialist come to speak at a meeting at this time and *not* refer to the war that is raging in Europe', he asked.[19] Maclean also wrote in the *Vanguard* that the Clyde Workers' Committee should be treated with the same suspicion that official trade union committees were and that 'if it still clings on to academic discussions and futile proposals, it is their [workers'] business to take the initiative into their own hands'. In contrast, the SLP offered uncritical support to the CWC.[20]

The clash between Maclean supporters and the CWC leadership came to a head in November 1915. Shortly after arriving in Glasgow as a BSP organiser, Peter Petroff attended a CWC meeting at Maclean's invitation.[21] Following a presentation by Muir on dilution, in which he argued that the government should 'take over' industry and give workers 'the right to take part directly and equally with the present managers in the management and administration in every department of industry', Petroff criticised this as tantamount to participating in the war effort and attacked the CWC leadership for not openly opposing the war. Gallacher, who was chairing the meeting, called Petroff's contribution an 'outrageous attack on Johnny Muir' and 'a deliberate attempt to disrupt the committee', and asked the meeting to vote to expel him. When James MacDougall protested that Gallacher was capitulating to wartime 'anti-alien' hysteria, Gallacher told him 'just to show there isn't anything racial about it I'll ask the delegates to add your name to the proposal'. When Maclean subsequently arrived at the meeting, he attacked Gallacher for his exclusion of Petroff and MacDougall, beginning a political break that would never heal.[22]

---

18   'Prepare for Action', *The Worker*, Jan 1916.

19   MacShane 1978, p. 77.

20   Milton 1973, pp. 107–8 (unfortunately Milton does not offer a date for this quote). For the SLP attitude, see the report of its national conference in *The Socialist*, May 1916.

21   The arrival date is from Ripley and McHugh 1989, pp. 85–6.

22   The quote is from Gallacher 1936, p. 61. MacShane 1978, p. 78. Gallacher 1966 describes the 'sinister' Petroff as having a 'hissing voice' and being a 'suave and cunning villain', pp. 72–3.

On 22 December Petroff was arrested under the Aliens' Registration Act when he arrived in Bowhill to speak at a meeting of the local BSP branch.[23] The following day, when Lloyd George was expected to begin his visit to Glasgow, the BSP's *Justice* published an article titled 'Who and What is Peter Petroff?' that denounced him as an enemy alien and called on the authorities to take action against him. Hyndman's supporters were true to their word about supporting the war effort. Hyndman accused the ILP of being German agents, his lieutenant Hunter Watts was employed as a government recruiting agent who threatened anti-war BSP members with prosecution, and Victor Fisher organised soldiers to attack anti-war meetings, going on to organise the British Workers' League, a proto-fascist group financed by Alfred Milner, Minister without Portfolio in Lloyd George's war cabinet.[24]

On 3 January 1916 Petroff came to court and was jailed for two months for entering a prohibited zone without permission. He was released pending appeal, and left the court to a rousing chorus of *The Red Flag*.[25] From that point, government repression intensified against Glasgow's working class. Petroff was interned under the Defence of the Realm Act, militants were arrested, and newspapers banned. This was part of a strategy to draw 'a sharp line of cleavage between the local workmen, who undoubtedly comprise the great majority of munitions workers, and the disloyal socialist minority', in the words of one of Glasgow's munitions commissioners, Lynden Macassey. Rumours of German gold and violence began to swirl, not least due to the propaganda of the Hyndmanites, and when Maclean appeared in court again in April, the prosecution's case included accusations that he encouraged the use of guns and his followers discussed assassinations.[26]

In this maelstrom the CWC's *Worker* decided to publish an article in its 29 January issue titled 'Should the Workers Arm?' which argued against calls for the arming of the working class. Why this was published at this particular moment bears some scrutiny. Walter Kendall suggests that it was a response to Lettish veterans of the 1905 Revolution exiled in Glasgow, while Harry Mac-

---

23   John Maclean letter in *Justice*, 30 Dec 1916. Petroff's trial is reported in the *Dundee Courier*, 24 Dec 1915.

24   *Justice*, 23 Dec 1916. The Hyndman article was reprinted in the SLP's *Socialist*, May 1915. Hunter Watts's activities were exposed in the *Worker* [Huddersfield] 30 Oct 1915. Fisher's activities are in the *Worker* [Huddersfield] 29 April 1916.

25   *Daily Record*, 4 Jan 1916. For the circumstances of Petroff's arrest, see Mary Adams Bridges' article in *Cotton Factory Times*, 17 March 1916.

26   Macassey quoted in Hinton 1973, p. 146. The police accusations against Maclean are in the report of his trial in *Forward*, 22 April 1916.

Shane remembered that it had been written by Catholic socialist ILPer Willie Reagan.[27] It is also quite possible that its intention was to distance the CWC from Petroff, whose leftist politics and experience of the 1905 Russian Revolution seemed to epitomise the British press's stereotype of a continental revolutionist, and by association Maclean. Whatever the intention of the article, it failed. The government did not care about the pacific intentions of the CWC, and it used the pretext of the article's headline to shut down the *Worker* and implement the government's plans to arrest Muir, Gallacher and the SLP's print-shop manager Walter Bell under the Defence of the Realm Act.[28]

Their arrests were answered by spontaneous strikes at a number of engineering factories including Muir and Gallacher's respective employers Barr & Stroud and Albion Motors. Although these quickly subsided, the next day a fresh round of strikes saw 10,000 workers down tools. Nevertheless, the CWC leadership told them to return to work: 'it was only the prompt action of the CWC in urging those who had not yet come out to refrain from doing so that averted a still more dangerous situation', argued the SLP's Arthur MacManus in defence of the CWC's opposition to solidarity action.[29] Seven weeks later, when Kirkwood, MacManus and three other shop stewards were arrested and deported, several left-wing CWC delegates called on it to organise strike action following a large protest demonstration in Glasgow city centre. Gallacher ruled their motion out of order and, along with Muir, told the press that the dispute at Parkhead Forge which precipitated Kirkwood's deportation had 'nothing to do with the Military Service Act, or the Munitions Act or the repeal of any Act of Parliament ... They are pure shop movements, caused by pure shop grievances, and no further significance attaches to them'. Instead, John Wheatley persuaded Gallacher and Muir to lobby the Ministry of Munitions, which of course got them nowhere.[30]

The trials of Maclean and Muir, Gallacher and Bell, held consecutively in April 1916, highlighted these political differences. Unlike his later, more famous

---

27   Kendall 1969, p. 124. MacShane 1978, p. 80. David Kirkwood claimed Muir pleaded guilty to protect the writer – whom he does not name – who had five children and could not afford to be jailed. Kirkwood also echoes Gallacher's denunciation of Petroff; see Kirkwood 1935, pp. 188–9.

28   For the government's search for a pretext under which to arrest the men, see Gallacher's secret service file 'Copy from S.F.300/2/Strikes UK/1. Vol. 1' in TNA KV 2/753.

29   Arthur MacManus, 'On the Clyde: A Study in Solidarity', *The Plebs*, vol. 8, no. 2, March 1916, p. 30.

30   *Daily Record*, 31 March 1916. See also Hinton 1973, pp. 156–9. When Muir and Gallacher returned from London, the SLP said naively 'it is difficult to understand why the government refused to deal squarely with the two delegates', *Socialist*, April 1916.

trial for sedition in 1918, Maclean pursued a cautious defence. He admitted that he opposed the war and conscription but denied the police witnesses' claims he had urged workers to strike, let alone take up arms, and he told the court that he opposed strikes in munitions factories. Although he did not renounce his beliefs, Maclean's attempt to backtrack and use legal sleight-of-hand to obscure his politics fooled no-one – George Chicherin later claimed that Maclean 'was not sufficiently well-versed in logical subtleties' to deal adequately with the prosecution's 'treacherous questions'.[31] He was found guilty and sentenced to three years' penal servitude. His supporters in court exploded into a rendition of the *Red Flag* and four of them were arrested when the police were ordered to clear the court.

If Maclean's shadow boxing with the law obscured his political message, Gallacher, Muir and Bell's appearance in the dock saw them leave their political principles at the courtroom door. Muir's defence included character witnesses Harold Jackson and Neil Maclean, two directors of his employer Barr & Stroud, with Jackson telling the court that Muir was someone whose 'influence tended to good order' in his factory. Inevitably the three were found guilty, whereupon they tendered a 'humble apology' to the court.[32] For this, the judge praised their 'unimpeachable characters' and told them they had exerted 'a very considerable influence, apparently, for good among your fellow workers, and against the application of physical force and the universal strike for the purpose of righting wrongs'. He sentenced Muir and Gallacher to a year's imprisonment, and Bell to three months jail, in marked contrast to Maclean's sentence of three years' hard labour. This time, the courtroom remained silent.

2   The Easter Rising and the British Left

The contrasting responses of Maclean, Gallacher, the SLP, and the leaders of the anti-Hyndmanite faction in the BSP to the events in Glasgow reflected a broader clash of political perspectives. These differences could also be seen in their responses to the Easter Rising in Ireland, which took place barely a week after Maclean and the CWC leaders had been jailed. The leadership of the British labour movement had traditionally stood alongside its 'own' ruling class when it came to Ireland. Despite significant Chartist support for Irish independence

---

31   The transcript of the trial can be found in the *Daily Record*, 13 April 1916. Chicherin's comment is in 'The Scottish Workers' Movement and Reaction', *Nashe Slovo*, 9 June 1916.

32   *Daily Record*, 14 April 1916.

in the 1830s and 1840s, and Marx and Engels campaigning for the British trade unions to take up the issue, trade union and Labour Party leaders had little sympathy for the Irish. The ILP's Bruce Glasier reflected this national chauvinism in his belief that 'there seems to be a flaw – a fatal lesion – in Irish character that unfits the people for rational and progressive life'.[33] It wasn't until 1913 that the Labour Party adopted a policy for Ireland; and then it merely followed in the wake of the Liberal Party and endorsed its Home Rule proposals, which ensured that Irish foreign affairs, police, and customs policy would remain under British control. Although the SDF and the SLP had traditionally supported Irish independence, they did little to campaign for it.

Just as the class struggle re-erupted in 1915 after the shock of the outbreak of war had faded, so too did the conflict in Ireland. On 24 April 1916 – Easter Monday – Dublin erupted in revolt against British rule as Irish Volunteers and Connolly's Irish Citizen Army seized key sites across the city in an attempt to liberate Ireland. After six days of fighting, the overwhelming military power of the British Army crushed the rising, leaving 485 people dead, over 2,600 wounded and much of Dublin city centre in ruins. In revenge, the British government unleashed a wave of repression across Ireland. More than 3,500 people were arrested or interned under martial law, and fifteen leaders of the rising were executed by firing squad. News of the executions was greeted with cheering by MPs in the House of Commons, including Labour Party leader Arthur Henderson.[34]

The failure of the British left to oppose its own government in August 1914 was replicated in their response to the Easter Rising. George Lansbury's *Herald* declared that 'no lover of peace can do anything but deplore the outbreak in Dublin' while the ILP's *Labour Leader* sought to 'condemn as strongly as anyone those who were immediately responsible for the revolt'.[35] The BSP, now led by the Fairchild/Fineberg group, described the insurrection as 'foolish, and like every such rising was doomed'. Despite a report on the 'terrible allegations' about British atrocities in Ireland in August, *The Call* carried no other reports of Ireland during 1916.[36] The SLP was even worse than the BSP, non-committedly observing that 'leaving the merits or demerits of the revolt aside, it will now be realised that armies are the force used by capitalists to maintain their undis-

---

33   Quoted in Bell 2016, p. 98.
34   For Henderson's ambiguous statement and a reply, see the ILP's *Forward* 11 and 25 Sept 1920. I am grateful to Jo Woodward for this reference. See also Bell 2016, p. 15.
35   *The Herald*, 29 April 1916.
36   *The Call*, 7 May and 10 Aug 1916.

puted sway'.[37] Other than this, *The Socialist* in 1916 made no other reference
to Ireland, or even the execution of James Connolly, its own party's founding
chairman.[38]

Although the SLP printshop had printed Connolly's *Irish Worker* in 1915 after
it had been banned by the government, the claim of Walter Kendall and Raymond Challinor that the SLP was involved in the preparations for the Easter
Rising is incorrect. Speaking in 1923 to the Communist International's English
Commission, Arthur MacManus recounted how he had gone to Dublin to link
up with Connolly and establish an SLP branch there but that Connolly had
criticised him for being 'ultra-internationalist' when he opposed Connolly's
plans for an insurrection.[39] As with the war itself, the SLP's insistence on the
primacy of workplace militancy meant it avoided political issues that could
threaten its alliances with those to its right, especially in its stronghold of
Glasgow where anti-Catholic sectarianism was a significant political factor.[40]
According to BSP member Harry MacShane, in Glasgow the Maclean-led BSP
supported the rising, the ILP opposed it, and the SLP was divided whether to
support or oppose it.[41] Nevertheless, there was clearly sympathy for the rising
among sections of the British working class. At the Manchester May Day rally
in 1917, mention of Connolly's name 'produced an indescribable response, the
whole audience rising to their feet spontaneously amid repeated cheers'.[42] The
heroism of Connolly also inspired young working-class militants such as Arthur
Horner, the future Communist Party miners' leader, for whom the rebels' 1916
Proclamation 'gave me the same inspiration, the same sense of a just struggle
and a righteous cause, as *The Miners' Next Step*' and led to him going to Dublin
to join the Irish Citizens' Army.[43]

The only leftist organisation that openly sided with the Irish rising was Sylvia
Pankhurst's ELFS.[44] The first issue of *The Woman's Dreadnought* published after
the Rising led on the front page with 'The Irish Rebellion: Our View' which
opened with the line 'Justice can but make one reply to the Irish rebellion

---

37   *The Socialist*, June 1916.
38   For an overview of the left's views of the Easter Rising, see McGuire 2018.
39   Transcript of Discussion, Communist International, English Commission (19 June 1923)
     RGASPI. F. 495. Op. 38. D. 1, Day 2, pp. 13–14.
40   Challinor 1977, p. 158. Kendall 1969, p. 373.
41   MacShane 1978, p. 83.
42   *Labour Leader*, 10 May 1917.
43   Horner 1960, pp. 26–9; Fishman 2010, pp. 59–61.
44   The ELFS changed its name to the Workers Suffrage Federation at its May 1917 conference
     and then to the Workers' Socialist Federation in May 1918.

and that is to demand that Ireland shall be allowed to govern herself'. The following week the *Dreadnought* became the only left-wing British newspaper to carry an eye-witness report of the events when it published 'Scenes from the Irish Rebellion' by Patricia Lynch, an 18-year-old ELFS member who managed to evade military restrictions and reach Dublin city centre.[45] This was published as a pamphlet and the ELFS continued to campaign for Irish independence throughout the war. 'Arthur Henderson was a member of the English cabinet that doomed James Connolly, a wounded prisoner of war, to death. He was in the government that strove to partition Ireland', wrote *Workers' Dreadnought* in March 1918, 'English Labour must get itself right with Ireland, imitate its zeal and take flame from its devotion.'[46] Even so, the ELFS remained tied to Pankhurst's personality-based politics, and printed an article by her friend Sir Francis Vane, the commander of the British Army's Portobello Barracks in Dublin during the Easter Rising. Vane had been dismissed from the army in the summer of 1916 for condemning British atrocities, but he also defended his role in suppressing the Rising because it had 'injur[ed] the cause of Ireland'.[47] It would not be until the Communist International's criticism of the fledging Communist Party of Great Britain in 1920 that the British left would begin to take an unambiguous position in support of the Irish struggle against British imperialism.

3   *Nashe Slovo*, the BSP and Revolutionary Internationalism

The failure of the newly installed Fairchild/Fineberg leadership of the BSP to support the Easter Rising was one more example of its distance from revolutionary politics. This was also seen in the debates about Britain that broke out in the Russian-language press of exiled Bolsheviks and Mensheviks in 1915. In September Theodore Rothstein argued in the Bolshevik journal *Kommunist* that the 'disorder' on Clydeside was essentially a defensive response by skilled engineers to the threat of dilution and the loss of their bargaining power. Denying that the strikes had any revolutionary implications, he suggested that the continued bureaucratic control of the trade unions had not been challenged and that the struggle against the war lay in the future. A few months later, he characterised the Clydeside struggles as 'the current, liberal phase of the

---

45   *TWD*, 6 and 13 May 1916.
46   *Workers' Dreadnought*, 30 March 1918.
47   *Workers' Dreadnought*, 26 Aug 1917.

movement'.[48] This view was also defended by Albert Inkpin, who wrote in *Nashe Slovo* that the events on the Clyde 'never had' a 'revolutionary character and aims'.[49] Yet even as Rothstein's article was being published, Glasgow was gripped by a rent strike, its major factories were so prone to strikes that employers openly discussed the imposition of martial law, and when Petroff made his first public appearance at the Glasgow Panopticon in October 1915, he drew a thousand people to hear him speak about the 1905 Russian Revolution.[50] Rothstein's correct observation that this was not a revolutionary situation obscured the reality that, at the very moment British jingoistic war fever was at its height, significant sections of Glasgow's working class were now openly receptive to revolutionary politics.[51]

Political passivity is, in the last analysis, an acceptance of the status quo. At the most immediate level, this could be seen in the BSP's refusal to campaign for Maclean's release from prison. Glasgow BSP's district council decided not to organise a movement for his freedom on the legalistic grounds that it would have to ask the courts for clemency, something that Maclean would not do. Instead, they called for his release on the grounds of 'common justice' and said that they would start a petition when the war was drawing to a close because 'his alleged offence was one arising out of war conditions, and these having passed, there was no reason why John Maclean should be longer kept in prison'.[52] That there could even be a debate about Maclean's release demonstrated the limits of the BSP's politics.[53]

That the Fairchild/Fineberg wing continued to co-exist in the BSP with Hyndman's rabid pro-war supporters until April 1916 became a significant point of conflict among those in the BSP who saw themselves as orthodox Marxists. In October 1915, Maclean's *Vanguard* reported on the Zimmerwald conference and argued for a split with the Hyndmanites: 'Faithful social democrats here have been led a sorry dance by the bourgeois members of the Central [Lon-

---

48   'Disorder in England', *Kommunist*, no. 1–2, Sept 1915. 'On the English Socialists', *Nashe Slovo*, 19 Jan 1916.

49   *Nashe Slovo*, 8 Aug 1916.

50   For martial law, see Hinton 1973, p. 116. For Petroff, see Milton 1973, p. 108.

51   Rothstein's analysis also parallels that of British 'revisionist' historians of the Clyde in World War One. For example, Maclean 1999. For a contrasting analysis, see Foster 1992.

52   *The Call*, 2 Aug 1916. See the issue of 13 July for the origins of the dispute. Mary Adams Bridges opposed the BSP stance in *Cotton Factory Times*, 30 June 1916. See Burke 1997, pp. 189–201, for the debate between the leftists and the BSP leadership on the release of Maclean.

53   For the split with Hyndman, see *The Call*, 4 May 1916 and the *Worker* [Huddersfield], 29 April 1916.

don] branch [which was controlled by Hyndman] of the BSP. Our business is to trust ourselves and our cause and line up with our world comrades as quickly as we can'. Peter Petroff followed this up in the December issue and suggested 'to those members of the E[xecutive] C[ommittee] who pose as the opposition in the BSP to sit down fast on one of the two stools between which they are wavering'. He further went on to say 'we must, therefore, purify our parties and immediately proceed to gather our forces'.[54] *Vanguard* would be the organising centre for the leftist opposition.

However, Rothstein opposed a split with Hyndman. He argued the preservation of party unity was the responsibility of the left, and highlighted a number of incidents where anti-war members had won victories on party committees which he believed showed the BSP was changing. A split would only weaken the anti-war opposition, he maintained, potentially leaving the BSP organisation in the hands of Hyndman. As evidence of the success of this approach, he pointed to the ILP's refusal to break with the parliamentary Labour Party and how this had helped it to avoid being isolated from the working class.[55]

But in reality the BSP was already split. The Hyndmanites had formed their own party within a party, the Socialist National Defence Committee, and the Fairchild/Fineberg faction launched their own newspaper, *The Call*, in February 1916. Talk of preserving organisational unity where none existed reflected a reluctance to break politically with the pro-war faction, and once again allowed the ILP to claim it was the only party unequivocally opposed to the war. In this, as he had done before the war, Rothstein followed Kautsky in seeking to maintain a 'party of the whole class' containing all shades of ostensibly socialist opinion regardless of their practical politics. This approach was stated explicitly by Rothstein's ally Zelda Kahan who reported that the German SPD's 1916 congress showed 'however much we may condemn its policy of August 4, 1914, the main section of the German majority is not so bad as it is generally represented. ... We still have faith in German social democracy'.[56] This was not the view of most German SPD members. Following the heavily stage-managed 1916

---

54   Peter Petroff, 'Rebuilding the International', *The Vanguard*, Dec 1915, p. 6. It was not until just before the break with the Hyndmanites that the BSP left declared its support for the Zimmerwald Manifesto. See *The Call*, 9 March 1916.

55   'English Socialism and War', *Nashe Slovo*, 7 December 1915. This ILP position was explicitly criticised by the Communist International in 1920; see 'The Communist International Answers the ILP' in *The Communist International*, no. 11/12, June–July 1920, col. 491.

56   *The Call*, 19 October 1916. Kahan may have followed the logic of her position and joined the ILP; a letter from her in the *Labour Leader* of 19 April 1917 gives her affiliation as Hackney ILP.

SPD congress, the right-wing began expelling its opponents. Within six months of Kahan's article, the centre and the left had broken away to form the Independent Social Democratic Party of Germany (USPD). Her subsequent article on the split wondered whether 'with a little more forbearance on both sides a split may have been avoided ... we cannot help regretting the break-up of the German party' and hoped 'after the war the best elements of both sides will come together again'.[57]

Rothstein's pro-unity article was published in *Nashe Slovo*, the Paris daily edited by Trotsky and Martov. This was a newspaper of left-wing Mensheviks who opposed the war but did not support Lenin's call to split from the Second International, and were characterised as 'conciliators' by the Bolsheviks.[58] *Nashe Slovo* circulated widely among Russian exiles in Britain and carried extensive coverage of British politics. Its most frequent contributor on Britain was George Chicherin, who began the war as a pro-war Menshevik but shifted to the left as the war progressed.[59] He came to Britain in the autumn of 1914 and was heavily involved in the defence of Russians exiled in Britain, forming the Russian Political Prisoners and Exiles Relief Committee in 1915. The committee sought to mobilise working-class support for its work, and established branches in Glasgow, Liverpool, Newcastle and at Woolwich Arsenal in south London.[60] More importantly, as he moved leftwards, he also became the most articulate spokesman of those BSP leftists who not only opposed Hyndman but also Rothstein and his supporters in the Fairchild/Fineberg group.

When *Justice* denounced Petroff to the British authorities in December 1915, Chicherin raised the call for the left in the BSP to split from Hyndman and the social patriots. He argued against Rothstein's 'gradualist' policy of slowly taking over the apparatus of the BSP, pointing out that this strategy had allowed the BSP to go even further down the path of national chauvinism. As the events in Glasgow demonstrated, significant sections of the working class had become receptive to Marxist politics and now was the time to raise the banner of an

---

57 On the consequences of the 1916 SPD Congress, see Riddell 1984, pp. 456–70. Kahan, 'Some Reflections on the German Split', *The Call*, 15 March 1917.

58 For the story of *Nashe Slovo*, see Deutscher 1954, pp. 220–4; Trotsky 1975, pp. 250–65; Rosmer 1959, vol. 1, ch. 9; Yamanouchi 1989, pp. 17–32. The debate between Lenin and the *Nashe Slovo* editorial board is in Riddell 1984, pp. 228–35. Its coverage of British politics is discussed in Thatcher 1999, pp. 243–52.

59 The only English-language biography of Chicherin is Debo 1964. His 'authorised biography' is in Haupt and Marie 1974, pp. 331–41. For his activities in war-time Britain, see Grant 1984, and McHugh and Ripley 1985, pp. 727–38.

60 Grant 1984, pp. 231–70.

openly revolutionary party.[61] *Nashe Slovo* reported that in early January a number of the BSP's Glasgow branches had decided to break away but 'subsequent events' as Chicherin described them, presumably Lloyd George's crackdown, caused them to retreat.[62] Lenin supported Chicherin against Rothstein, praising him for his 'very good internationalist work in Britain' and because he 'came out in the conciliatory *Nashe Slovo* in Paris for an immediate split there. We are naturally in full agreement with [him] in his polemic with T. Rothstein, a correspondent of *Kommunist*, who takes a Kautskyite attitude'.[63]

Chicherin, who moved closer to the Bolsheviks as the war drew on, continued to cross swords with Rothstein and his supporters in the BSP leadership. In July 1916 he attacked Rothstein's refusal to oppose the imperialists' forcible annexation of smaller nations. Writing under the pseudonym John Bryan, Rothstein argued that socialists 'cannot indulge in practical demands which go against the inherent tendencies of capitalist development' and therefore had to adopt a stance of 'political agnosticism' towards annexations. He buttressed his argument by borrowing from Kautsky's idea of a peaceful, co-operative imperialism by suggesting it was possible the war could end with the capitalists trying 'to pool their interests together after the manner of a gigantic trust and exploit them on joint account'. In response, Chicherin, now writing explicitly from the perspective of the Zimmerwald Left, argued that 'proceeding from its class standpoint, the proletariat is the adversary of every oppression, of every domination by force. It is thus also against national oppression, and also against subjugation of new territories against the will of their inhabitants by brutal force'. The article ended by pointing out that Rothstein's position would lead to 'renewing the disintegration of international socialism'.[64] Chicherin returned to the issue again in January 1917, presenting the clearest statement of revolutionary opposition to the war that would be published in *The Call*, declaring that

> the military defence of the country in imperialist war is not a task to which the organised conscious working class should in any way concur. The proletariat's task, its present historical mission – the international struggle against war; against imperialism; against the very foundations of

61   'Denunciation by *Justice*', *Nashe Slovo*, 7 Jan 1916.
62   'The Scottish Workers' Movement and Reaction in England', *Nashe Slovo*, 16 May 1916.
63   Lenin 1916a, pp. 180–1.
64   Rothstein as John Bryan, 'Technicals of A Durable Peace', *The Call*, 29 June 1916. Chicherin letter in *The Call*, 13 July 1916. For Kautsky's position on imperialism, see Salvatori 1979, pp. 181–203.

the capitalist system – must be carried on without taking the least notice of the interests of the military defence of the respective countries. If, in our international fight, we damage these interests, it will not stop us, as it did not stop Liebknecht and his friends in Germany.[65]

4 The Zimmerwald Debate in Britain

The *Nashe Slovo* exchange between Chicherin and Rothstein demonstrated once again that the debate about the industrial struggle in Glasgow was inseparable from the debate on the war. *Vanguard* was not only the voice of the most class-conscious workers in Scotland, it was the only British newspaper to call for a clear break with the Second International. Petroff, the regular author of the *Vanguard*'s articles dealing with international questions, was openly in favour of splitting from the International and creating a new international, writing in a November 1915 front-page article that 'the war has revealed all that was bad in the Labour and Socialist movement. The progress of the war, with all that is accompanying it, is strengthening those elements who will build a new International on a more sound basis'.[66]

Petroff's analysis of the Zimmerwald conference was in some aspects similar to that of Lenin. He criticised the 'very mild' Zimmerwald manifesto, which had been written by Trotsky, for its failure to call for revolutionary action against the war, attacked its 'liberal phrases', and accused it of bearing 'a strong resemblance to the platitudes of which many of the leaders of the Old International were so enamoured'.[67] However, the *Vanguard* also published a model resolution for circulation to BSP branches that supported the Zimmerwald conference but said nothing about the pacifist sentiments of the manifesto nor the need to build a new international.[68] Petroff also remained vague about the way in which peace could be won, suggesting that 'peace must be obtained by the pressure of the mass movements of the people who would be able to dictate the terms of peace'.[69] This differed significantly from the Zimmerwald Left, for whom Karl Radek had submitted a resolution to the conference that argued that the task of revolutionaries was to:

---

65   *The Call*, 4 Jan 1917.
66   Petroff, 'The Breakdown of the International', *Vanguard*, Nov 1915, p. 2.
67   Petroff, 'Rebuilding the International', *Vanguard*, Dec 1915, p. 5.
68   'Resolution on Zimmerwald', *Vanguard*, Dec 1915, pp. 7.
69   'Resolution on Zimmerwald', and Petroff, 'Rebuilding the International', *Vanguard*, Dec 1915, pp. 7 and 6.

organize anti-government street demonstrations, carry out propaganda of international solidarity in the trenches, promote economic strikes, and, where conditions are favourable, to turn them into political strikes. 'Civil war, not civil peace' is our slogan. In opposition to all illusions that decisions of diplomats and governments can somehow create the basis of a lasting peace and initiate disarmament, the revolutionary Social Democrats must always explain to the masses that only social revolution can achieve a lasting peace and the liberation of humanity.[70]

No political tendency in Britain held such an unambiguous position of opposition to the war or endorsed Lenin's call to turn the imperialist war into a civil war. Even Chicherin's January 1917 article in *The Call*, quoted above, did not argue that the war could be used to intensify the class struggle. For Lenin, the position espoused by Chicherin was only the beginning of wisdom: 'in each country, the struggle against a government that is waging an imperialist war should not falter at the possibility of that country's defeat as a result of revolutionary propaganda', he argued in March 1915, before advocating what became known as a revolutionary defeatist position. 'The defeat of the government's army weakens the government, promotes the liberation of the nationalities it oppresses, and facilitates civil war against the ruling classes'.[71] Only James Connolly understood that the war offered an opportunity to strike back against the British ruling class, although this was in the context of Irish independence rather than workers' revolution, as expressed through the slogan 'Britain's difficulty, Ireland's opportunity'.

The SLP largely endorsed the Zimmerwald manifesto, regretting only its failure 'to grasp the significance of revolutionary industrial organisation' and stressing 'the need for industrial and well as political action as an effective method of combating the militarist schemes of the ruling class', a somewhat hollow criticism given the refusal of its own members to raise the issue of the war in the CWC.[72] In contrast, the WSF's eclectic leftward trajectory led it by early 1918 to argue that 'a capitalist peace under any circumstances means that the workers of Europe lose the war. A capitalist peace means the continuance

---

70 Karl Radek, 'Draft Resolution on the World War and the Tasks of Social Democracy' in Riddell 1984, p. 299. Written by Radek, this resolution was presented by Radek and Lenin to the Zimmerwald conference held on 5–8 September 1915.

71 'The Conference of the RSDLP Groups Abroad', *CW* vol. 21, p. 163. For the debate on the slogan of defeatism, see Pearce 1961; Draper 2014; Slaughter 1967. I am grateful to David Scott for his comments on this and many other sections.

72 1916 SLP conference resolution on Zimmerwald, *The Socialist*, May 1916.

of capitalism and the exploitation of the workers; and it will be an armed truce that will lead to more war. ... A capitalist peace will have for its aim the repression of revolution in Europe' although when it came to how a 'workers' peace' could be achieved it the WSF struggled to break out of its pacifist framework.[73]

Petroff's ambiguity on Zimmerwald was a reflection of his attitude to the Bolsheviks, whose revolutionary defeatist programme he criticised obliquely in the *Vanguard* in an attack on those who:

> are talking about the social revolution as the immediate step. They do not trouble as to whether this can be accomplished without the necessary forces, but rest content so long as it is stated in resolutions. These people, who are more 'revolutionary' than reason permits, suggest the formation of an omnipotent Central Committee to control the whole world. Just in the same way as the Hegelian 'idea' was considered the driving force of history, so, in the mind of Socialists, this 'Committee' will become the driving force of the revolution irrespective of the balance of power in the various countries.[74]

This attack on Lenin, which echoed the young Trotsky's claim that Lenin's conception of the revolutionary party would lead to the central committee substituting itself for the party and the masses, undoubtedly passed over the heads of any non-Russian readers of the *Vanguard*.[75] However, by opposing the need for a centralised party Petroff inadvertently highlighted the weakness at the heart of Maclean's and the leftist opposition's politics; their inability to build an organisation that could both wage a factional struggle against the BSP's centrists and build a party for militant workers based on an openly revolutionary programme. And, although no-one could know it, the next few months would demonstrate just how important such a party was for the achievement of revolutionary goals.

---

73   *Workers' Dreadnought*, 20 April 1918.
74   Petroff, 'Rebuilding the International', *Vanguard*, no. 4, Dec 1916. Chicherin made a similar point in *Nashe Slovo*, 'The Scottish Workers' Movement and Reaction in England', 16 May 1916.
75   For example, see part three of Trotsky's 1904 *Our Political Tasks*.

CHAPTER 6

'Lads Like Me Had Whacked the Bosses': The Coming of the Russian Revolution

On 22 January 1917, 150,000 workers across the city of Petrograd went on strike to mark the twelfth anniversary of Bloody Sunday, the day when Russian troops shot hundreds of demonstrators who were peacefully marching to the Tsar's Winter Palace in 1905.[1] Barely a month after the strike, to coincide with the opening of the Duma, the Russian parliament, workers in dozens of factories downed tools in protest against falling wages, rising prices and shortages of food. As March began, 30,000 workers at Petrograd's huge Putilov engineering works were faced with starvation after being locked out by management because they had asked for a wage increase to cope with war-time inflation. On 8 March, International Women's Day, protests against bread shortages rapidly flared into massive demonstrations calling for the overthrow of the Tsar and an end to the war. A week later, Tsar Nicholas II abdicated. The Russian Revolution had begun.[2]

In Britain, news of the downfall of the Romanovs reverberated across all society. *The Times* praised the Tsar as a 'monarch of ideals' but also claimed that 'British public opinion has helped a very great deal' in the movement towards democracy.[3] Liberals who had campaigned against the anti-Semitism and police state repression of Tsarism – many of whom had then ignored these characteristics of the Romanov regime during its war-time alliance with Britain – believed that Russia would adopt British constitutional principles. But for working-class militants in Britain, the toppling of the Tsar through strikes and demonstrations was an example to be emulated in their fight against war, censorship and industrial repression.

A few days after the Romanovs were consigned to the dustbin of history, the Committee of Delegates of the Russian Socialist Groups in London, of which Chicherin was the secretary, announced a meeting to welcome the Russian Revolution for the following Saturday, 24 March. An astounding 7,000 people crammed into the Mile End Road's Assembly Hall in London's East End, with

---

1 Estimates of deaths range from the government's 96 to 4,000. I have converted Russian dates to the Gregorian calendar, which by 1917 was 13 days ahead of the Julian calendar.
2 See Hasegawa 1981 among many hundreds of books on the subject.
3 *The Times*, 17 March 1917.

many others locked out, to hear Transport Workers' Federation leader Robert Williams, the BSP's Edwin Fairchild and Joe Fineberg, and prominent anti-Tsarist campaigner Mary Bridges-Adams (a close associate of Chicherin) hail the overthrow of Tsarism. A resolution calling for the immediate release of Peter Petroff and the other Russian leftists interned by the British was unanimously passed.[4]

The following week 20,000 people crushed themselves into the Albert Hall – named after the husband of one the Tsar's relatives – to hear a wide range of liberals and socialists welcome the revolution. Henry Nevinson, a supporter of Sylvia Pankhurst, gave an eye-witness account of Bloody Sunday in 1905, and miners' leader Robert Smillie denounced the 'industrial slavery' that the British government had introduced at home.[5] One of the evening's loudest ovations came when Robert Williams declared 'those of us who are internationalists find our minds and souls exultant at the glorious message which had come through from the Russian Workmen and Soldiers Delegates – in my judgement it is the tocsin of revolt in every country in Europe!' The meeting ended by passing a resolution calling on the British government to follow the lead of the Provisional Government and allow: 'industrial freedom, freedom of speech and the press, the abolition of social, religious and national distinctions, an immediate amnesty for political and religious offences, and universal suffrage'.[6]

The outpouring of support for the Russian workers' struggle was repeated across Britain. In Glasgow 70,000 marched through the city on May Day from George Square to Glasgow Green. Among the 215 organisations represented were Jewish, Lithuanian and Latvian socialist groups.[7] 'Glasgow and Petrograd, the Clyde and the Neva, were linked together on Sunday in the hands of international brotherhood, never again to be separated by the Georges or the Miliukoffs', wrote local ILP councillor Patrick Dollan in a *Labour Leader* article which proclaimed 'Glasgow the British Petrograd'.[8] In Liverpool, a May Day demonstration in Edge Hill was led by 150 Russian Sailors in full dress-uniform carrying the Red Flag at the their head. Manchester's May Day celebrations saw a crowd of thousands pack into the Free Trade Hall to unanimously affirm:

---

4 *Labour Leader*, 29 March 1917. *The Herald*, 24 and 31 March 1917. During the war the *Daily Herald* became a weekly and accordingly dropped 'Daily' from its title.

5 *Labour Leader*, 5 April 1917.

6 *The Herald*, 7 April 1917.

7 A Lithuanian community existed in Bellshill, just outside Glasgow, where a branch of the Lithuanian Social Democratic Party had been formed in 1903; see White 2004.

8 10 May 1917. Dollan wrote under the pseudonym Myner Collier.

its unfaltering belief that the glorious Russian Revolution is a warning to all those reactionaries in this and other countries who desire to diminish and restrict democratic liberty, and that it is the precursor of greater movements at home and abroad to secure the complete emancipation of the workers of the world.[9]

In Leicester, 10,000 marchers on the Trades Council's May Day demonstration voted' without dissent' to send 'fraternal greetings to the people of Russia and congratulate them on the success of their revolution'. Over a thousand people assembled in Leeds' Victoria Square to send 'a message of support to the Workers' and Soldiers' Committees in Russia', while in Wales a meeting of over 2,500 in Merthyr Tydfil endorsed the resolution of the Albert Hall meeting, sending 'its congratulations to the Russian proletariat'.[10] Looking back in 1951, Aneurin Bevan recalled seeing Welsh miners 'when they heard that the Tsarist tyranny had been overthrown, rushing to meet each other in the streets with tears streaming down their cheeks, shaking hands and saying: "At last it has happened" ... the revolution of 1917 came to the working class of Great Britain, not as social disaster, but as one of the most emancipating events in the history of mankind'.[11]

The popularity of the revolution was more than symbolic. Despite Lloyd George's repression on Clydeside and the suppression of the Easter Rising in 1916, industrial conflict continued throughout Britain. The introduction of military conscription early in 1916 and the government's drive to dilute skilled labour by replacing it with unskilled workers, alongside the 'combing out' of men to serve in the army, meant that workplaces increasingly operated almost under martial law conditions. A number of disputes broke out when workers were threatened with being sent into the army if they did not submit to the discipline of their employers. For men and women working long, backbreaking hours in a factory, mine or shipyard, deprived of their right to strike or even to change jobs in munitions' industries, the freedoms won by Russian workers were a shining beacon.

---

9   *Labour Leader*, 10 May 1917.
10 *Leicester Daily Post*, 7 May 1917. *Pioneer*, 12 May 1917. *Yorkshire Post*, 7 May 1917. *Labour Leader*, 10 May 1917.
11 Speech at the 1951 Labour Party conference, *Labour Party Annual Conference Report*, 1951, p. 121.

1   **Repression and Revolt**

By the start of 1917 the flashpoint for government attacks on working-class
organisation was focused on Sheffield. As in Glasgow, it was the highly skilled
men of the Amalgamated Society of Engineers (ASE) who led the resistance to
Lloyd George's assault on workplace rights. Military conscription now meant
that an ever-present fear of being drafted into the army hung over the head of
every worker. During the summer of 1916 the Sheffield district committee of the
ASE dealt with 300 cases of members threatened with conscription by factory
managers.[12] In October Leonard Hargreaves, a fitter at the Vickers' engineering
factory, was conscripted into the army despite having a badge of exemption due
to his work as an engineer in the munitions industry. However, he did not have
a certificate of exemption and this lack of paperwork was enough to have him
sent into the Army Service Corps.

On 8 November 1916, a mass meeting of Vickers' workers voted to 'down
tools' if Hargreaves wasn't released from the army within seven days, a decision
communicated directly to Prime Minister Herbert Asquith by the leader of the
shop stewards, J.T. Murphy, who worked alongside Hargreaves at Vickers. No
response was forthcoming and a week later 12,000 Sheffield engineers went on
strike, many proclaiming 'No Hargreaves, No Work'. The shop stewards sent out
motorcyclists across the country to argue for solidarity action from ASE members and three days' later engineers at the Vickers' plants in Barrow-in-Furness
walked off the job. Faced with a shutdown in two of England's most important
engineering centres, the government retreated. On 20 November Hargreaves
was on his way back home to Sheffield.[13]

This was a significant victory. Not only was Hargreaves released from the
army, but the government also agreed to the ASE's demand that the union
should be allowed to issue 'Trade Cards' for its members in the munitions'
industry exempting them from conscription, giving rise to the slogan 'You can't
take me, I'm ASE'. The Sheffield success sent a surge of confidence through
engineers and other workers across Britain. At the same time, the inability
of British forces to make a decisive breakthrough in the war led to a crisis of
confidence in Asquith's premiership. On 6 December 1916 he resigned and was
replaced by Lloyd George who announced his muscular new regime by reject-
ing Germany's offer of peace talks, unveiling a scheme of industrial conscription, and making Labour Party leader Arthur Henderson one of five members
of his newly created war cabinet.[14]

---

12   Mustill 2016, p. 16.
13   As well as Mustill, see also Moore 1960, p. 8, and Darlington 1998, pp. 18–23.
14   *The Times*, 20 Dec 1916.

It made little difference to the industrial situation. Indeed, 1917 would see the highest number of industrial disputes since the war began. Over 5.6 million working days were lost that year through stoppages, a figure that exceeded the aggregate total of all days lost between August 1914 and December 1916.[15] Throughout the spring of 1917, strikes broke out with increasing frequency and size. In March, Barrow was once again paralysed by a strike of 10,000 munitions workers. The following month, an attempt by the anti-union management of Tweedale & Smalley in Rochdale to introduce 'dilution' into non-war engineering work led to a strike that quickly spread to 60,000 other Lancashire engineers. Within another four weeks, 200,000 workers in London and dozens of other towns had downed tools in support of the Rochdale workers in what became known as the 'May Strikes'. Other smaller scale disputes also ignited across Britain, spurred not merely by wages and working conditions but also by a growing sense of an inequality of wartime sacrifice. 'The redistribution of national income in favour of those who were already wealthy', the moderate ILPer Jimmy Mallon warned the government in July 1917, 'is a profound and indeed fundamental cause of industrial unrest, causing, as it has, a more acute sense of social inequalities'.[16]

The government had become especially concerned by the growing influence of the shop stewards' movement in this latest wave of strikes. The Hargreaves dispute had been led by a network of shop stewards in Sheffield's engineering factories, which emerged from an unofficial committee set up by highly skilled engineers in late 1915 to demand a wage rise due to extra work caused by dilution. Although their pay claim was turned down by the employers, the government agreed to meet the shop stewards to try to avert a strike. This unexpected victory for the engineers led the ASE's Sheffield District Committee to encourage every factory shop-floor unit to elect shop stewards, and so by November 1916 around sixty stewards had been elected and a city-wide engineering shop stewards committee had been set up. This was the infrastructure upon which the victory in the Hargreaves case was won.[17]

At the same time as the Hargreaves dispute, the SLP's Arthur MacManus organised the first national conference in early November 1916 of what would

15   Office for National Statistics, https://www.ons.gov.uk/employmentandlabourmarket/peo
      pleinwork/workplacedisputesandworkingconditions/datasets/labourdisputeslabourdisp
      utesannualestimates – accessed 2 November 2018.
16   J.J. Mallon, 'Note to the Report of the Commissioners for the Yorkshire and East Midlands
      Area', p. 7. appendix to G.N. Barnes MP, *Commission of Enquiry into Industrial Unrest. Summary of the Reports of the Commission*, CAB 24/23/59.
17   For background, see Hinton 1973, pp. 166–70, and Darlington 1998, pp. 15–23.

become the Shop Stewards and Workers' Committee Movement (SSWCM), bringing together a small number of shop-floor militants from Merseyside, Clydeside, Barrow, Manchester and London. On 15 May 1917 the SSWCM held a strikers' delegate conference in London where a hundred delegates from across Britain met to co-ordinate the engineering strike wave. Although there appears to have been a significant number of delegates who wanted a settlement, the strikes continued to spread. On 17 May, the SSWCM sent Dave Ramsey, a SLP member from Leicester, and William Watson, a leading member of the London Workers' Committee and a regular contributor to the *Workers' Dreadnought*, to Scotland to persuade the Glasgow workers to support the strikes. At this point, confronted by the potential rekindling of Clydeside militancy, the government arrested 10 of the central leadership of the SSWCM, a decision made at a War Cabinet meeting supported by Arthur Henderson. However, when many strikers refused to return to work until the imprisoned 10 had been released, the government withdrew the charges and released the men less than a week later.[18] When Glasgow council provocatively made Lloyd George a freeman of the city at the end of the month, 30,000 Glaswegians demonstrated in protest; at the head of the march were one hundred Russian sailors carrying the red flag.

This tide of discontent rose at such an alarming pace that on 25 May Lloyd George announced he was appointing a 'Commission of Enquiry into Industrial Unrest', comprising senior civil servants, industrialists and trade union officials. It quickly reported back, telling him that working-class people were dissatisfied with deteriorating working conditions, attacks on personal freedom, military and industrial conscription, and the inflationary costs of living. An earlier report from March had already informed the government that food prices had risen by 92 per cent since August 1914, with bread rising by 100 per cent.[19] The chair of the commission, pro-war Labour M.P. George Barnes, stated that the key factor was 'the feeling that there has been inequality of sacrifice, that the government has broken solemn pledges, that the trade union officials are no longer to be relied upon, and that there is woeful uncertainty as to the industrial future'.[20] Most concerning for Barnes and his fellow commissioners was the fact that many workers now had no confidence in the trade union leadership and openly 'expressed distrust in, and total indifference to, any promise that government may make, while some referred to Russia and openly declared

---

18   Hinton 1973, pp. 204–7.
19   Wrigley 1976, p. 180.
20   G.N. Barnes MP, *Commission of Enquiry into Industrial Unrest. Summary of the Reports of the Commission*, p. 7. CAB 24/23/59.

the one course open for labour was a general down tools revolutionary policy to secure reforms that constitutional action was failing to effect'.[21]

Barnes may well have been referring to the SSWCM. The shop stewards' movement had grown precisely because the war highlighted the gap between the interests of trade union officials and those of their members. Unlike the constricting class collaboration of the trade union leadership, direct action from the shop floor got results, precisely the point the SLP and the syndicalists had been arguing since before the war. Moreover, the SSWCM leaders openly identified with the revolution in Russia. Its president (MacManus), secretary (J.T. Murphy), and assistant secretary (George Peet) would all become members of the Communist Party, and at least three of the eight other members of its National Administrative Council elected in January 1918 were associated with the SLP or Sylvia Pankhurst's WSF.[22] The main leader of the SSWCM was J.T. 'Jack' Murphy, a skilled engineer at the same Vickers factory as Leonard Hargreaves and the leader of the Sheffield shop stewards' movement. A former preacher in the Primitive Methodist movement, Murphy had been won to syndicalism when he met James Connolly during the Dublin lockout, and his intellectual self-assuredness and organisational abilities meant he became a senior union negotiator in his plant while still in his twenties.

Murphy's ideas about syndicalism were laid out in his March 1917 pamphlet *The Workers' Committee*, which argued that the shop-floor committee was the basis for working-class organisation. Clearly influenced by *The Miners' Next Step*, Murphy argued that such committees would replicate upwards in a pyramid fashion, so that the shop committee would elect delegates to a factory committee, which would send delegates to a local workers' committee, all the way up to a national workers' committee. 'Once such a body or structure is erected', he wrote in 1917, 'the workers will have made possible the complete transition from the old form of trade unionism to industrial unionism'.[23] In some ways this appeared to resemble the soviet structure which emerged during the Russian Revolutions, but Murphy stepped back from arguing that the committees should exercise soviet-style power: 'these committees should not have any governing power, but should exist to render service to the rank and file, by providing means for them to arrive at decisions and to unite their forces'.

---

21 'Report of the Commissioners for the Yorkshire and East Midlands Area', p. 7. appendix to G.N. Barnes MP, *Commission of Enquiry into Industrial Unrest. Summary of the Reports of the Commission*, p. 3. CAB 24/23/59.

22 See the report of the conference published as an appendix to Tom Bell 1941, p. 304. George Peet should not be confused with future CPGB leader Fred Peet.

23 'The Gathering Storm', *Solidarity*, vol. 1 no. 5, April 1917.

Murphy also ignored the question of political leadership: 'it matters little to us whether leaders be official or unofficial [because] so long as they sway the mass, little thinking is done by the mass'. Nor did *The Workers' Committee* say anything about the Labour Party. Beyond workplace militancy the pamphlet's political content was a melange of voguish ideas. Quotations from Walt Whitman, Henrik Ibsen and John Stuart Mill opened the pamphlet, which also contained the statement 'the future of the race becomes a story of race deterioration'.[24]

Murphy's ideas about the centrality of shop floor organisation to the conquest of power by the working class were echoed by Willie Gallacher. In his widely read pamphlet of 1917, *Towards Industrial Democracy: A Memorandum on Workers' Control*, Gallacher argued that 'the movement for the overthrow of capitalism by an abolition of the wages system must begin, not at Westminster, not in the trade union executive, nor yet in the trade union branches, but in the workshops. And it should take the form of the assumption by the workers of an ever-increasing share in control'. But whereas Murphy was close to Daniel De Leon's idea that control of industry would enable the workers to lock-out the bosses and run society themselves, Gallacher's idea was that having taken control of industry, workplace committees could 'force up contract prices to a point that would approximate to the full exchange value of the product, and put the profiteer out of business. In short, we shall have taken to our hands a powerful economic lever which, intelligently and resolutely applied, is easily capable of overthrowing the entire structure of capitalism, and substituting for it a real Industrial Democracy'.[25]

Both Murphy and Gallacher remained conspicuously silent on the question of opposition to the war. This was something of which Murphy was clearly aware, writing in his 1941 memoir *New Horizons* that 'none of the strikes which took place during the course of the war were anti-war strikes. ... Had the question of stopping the war been put to any strikers' meeting it would have been overwhelmingly defeated'.[26] However, putting a vote to a mass meeting is a different question from patiently arguing against the war on the shop floor. Moreover, by late 1916 working-class attitudes towards the war were changing – as the government itself acknowledged in private. During the Hargreaves dispute, the district secretary of the ASE told the Ministry of Munitions that many of his members 'were joining the No Conscription Fellowship' and that 'the movement is against conscription of any kind'. The following month an internal

24   Murphy 1917.
25   Gallacher and Paton 1917, pp. 8 and 11.
26   Murphy 1941, p. 41. This is also discussed in Darlington 1998, pp. 42–4.

Cabinet note observed that in Sheffield 'the driving force behind this agitation is not an economic question at all but has its roots as well as its cohesive
force in a widespread antagonism to the Military Service Act'. In October 1917
George Barnes told Lloyd George that although the majority of workers still
supported the war, 'the pacifist element is amongst them and there is a good
deal of war weariness which might easily be turned to disaffection by any great
reverse or untoward circumstance here at home'.[27] And at the start of 1918 the
question of stopping the war was actually put to a meeting of striking members of the Workers' Union in Sheffield who passed a resolution opposing 'a
further comb-out [of factory workers for the army] being applied until the government gives a guarantee of its intention not to continue the war longer than
necessary to secure the policy laid down by our brother democrats in Russia'.[28]

It was this growing demand for peace that presented revolutionary opponents of the war with significant opportunities to win workers to their programme. But *Solidarity*, the SSWCM monthly journal, made no statement in
opposition to the war until February 1918. When it did, it blamed the German
workers for British workers' failure to oppose the war and called for war against
the Germans if they did not support a general strike:

> if we could only be certain that the German workers would follow suit,
> we should have no hesitation in calling for an immediate policy of 'down
> tools, and damn the consequences'. But we are not in touch with our fel-
> low workers in Germany, and do not know what would happen over there
> in the event of a big strike here. It might mean that the German workers
> would be willing to do the bidding of their war lords, and take advant-
> age of the situation by attempting to invade these islands. In which case,
> they would get the surprise of their lives. For, apart from defending these
> shores, the revolutionary element here would take the keenest delight in
> administering such a pasting to the Germans for their perfidy and stupid-
> ity in not taking up the socialist lead, that they would be soon wishing
> they were back home again.[29]

Murphy himself actively opposed making the war part of the SSWCM's platform. At the April 1918 SSWCM conference Murphy, now a member of the SLP,

---

27   See Wrigley 1976, p. 182 for the first two quotations and p. 222 for the third.
28   *Workers' Dreadnought*, 12 Jan 1918.
29   'The Great Revolt', *Solidarity*, vol. 2, no. 3, Feb 1918.

argued against a motion from its National Administrative Council calling for a referendum on the war, arguing that:

> the workers were not ready for a peace movement. When the programme was drafted there was a possible chance that it might succeed, but the great offensive had changed the temper of the people. Events were moving very rapidly, and before long there might be a better chance for an advanced programme. In the meantime, we should discuss workshop organisation.

When WSF supporter William Watson proposed that the SSWCM should call for an immediate armistice on the basis of 'no annexations, no indemnities and self-determination for all nations', he was opposed by SSWCM secretary George Peet who argued 'we should leave questions of peace and war alone and devote our energies to building up a class organisation'. When the report of the conference appeared in *Solidarity*, there was no mention of this debate on the war.[30]

2   Follow Russia! The Leeds Convention

Other tendencies in the labour movement were not so agnostic, as could be seen at Leeds' Coliseum theatre on Sunday 3 June 1917 where 1,150 delegates from across Britain gathered to hail the Russian Revolution, call for peace, and protest against the anti-working-class policies of the government. Organised under the slogan 'Follow Russia!' the convention was called jointly by the BSP and ILP under the auspices of the United Socialist Council, which the two parties created in 1913 and had revived in August 1916. Addressed to trade union branches, trades councils, local Labour Parties, branches of socialist organisations, and women's industrial and political organisations, the convention call said it would 'congratulate and encourage our Russian comrades upon the success they have achieved in overthrowing the reactionary forces of that country' and 'ascertain and pronounce upon the opinions of the working class of this country upon the developments which have taken place, and are taking place,

---

30   A full report on the conference can be found in *Workers' Dreadnought*, 20 April 1918, from where the above quotations are taken. The official report is in *Solidarity*, vol. 2, no. 6, May 1918. Murphy had joined the SLP in August 1917 according to *New Horizons*, p. 59, having been recruited by Arthur MacManus; see his letter to Walter Kendall, 27 November 1960, at PHM CP/IND/MURP/01/09.

in Russia'. At its heart was opposition to the war: 'it is our duty to work for a complete and real international peace based upon working-class solidarity, and therefore calculated to be honourable and enduring'.[31]

When the delegates assembled on the Sunday morning, they listened to a telegram of greetings from the executive of the Petrograd Soviet before Ramsay MacDonald and the BSP's Dora Montefiore moved the first resolution, 'Russia Hail!', welcoming the revolution. The ILP's Philip Snowden and the BSP's Edwin Fairchild then proposed the resolution on peace, supporting the Russian Provisional Government's call for peace 'without annexations or indemnities and based on the right of nations to decide their own affairs'. There was no dissent about support for the Russian Revolution but the peace debate saw pro-war interventions from Edward Tupper of the Seamen's Union and the rising trade union official Ernest Bevin who denounced the ILP as 'fatuous friends'. From the left, William O'Brien, a comrade of James Connolly who had been active in the Dublin Lockout, questioned whether the call for peace extended to freeing the 127 Irish republican prisoners in British jails, pointing out that many of those who supported the Russian Revolution 'did not acclaim the revolution in Ireland, where the leaders were taken out and shot like dogs'.[32]

A third resolution demanded full civil and political liberties for men and women, freedom of the press, an end to labour compulsion, and the release of political prisoners. The fourth and last resolution of the convention was moved by Sheffield ILP MP Will Anderson, and called on delegates 'to establish in every town, urban, and rural district, Councils of Workmen and Soldier's Delegates for initiating and co-ordinating working-class activity ... and to work strenuously for a peace made by the peoples of the various countries, and for the complete political and economic emancipation of international labour', and establish a national Provisional Committee to lead their work. Anderson's oratory in proposing the resolution had rarely flown higher: 'if revolution be that we are not going to put up in the future with what we have put up with in the past, we are not going to have the shams and the poverty of the past, then the sooner we have revolution in this country the better'. Transport workers' union leader Robert Williams went one better with: 'I want to accept the resolution in its very fullest implication. The resolution, if it means anything at all, means that which is contained in the oft-used phrase from Socialist platforms: The dictatorship of the proletariat'.

---

31 *Labour Leader*, 17 May 1917.
32 All quotes in this and the following two paragraphs are from Coates 1974. See also White 1974b.

In response, the syndicalist South Wales miners' leader Noah Ablett asked what practical measures were proposed to organise workers and expressed disappointment that no future plans had been announced. Sylvia Pankhurst attacked the idea that Britain was the home of liberty – 'we have never had real liberty in the country' – and called for the inclusion of working women on the Provisional Committee, while Huddersfield BSP leftist Fred Shaw said that 'The time is ripe for the working classes to take things into their own hands and follow Russia. This war has driven out of the minds of the workers many of the old middle-class ideas about the state. We must go forward and ignore all the coercion that the capitalist state can bring upon us'. After passing this resolution 'with only two or three dissentients', the convention ended in a jubilant mood by setting up 13 district 'workers councils' and sending its greetings to the Petrograd Soviet.

But the enthusiasm of the delegates was not directed towards action. The reality was that the Convention had been carefully controlled by the ILP leadership. All of the resolutions were proposed by senior ILP figures: MacDonald, Snowden, Anderson and Ammon. The thirteen-person Provisional Committee comprised only the original signatories of the call for the Convention, namely nine ILP members, including the MPs MacDonald, Snowden, Anderson and Fred Jowett, plus the BSP's Fineberg, Fairchild, Tom Quelch, and Harry Alexander, Fairchild's co-thinker, all of whom were on the centre or right of the party. Most notably, as Noah Ablett pointed out, no practical political campaigns were organised, and there was no commitment to support current industrial struggles. This contrasted with the earlier rallies in support of the February Revolution that routinely called for the release of political prisoners, most notably of John Maclean. And as Willie Gallacher suggested in his short speech, many at the Convention were content with the achievements of the February Revolution and had no desire to see Russian workers assert their own power. It was only at the end of the conference that militants such as Gallacher and Shaw could speak.[33]

The ILP's intentions for the Convention had been made clear three weeks earlier by Anderson in the House of Commons, when he protested against government suppression of an article about a strike in Woolwich written by an engineering union official. Such censorship, he claimed, played into the hands of 'extremist' militants:

---

33   Arthur MacManus and J.T. Murphy also attended the Convention but did not speak. See
       Murphy 1934, p. 152.

The old policy on the part of the rulers here used to be that when grievances had reached a certain point concessions were made, and very
largely the steam taken out of the movement, so far as the extreme elements were concerned. What you are now doing by coercive laws, by
repressive laws, by the penal side of the Munitions Act, and so on, is to
try to dam up all the current of discontent, but the current will not be
dammed up. I do assure you that you will be astonished and, unless you
are very careful, you will bring the country to the very verge of revolution.[34]

Others soon began to backtrack on the rhetoric of Leeds. 'There is and never
has been any question of advocating or suggesting a physical force revolution',
explained an editorial in *The Herald* about the Convention. Needless to say,
the Convention's promise to establish workers' councils across Britain quickly
evaporated. Only four regional meetings were held, although four others were
stopped by bans or, as happened in London, by a reactionary mob. The National
Council held just a single meeting. For Anderson, MacDonald and their ILP co-
thinkers, the purpose of the Leeds Convention had fulfilled its task: to take the
steam out of the movement.

3   Labourism Responds to the Russian Revolution

The authority that MacDonald, Snowden and the ILP had won in the labour
movement because of their anti-war stance was used to its fullest extent at
Leeds. Yet the ILP's opposition to the war was more ambiguous than it appeared. The Convention call played on fears that the Russians might strike a
deal with Germany if Britain did not support the Provisional Government's
peace proposals: 'if the Russian people receive no sympathetic response to their
call for an international peace from the people of the allied countries, they may
be driven into a separate peace with the Kaiser's reactionary government'.[35]

     In January 1917 the ILP proposed to the Labour Party conference that it
organise an international congress of socialist parties to discuss a peace programme. This was defeated by the Labour leadership's proposal for a meeting
of socialist parties in the Allied countries. However, on 27 March 1917, the Menshevik and Socialist Revolutionary-led Petrograd Soviet issued the statement

---

34   H.C. Deb, 93, 5s, 14 May 1917, c. 1395–6.
35   *Labour Leader*, 17 May 1917.

'To the Peoples of the Entire World', which called for an end to the war and appealed to the workers of Europe to 'speak and act out jointly and resolutely to foster peace'.[36] Five weeks later, on 2 May, it issued 'To Socialists Abroad: For an International Socialist Conference' echoing the ILP's call for a meeting of socialist parties of all nations to agree a programme to end the war. At the same time, it also ordered Russian soldiers not to fraternise with German troops.[37] The call for a conference was inspired by a visit to Petrograd from the pro-war Danish social-democratic leader Frederik Borgbjerg who, along with the Norwegian, Swedish and Dutch parties, called for social democrats of all the belligerent nations to meet to discuss peace terms in Stockholm in mid-May.[38] Denounced by Lenin as 'a colloquy of ministers of imperialist governments' and an 'amnesty for the social-imperialists', the Stockholm initiative gained considerable support among social democrats and pacifists who wanted to reconstruct the pre-war Second International.[39]

In Britain, the February Revolution did nothing to shake the Labour Party leadership's support for the war. However, the worsening situation in Russia and at home now required a different approach. Arthur Henderson, as he did with all major issues in the labour movement, discussed the Labour Party's attitude to the events in Russia in Lloyd George's War Cabinet in late March. The Prime Minister agreed that Labour should seek to persuade the Russian social democrats to stay in the war. Consequently, the Labour parliamentary group chose the pro-war MPs Will Thorne and James O'Grady, plus Fabian Society secretary William Sanders, to travel to Russia with an equally pro-war delegation of French socialist deputies (which included Marcel Cachin, a future leader of the French Communist Party) and meet the leaders of the Petrograd Soviet.[40] The visit was, in the words of the British Consul-General in Moscow Robert Bruce Lockhart, 'a farce', in which Thorne and O'Grady were regarded by even moderate Mensheviks as lackeys of Lloyd George.[41] However, the growing popularity of the call for the Stockholm conference and a fear that the Germans would use it to gain a diplomatic advantage persuaded Lloyd George that Henderson

---

36 An English translation is in Allen 2018, p. 59.
37 'Military Strength Serves the Cause of Peace' reprinted in Allen 2018, pp. 62–5.
38 The somewhat tortuous history of the failed Stockholm congress can be found in Meynell 1960 and Kirby 1982.
39 Lenin, *CW* vol. 25 – the first quote is from the article 'The Stockholm Conference', p. 269, and the second from 'Kamenev's Speech in the C.E.C.', p. 241. Kamenev wanted to participate in the conference. See also Gankin and Fisher 1940, pp. 583–609.
40 See Wrigley 1976, pp. 206–7.
41 Bruce Lockhart 1932, pp. 120–1.

himself should visit Russia. The cabinet also agreed to issue the ILP's Ramsay MacDonald and Fred Jowett passports to visit Russia, although their trip was scuppered when the National Sailors' and Firemen's Union, led by the pro-war Havelock Wilson, refused to allow them passage.[42]

When Henderson arrived back in England on 24 July he was a chastened man. Just as Lord Liverpool's witnessing of the fall of the Bastille in 1789 had imbued him with a visceral fear of popular revolt that defined his reactionary premiership, Henderson's experience in revolutionary Russia would define the rest of his political career. Shocked at the collapse of the Russian state, he was shaken to the core by the inexorable rise of 'the extremists' as he labelled the Bolsheviks. The choice facing Russia, he told Lloyd George, was between 'direct action on [sic] Western proletariate [sic] to provoke uprising against capitalism and war together. The other is for constitutional action by first converting labour and [social]ist parties and then trusting the pressure they will exercise on the Government'.[43] The Allies' only hope of keeping Russia in the war and averting a second revolution was to bolster the authority of the moderate socialists in the government, which meant supporting the Stockholm conference. Henderson therefore now threw his weight behind it and committed Labour to attending.[44] This was not what Lloyd George wanted and, using the excuse of Henderson's attendance at a meeting in Paris to organise the Stockholm conference, forced him to resign from the cabinet on 11 August.[45] The Stockholm conference never took place, but the clash with Lloyd George rebuilt Henderson's credibility with a labour movement that was questioning the war.

Henderson's visit to Russia had given him a glimpse of a future which he was determined not to let happen in Britain. This desire to stop revolutionary developments defined his plans to modernise the Labour Party for the postwar age. The coming of peace, he argued, would see the world enter 'an era of revolutionary change to which there is no parallel in history'.[46] But this would bring immense dangers and 'the prospect of social convulsions on this scale is enough to appal the stoutest heart'. He continued:

> Never before have we had such vast numbers of the population skilled in the use of arms, disciplined, inured to danger, accustomed to act together

---

42 Wrigley 1976, p. 208, notes the absence of animosity to MacDonald in the privacy of Cabinet discussions despite its public denunciation of him.

43 Henderson to Lloyd George, 1 July 1917, quoted in Winter 1972, p. 766.

44 For Labour's role in the conference, see Wade 1967.

45 Graubard 1956, p. 30.

46 Henderson 1918, p. 1.

under orders. When the war ends this country and every other will be flooded with hardy veterans of the great campaigns. Among them will be thousands of men who have exercised authority over their fellows in actual warfare, and who will be capable of assuming leadership again if insurrectionary movements come into existence. We may be warned by a perception of these facts that if barricades are indeed likely to be erected in our streets they will be manned by men who have learned how to fight and not by ill-disciplined mobs unversed in the use of modern weapons, likely to be easily overcome by trained troops. Revolution, if revolution is indeed to be forced upon democracy, will be veritable civil war.[47]

The Labour Party therefore had to be a bulwark against revolution in Britain, which meant 'its form of organisation must be completely changed if it is to be enabled to meet the requirements of the new situation'. These requirements were 'ordered social change by constitutional methods', because 'the natural bias of organised Labour lies in the direction of smooth, orderly progress'.[48]

Henderson was not the only Labour Party leader with this perspective. Earlier in 1917 Ramsay MacDonald warned the Leicester May Day rally that 'the Lenin party ... was composed of thoughtless anarchists, who had no definite policy, whose minds were filled with violence and hatred'.[49] Henderson, MacDonald and Sydney Webb led the development of a new party constitution and programme for peacetime. The new programme was drafted with one eye on the general election that would follow the war and the other firmly on the events unfolding in Russia. The famous 'clause four' of the party's new constitution written by Sydney Webb read:

> to secure for the workers by hand or by brain the full fruits of their industry and the most equitable distribution thereof that may be possible upon the basis of the common ownership of the means of production, and the best obtainable system of popular administration and control of each industry and service

and was designed to inoculate the party against the revolutionary spirit of Russia which he and his co-thinkers feared would soon possess the British working class.

---

47   Henderson 1918, p. 59.
48   Henderson 1918 p. 59.
49   *Leicester Daily Post*, 7 May 1917.

Henderson, MacDonald and Webb's reform plans were not just confined to Labour's written programme. The party was to be restructured as a national organisation based on individual membership, replacing its ad-hoc local Labour Representation Committees with local branches based on parliamentary constituencies. Moreover, they also sought to alter the social composition of the party by attracting members of the middle classes, especially from the Liberal Party. The Liberal Party had haemorrhaged 'progressive' members during the course of the war, many of whom joined the Union Of Democratic Control, formed in September 1914 by dissident Liberals and the MacDonald wing of the ILP to campaign for a negotiated end to the war.[50] Clause Four had been designed to appeal to these people – hence its reference to 'workers by brain' – and its woolly sentiments were little different from those of liberals who agonised over 'the social question' in the years before the war. In the words of Sydney Webb, Clause Four represented 'a socialism which is no more specific than a definite repudiation of the individualism that characterises all the political parties of the last generation'.[51] Labour's regroupment with 'the liberal wing of the Liberal Party' would be extremely successful, bringing into its ranks significant figures such as Arthur Ponsonby, Charles Trevelyan, William Wedgwood Benn (father of Tony Benn), and Lloyd George's former lieutenant at the Ministry of Munitions, Christopher Addison.

On 10 October 1917, the new draft constitution of the Labour Party was circulated to the party's national executive committee. It endorsed Webb's Clause Four and asked Henderson, MacDonald and Webb to draw up a programme for post-war reconstruction, which Webb would shortly publish as *Labour and the New Social Order*. In February 1918 the new constitution was ratified by a special party conference.[52] The Labour Party had been reborn, as much a product of the Russian Revolution as the Communist Party of Great Britain.

4   Bolshevism and the British Left

While the Labour Party re-defined itself through its opposition to workers' revolution in Russia, the organisations to its left wholeheartedly identified with that revolution. As Harry Pollitt later recalled:

The thing that mattered was that lads like me had whacked the bosses
and the landlords, had taken their factories, their lands and their banks
.... All I was concerned about was that power was in the hands of lads like
me and whatever conception of politics had made that possible was the
correct one for me.[53]

As with opposition to the war, support for the revolution encompassed every
shade of opinion from reform to revolution. The BSP's coverage of the revolution tended to follow that of the moderate Mensheviks in the Russian socialist
movement. *The Call*'s first response to the momentous events was a front page
declaring 'Long Live the Revolution!' and it enthusiastically took part in organising rallies across the county in support of the revolution.[54] Yet this and its
subsequent statements said little about the struggle against capitalism and generally focused on praising the Provisional Government's peace declarations.
The BSP was a strong supporter of the government, approvingly quoting Alexander Kerensky and Nikolai Chkheidze, the Menshevik president of the Petrograd Soviet (it even sold portraits of Chkheidze) and defending their decision
to continue the war. '[Russia] cannot withdraw from the war at present without
assisting the greed and the lusts of Austro-German imperialism which, on
being freed from all fear in the East, would at once concentrate its forces in the
West and Near East, and probably succeed in defeating all its rivals and in establishing its own hegemony in the world', *The Call* told its readers in June 1917.[55]

This position was not something that could be ascribed to lack of knowledge
about the situation in Russia. Theodore Rothstein, perhaps the best-informed
person in Britain due to his personal contacts and work as a government translator of the Russian press, analysed the course of the revolution in August 1917
under the pen name John Bryan. As with much of Rothstein's literary output,
the article was laced with several degrees of ambiguity. The entry of the Menshevik leaders Tsereteli and Skobelev into the Provisional Government in early
May 1917 was, he argued, 'a great step which marked the official triumph of
the revolutionary proletariat' but also something that 'weakened its opposition
to the bourgeoisie'. He acknowledged 'the violent opposition of the Leninites'
to the Mensheviks joining the government and suggested that if it 'fail[ed] to
achieve real success' the 'Jacobins' could come to power 'who will then apply

---

53   Pollitt 1947, pp. 41–2.
54   *The Call*, 22 March 1917.
55   'Russia's Call to Democracy', *The Call*, 20 June 1917. Chkheidze's portrait was advertised in
      the 26 July issue.

a drastic solution to all the problems of the day'.[56] However, in an editorial in late July *The Call* said it disapproved of Mensheviks joining the government and accused them of 'carrying out the policy of their enemies in the guise of revolutionary action'.[57]

Rothstein's comrade Zelda Kahan explicitly opposed the Bolsheviks in May in an article on the impact of the revolution on the Second International. Criticising Lenin personally – probably the first time his name was mentioned in *The Call* in 1917 – Kahan accused him of wanting a new international that consisted only of those 'who are purely internationalists, and in no way support their governments'. In contrast, she wanted to bring together all wings of the Second International, even including the German SPD's pro-war leader Philipp Scheidemann:

> There is scarcely a country where the national sections of the International or parts of it have not sinned against the principles of the International as much as in any other. We are all in glass houses and none can afford to throw stones. If only those who adhere to Zimmerwald and Kienthal meet, they may pass excellent resolutions but unfortunately there does not seem much probability of the exerting any comparatively effective influence in promoting peace.[58]

It should not be surprising that the BSP's first considered response to the October Revolution echoed that of the Mensheviks. Its initial article had merely declared it to be 'The Second Russian Revolution' that 'brings the immediate objects of the revolution back to what it was at the commencement'. The following week it supported the Menshevik-dominated railway workers' union, Vikzhel, which had organised a strike against the new Bolshevik/Left Social Revolutionary government in favour of a coalition government of all socialist parties. 'The proposals of the railway union provide the most hopeful means of dealing with the situation', explained *The Call*. 'Control in the hands of a socialist government would serve the best interests of Russia and the Russian people', it explained, while also admitting that 'no agreement could be reached on the inclusion of the Bolsheviks in the proposed government', among the oppon-

---

56   John Bryan, 'The Struggle of the Classes in Russia' in *The Plebs Magazine*, August 1917, v. 9, no. 7, pp. 145–7. The article is debated in Challinor 1977, p. 226, and in John Saville's introduction to Rothstein 1983, pp. xiii–xiv.

57   *The Call*, 27 July 1917.

58   *The Call*, 31 May 1917.

ents of the new government.[59] It was only the following week, when it became clear that the Bolsheviks had consolidated their position, that *The Call* came out unequivocally in support of them.

In contrast, the Socialist Labour Party sided with the Bolsheviks from the very start of the revolution. The SLP published a special supplement in the first issue of *The Socialist* after the February Revolution, characterising it as a 'middle-class revolution' and siding with 'the Bolshevik section [which] endorses the irreconcilable Marxian position'. Thanks to the translations of Alexander Sirnis, who worked with the SLP despite being a member of the BSP until September 1917, the SLP was also able to publish a number of works of Lenin, including his *Opportunism and the Collapse of the Second International* in June 1917.[60] *The Socialist* greeted the October Revolution with the headline 'Hail! Revolutionary, Socialist Russia'. Despite this unequivocal support, the SLP did not fully understand the politics of the Bolshevik Party, sometimes presenting them in terms more appropriate to the Menshevik position: 'it does not aim at the immediate establishment of Socialism, which at present is impossible in such an economically backward country as Russia; but it sought to use its power to strike a blow for international peace and to win the maximum concessions possible for the Russian workers', wrote *The Socialist* in October 1917.[61]

Yet the SLP's solipsistic parochialism was never far from the surface. Its supplement on the revolution eccentrically told readers that 'the SLP is closely watching events in Russia to learn where its policy is weak or where its tactics are wrong. But so far as the press is concerned, we can proudly claim that [the importance of] party control of a printing press has emphatically been demonstrated by the events in Russia'.[62] For the casual reader it may have seemed that the Russian proletariat had overthrown capitalist state power merely to prove that the SLP had been right all along: a March 1918 article was titled 'Triumph of the SLP Tactics in Russia' and proclaimed that 'for years the SLP has been sneered at and jeered at, but now Russia, in the transition towards the Socialist Republic, shows the SLP is right'.[63]

Sylvia Pankhurst's Workers' Socialist Federation also leapt to support the February Revolution, pointing out in an editorial titled 'Whose Russian Revolution?' that 'at present there are virtually two governments in Russia – the Provi-

---

59   *The Call*, 22 Nov 1917. For an outline of the Vikzhel position see Rabinowitch 2007, pp. 26–31.
60   Sirnis's resignation letter from the BSP appeared in *The Socialist*, Nov 1917.
61   *The Socialist*, Oct 1917.
62   *The Socialist*, April 1917.
63   *The Socialist*, March 1918.

sional Government appointed by the Duma and the Council of Labour Deputies, which is responsible to the elected representatives of the workers and the
soldiers'. Although it favoured a socialist outcome for the revolution, the WSF
had little idea how that could be accomplished, but by June it had come down
on the side of Lenin: 'The Maximalists [as the Bolsheviks were often called in
the British press] and Leninites, on the other hand, desire to cut adrift from
the capitalist parties altogether, and to establish a Socialist system of organisation and industry in Russia, before Russian capitalism, which is as yet in its
infancy, gains power and becomes more difficult than at present to overthrow.
We deeply sympathise with this view'.[64]

As the revolution progressed, the WSF increasingly identified with the Bolsheviks and printed numerous articles by and about Lenin. By the end of
September *Workers' Dreadnought* reported that it was 'a cause for great satisfaction' that the Bolsheviks had won a majority in the Petrograd Soviet; 'the
Maximalists are the international socialists who recognise that this is a capitalist war and demand an immediate peace, and who desire to establish in Russia
not a semi-democratic government and the capitalist system such as we have
here in England but a socialist state', it explained.[65] Even so, the contradictions
of the WSF's politics were demonstrated shortly after when it organised a peace
picket at Westminster Abbey with the slogans 'Support the Pope's Move for
Peace' and 'Negotiate for Peace on Russian Terms, No Annexations, No Indemnities'.[66] Nevertheless, the WSF nailed its colours firmly to the mast of the October Revolution. It greeted 'the Lenin Revolution' with 'our eager hopes are for
the speedy success of the Bolsheviks of Russia: may they open the door which
leads to freedom for the people of all lands'.[67] Nor did it have doubts about supporting the Bolsheviks' dispersal of the Constituent Assembly in January 1918,
arguing that it consisted of 'a large proportion of capitalist wolves clothed in
the bright promises of the socialist lamb', while noting that 'some complain
that the Soviets only represent the working classes; if they are to rule, the opinions of other classes will be ignored. ... To those who object, we need ask but
one question: "Are you a socialist?"'[68]

With those words, Pankhurst had highlighted the division between revolutionaries and reformists that would define the post-war politics of the British
labour movement.

---

64   *Woman's Dreadnought*, 30 June 1917.
65   *Workers' Dreadnought*, 29 September 1917.
66   *Workers' Dreadnought*, 13 October 1917.
67   *Workers' Dreadnought*, 17 November 1917.
68   *Workers' Dreadnought*, 26 January 1918.

1919: The Question of Power

As the final details of the German surrender were being negotiated on the evening of 10 November 1918, Britain's war cabinet met in Downing Street. Chaired
by Lloyd George, the meeting began by reviewing two telegrams from French
prime minister Georges Clemenceau. A German request for a further twenty-
four hours' consultations had been refused and Clemenceau was confident
the Allies' surrender terms would shortly be accepted. As the meeting pro-
ceeded, First Lord of the Admiralty Eric Geddes interrupted the discussions
to announce that a telegram had just been received saying that the German
government had resigned. The end was at hand.

But it wasn't.

Lloyd George then told the meeting that he had been reading telegrams
about the situation in Berlin and 'it would seem that events were taking a similar course in Germany to that which had taken place in Russia'. In response,
Henry Wilson, the Chief of the British Imperial General Staff, suggested the
British Army should advance no further than the Rhine, so as not to get 'involved in Bolshevik outbreaks in Germany'. Winston Churchill, who was now
Minister of Munitions, suggested that Britain 'might have to build up the German Army, as it was important to get Germany on her legs again for fear of the
spread of Bolshevism'. The Prime Minister urged caution, describing Germany
as a 'cholera area' infected with the 'virus' of Bolshevism and that 'it would be
most undesirable to march British miners to Westphalia if Westphalia was controlled by a Bolshevist organisation'.[1] The fear of 'Bolshevist infection' was now
at the forefront of government thinking.

The collapse of the German war effort was the direct result of that revolutionary infection. In March 1918 its High Command had launched a spring
offensive but its failure allowed the Allies, now reinforced by American forces,
to seize the initiative. As autumn came the German army and its allies were
in retreat on all fronts. A mutiny among troops of its Bulgarian ally in September forced that country out of the war, and the Hapsburg dynasty was finally
despatched to oblivion when workers in Budapest and Vienna overthrew the
imperial governments of Hungary and Austria. On 3 November sailors at the

---

1 All quotes are from the minutes of War Cabinet meeting 500A, 10 November 1918, at TNA
CAB/23/14/45.

Kiel naval base in northern Germany threw aside their officers and established a workers' and sailors' council. Five days later, Berlin was informed that workers' councils had taken control of Cologne, Frankfurt-am-Main, Dusseldorf, Halle, Leipzig, Magdeburg, Stuttgart and many other smaller towns. 'All Red', noted the War Ministry's report laconically.[2] Workers in Bavaria deposed the state government and proclaimed a new 'Bavarian Peoples' State'. The following day, Berlin itself was brought to a halt by a general strike. The authority of the government and the Hohenzollern monarchy had turned to dust under the blows of working-class insurrection. The Kaiser abdicated, the cabinet resigned, and a Council of Peoples' Deputies took charge. Power was now in the streets – all that was needed was a force to wield it.

In Britain, the cabinet's fear of the Bolshevik contagion was not simply scaremongering. During the war, strikes were more frequent in Britain than in Germany. In 1916, over twice as many British workers took part in twice as many strikes than their German counterparts, while in 1917 there were 730 British disputes involving 872,000 strikers compared to 562 strikes in Germany involving 651,000 workers.[3] Although there were no military mutinies to compare with those in Germany or in France, the mutiny by British and Empire troops at Étaples in Northern France that September had shaken the usually implacable self-confidence of the High Command.[4] Autumn 1917 also saw strikes by Chinese and Egyptian workers in British army labour battalions at Boulogne and Fontinettes, on the outskirts of Calais. These were bloodily suppressed, with 36 men shot dead and dozens more wounded.[5]

In 1918 more strikes took place in Britain and more workers struck than in any other year since records began in 1891, with the exception of 1913. Trade union membership leapt by almost two-thirds since 1914 to a total of 6.5 million members.[6] Calls to end the war became increasingly popular, and were given further impetus when the Bolsheviks issued their 'Decree on Peace' at the end of October 1917 and began publishing the secret diplomatic treaties of the Allies. In January 1918 the Labour Party conference was addressed by Maxim Litvinov, now the official representative of the Bolshevik government

---

2 Watt 1973, pp. 208–9.
3 For German figures, see Carsten 1982, p. 124. British statistics can be found at https://www.ons .gov.uk/employmentandlabourmarket/peopleinwork/workplacedisputesandworkingconditi ons/datasets/labourdisputeslabourdisputesannualestimates
4 Despite press censorship, the Étaples mutiny was mentioned in the *Workers' Dreadnought*, 3 Nov 1917.
5 Gill and Dallas 1975. See also, among many others, Rothstein 1985; Dallas and Gill 1985; Putkowski 1998; Lamb undated.
6 Wrigley 1990, p. 131.

itself. 'For the first time', he told the delegates, 'the working class has attained supreme power in one of the largest states in the world. ... They had revolted not against the unsuccessful conduct of the war, but against the war itself'.[7]

Three days after the end the war, Lloyd George called a general election for 14 December 1918. His coalition of the Conservative Party and personal retinue of Liberals was returned with an overwhelming majority. But, although it gained only fifteen new MPs, the Labour Party's share of the vote shot up to over 20 per cent, making it the second most popular party. In Ireland, Sinn Fein won 73 seats, leading it to establish the Dáil Éireann and declare Irish Independence on 21 January 1919. The 'great industrial trouble' and 'civil strife in Ireland' that Lloyd George forecast in July 1914 was about to re-emerge. January 1919 would be the September 1914 that never was.

1   'Are You Ready to Take Power?'

As soon as the war ended, the suppressed social tensions of war-time exploded. In December 1918, two battalions of black troops in the British West Indies Regiment stationed in Taranto in Italy, revolted against their conditions and racist treatment by officers. On 3 January 1919 two thousand soldiers at the military base in Folkestone in Kent refused to board ships taking them back to France and demanded to return home. The following day troops at Dover demonstrated in support of the mutineers, and 10,000 men marched through Folkestone calling for immediate demobilisation. Two days later, 1,500 Army Service Corps (ASC) troops at Osterley Park in West London commandeered the base's lorries and drove in them to Whitehall to press their call to return to civvy street. Within a few days, strikes and demonstrations had broken out at military bases across southern England. 'Everywhere the feeling is the same', reported the *Daily Herald*, 'the war is over, we won't have to fight in Russia, and we mean to go home'.[8]

As these cracks appeared in the armed forces, intense class conflict erupted in Belfast and Glasgow. Calls had been growing among engineers throughout 1918 to reduce the regular 54-hour working week to 40 hours. To avoid disruption to the munitions industry, the government proposed to introduce a 47-hour week at the start of 1919. This satisfied no-one, and in Belfast more than 90 per cent of 22,000 engineers voted to strike for a 44-hour week. On

---

7   *Labour Leader*, 10 January 1918.
8   *Daily Herald*, 11 Jan 1919. For details of the mutinies, see Butler 2019; Wintringham 1936; Dallas and Gill 2002.

25 January the strike began and over the next few days industrial Belfast gradually fell silent. A strike committee was elected and began to publish its own daily *Workers' Bulletin*, and by the first week of February the shipyards, textiles factories, gas and electricity were shut down. But the dispute remained under the control of men who did not want to extend the strike to challenge the employers. They did not ask the local transport workers and dockers to strike with them, and when George Cuming, the managing director of the Harland and Wolff shipyard died unexpectedly on 1 February, the strike committee urged strikers to join his funeral cortege. Increasingly isolated by the union leaders' refusal to give official support to the strike, denounced by the Labour Party leader William Adamson, and fatally weakened by many strike leaders being members of the sectarian Orange Order, the militancy of the strikers was finally beaten down when British troops were mobilised to re-open the electric power stations and gas works. Shop stewards were threatened with arrest under the Defence of the Realm Act, and eventually the strikers voted to accept the 47-hour week and return to work. The defeat ruptured the working-class unity forged by the strike and opened the door for the purge of thousands of Catholics and leftists from Belfast's shipyards in July 1920, which left 22 workers dead and helped consolidate Britain's partition of Ireland.[9]

In Glasgow, the strike for a 40-hour week began on 27 January. Within three days it was 40,000 strong and spreading to the Scottish coalfields, where 36,000 miners walked out in support of the strikers. The militancy of the Clydeside working class during the war meant the government was acutely aware that Glasgow could quickly become a beacon for working-class revolt across Britain. On 30 January Chancellor of the Exchequer Bonar Law told Lloyd George that 'everything depends on beating the strike in the Glasgow area as, if the strikers are successful there, the disorder will spread over the country'.[10] The Glasgow strike committee, chaired by ILPer Manny Shinwell, the local leader of the Seaman's Union, met with Glasgow's Lord Provost, the equivalent of the city mayor, and asked him to persuade the government to agree to a 40-hour week. Bonar Law interpreted this as a sign of weakness, but the War Cabinet was also concerned about the reliability of using troops to suppress the strike. Robert Munro, the Scottish Secretary, felt that the police would be 'more reliable, and suitable than soldiers'.[11] Even so, the situation was deemed so dire the Army made 12,000 troops available if the situation required them.

---

9   Munck 1985; O'Connor 1992, pp. 104–5.
10   Wrigley 1990, pp. 108–10.
11   Wrigley 1990, p. 109.

On a chilly Friday morning on 31 January over 20,000 demonstrators gathered in Glasgow's George Square in support of the strike committee delegation that was to meet the Lord Provost in the City Chambers to hear him report about his discussions with the government. Shortly after noon, in what seemed to be a pre-planned move, while the delegation was kept waiting inside the City Chambers, the Riot Act was read to the crowd outside. The demonstrators had twice ignored orders to leave and the Riot Act gave the police the right to use force to disperse them. The police then baton-charged the crowd, injuring 53 of them. Shinwell and his fellow strike committee leader David Kirkwood rushed outside to protest the violence, whereupon Kirkwood was beaten unconscious by police truncheons. Willie Gallacher was also attacked by the police and taken into the City Chambers for first aid. As demonstrators forced the police back, Gallacher was asked by the authorities to appeal to the crowd for peace. This he did, asking them to obey police instructions and march away from George Square to Glasgow Green.[12] Nevertheless, the police continued their attack, and the Glasgow ILP's *Forward* described how they 'made a mad rush with drawn batons on the defenceless crowd. The infuriated men in uniform struck whenever they saw a head'.[13]

Just as at his trial in 1916, Gallacher had buckled under pressure and his weakness only emboldened the local authorities. In later life, he claimed he should have told the crowd to march to the army barracks at nearby Maryhill to try to win the soldiers over to their side, but this was the braggadocio of hindsight. Shinwell and other strike committee members were arrested and Glasgow erupted in running violence as police continued to attack demonstrators in a day that became known as 'Bloody Friday'. Order was restored, wrote the *Daily News'* reporter in Glasgow, 'by a display of overwhelming military force. Some thousands of Scottish and English troops were brought into the city during Friday night ... The City Chambers, railway stations, electric power stations, gasworks, bridges and many other places are guarded by soldiers with field equipment and wearing steel helmets. Machine guns, coils of barbed wire, and other materiel are located at convenient points. ... I have never seen such extensive preparations for repression'.[14] Under mortal threat, refused solidarity action by trade union officials, and lacking any leadership, the strikers returned to work a few days later. Ominously, Bonar Law told Lloyd George he thought the Lord Provost had been 'timid'.[15]

---

12   For his personal account of Bloody Friday, see Gallacher 1936, pp. 227–35.
13   *Forward*, 8 Feb 1919. See also MacShane 1978, pp. 106–7.
14   *Daily News*, 3 Feb 1919.
15   Wrigley 1990, p. 111.

Unlike the Belfast strike, the leadership of the Glasgow forty hours' movement was avowedly left wing, yet the end result was also acceptance of the same 47-hour week as Belfast. But the SLP's Arthur MacManus viewed the strike as a victory: 'all the old bitter enemies of the past forgetting their differences of craft, creed, sex, etc., and finding a common fighting front in the realisation that they are workers first and graded labour afterwards – yes! That is Victory'.[16] The only lesson he drew was to 'solidify the organisation in the workshop. Every shop, yard and factory must have its shop organisation linking all workers together'. Although the SLP sent speakers out to other engineering centres to try to spread the strike, its strategy was indistinguishable from that of the Strike Committee, which was dominated by Labour Party figures such as Shinwell, Kirkwood and the MP Neil Maclean. The strike committee's *Bulletin* argued that 'there is no need for violence to combat violence if all withdraw their labour and paralyse industry. This will have the effect of closing the source of profit to the profiteers, and when that is effected, they will be compelled to concede our demands'.[17] But this overlooked the 'profiteers' having the machinery of the state at their disposal which could impose their will by force.

Despite passing a resolution supporting industrial unionism at its April 1918 conference, the BSP was instinctively uncomfortable with the events on the Clyde. *The Call* explained that it would have preferred 'a movement on a universal scale' to campaign for a shorter working week, rather than 'local sporadic efforts'. Moreover, it thought that the workers had made a mistake merely going on strike: 'it would have been much better to have captured the civil government of Glasgow, for instance, as the control of the police would then have been in the workers' hands, and they would not have been ordered out to baton the workers on strike'. By 'capture' it meant gain a majority on the city council. Even better, *The Call* continued, would have been for 'the workers to have captured parliament, as the latter have control of the military'.[18] The BSP's desire to funnel industrial militancy into parliamentary channels was no different from the position of the leadership of the Labour Party.

Despite victories in Glasgow and Belfast, the government still faced spiralling discontent. As army discipline continued to splinter in January, the war cabinet agreed to speed up demobilisation. Announced at the height of the Glasgow strike, it came too late to prevent Army Service and Ordnance Corps troops at Calais going on strike in protest against working conditions. As at

---

16   'The Strike: A Retrospect', *The Worker*, 1 March 1919.
17   *Clyde Strikers' Bulletin*, reprinted in *Workers' Dreadnought*, 8 Feb 1919. For the SLP and the Forty Hours Strike, see Challinor 1977, pp. 208–10.
18   *The Call*, 13 Feb 1919.

Folkestone, troops elected their own soldiers' committee and refused orders from officers and NCOs. They also contacted French railway workers and were demanding the right to send delegates to the 'Hands Off Russia' conference at the Royal Albert Hall on 8 February. As Calais was one of the main nodal points for troop movements from Britain to Europe, the mutiny could reach tens of thousands of military personnel who passed through it. None other than Field Marshall Douglas Haig himself ordered the camp commander to use any means necessary to stop the spread of the revolt. Early on 30 January the camp was surrounded by three brigades with machine-gunners placed around the perimeter and in the camp offices. The mutineers were ordered to end their strike or face the consequences. Despite a brave appeal to continue by the soldiers' committee, the overwhelming show of force succeeded and the strike collapsed.

Nevertheless, these mutinies punctured the idea of immutable military discipline, and their spirit soon appeared among British soldiers in Soviet Russia. Direct British intervention against the revolution began on 2 August 1918 when troops established a regional puppet government at Archangel. However, in February 1919 soldiers of the 6th British Yorkshire Regiment based in Archangel refused their officers' orders. Their two spokesmen were sentenced to death, later commuted to life imprisonment. A further ninety Royal Marines also refused to fight. In June, men of the Hampshire Regiment refused to engage with Red Army troops.[19] In India that same month, soldiers of the Royal Connaught Rangers in Punjab mutinied in protest at the atrocities committed by the Black and Tans in Ireland, a rebellion hailed by John Maclean's *Vanguard* as 'the greatest deed in British history'. Sixty-nine troops were court-martialled and one of the leaders, James Daly, was shot by a firing squad. At the same time in Britain, soldiers in Dover once again refused to embark for France, while 1,800 men went on strike at the Eastern Command Labour Centre in Sutton.[20]

It was not merely discipline that was being undermined, so too was patriotism. In July 1919 official celebrations to mark the signing of the Versailles Treaty took place across Britain. In many areas they were met by demonstrations of demobilised soldiers, often unemployed and angry at their treatment by the government. Luton Town Hall was ransacked and burned down in protest at the local council ban on a Discharged Soldiers' and Sailors' Federation

19   Ullman 1968, pp. 201–3.
20   Ullman 1961, pp. 235–8; Lockley 2003; Butler 2018, p. 24; *Vanguard*, Aug 1920; Pollock 1969; Wrigley 1990, p. 47.

memorial service that was organised in opposition to the official parade.[21] Similar disturbances also took place in Bilston, Coventry, Fareham and Swindon, while demonstrations against the celebrations were held in Barrow, Glasgow and Manchester. The erosion of discipline and patriotic morale in the armed forces was not simply a military issue, but had a direct bearing on the industrial situation. When the war cabinet discussed using troops against strikers at the end of January, its concerns were highlighted by General Wyndham Childs' acid comment that in the past 'we had a disciplined and ignorant army, whereas now we had an army educated and ill disciplined'.[22] On 4 February the war cabinet set up an Industrial Unrest Committee to co-ordinate action against a strike on the London Underground and the anticipated inevitable tidal wave of strikes, particularly the imminent threat of a national miners' strike.

Industrial relations in the mines had been in a state of mutually suspicious suspended animation since the national coal strike of 1912. Both sides knew the 1915 settlement that had been forced on Lloyd George by the South Wales miners' strike was only a temporary truce. Thus the start of 1919 was gripped by a wave of local strikes by miners who decided not to wait for the national leadership and took action themselves. On 14 January a special conference of the Miners' Federation of Great Britain (MFGB) reiterated its demands for nationalisation of the mines, a six-hour day and a 30 per cent pay rise, only to be fobbed off by the government with an offer of a shilling per day increase and an inquiry into the industry. This was rejected by another MFGB conference the following month, which decided to ballot the membership on strike action.

There was no doubt how the miners would vote. The only question was the size of the majority. When the result was announced on 25 February over 85 per cent of the 720,246 miners voting wanted strike action. But between the ballot and the announcement of its result, Lloyd George had returned from negotiating the Versailles Treaty and taken charge of the negotiations with the MFGB. This was, he told his ministers, a matter of power that had to be fought to the end, as the cabinet minutes recorded:

> he had given a good deal of consideration to the possibility of the miners holding up the life of the community, and if they use starvation as a weapon they must not complain if society made use of the same weapon.

21   Luton coverage in *Daily Herald*, 31 July 1919. The other disturbances as recorded in *Report on Revolutionary Organisations in the UK*, 24 July 1919 (TNA CAB/24/84/90).

22   Wrigley 1990 p. 109.

We could control the bread and foreign supplies and we had sufficient troops to guard the main centres ...[23]

On 20 February the MFGB leaders were summoned to a meeting in Downing Street. Lloyd George asked them to postpone the strike, due to begin on 15 March, and take part in a committee of inquiry instead. The MFGB refused. It was at this point that Lloyd George made the most famous challenge in the history of the British labour movement, as recounted by miners' leader Robert Smillie to Aneurin Bevan:

I feel bound to tell you that in our opinion we are at your mercy ... if you carry out your threat and strike you will defeat us ... But if you do so, have you weighed the consequences? The strike will be in defiance of the Government of the country, and by its very success will precipitate a constitutional crisis of the first importance, for if a force arises in a state which is stronger than the state itself, then it must be ready to take on the functions of the state, or withdraw and accept the authority of the state.[24]

With a customary theatrical flourish, he ended by asking 'Gentlemen, ... are you ready?' 'From that moment on', Smillie continued, 'we were beaten and we knew we were'.

The reality was somewhat less dramatic but no less portentous. According to the verbatim transcript of the meeting published the following day, Lloyd George warned the miners that:

if there is a conflict, it will not be between mine-owners and miners, it will be between one industry and the whole of the state. I cannot conceive of anything graver than that. The state could not surrender if it began, without abdicating its functions. It is not a question of this government or that government, but of government – every government. ... We have thought out what it means. I am perfectly certain each and all of you have done so.[25]

The MFGB representatives replied in the affirmative, and Lloyd George went on to make a not-so-veiled threat of starvation: 'The government is directly

---

23   10 Feb 1919, quoted in Wrigley 1990 p. 147.
24   Bevan 1952, pp. 20–1.
25   *The Times*, 22 Feb 1919. Smillie makes no mention of the incident in his autobiography; Smillie 1924.

responsible for the feeding of the community. All of the food in the country is practically under government control. We command all the food supplies, and we should have to distribute it according to the best of our ability'. If conflict did break out, 'it would be impossible ... for any government to give in without surrendering the functions of all government'. Far from saying that the government was powerless, as Smillie told Bevan, Lloyd George was threatening the miners with civil war. Both he and the MFGB understood he was not bluffing.

Face-to-face with a struggle for power, the MFGB leadership baulked and accepted a role on the Royal Commission on the Coal Industry to be chaired by Sir Herbert Sankey, which Lloyd George had created to drag out negotiations.[26] This provided Smillie with an excuse to postpone industrial action and channel the combativity of the miners into the Sankey Commission hearings. Significant numbers of miners opposed this course and supporters of the *Workers' Dreadnought* in the South Wales Miners' Federation argued against the Sankey Commission at a special delegate conference at the end of March.[27] But the momentum generated by the February ballot victory had been stalled by withdrawal of the strike threat. On 19 April a ballot overwhelmingly voted for the MFGB leaders' recommendation to accept the government's offer of a two shillings a day pay rise, an hour off the day, and another report in May on the question of nationalisation of the mines. *The Call* greeted Sankey's report as 'a great victory' for the miners, but in reality it was 'a farce to stave off revolt' as belatedly characterised by John Maclean's *Vanguard*.[28] Lloyd George had won a decisive battle.

While the miners were being side-tracked by Sankey, Lloyd George was also hard at work trying to weaken the potential strength of the Triple Alliance of mining, railway and transport unions. Not wanting to fight on two fronts at once, the government, which still continued its war-time role of running the railways, conceded the railworkers' demand for an eight-hour day. However, when it was introduced, traditional paid breaks for washing and eating were abolished, raising the temperature of industrial relations. Desperate to defuse the situation, Lloyd George flew NUR leader J.H. Thomas to Paris to negotiate personally during breaks in the Versailles Treaty talks. Thomas was only too keen to reach an agreement. On 19 March, the day before the release of Sankey's

---

26 The full extent of Lloyd George's manipulation of the MFGB leadership is in Wrigley 1990, pp. 151–2.

27 *Workers' Dreadnought*, 12 April 1919.

28 *The Call*, 27 March 1919. *Vanguard*, May 1920.

interim report, the government accepted most of the NUR's demands, averting the threat of a joint coal and rail strike. Even so, Lloyd George was so worried about a miners' strike breaking out when the Sankey Report was published he ordered that food held by the Co-operative Society should not be moved to mining areas during a strike: 'Once the strike begins it is imperative that the state should win. Failure to do so would inevitably lead to a Soviet Republic', he told Bonar Law.[29]

2   The Police Strikes

Alongside military and naval forces, the state also deployed the police on a huge scale against strikers, demonstrators and leftists. This led to dissatisfaction among policemen about long working hours and low pay. In August 1918 the National Union of Police and Prison Officers (NUPPO) threatened to strike for increased bonus payments, official recognition, and the reinstatement of its sacked organiser PC Thomas Thiel. Finding its demands ignored, it declared a strike on 30 August that was supported by most constables across London. The next day the Cabinet agreed to a pay rise, Thiel was reinstated, and Lloyd George met NUPPO representatives, charming them to the extent the strike was called off despite no recognition being given to the organisation.[30]

Dissatisfaction among the police during industrial conflicts was common. NUPPO was formed in the aftermath of the 1912 London dockers' strike, when the Home Office reneged on a pledge to pay a bonus for work during the strike. Writing in the *Police Review*, 'Sam Buck' complained that 'at the start of the strike we were cheered by rumours that if we succeeded in quelling the strike we should be remunerated with a substantial rise of pay. With this in mind we stood shoulder to shoulder ... Is it not incumbent on the powers that be that their servants and allies should be well-looked after?'[31] This belief that the police were not adequately compensated for their duty of 'quelling' strikes was NUPPO's raison d'être. Its London city organiser, John Zollner, emphasised that 'in the event of anything happening with the other trade unions, it is the duty of every policeman, whether he was in the streets, on the railway, or at the

---

29   Quoted in Wrigley 1990, p. 160.
30   For a history of NUPPO see Allen 1958, pp. 133–43. For the genesis of NUPPO see the editorial in *Police and Prison Officers' Magazine*, 6 February 1920 (hereafter *PPOM*). For a general survey, see Emsley 2000, pp. 89–110.
31   *Justice*, 25 Oct 1913.

docks, to maintain law and order'.[32] One of NUPPO's 'chief objects', P.C. Janes told a recruitment meeting in February 1919, 'was the protection of life and property'.[33] NUPPO also recruited prison officers and publicised how its members administered jails across Britain and Ireland. These included Glasgow's Duke Street prison, where John Maclean was detained in 1918, and Dublin's Mountjoy, in which trade unionists had been incarcerated and Republicans executed.[34]

In May 1919 the government finally announced it would not recognise NUPPO and would sack any policemen who went on the strike. On 31 July NUPPO declared a strike, but it was supported by barely 3,000 policemen, largely in London and Liverpool, and petered out after a week. With the exception of the Nine Elms NUR branch in South London and some Liverpool tram workers, the police received no support from trade unionists.[35] This lack of support was not difficult to understand. When Harry Pollitt, then a supporter of the Workers' Socialist Federation, encouraged London dockers to support the police strike he met with stiff opposition. 'I would not go so far as to say that as a general rule policemen are popular with the masses, especially with London's dockers, and the dockers in particular kept interrupting me with "Harry, how can you stick up for the coppers? They batoned us down in the dock strike in 1912"', he later recalled.[36]

This was a common response of working-class people to their daily experience of the police, but it was not a position that was held widely on the left. The BSP had historically supported the police. The 1890 pay strike at London's Bow Street police station took place with the involvement of two SDF policemen, George Walden and Jack Williams.[37] But, as the pseudonymous 'Working Journalist' argued in *Justice* in 1913 after the dockers' strike, discontent among the police was an expression of their hostility to the working class, not evidence of common interests. 'I hope that it is now fully realised that the policeman exists for the purpose of protecting property, and that all his other duties are subordinate to that. ... I have never known a body of police in this country who

---

32   *PPOM*, 23 Jan 1919.

33   *PPOM*, 20 Feb 1919.

34   *PPOM*, 6 Feb 1919.

35   Harry Wicks, then a local railway worker, recalled this support was not reciprocated by the police who 'savagely attacked' Nine Elms rail workers during the 1926 General Strike; Wicks 1992, p. 6.

36   Pollitt 1947 or 1940?, p. 107.

37   *Justice*, 1 Jan 1914. There had also been disputes over police pay and conditions in Newcastle in 1870 and in London in 1872.

were not prepared to bludgeon their own mothers and wives if they thought it would please their governors. Their whole scheme of life and work fosters this'.[38]

Such opposition was rare in the BSP. At the end of January 1919, in the same week as police attacked demonstrators on Glasgow's 'Bloody Friday', *The Call* published an article by NUPPO founder and former police inspector John Syme. Headlined 'A Blue Bolshevik' Syme claimed the police's role was 'to protect and help members of the public'.[39] During the August 1919, strike, *The Call* trumpeted 'Help the Coppers' and 'Help for the Police'.[40] This was also the position held by the WSF, which told police strikers that 'you belong to the working-class army now, policemen; you have gained class-consciousness' and asked them to 'to show solidarity with the workers on any and every occasion'.[41] NUPPO delegates even took part in the March 1920 rank and file conference called by the Willie Gallacher and J.T. Murphy-led Shop Stewards' and Workers' Committee.[42]

Only the SLP hesitated to support the police: 'No doubt they are labouring under grievous wrongs that want righting, but we cannot forget Glasgow, Liverpool, Belfast, London, etc., where innocent working men have been mercilessly clubbed for daring to strike', it wrote in May 1919, before going on to say unless the police went on strike for socialism 'we can only regard them for what they so far have proved themselves to be – part of the physical forces of capitalism'. The following week J.T. Murphy was more sympathetic to the police constable, who 'belongs to the industrial working class, is drawn from it, and his conditions are determined by the conditions existing among the rest of his class'.[43] One of the few unambiguous opponents of the police was leftist BSP organiser George Ebury who, speaking alongside John Maclean in Glasgow in June 1919, called the police 'a bunch of ignorant hogs who wanted to form a union and join the Labour Party, but he for one would strongly oppose it, as there was no difference between a union and a non-union baton'.[44]

---

38   *Justice*, 25 Oct 1913.
39   Syme's belief in the fairness of the British state led him to assure Agnes Maclean that her husband John would not be force-fed in secret when he was imprisoned in 1918. He was. Milton 1973, p. 178.
40   *The Call*, 20 Jan, 7 Aug and 21 Aug 1919.
41   *Workers' Dreadnought*, 7 Sept 1918 and 1 March 1919.
42   Bell 1940, pp. 306–7.
43   *The Socialist*, 15 and 22 May 1919.
44   Report on 9 June Glasgow Demonstration in *Fortnightly Report on Revolutionary Organisations in the UK*, no. 7, 12 June 1919. TNA CAB/24/81/63.

3   Leadership, the Lefts and the Left

The government's reassertion of its authority throughout 1919 added to its growing self-confidence. In September, it abandoned the temporary compromise
with the railway workers and demanded pay cuts. Once again, this was an
opportunity for the Triple Alliance to take united strike action in support of
the railworkers, something that was still deeply feared by the government. The
Daily Herald revealed in May that army regiments had been asked if their troops
would break strikes or serve in Russia. As an NUR strike loomed, Field Marshall
Haig chaired a meeting of Army commanders to discuss how to deal with a
general strike.[45] Faced with such a provocative pay cut, even J.H. Thomas had
to respond, realising that if he failed to take action the anger of his members
would threaten his authority. So, on 27 September, the NUR declared a national
strike. Inundated with offers of solidarity from other unions, the NUR leadership refused to meet the other Triple Alliance unions and fought to keep
the dispute strictly about wages. In the midst of the strike, right-wing dockers'
leader Ernest Bevin warned that if a general strike happened 'I think it must
be civil war, for I cannot see how it is possible, once all the trade unions are
brought in, for the government to avoid fighting for the supremacy and power,
and I do not believe that our people, if they knew what it meant, would be prepared to plunge into it'.[46]

The rail strike ended a week after it began, when the government rescinded
the pay cut and guaranteed to maintain wage levels for another 10 months. In
return, the NUR agreed to a 'no strike' pledge until the following September.
Although the NUR leadership claimed this was a victory, in reality the dispute
showed the government that the Triple Alliance was a dead letter: none of the
leaders of its component unions sought to organise co-ordinated strike activity.
'That breaks up the Triple Alliance', Lloyd George triumphantly told his friend
Sir George Riddell, 'We have detached the railwaymen. I think the result of the
strike will have a most salutary influence'.[47] The government had also been able
to 'stress test' its strikebreaking preparations, and nine days after the end of the
strike the Industrial Unrest Committee was reorganised as a cabinet committee called the Supply and Transport Committee. A year that had begun with the
government fearful of its ability to contain a combative proletariat ended with
it confident of winning a major confrontation with the working class.

---

45   *Daily Herald*, 13 May 1919. See also Jeffrey and Hennessey 1983, p. 14, chapter one covers
      the government's attempts to organise against industrial unrest; Desmarais 1975.
46   Quoted in Bullock 1969, pp. 108–9.
47   Quoted in Wrigley 1990, p. 225.

This was not merely a triumph for the wiles of Lloyd George or the British ruling class's centuries of dealing with rebellious subjects. Although the NUR was led by the right-wing J.H. Thomas, the MFGB was led by Robert Smillie and the National Transport Workers' Federation leader was Robert Williams, both avowed left-wingers elected in 1912 as representatives of the wave of pre-war militancy. Williams was an advocate of 'direct action' and would even be a founding member of the CPGB. In March 1919 he declared that 'we are on the eve of the proletarian revolution' and called for a 'Committee of Public Safety' in opposition to 'the House of Pretence at Westminster'.[48] Yet when it came to turning rhetoric into action, both men fell short. Neither challenged Thomas's refusal to collaborate with the Triple Alliance during the NUR strike, and both sought to pass responsibility for organising action to the TUC. On the left, only Sylvia Pankhurst's WSF appeared to grasp the role of the left-wing trade union leaders. Highlighting the failure of 'the half-hearted officials who pretend to lead the workers' to organise action against British intervention in Soviet Russia, *Workers' Dreadnought* asked of the self-professed leftist trade union leaders 'what are these men doing in this hour of crisis? ... If Smillie, Williams, Cramp, Hodges and Bromley were in truth keenly alive to the workers' interests, far-seeing and earnest to serve them well, they would denounce the traitors within the movement as more dangerous to the cause of working class emancipation than the very capitalists themselves!'[49]

In contrast to the *Dreadnought*, the BSP's *Call* offered no criticisms of the left-wing trade union leaders. The BSP argued the failure of the Triple Alliance in the Spring and Autumn of 1919 was due to a lack of centralised organisation. Its solution was to call for a 'general staff for all the forces of labour'. Tom Quelch had first raised this call in late 1917 but it became the BSP's central demand in April 1919 and was its main campaigning axis during the September rail strike when it called for a 'central executive ... just as a general staff centrally directs a fighting army'.[50] The slogan, which was based on the Triple Alliance's own call for the TUC to hold a national labour convention to discuss the Hands Off Russia campaign, was the forerunner of the Communist Party's slogan of 'All Power to the General Council' in the period before and during the 1926 General Strike. Far from strengthening militancy, the creation of the TUC General Council in

---

48   *Daily Herald*, 29 March 1919.

49   *Workers' Dreadnought*, 25 Oct 1919. See also the *Dreadnought* for 14 May 1919 on the same issue: 'Mr Williams is the secretary of the Transport Workers' Federation. Why does he not publicly use his influence with the transport workers to down tools?'.

50   *The Call*, 23 Aug and 13 Dec 1917; and 24 April and 9 Oct 1919.

1920 was led by Ernest Bevin, who drew up the proposal that was adopted by the TUC at its congress in Portsmouth.[51] As BSP shop steward William McLaine predicted, this was 'a committee of general secretaries, presidents and "dead heads" generally'. His alternative was 'a General Staff by all means but it must be drawn directly from the rank and file'.[52]

This of course begged the point of what the general staff would do. The problem facing the British working class was not one of organisation, of which there was plenty, but of politics. As was shown when Smillie and the MFGB leadership met Lloyd George in February, even the most left-wing of trade union leaders were not prepared to pursue the class struggle to the extent of overthrowing capitalism. Confronted with the opportunity to take a path towards working-class power, the lefts shrank back. When the right-wing dockers' leader James Sexton asked at the 1919 Labour Party conference 'supposing they destroyed the government by a national strike, what were they going to put in its place? ... they had no machinery to replace what they had destroyed', the Labour and trade union lefts had no answer.[53] Smillie's timidity when confronted with Lloyd George's gauntlet in February might be contrasted with Lenin's response at the first All-Russia Congress of Soviets in June 1917 when the Menshevik minister Irakli Tsereteli claimed there was no political party which wanted to take power in Russia: 'Yes, there is', replied Lenin. 'No party can refuse this, and our Party certainly doesn't. It is ready to take over full power at any moment'.[54]

The major lesson of 1919 was that it demonstrated how left-wing leaders of the Labour Party and the trade unions would sooner demobilise workers rather than directly confront the ruling class and its state, even when in a position of strength. Anticipating the actions of the lefts in the 1926 General Strike, Smillie, Williams and others showed that however militant their rhetoric – or even their personal convictions (there could be no doubt that Smillie in particular was a sincere man) – at each and every stage of the class struggle during 1919 they drew back from pursuing the interests of the working class to their revolutionary conclusion. This was still not fully appreciated by the revolutionary Marxists. John Maclean, who knew Smillie through the latter's support for his Scottish Labour College, still believed in the good intentions of the miners' leader even after the MFGB's failure to strike or unify the regional strikes in

51   Bullock 1969, p. 147.
52   *The Call*, 16 Oct 1919. J.T. Murphy also opposed the call for a 'general staff' of labour, see *Solidarity*, Dec 1919.
53   Hinton 1973, p. 315.
54   'Speech On The Attitude Towards The Provisional Government', *CW* vol. 25, p. 20.

summer 1919. 'Let us back Smillie in the process of getting labour united on the industrial field with the object of pressing the class war to victory for our side', argued Maclean. 'Smillie knows the importance of the vote, but only as an agency auxiliary to that of industrial pressure'.[55] Even the Communist International's Karl Radek speculated that, although they were not communists, Williams and the other lefts 'are playing, to a certain extent, a revolutionary part [in events], and some of them are perchance capable of acting as wholehearted communists in the future', foreshadowing the CPGB's position on the Labour Party and TUC left-wingers in 1926. A surprised Sylvia Pankhurst doubted that Radek really knew Williams and company: 'he certainly places them very much further to the left than we were able to consider justifiable'. This was an opinion shared by Lenin, who told Joe Fineberg that Williams 'has complete mush for brains'.[56]

It was not just the left wing of Labour and the trade unions that was found wanting in 1919. Industrial unionists and advocates of direct action also found themselves inadequately armed for the intensity of the class struggle. Former leader of the Unofficial Reform Committee Noah Ablett 'failed to give any direct lead' to the opposition to the Sankey Report according to Welsh supporters of the *Workers' Dreadnought*.[57] Nor did the SLP and the other advocates of industrial unionism have political answers for the challenges of the period. As we have seen, Arthur MacManus thought the solution to state repression in Glasgow in January 1919 was to increase workplace organisation. The SLP was critical of the BSP's call for a general staff of labour, arguing that 'all talk of a real general staff is beside the question until the industrial and political movement of labour is inspired with the single determination to put an end to private exploitation in every shape and form'. The SLP's solution was that 'there must be a strong rank and file movement – unofficially if not officially, officially if not unofficially – bent upon exercising vigilance over labour affairs'.[58] But other than abstract calls for workers to take over industry and put an end to capitalism, the SLP said nothing about how to organise the working class to take power. During the autumn rail strike *The Socialist* did not criticise the Triple Alliance leaders nor discuss the possibility of a general strike or the need for a new leadership for the labour movement.[59] As with the outbreak of the war, *The*

---

55   'The TUC and After', *The Call*, 25 Sept 1919.

56   Karl Radek, 'The British Delegation to Russia', *Workers' Dreadnought*, 3 July 1920. Lenin quoted in Tosstorff 2016, p. 137.

57   *Workers' Dreadnought*, 12 April 1919.

58   *The Socialist*, 16 Oct 1919.

59   For example, see 'The Crisis', in *The Socialist*, 2 Oct 1919.

Socialist often conveyed the sense that the SLP viewed external events as distraction from its long-term educational work. When John Maclean was arrested in April 1918, the SLP called for his release but saw fit to remind its supporters that 'we, too, advocate the establishment of a Socialist Republic. But there is a difference between us and Maclean, that we do not advocate action until the conditions are ripe for such action'.[60]

When those conditions would be ripe the SLP was never able to say. Yet, even without the benefit of hindsight, no-one could deny that the level of industrial conflict, the depth of the social crisis confronting the ruling class, and the revolutionary example of Soviet Russia, meant that the conditions had never been more ripe for the building of a revolutionary working-class party in Britain than in 1919. This is not to say, as some historians have argued, that 1919 represented a revolutionary situation in Britain. At no point did the working class take any action that threatened the capitalist state, even temporarily. There was no uprising in Glasgow in response to Bloody Friday. There was no general strike in support of the miners in March or for the rail workers in September. It was only in Ireland where the British state found itself confronted by a determined opposition, but this was led by nationalists rather than socialists. Fortunately for British capitalism, the post-war economic crash did not occur until late 1920, by which time the febrile political conditions of post-war Britain had somewhat stabilised. Yet, although British workers faced the most experienced capitalist class in the world, the primary responsibility for the failure to transform the deep working-class discontent into revolutionary feeling lay with the existing left-wing leadership of the labour movement. Despite the militant rhetoric of leaders like Bob Smillie and Robert Williams, they turned away from marshalling the industrial strength of the working class for fear that they would be confronted by a struggle for state power. The question of how to deal with these left-wing leaders would be at the heart of the struggle to build a communist party over the next decade.

4   Racist Scourge in Europe

Such a party would have to confront the deep racism of British society. At the heart of the British war effort was the defence of its empire, which meant that race and the defence of the imperial racial hierarchy was a constant factor in

---

60   *The Socialist*, May 1918.

the social tensions of war-time. By the end of 1916, the labour shortage was so acute that the government floated the idea of importing black workers from South Africa.[61] The proposal was denounced by, among others, George Lansbury's *Herald*, as the now weekly *Daily Herald* was known during the war. One *Herald* writer suggested that 'before our coloured brethren are introduced to this favoured clime, their would-be employers should endeavour to persuade the authorities to make whip-manufacturing a starred trade'.[62] The *Herald*'s position was inspired by E.D. Morel, a leader of the Union for Democratic Control who joined the ILP in April 1918. In 1917 he published *Africa and the Peace of Europe*, which the *Herald* advertised with the lurid headline '25 Million Armed Negroes for Europe'. It accused 'European statesmen' of wanting to 'conscript Africa's teeming millions for war in Europe' and creating 'a hideous danger'.[63] Morel had been a prominent campaigner against Belgian atrocities in the Congo, but this was because he believed that 'races' should live separately and feared that the horrific treatment of Africans by imperialism would lead inevitably to a violent backlash against their oppressors. He therefore utterly opposed any black immigration to Europe.

Sadly but unsurprisingly, the BSP outdid the *Herald*'s racist rhetoric. Party leader Tom Quelch, the son of SDF stalwart Harry and a future founding leader of the CPGB, claimed in a major article in *The Call* that 'a grotesque shadow has been flung across the economic milieu of the workers – a shadow, dark and menacing – the shadow of the Negro labourer'. He complained that 'the hell of our suffering and degradation is not complete. We have not been hounded low enough. Black men, say our rulers, must be brought here to challenge our right to live, to offer themselves alongside of us in the labour market', before going on to warn soldiers that their wives and daughters were to be 'delivered into the arms of the vigorous Othellos of Africa while they are in the trenches'. He ended by complaining that 'the masters are not concerned as to racial purity, patriotism or anything else'.[64] This attitude was repeated in an article in the *Woman's Dreadnought* by prominent liberal Ethel Wedgwood, who described African workers as 'converted cannibals'. She argued that if black workers were brought to Britain they should be kept in 'a convict prison' that offered 'no possibility of leaving', based on the labour camps for Chinese workers used by the British

61   Asquith's statement on the importation of South African workers is in *The Times*, 22 Nov 1916.
62   'The Human Comedy: Uplifting the Native', *The Herald*, 20 Jan 1917.
63   *The Herald*, 15 Sept 1917.
64   *The Call*, 25 Jan 1917.

in the Transvaal.[65] Despite a consistent record of opposing anti-Semitism, the *Dreadnought* does not appear to have challenged Wedgwood's views.[66]

The backwardness of Britain's ostensible Marxists was opposed by Georges Chicherin. He attacked Quelch's acceptance of 'racial distinction between workers' and pointed out that 'racial distinctions and restrictions are the greatest hindrance to the universal development of labour solidarity. How can the masses of the backward countries be drawn into the international labour movement if the labour organisations of the more developed countries consider them as inferior beings and exclude them?'[67] In response, Quelch reiterated his stance, claiming Africans 'belong to a different evolutionary epoch', and praised anti-Chinese legislation in America and the 'White Australia' policy of the Australian Labour Party. Chicherin pointed out that '"racial" differences are in reality economic differences' and argued that 'when the workers of the "backward" exploited countries see the organised workers of the "advanced" exploited countries shutting them out, the labour movement itself becomes in their eyes a weapon of the exploiters directed against them'. To accept such divisions, he warned, 'means identification of labour with the capitalist divisions of the world'.[68] Chicherin's stance was shared by the SLP. An article in the September 1917 issue of *The Socialist* under the byline of 'A Negro' insisted that:

> the workers of the so-called subject races are part and parcel of the international working-class movement. ... How must the coloured labour problem be met? By organisation! By class organisation!! ... if coloured men are brought to compete with us, we will organise them alongside ourselves, and with greater unity continue the fight against capital. The moment white labour fights black labour, that moment Capital beats both. The moment white and black labour unite, that moment the defeat of Capital has commenced.[69]

It is also important to realise that racism did not always go unchallenged by rank-and-file trade unionists. In October 1917 members of the Workers' Union in Birmingham began a recruitment campaign among Chinese workers in the local metal industries. Union official John Beard told its monthly *Workers Record* that 'these men are workmen, circumstanced like every other workman,

---

65   'Coloured Labour', *Woman's Dreadnought*, 23 June 1917.
66   For the *Dreadnought*'s opposition to anti-Semitism, see 'A Pogrom in London', 26 May 1917.
67   *The Call*, 8 Feb 1917.
68   *The Call*, 15 Feb 1915 (for Quelch) and 22 Feb 1917 (for Chicherin).
69   'Colour is Only Skin Deep', *The Socialist*, Sept 1917.

and I record it to the credit of several of our branch officials who took the initiative of enrolling them in our union ... so far as I am concerned I will be no party to hounding a man simply because his colour, creed or civilisation is different to mine'.[70]

Although the government did not pursue the idea of importing African workers, the issue of racism once again flared up at the start of 1919. The end of the war led to shipowners laying off huge numbers of seamen as the demand for merchant shipping collapsed. Many seamen from the West Indies, West Africa and North Africa found themselves abandoned in Britain with no prospect of a passage home, while the employment market was saturated with demobilised Royal Navy sailors. Long-established Chinese, African and West Indian communities of sailors in British towns quickly became the focus of racist hostility.[71] The situation was further enflamed by the racist rhetoric of the shipowners and the right-wing leaderships of the seamen's unions, most notably Havelock Wilson, the leader of the National Sailors' and Firemen's Union.

On 23 January 1919 the desperate employment situation erupted in open violence at Glasgow's merchant marine office, when fighting broke out between white and black seamen seeking jobs. The previous day local seamen's leader Manny Shinwell spoke at a seamen's meeting and blamed unemployment on the government's refusal to exclude Chinese labour from British ships. 'It was essential', he said, 'that action should be taken at once'. It should be noted that Willie Gallacher also appears to have spoken at this meeting although there seems to be no record of what he said.[72] Shinwell's speech was a green light for racist violence, and the following day white racist mobs surged through streets where black residents lived, attacking them and invading their homes. The pogrom only ceased when police arrested 30 black seamen. Needless to say, none of the white pogromists were detained.[73]

The following month Arab seamen in South Shields (where Havelock Wilson was the Liberal Party MP) were denied work and subject to racist attacks led by an official of the National Union of Ships' Stewards, Cooks, Butchers and Bakers. Once again, it was the attacked Arab sailors who were jailed.[74] In May, escalating unemployment among seamen in Liverpool emboldened racist

---

70   *Workers Record*, Dec 1917, p. 14. *Workers' Dreadnought* also opposed a later wave of anti-
      Chinese racism; see 'Yellow Peril', 16 Oct 1920.
71   For an overview, see Fryer 1984, pp. 293–312.
72   [Glasgow] *Evening Times*, 23 Jan 1919, quoted in Jenkinson 2008, p. 38. See p. 40 for Gal-
      lacher's presence at a seamen's meeting with Shinwell on 28 January.
73   Jenkinson 2009, ch. 3.
74   Auerbach 2009, pp. 105–6.

mobs, and in early June a week-long pogrom saw racists run amok throughout the long-established black community in the Toxteth area, leaving dozens injured and murdering ship's fireman Charles Wootton. That same month saw racist riots break out in Cardiff, as Australian soldiers using live ammunition led mobs into the black, Arab and Chinese communities in the city's docklands. Scores were injured and Mahommed Abdullah killed by a blow to the head. Tellingly, the inquest into his killing could not decide whether his death was caused by the mob or the police.[75] Racist attacks on non-white workers also took place in the docklands of Hull, Salford and London's East End.

The response of the left groups mirrored their reactions to proposed importation of African workers during the war. The BSP seems to have said nothing in response to the outbreaks of racist violence in the first half of 1919. No-one followed Chicherin's lead, who by this time had returned to Russia to become Soviet Commissar for Foreign Affairs. It also appears that no left-wing newspaper addressed the Glasgow racist attacks on black seamen. However, the organisations to the BSP's left did oppose the wave of racist violence across the summer of 1919. In *The Socialist*, William Paul stated: 'The SLP has always insisted, despite the sneers of the so-called socialists, that no worker should be debarred from working at any job. It does not matter what the colour, sex or skill of the worker may be. ... There is no yellow peril, there is no Asiatic problem. These things only exist because capitalism exists'.[76] The SLP and James Connolly had spoken out against racist treatment of Chinese and Lascar (Asian and Arab) seamen by the Seamen's and Transport Workers' union leaderships during the 1914 Head Line Strike.[77] *The Worker*, the newspaper of the Clyde Workers Committee which was suppressed in 1916 but revived in late 1918, took an equally robust line against the 1919 pogroms. It also addressed lynch-mob paranoia about white women having sex with black men, asking 'well what if they should? The colour of the skin is not a factor in deciding whether a man can make a woman happy'. The article ended with an appeal to 'fellow workers, drop all this racial warfare, recognise the black man as being a victim of capitalism just as you are; join up your forces with him, and fight to destroy that which makes slaves of you just as it makes a slave of him'.[78]

---

75   Fryer 1984, p. 307. Evans 1980, pp. 5–29.

76   'Race Riots and Revolution', *The Socialist*, 10 July 1919. The following year Paul gave a series of lecture on racism and internationalism in the South Wales' coalfields, see *The Socialist*, 1 April 1920.

77   'Union Scabs and Chinese Labour', *The Socialist*, May 1914.

78   *The Worker*, 12 July 1919.

The Workers' Socialist Federation initially opposed racism from a largely liberal perspective, asking 'those who have been negro hunting' if they were aware of how they were doing the capitalists' work for them and suggesting that black workers 'would have probably stayed in Africa if the capitalists had left him and his country alone'.[79] However, this stance changed when the revolutionary Jamaican poet Claude McKay began writing for the *Workers' Dreadnought* in 1921. In January that year he wrote *Socialism and the Negro* which argued that:

> today, the British Empire is the greatest obstacle to international socialism, and any of its subjugated parts succeeding in breaking away from it would be helping the cause of world communism. In these pregnant times no people who are strong enough to throw off an imperial yoke will tamely submit to a system of local capitalism. The breaking up of the British Empire must either begin at home or abroad: the sooner the strong blow is struck the better it will be for all communists.[80]

This was not a position held widely by the British left. In April 1920, the *Daily Herald* published a front-page article by E.D. Morel headlined 'Black Scourge in Europe. Sexual Horror Let Loose by France on the Rhine'. Morel described the Senegalese troops in the French Army occupying the Rhine as 'black barbarians' from 'tribes in a primitive state of development' who were 'raping women and girls – for well-known physiological reasons', and the article told lurid stories of brothels, venereal disease, and the 'unrestrained and unrestrainable' sexual appetites of Africans.[81] In the same issue, a *Herald* editorial (George Lansbury was the editor) claimed to oppose racial prejudice but declared:

> It is an odious outrage to bring thousands of children of the forests from Africa to Europe without their womenfolk ... Are the Christians of Europe, who raise millions of pounds annually to teach the heathen the blessings of monogamy, going to remain silent before the sexual outrages that are being committed?[82]

This was the start of the newspaper's campaign against black troops in Europe. Two days later, another *Herald* editorial said 'We want them sent home, to their

---

79   'Stabbing Negroes in the London Dock Area', *Workers' Dreadnought*, 7 June 1919.
80   *Workers' Dreadnought*, 31 Jan 1920.
81   *Daily Herald*, 10 April 1920.
82   Shepherd 2002, p. 180, says the Morel article is 'a mystery in relations to Lansbury's editorship'.

own places, from which they should never have been brought. This is a vital matter for women of all countries – and for the workers all countries. ... we shall have savages used to blackleg, and to coerce, the workers in all European countries'. A mass meeting in Westminster's Central Hall was called to protest 'Against the Use of Black Troops in Europe', and was addressed by Morel and future Labour MP Margaret Bondfield, and supported by, among others, the Women's International League for Peace and Freedom.[83]

In response, Claude McKay immediately sent an article to Lansbury for publication in the *Daily Herald*. Lansbury refused to print it, whereupon it was quickly published by the *Workers' Dreadnought*.[84] McKay asked why the 'Christian-Socialist-pacifist *Daily Herald*' was publishing 'all this obscene, maniacal outburst about the sex vitality of black men in a proletarian paper?' He went on to expose how Morel and the *Herald* were inflaming racism: 'I feel that the ultimate result of your propaganda will be further strife and blood-spilling between the whites and the many members of my race, boycotted economically and socially, who have been dumped down on the English docks since the ending of the European War'.[85] McKay's skewering of Lansbury's Christian piety continued later that year when he discovered that Lansbury, who owned a sawmill business, employed non-union labour, some of whom scabbed on a sawmill workers' strike. He wrote an exposé for the *Dreadnought*, only to find that Sylvia Pankhurst would not print it because she owed money to Lansbury.[86]

There would later be one final source of support for Morel's racism. In April 1922, the Communist Party of Great Britain's weekly newspaper *The Communist* revived the issue by publishing an article titled 'Outcry Against the Black Horror'. It once again decried the 'the awful disgrace which is being done to our white women on the Rhine by the eager lust of African savages', complained about mixed-race 'bastards' being born, and denounced the supposed sexual abuse of white boys by black soldiers.[87] The CPGB published this without comment and, as far as can be ascertained, without opposition. Even more lurid than Morel's diatribes, the article showed to what depths such racism would lead: although not stated by *The Communist*, the article was a reprint of a leaflet distributed by the German fascists of the Deutscher Fichte-Bund.[88]

---

83   Reinders 1968, pp. 6 and 15. The issue is also discussed in Marks 1983, pp. 297–333; Wigger 2010; Campbell 2014.
84   McKay 1985, p. 75.
85   'A Black Man Replies', *Workers' Dreadnought*, 24 April 1920.
86   McKay 1985, pp. 77–9.
87   *The Communist*, 8 April 1922.
88   The DFB leaflet is reprinted in Collar 2012, p. 157.

5   Ireland's Tragedy, Labour's Disgrace

When it came to British colonial rule, the SDF had traditionally voiced concern about the terrible impact of British imperialism on the peoples of the world. Hyndman himself wrote regularly about the poverty and oppression caused by imperialism in India, yet this never transcended that strain of British liberal opinion which had recoiled from the grim reality of the British Raj. Although he regularly spoke of the need for 'self-governance', this was not a call for self-determination.[89] At the 1904 congress of the Second International Hyndman had successfully moved a resolution which called 'on the workers of Great Britain to compel their government to abandon its present infamous and degrading colonial system and to introduce the perfectly practicable system of self-government for the Indian people under English sovereignty'.[90] Of course, the final three words meant the continuance of British rule, and the policy was essentially identical to that which the Labour Party would adopt towards Ireland.

After the departure of Hyndman, the BSP largely continued his colonial politics. In September 1916, a front-page article by Arthur Sifleet attacked British policy in India and Ireland, arguing that a socialist government would 'proffer sympathetic assimilation to our more highly developed black brothers, and peaceful self-development to the rest'. Although he claimed that 'colour hatred will be dissolved by socialism' the article was headlined 'Hands Off the Darkies'.[91] As with much else in its programme, the BSP saw opposition to imperialist rule in India and elsewhere as a moral question, which it opposed on paper but was not prepared to actively campaign against. The same was also true of the SLP, which would mention India as an example of the rapaciousness of British capitalism but never made it part of its day-to-day factory work. This attitude would be inherited by the young Communist Party of Great Britain, and would be a cause of constant criticism from the Communist International.

The relationship between the British Empire and the class struggle was nowhere more acute for the British labour movement than in Ireland. Industrial militancy was intimately connected to the conflict in Ireland, a point reiterated by Lloyd George in August 1919: 'The Irish question ... had more to do with the existing industrial unrest than the great majority of people imagined.

---

89   Morris 2014.
90   Braunthal 1967, p. 312.
91   *The Call*, 7 Sept 1916.

... A satisfactory settlement of the Irish question was most important'.[92] A significant proportion of the industrial working class in Britain had Irish roots, and support for the Irish cause grew as the War of Independence intensified. In March 1920, the 200 delegates at the Shop Stewards' and Workers' Committee's rank and file conference called for Irish independence and the withdrawal of British troops. Three weeks later the London district council of the NUR called on the Triple Alliance to take action in support of IRA hunger strikers at Mountjoy Prison. On 18 April 4,000 people marched in Glasgow in opposition to British military rule in Ireland, while the Labour Party's J.R. Clynes was roundly booed for his party's refusal to act in support of Ireland at the Manchester May Day demonstration.[93]

The following month around 2,000 dockers and 300 coal heavers at Liverpool docks went on strike in support of Irish political prisoners in Wormwood Scrubs. In May, Dublin members of the National Union of Railwaymen (NUR) at North Wall refused to handle munitions or transport troops for the British Army and were sacked. Outrage spread quickly among trade unionists and calls for solidarity strikes became so loud that a special conference of the TUC was convened in July to discuss the situation in Ireland. At the conference J.H. Thomas called for an end to war in Ireland and for it to be given 'Dominion' status in the British Empire, but pointedly refused to endorse action in support of his sacked members in Dublin. Opposing this, the Miners' Federation called for the withdrawal of all British troops, for the 'cessation of the production of munitions of war destined to be used against Ireland and Russia', and for 'a general "down tools" policy' if the government refused. In a classic TUC fudge, both resolutions were passed, but as the Home Office's Director of Intelligence Basil Thomson astutely noted, the MFGB's call to put to the issue to a ballot was 'a very different thing from a threat of immediate action'.[94] No action by the TUC or the trade union leaders was forthcoming, but the Dublin NUR embargo on British munitions and troops lasted until the end of December.[95]

Nevertheless, the desire for action to support Irish self-determination did not evaporate. For many, the fight against British intervention in Soviet Russia was linked to the demand to get British troops out of Ireland. On 23 June

---

92   Wrigley 1990, p. 216.
93   *Report on Revolutionary Organisations in the UK*: 5 April 1920 (TNA CAB/24/103/86), 22 April 1920 (TNA CAB/24/104/30) and 6 May 1920 (TNA CAB/24/105/39).
94   Bell 2016, pp. 145–6. Thomson in *Report on Revolutionary Organisations in the UK*, 15 July 1920 (TNA CAB/24/109/35).
95   Townshend 1979.

a demonstration calling for 'Hands Off Russia and Ireland!' marched through Liverpool, and of the 350 local Councils of Action that were set up in August 1920 to stop British involvement in the Russo-Polish war, seventy-eight explicitly called for a 'down tools' policy to force British troops out of Ireland.[96] In response, the June conference of the Labour Party voted to support the 'absolute and free self-determination of Ireland'. Although this appeared to shift Labour away from its traditional pro-imperialist stance, it was intended to draw the sting from calls for action to force withdrawal from Ireland. Barely was the ink dry on the resolution when a special Labour Party conference in December 1920 reversed the demand for Irish self-determination and called instead for an Irish constituent assembly, with the proviso that it 'should prevent Ireland from becoming a military or naval menace to Great Britain'. As Sylvia Pankhurst noted, this differed little from the policy of former Liberal prime minister Herbert Asquith.[97]

The positions taken by British left towards the Easter Rising were replicated during the War of Independence. The BSP supported Irish independence and opposed British imperialism in the pages of *The Call* but appears to have done nothing in practice to promote it. The first time *The Call* mentioned stopping munitions shipments to Ireland was when the Miners' Federation proposed it at the 1920 TUC conference.[98] The SLP was much more vigorous, calling on the TUC to turn its resolutions of support for Irish independence into trade union action. It established links with revolutionary socialists in Belfast and Dublin and in 1920 organised a speaking tour for Sean McLoughlin, a communist and veteran of the Easter Rising who was briefly a member of the SLP.[99] Mcloughlin appears to have been the only person to raise the issue of Ireland during the discussions to create a British communist party, arguing in *The Socialist* that Irish and Irish-descended workers in Britain were a crucial section of the working class and that 'to clear the way for the class struggle [in Britain], the question of Ireland's independence must be settled soon. A general strike for 24 or 48 hours would bring the Army of Occupation out of Ireland. ... No more speeches, a general strike to remove the troops from Ireland, and ... the workers of Irish extraction will flock into the labour and socialist movement if the strike for Ireland is successful'.[100] Even so, the SLP did not see Ireland as a cent-

---

96   *Report on Revolutionary Organisations in the UK*, 1 July 1920 (TNA CAB/24/108/66).

97   Quoted in Bell 2016, p. 54. *Workers' Dreadnought*, 16 Oct 1920.

98   'Direct Action on the TUC', *The Call*, 15 July 1920.

99   For McLoughlin, see McGuire 2011. For the early history of communism in Ireland see O'Connor 2004.

100   'Unity, Ireland and the Revolution', *The Socialist*, May Day supplement 1920.

ral issue in its programme; its Paisley branch in Glasgow mentioned Ireland barely in passing in its manifesto for the parliamentary by-election in February 1920.[101]

Unlike the BSP and SLP, Sylvia Pankhurst and her supporters placed great emphasis on the Irish struggle. The *Woman's Dreadnought* had distinguished itself during the Easter Rising with Patricia Lynch's eye-witness reporting, and this continued throughout the war. In the summer of 1918 'self-determination for India and Ireland' was one of the seven points of the programme of the newly launched Workers' Socialist Federation. In the same issue of *Workers' Dreadnought* in which this was announced, an editorial from Pankhurst called for independence for Ireland and praised Bolshevik policy on nationalities, quoting extensively from Trotsky's booklet *War and Revolution*.[102] Throughout 1920, as British repression in Ireland intensified, *Workers' Dreadnought* carried regular coverage of the struggle for independence. 'We desire to see a Workers Communist Soviet Republic in Ireland', it declared in January 1920, going on to say 'as a step thereto and as a blow at the strength of capitalism in Britain, we welcome the brave struggle of the Irish people for independence'.[103] It was insistent in warning against the role of the Labour Party in derailing the fight for Irish independence, opposing the call for a constituent assembly and denouncing Labour's Irish policy as following 'the worst traditions of capitalist diplomacy'.[104] It also warned against illusions in Sinn Fein: 'even if the grant of independence under the capitalist system could ever mean genuine independence to small countries like Ireland, the workers can never be emancipated so long as they remain under the rule of their native capitalists. The Sinn Feiners are not fighting for a workers' republic, but an Irish republic; they are not Red Guards, but Green Guards'.[105]

The only other voice on the left that consistently agitated against British imperialism in Ireland was that of John Maclean. In July 1919 he was invited to Dublin to speak in support of the campaign against intervention in Soviet Russia. He provoked controversy among Republicans by arguing that 'Irish labour would not be free under a Sinn Fein republic, and that ... Irish labour should support British labour in the campaign against intervention in Russia' and suggesting that Irish socialists 'should not antagonise the soldiers of occupation in

101   *The Socialist*, 26 February 1920. For a discussion of the SLP and Ireland in this period, see McGuire 2018, pp. 152–6. For a broader perspective, see Redfern 2005.

102   *Workers' Dreadnought*, 1 June 1918.

103   *Workers' Dreadnought*, 9 Jan 1920.

104   *Workers' Dreadnought*, 27 Nov 1920.

105   *Workers' Dreadnought*, 24 April 1920.

Ireland but should try to win them over to the Irish point of view'.[106] Following his visit, in the summer of 1920 he published *The Irish Tragedy: Scotland's Disgrace*, a pamphlet that reportedly sold 20,000 copies as Maclean spoke across Scotland in support of the Irish fight for independence. In it, he detailed the crimes of Britain in Ireland, called for a general strike to force the withdrawal of British troops, and concluded

> should Ireland get a Republic the class war will then burst out and be fought out till Irish Labour wins and establishes Communism finally again in the 'Ould Counthrie'. This new phase in Irish life ought to be the inciting influence to British Labour, for Labour everywhere must ally against the common enemy, Capitalism, and destroy it to make way for World Communism.[107]

Just as Lloyd George predicted in July 1914, Britain had become gripped by massive industrial conflict and turmoil in Ireland. The outbreak of war had delayed their coming, but the British ruling class was confronted by its deepest social crisis since the 1840s. The question now was how that crisis would be resolved.

---

106   'Impressions of Dublin', *The Worker*, Aug 1919.
107   Maclean n.d., p. 9.

CHAPTER 8

Between Labourism and Bolshevism: Towards A Communist Party

British military intervention in Russia began even before the Bolsheviks came to power. On 9 September 1917 General Kornilov, commander-in-chief of the Russian Army, marched on Petrograd to suppress the workers' soviets. Alongside him was a British armoured-car squadron, led by the Conservative MP and future Mussolini supporter, Oliver Locker-Lampson.[1] Many in the British government, including the British ambassador Sir George Buchanan, were supportive of Kornilov's coup attempt. Brigadier-General Alfred Knox told the War Cabinet that 'General Kornilov should be fully supported in the measures which he wished to take to restore discipline at the front, on the railways, and in Petrograd'.[2] The cabinet concurred and informed Alexander Kerensky, the Provisional Government's prime minister, that he should 'come to terms with General Kornilov'.[3] Determined opposition by Petrograd workers caused the coup to quickly collapse, but this did not deter the interventionist impulses of the British government.

Less than four weeks after the October Revolution, the war cabinet decided to provide unlimited financial support to Kornilov's ally, the White Cossack general Alexey Kaledin.[4] On 6 March 1918, three days after the signing of Brest-Litovsk peace treaty between Russia and Germany, Royal Marines occupied Murmansk, Russia's strategically vital port 600 miles north of Petrograd. On 1 August, British forces seized the major seaport of Archangel in northern Russia. Martial law was imposed under Major-General Frederick Poole, a man who dismissed his Bolshevik opponents as 'mostly Jews'.[5] His successor was Brigadier-General Edmund Ironside, whose regime shot anyone caught distributing Bolshevik propaganda, confined Russians to their homes, and on 17 July

---

1 The story can be found in Perrett and Lord 1981. The definitive account of British intervention against the Soviet republic remains Richard Ullman's three-volume *Anglo-Soviet Relations*, published by Princeton University Press. See also Kinvig 2006. For Locker-Lampson, see Collins 2016.
2 Quoted in Page Arnot 1967, p. 75.
3 Quoted in Ullman 1961, p. 12.
4 Occleshaw 2006, pp. 28–38; Ullman 1961, pp. 42–7.
5 Quoted in Lockley 2003, p. 47.

1919 machine-gunned 25 Red Army servicemen as 500 local people were forced to watch.[6] In March 1919, British forces used poison gas against the Red Army and Russian civilians. Initially the gas was sprayed out from aeroplanes, but in 1918 British scientists developed shells that released poison into the air when they exploded. Fifty thousand of these 'M Devices' were sent to Russia and used on at least seven villages that supported the Bolsheviks. When criticised in parliament for the use of chemical weapons, Secretary of State for War Winston Churchill – who declared that Russia was under the control of 'Jew-Commissars' – blithely stated that 'it is a very right and proper thing to employ poison gas against them'.[7]

Alongside their own forces, the British also provided extensive amounts of war materiel to the counter-revolutionary armies of Generals Denikin and Kolchack.[8] 'I am myself carrying out Kolchak's orders', Churchill assured a meeting of Tsarist generals in May 1919.[9] By September 1918, Denikin estimated that Britain was supplying half of the total munitions received by the White forces, including one hundred tanks, two hundred aeroplanes, and hundreds of thousands of guns.[10] Wherever Denikin established his superiority, his troops took the opportunity to unleash their anti-Semitism. As the historian W. Bruce Lincoln noted, 'as the pogroms of 1919 burst upon the Jews of the Ukraine with incredible ferocity, the enemies of Bolshevism committed some of the most brutal acts of persecution in the modern history of the Western world'.[11] British financial and political support was crucial in facilitating the barbarity of the White armies, a fact highlighted by supporters of the Bolsheviks in Britain.[12]

Within a few weeks of the October Revolution, the BSP, WSF and SLP began campaigning to defend Soviet Russia against British intervention. On 10 January 1918, *The Call* published Maxim Litvinov's 'To The Workers of Great Britain' calling for working-class defence of the revolution. In the autumn of 1918 Sylvia Pankhurst established the People's Russian Information Bureau (PRIB). This brought together the WSF, BSP, SLP, the left-wing of the ILP, the London Work-

---

6   Lockley 2003, p. 53; Balbirnie 2016.

7   Ullman 1968, pp. 181–2. Neither Ullman nor Martin Kettle found any evidence to support Churchill's contention that the Bolsheviks used poison gas; Kettle 1992, pp. 76–7. For Churchill's anti-Semitism, see White 1979, p. 57.

8   For Kolchak, see Occleshaw 2006, pp. 278–9.

9   *Daily Herald*, 3 July 1920. For more on the context of this remark, see Graubard 1956, p. 99.

10   Lincoln 1990, p. 198.

11   Lincoln 1990, p. 317.

12   See, for example, 'The Massacre of the Jews by Denikin's Bands', *The Worker* [Glasgow], 20 December 1920. For the British government's attitudes to the pogroms and its own anti-Semitism, see Kadish 1992, pp. 12–20.

ers' Committee and branches the National Union of Railwaymen to distribute pamphlets and leaflets to counter anti-Soviet propaganda. Its weekly bulletin carried news from the civil war, developments in Soviet society and extracts from Russian revolutionary newspapers. It also distributed *Are You a Trade Unionist? An Appeal to British Workers* by Lenin and Chicherin. At its first conference in July 1919 the PRIB brought together around 220 delegates from a wide variety of organisations.[13] In November 1918 a mass rally at a packed Royal Albert Hall in London saw Labour Party leaders and trade union officials call for British troops to be withdrawn from Russia, and on 18 January the London Workers' Committee, two of whose key leaders were the WSF-supporting shop stewards William Watson and Harry Pollitt, and the SLP's London District took the initiative to form a 'Hands Off Russia' committee. Lenin was asked to be honorary president, and Trotsky, Karl Liebknecht and Clara Zetkin invited to be vice presidents.[14]

Such solidarity did not come without a cost. The SLP offices were raided by police for printing the new Soviet constitution, the BSP's for publishing Lenin's pamphlets, and the PRIB was subject to constant police harassment.[15] Across Britain, individuals and organisations were persecuted for supporting the Bolsheviks. In March 1919, William Scott of North Shields was jailed for six months for distributing a pamphlet about the dictatorship of the proletariat. The same month six Lithuanian socialists were deported for attending a meeting about the October Revolution. In May Arnold Yates was fined £50 for handing out a leaflet titled 'To British Sailors' opposing intervention in Russia. In June, the home of the translator J.T. Lyne was raided and manuscripts of Lenin's articles he was translating were seized. The following month, WSF member 'Miss O'Neill' was jailed for 11 days and Matt Kavanagh fined £2 for 'insulting behaviour' in Hyde Park, while Bristol's 'Bomb Shop' bookstore was raided and writings by Lenin and Chicherin confiscated. These continuous police actions against leftists established a pattern of harassment that would continue throughout the next decade.[16]

---

13   A collection of PRIB leaflets and bulletins can be seen in file IWSA/1/61 in the Archive of the International Woman's Suffrage Alliance, John Rylands Library, Manchester. *Fortnightly Report*, 15, 7 Aug 1919, TNA CAB 24/86/35.

14   *Workers' Dreadnought*, 28 Dec 1918. 'The "Hands Off Russia" Conference. Official Report' at PHM CP/IND/POLL/1/8.

15   *Daily Herald*, 26 Oct 1918.

16   For details of these arrests and surveillance of leftists, see Basil Thomson's *Fortnightly Report* throughout 1919. The background to his work is in his 1922 autobiography, *Queer People*.

But harassment did not deter supporters of the revolution. On 18 January 1919 almost 500 delegates met in London to organise a national 'Hands Off Russia' campaign. Harry Pollitt moved the main resolution calling for a general strike to force the British government to withdraw its troops from Russia and end its support for the White armies. Opposition to a new war in Russia ran deep throughout the labour movement, and as British intervention in Russia increased, the issue moved to the centre of working-class politics. In February *Workers' Dreadnought* reported that dockers in Bristol had refused to load military supplies onto a ship bound for Russia. In July miners in Merthyr Tydfil in South Wales went on a one-day strike which called for hands off Russia, while dockers at London's Victoria and Albert Dock also walked off the job in protest against British intervention.[17] The Miners' Federation called for strike action to force the withdrawal of British troops from Russia in March, as did a joint Labour Party/TUC conference in April, and the Labour Party itself in June 1919. This official support led the 'Hands Off Russia' campaign to broaden its committee to include senior trade union leaders such as the NUR's Charlie Cramp, Tom Mann, now the ASE general secretary, John Bromley, general secretary of ASLEF (the train drivers' union), and John Hill, general secretary of the boilermakers' union. On 25 July, with hundreds of thousands of miners across Britain on strike, the Triple Alliance voted overwhelmingly to ballot its members on whether to take strike action to force British withdrawal from Russia. Four days later, Winston Churchill announced that all British troops would leave Russia before the winter, conscription was to end, and all conscientious objectors had been released from prison. 'Churchill Admits Defeat' announced the *Daily Herald*.[18]

Churchill's decision reflected the Western powers' recognition that they could not militarily defeat Soviet Russia. Three days after the British withdrew from Archangel, the Supreme Council of Allied Powers decided on 30 September 1919 to organise a 'peaceful blockade' of Russia, while continuing to pour money and arms into the White armies.[19] The 'Hands Off Russia' campaign continued to hold rallies and demonstrations throughout the spring of 1920. Then, at the end of April, Poland's Marshall Józef Piłsudski attacked Red Army troops in the Ukraine as part of his plan to return to Poland's pre-1722 boundaries, which encompassed Ukraine, East Prussia, Lithuania, White Russia and half of Latvia. Taken by surprise, the Red Army retreated and on 7 May Pilsudksi cap-

---

17   *Workers' Dreadnought*, 1 Feb 1919. *Pioneer* [Merthyr], 26 July 1919. *Daily Herald*, 22 July 1919.

18   *Daily Herald*, 30 July 1919.

19   The Allied Blockade was formally lifted on 16 January 1920. For the history of the economic blockade, see Gawore 1975, pp. 39–69.

tured Kiev. Given the support provided to Pilsudski by Britain and France, war with Soviet Russia appeared to be inevitable.[20]

However, on Monday 10 May dockers at London's East India Docks – next to the site of the 1889 strike – noticed that guns and ammunition destined for Poland were due to be loaded onto the ss *Jolly George* steamship. They immediately refused to touch the ship or refresh its coal stocks. The ship's crew also refused to sail until the munitions were removed, and the local branch of the Wharf, Riverside and General Workers Union ordered its 4,000 members not to allow the ship to set sail, and to stop all munitions intended for nations at war with Russia.[21] Such was the level of opposition to war that, at the dockers' national conference in Plymouth that month, it was right-winger Ernest Bevin who congratulated the Jolly George dockers and called for blanket action to stop 'these wicked acts'. Three days later, the National Union of Railwaymen instructed its members not to handle any military supplies for Poland, and on 9 June the Miners' Federation linked the struggle against war in Russia with the fight for Irish self-determination, arguing that 'the most effective way in which a protest can be made is for the organised workers to refuse to manufacture or transport munitions of war for Ireland or Poland'.[22] In July this was endorsed by the TUC and the Labour Party.

By now the Polish offensive had been repulsed and, led by the 27-year-old general Mikhail Tukhachevsky, the Russians made rapid progress towards Poland. On 3 August, with the Red Army approaching Warsaw, the British announced that they would come to the aid of Poland if the advance was not halted. War seemed only days away. 'We cannot hide from ourselves that the outlook is very dark', a leader in *The Times* explained ominously, 'we must face it with the same unanimity and the same courage with which we faced the crisis of 1914'.[23] However, the leadership of the Labour Party understood how deeply British workers opposed war against Soviet Russia. The day after the British ultimatum to the Russians, Arthur Henderson sent a circular to all Labour Party branches and local Trades Councils urging them to organise anti-war demonstrations on Sunday 8 August.

The response was overwhelming. Hundreds of meetings and demonstrations took place across Britain. For the only time in its history, the *Daily Herald*

---

20   Details of British involvement in the Polish war, direct and indirect, can be found in Macfarlane 1967.
21   *Daily Herald*, 13 May 1920, *Workers' Dreadnought*, 15 May 1920. *Fortnightly Report*, no. 54, 13 May 1920, TNA CAB 24/105/81.
22   *Daily Herald*, 19 May 1920.
23   *The Times*, 6 Aug 1920.

published a Sunday edition, bearing the headline 'Not a man, not a gun, not a sou' for the war.[24] Home Office Director of Intelligence Basil Thomson told the cabinet 'there were remarkable demonstrations against war in practically every part of the country and, in spite of the holiday season, audiences which generally number a hundred or so grew to thousands'. One of his spies in Lancashire reported that 'never have we known such excitement and antagonism to be aroused against any project as has been aroused amongst the workers by the possibility of war with Russia. In every hand ex-servicemen are saying they will never take part in any war again. The workers are dead against a war with Russia'.[25]

On Monday 9 August, the TUC, Parliamentary Labour Party, and the Labour Party National Executive Committee met at the House of Commons. They declared that 'the whole industrial power of the organised workers will be used to defeat this war' and set up a Council of Action. Within days 350 local councils of action had been established. That Friday, over a thousand delegates attended a hastily-called national conference and heard arch right-winger J.H. Thomas declare that 'only desperate and dangerous methods will provide a remedy' to the threat of war, which might require 'a challenge to the whole constitution of the country'.[26] The delegates voted for the Council of Action to take 'any steps that may be necessary and not to disband until it had secured peace'.[27] 'Peace with Soviet Russia. End the Wars! End the Blockade' proclaimed its leaflets.[28] The following day the Council of Action met Lloyd George for the second time, and Ernest Bevin told the prime minister they wanted to meet Russian ministers Lev Kamenev and Leonard Krassin, who were visiting Britain on a trade mission, to hear the Russian viewpoint.

However, as Britain spiralled towards a general strike, Polish forces led by the French general Maxime Weygand began to push the Russians back and on 18 August Tukhachevsky ordered the Red Army to withdraw. The crisis was averted, the Labour Party and trade union leaders breathed a sigh of belief, and the Council of Action was quietly dismantled. It may not have stopped the war, but

---

24   *Daily Herald*, 8 Aug 1920.

25   *Fortnightly Report*, no. 67, 12 Aug 1920, TNA CAB 24/110/72. Although some historians have cast doubt on the reliability of Thomson's reports, on this occasion the impressions of his agent are at one with newspaper and other contemporary reports.

26   Council of Action, *Report of the Special Conference on Labour and the Russian-Polish War* (London, 1920), p. 14.

27   *Daily Herald*, 13 Aug 1920.

28   See the official leaflet 'Peace with Soviet Russia' dated 17 Aug 1920, at PHM CP/IND/POLL/1/8.

the wave of working-class action against intervention sent a shiver of existential fear down the spine of the British ruling class.[29]

1   Towards Unity ... and the Labour Party?

The united front campaign to defend Soviet Russia inevitably led to discussions among Marxist groups about creating a united party based on the example of the Bolsheviks. For the BSP, this was part of a process that began before the war when they created the United Socialist Council (USC) with the ILP and the Fabian Society. In August 1916 the BSP and the ILP revived the USC, albeit without the Fabians. The BSP's Easter 1917 conference endorsed the reborn USC and the following year the BSP conference voted to seek unity with both the ILP and the SLP, and the three organisations met in November 1918.

At the same time, the leftward evolution of Sylvia Pankhurst's Workers' Socialist Federation brought it into to the orbit of the BSP, and in the spring of 1918 the two organisations also began unity discussions. By now the WSF had extended its reach beyond its base in the East End of London – where it had an almost daily cycle of meetings and other activities – with 22 branches across Britain, including Birmingham, Glasgow, Leeds, Manchester and Mid-Rhondda in the heart of the South Wales coalfield.[30] To what extent the members of the WSF shared Pankhurst's movement towards Marxism is unclear; with the exception of campaigning for Soviet Russia, the work of the branches continued the propaganda meetings and community work that the ELFS did before the war. The WSF was, in the words of Claude McKay, 'a one-woman show, not broad-based enough to play a decisive role in the labour movement' and its politics were almost entirely dictated by Pankhurst.[31] Nevertheless, its leftism became a pole of attraction for serious militants such as engineering shop-stewards William Watson and Harry Pollitt, not to mention McKay himself. Even after it had ceased to view itself as a women's suffrage group, the WSF had a significantly higher proportion of female members and leaders than almost any other organisation in the labour movement. At its 1918 conference thirteen of its fifteen national committee members were women.[32]

---

29   For the history of the Council of Action see White 1974a.

30   *Workers' Dreadnought*, 23 Feb1918, and 'WSF Report from 1 January to 31 March 1917' in E. Sylvia Pankhurst papers 1863–1960, International Institute of Social History, Amsterdam, Reel 25, File 217.

31   McKay 1985, p. 87.

32   *Workers' Dreadnought*, 1 June 1918.

According to Pankhurst, the BSP was the suitor in the unity discussions. It approached the WSF in the spring of 1918, shortly after conscription was extended to all men below fifty years old, because it feared its entire leadership would be conscripted. Pankhurst recalled 'the tentative offer of fusion was very cordially received', and she wrote *The Call*'s front-page article for its May Day issue.[33] At that year's Labour Party conference she proposed the BSP's motion demanding the Labour Party withdraw from the war-time coalition. There was also some collaboration at local level, such as when the WSF's Sheffield branch held a joint meeting with the BSP in February 1918.[34] Even so, in late April the WSF committee turned down a merger proposal.[35] The WSF finance committee discussed the issue two weeks later, where Pankhurst complained that merger would mean 'our amalgamating the paper and organisation with it'.[36] This was not an acceptable outcome for her, and was no doubt exacerbated by the BSP's suggestion that the openly reformist Edwin Fairchild should edit the unified newspaper.

Pankhurst and the WSF were continuing to move leftwards towards the Bolsheviks. Whereas the BSP congratulated the Labour Party's November 1918 conference for ending its alliance with Lloyd George and called for Labour to be transformed 'into an effective and revolutionary weapon in the emancipation of the British proletariat in this period of social revolution', Pankhurst dismissed the same conference as 'a play' and wondered 'how soon the parliamentary game would end altogether'.[37] By the December 1918 General Election the WSF had moved considerably to the left of the BSP. The only election candidates it supported were John Maclean, who picked up a third of the vote against Labour leader George Barnes in Glasgow's Gorbals' constituency; ILP shop steward David Kirkwood, whose manifesto pledged 'public ownership and democratic control' of industry; and the SLP's three candidates. Pankhurst herself refused to stand as a candidate, despite rumours she would contest Sheffield's Hallam constituency, because she 'regards parliament as an out of date machine, and joins the [Workers' Socialist] Federation in working to establish soviets in Britain'.[38] Pankhurst thus became an 'anti-parliamentarian', opposed to participation in parliament or in parliamentary elections. In June 1919 the WSF decided to withdraw all its members from the Labour Party, and the fol-

---

33   'Towards a Communist Party', *Workers' Dreadnought*, 21 Feb 1920.
34   *Workers' Dreadnought*, 23 Feb and 6 July 1918.
35   WSF committee minutes, 26 April 1918, Pankhurst Papers, IISH.
36   WSF finance committee minutes, 9 May 1918, Pankhurst Papers, IISH.
37   *The Call*, 21 Nov 1918. *Workers' Dreadnought*, 23 Nov 1918.
38   *Workers' Dreadnought*, 7 Dec 1918.

lowing month the WSF's Melvina Walker and Norah Smyth were expelled from Poplar Labour Party.[39] Under the slogan of 'no affiliation to the Labour Party', the break was completed when the WSF formally changed its name to the Communist Party at its 1919 conference, although it soon dropped the title as a show of good faith during the communist unity discussions.[40]

For the BSP, the 1918 general election emphasised its growing closeness to the Labour Party. *The Call* 'congratulated [Labour] upon its election manifesto', and thirteen of its members ran as Labour Party candidates. John Maclean stood under the BSP banner but *The Call* insisted on describing him as Labour. None were elected, although a year later the Liberal MP Colonel Cecil L'Estrange Malone defected to the BSP after visiting Soviet Russia. For the BSP right wing led by Edwin Fairchild and Henry Alexander, the Labour Party was the vehicle for socialism. 'Like the elephant's tread', Alexander wrote in the summer of 1919, 'the pace of Labour may lack something in rapidity, but its surety of footing is a guarantee that every forward step taken consolidates the position preparatory to the final attack'.[41] Much of this analysis was also shared by BSP members who saw themselves as supporters of the Bolsheviks. In the run-up to its 1918 conference Joe Fineberg, the de facto leader of the Rothstein tendency, argued that the BSP must stay in the Labour Party:

> We can do one of two things. Come out of the Labour Party and leave the field to the non-socialist elements that control it now; or remain in, taking part in this political expression of the class conflict, striving to impress it with a Socialist character. If we leave the Labour Party we delimit the future of the BSP, and voluntarily condemn ourselves to hover round the fringes of Labour's action, holding street-corner meetings and drifting to stagnation.[42]

This was based on his belief that 'the Labour Party is the political expression of the working-class movement'. As it was before the war, this phrase became the primary justification for the BSP's stance towards Labour. Fred Willis, who replaced Fairchild as the editor of *The Call*, took the same tack: 'For good or ill the Labour Party is the political expression of working-class thought in this

---

39   *Workers' Dreadnought*, 14 June 1919. WSF committee minutes, 7 Aug 1919, Pankhurst Papers, IISH.

40   WSF committee minutes, 12 June 1919, Pankhurst Papers, IISH.

41   'Soviets as a Practical Proposition: A Reply to John Bryan', *The Call*, 9 June 1919.

42   'Marxism and the Labour Party', *The Call*, 7 March 1918.

country ... Ours is the task to give it socialist clarity and revolutionary leading'.[43] The debate was the centrepiece of the Easter 1918 BSP conference. Fineberg and Fairchild both spoke in favour of remaining in the Labour Party, while John Maclean and Albert Ward called for leaving. Pointing out that the Labour Party was a member of Lloyd George's cabinet which was trying to crush socialism in Russia, Maclean argued 'Labour members were an important part of the cabinet ... The BSP could run its independent candidates and fight every Labour member who stood by that government. The BSP had now the chance of leading the workers and sweeping aside the Labour Party'.[44] The conference eventually agreed to hold a referendum of the membership on the issue, which resulted in a four to one majority voting to stay in the Labour Party.

For the SLP, the 1918 general election ushered in a new era for its politics. J.T. Murphy stood as a candidate in Manchester's Gorton constituency, picking up 6.7 per cent of the vote against Labour's John Hodge, Lloyd George's former minister of pensions. William Paul contested Ince, near Wigan, winning 13 per cent of the poll in opposition to Stephen Walsh, the Labour MP who was the war-time secretary to the Ministry of National Service. In Halifax, Arthur MacManus won 15 per cent against J.H. Whitley, the Liberal who proposed class collaborationist works councils as an answer to industrial unrest in 1917. The SLP's election manifesto was militantly socialist. 'We affirm that so long as one section of the community own and control the means of production, and the rest of the community are compelled to work for that section ... there can be no peace between them', it stated unambiguously, and called for a soviet-style 'Federal Congress of People's Administrative Councils, composed of delegates from the toiling masses' to wield state power. However, it was still rooted in the abstract propaganda of the pre-war SLP. There was no mention of Soviet Russia, Ireland, nor anywhere else, despite the manifesto's '14 points' echoing US President Woodrow Wilson's 14-point peace programme to end World War One. And apart from one passing reference, it said nothing about the Labour Party or the trade unions.

For Murphy, MacManus, Paul, and Tom Bell, the campaign demonstrated the possibilities beyond the SLP's narrowly industrial focus. The party grew quickly after the war and by December 1919 it had 45 branches across Britain, including five in Wales and 17 in Scotland.[45] Recognising the rapidly changing political situation, in January 1919 Murphy published a major article in *The*

---

43   *The Call*, 10 July 1919.
44   *The Call*, 4 April 1918. *The Worker* [Huddersfield], 6 April 1918.
45   *The Socialist*, 11 Dec 1919.

Socialist called 'A Manifesto. A Plea for the Reconsideration of Socialist Tactics and Organisation'. This offered a covert critique of the SLP's pre-war ideas about the struggle for socialism. It began by restating the SLP's general election manifesto and went on to argue that the traditional division between political and educational organisations in the British working class – including by implication John Maclean's conception of independent working-class education – was mistaken: 'today we have the confusing spectacle of one body seeking to educate another how to act, while the elements leading up to action are outside the scope of the former body's control. Whereas if education and the machinery of action were parts of the one organisation the latter would respond in terms of the former'.[46]

Murphy went on to argue the war had 'shown that it is impossible to separate the political and industrial character of any grave issues'. In a passage that seemed to offer a self-criticism of his own war-time politics, he argued that 'the war has revealed that the industrial agitation of today can become the political issue of tomorrow, and vice versa', and what was needed was 'the immediate creation of a movement which will combine both the industrial and the political functions'. Despite saying little about the leadership of the Labour Party or the trade unions, Murphy's manifesto was the first time that anyone had sought to grapple with either the traditional conceptions of British Marxism or the political implications of the October Revolution. It ended with a ringing call to re-examine previous attitudes and activities, and 'banish the bias of party, the formula of tradition, the superstition of theory and the fetishism of the doctrinaire. Let us educate for revolution, let us work for revolution, and thereby achieve revolution'.

The BSP, SLP and the ILP had met again in November 1918 to discuss the potential for a united party. Once again, talks with the ILP proved fruitless, but now it was the leadership of the SLP which took the initiative towards unity. In June 1919 Murphy published 'An Appeal for a United Socialist Effort And Open Letter to Socialists' which called for all revolutionaries to unite in a single party supporting the Communist International. 'I appeal, therefore, to every socialist [to] make one further effort to create a society in this country worthy of revolutionary international socialism', he wrote.[47] To demonstrate its appetite to deepen the political re-alignment of the left, the SLP announced it was suspending its constitution to remove any organisational barriers to unity.

---

46   *The Socialist*, Jan 1919.

47   The discussions with the ILP took place on 6 and 19 March 1919; Bell 1937, p. 51; *The Socialist*, 27 March 1919; *Workers' Dreadnought*, 7 June 1919.

2   The Coming of the Communist International

As Murphy's article implied, the desire for revolutionary unity in Britain was sharpened by the formation of the Communist International in Moscow on 2 March 1919. The movement for a new revolutionary international had begun on 4 August 1914, when the German SPD voted for war credits in the Reichstag, and less than two months later Lenin wrote that 'the Second International is dead, overcome by opportunism. Down with opportunism, and long live the Third International ... To the Third International falls the task of organising the proletarian forces for a revolutionary onslaught against the capitalist governments, for civil war against the bourgeoisie of all countries for the capture of political power, for the triumph of socialism!'[48] The Bolsheviks drew a line separating revolutionaries, such as themselves, Maclean, and Liebknecht and Luxemburg in Germany, from 'social patriots' who had supported the war and 'centrists' who refused to make a clear break with them. For Lenin, the key political division was between those who sought to build a new international, and those who sought unity, even at arm's length, with those who had led the proletariat into the imperialist slaughter.

This was the basis for the call for the creation of the Communist International, which became known as the Comintern. A radio broadcast on Christmas Eve 1918 called for 'communists of all countries' to 'rally around the Third International' and on 24 January 1919 Trotsky's 'Letter of Invitation to the First Congress of the Communist International' was published. Scheduled to take place on 15 February, the difficulties of travelling to Moscow meant that the congress did not convene until 2 March. Both the broadcast appeal and Trotsky's letter invited British revolutionaries by name. 'The co-thinkers of Maclean in England [sic]' were among those in whom the radio declared 'the Third International already exists and leads the world revolution'. Of the 39 organisations invited to the founding congress, five were from Britain, along with 'revolutionary forces in Irish workers' organisations'. The five British groups were the 'left forces in the British Socialist Party (in particular, representatives of the Maclean current); the British Socialist Labour Party; the Industrial Workers of the World in Britain; the Industrial Workers group in Britain; revolutionary forces in the shop stewards' movement (Britain)'.[49]

This was a slightly confusing list, a consequence of the Bolsheviks' lack of recent knowledge of the British left. While the BSP left wing, the SLP, and

---

48   'The Position and Tasks of the Socialist International', *CW* vol. 21, pp. 40–1.
49   Riddell 1986, p. 442, which also contains Trotsky's letter. For further background, see Hulse 1964.

the revolutionary shop stewards were obvious choices, the 'Industrial Work-ers of the World in Britain' presumably meant the SLP's now defunct Industrial Workers of Great Britain and the 'Industrial Workers Group' may possibly have meant the tiny Workers International Industrial Union. Most surprising was the omission of the Workers' Socialist Federation. It is possible the list was influenced by the Bolsheviks' reliance on the BSP's Joe Fineberg for much of their information. He had returned to Russia in May 1918, where he became an important source of information about Britain for Lenin and seems to have been involved in at least one of the meetings that led to the drafting of the Christmas Eve radio broadcast.[50] Fineburg was the only British delegate at the founding Comintern congress, attending with a consultative vote for 'the British Communist Group'. His report on Britain, given on the second day, described the state of the class struggle in Britain since 1910 but said noth-ing about the organisations of the revolutionary left or the Labour Party, apart from a passing comment on 'the peculiar structure of the Labour Party con-ferences'.[51] This was a notable omission given that Moscow's December radio appeal began by denouncing Arthur Henderson and the British Labour Party's call for a conference in Lausanne to revive the Second International, but of course it reflected Fineberg's attitude to the Labour Party.

Details of the founding of the Comintern took some time to reach Britain. A short report appeared in *The Call* on 3 April and it wasn't until May that the SLP announced it had been invited by name to the congress. However, when the news did finally arrive it fundamentally altered the nature of left-wing polit-ics in Britain.[52] Firstly, it underlined the need for a single united communist party that would be part of the new international. Trotsky's 'Letter of Invitation' had stressed that the Comintern would give revolutionaries 'systematic lead-ership, subordinating the interests of the people in each country to the com-mon interests of the revolution on an international scale' and that 'the various parties [would] become its sections'. Secondly, Trotsky stressed that this meant a break with the 'centre' of the workers movement who refused to split from those who had supported the war. 'Our tactic', he wrote uncompromisingly, 'is to break away from it [the centre] the most revolutionary forces, while ruth-

---

50   The background to Fineberg's departure is laid bare in his secret service file at TNA KV-2-780 and in *Communist International* (April 1929), pp. 443–4. On Fineberg's relationship with Lenin, see Lenin's reply to Chicherin's note of 6 April 1920 in Pipes 1998, p. 80.

51   Fienberg's speech is in Riddell 1987, pp. 106–11. The British writer Arthur Ransome also attended the congress, albeit in a non-political capacity, as described in his *Russia in 1919*, pp. 213–23.

52   Bell 1937, p. 51. *The Socialist*, 15 May 1919.

lessly criticising and exposing its leaders. At a certain stage of development an organisational separation from the centrists is absolutely necessary'.[53]

In the BSP, this immediately fractured unity between the supporters of the Bolsheviks and the openly reformist tendency led by Edwin Fairchild and Harry Alexander. When shop stewards' leader William McLaine proposed that the BSP join the Comintern in April 1919, Fairchild and Alexander both opposed the motion, and Fairchild also spoke against the call for workers rule through soviets.[54] Outvoted, Fairchild resigned the editorship of *The Call* the following month, and he and Alexander left the party because of their 'emphatic disagreement with the advocacy of forcible revolution in preference to action through parliament'.[55] The shedding of its openly reformist wing meant that the BSP was now, like the SLP and the WSF, united in support of the Comintern, and the path seemed to be clear to form a unified communist party.

The only obstacles to unity were the questions of participation in parliamentary elections and affiliation to the Labour Party. Even though the WSF opposed the BSP and SLP tactic of standing in parliamentary elections, no-one saw this as an insuperable barrier to unity. The WSF even admitted that 'their views regarding parliamentary action would not be allowed to stand in the way of the formation of a united party'.[56] It was only the Labour Party question that remained to be solved. But this was the defining issue for British Marxism and the gulf that separated the BSP, SLP and WSF became obvious in June 1919 when they and the South Wales Socialist Society – which had been formed in February 1919 by leftists around the miners' Unofficial Reform Movement on the basis of opposition to the Labour Party – met to map out a route to a unified British communist party.[57] The BSP delegates pointed out its members had voted four to one against leaving the Labour Party in 1918 and told the meeting that it was 'conditional upon any steps in the direction of unity that the basis of amalgamation should include the affiliation of the new organisation to the Labour Party'.[58] Affiliation was a principle which the BSP would not abandon, and this would become the determining factor throughout the unity

---

53   Quoted in Riddell 1986, pp. 450–1.

54   The April 1919 BSP conference is reported in *The Call*, 24 April 1919.

55   MacFarlane 1966, p. 22, says they resigned because of 'outside' interference in the BSP, but their statement in *The Globe* of 20 Oct 1919 clearly states they left because of political differences. Fairchild later joined the ILP, see *Labour Leader*, 23 Sept 1920.

56   *The Call*, 21 Aug 1919.

57   For the South Wales Socialist Society, see *Merthyr Pioneer*, 22 Feb 1919; *Workers' Dreadnought*, 19 June 1920; Pankhurst 1932, pp. 412–14; Leeworthy 2018, pp. 228–30; Jones 2010, pp. 17–24.

58   *The Call*, 21 Aug 1919.

discussions. As the other three organisations opposed joining the Labour Party, negotiations immediately hit a brick wall. As a compromise, the SLP delegates appear to have proposed holding a referendum on affiliation to Labour one year after the new party's founding congress, and the meeting eventually agreed to a motion stating:

> That the membership of the various organisations be consulted as to their willingness to merge the existing organisations in a united party having for its object the establishment of communism by means of the dictatorship of the working class working through soviets; and that the question of the affiliation of the new party to the Labour Party be decided by a referendum of the members three months after the new party is formed.[59]

However, this compromise collapsed as soon as the non-BSP delegates reported back to their organisations. Only the South Wales Socialist Society seems to have accepted the proposal but the Society was a loose and unstable organisation with little political authority. It collapsed by the time of the CPGB unity convention – it had no delegates at the convention – and its leading members formed the Communist Party of South Wales which was allied with Sylvia Pankhurst.[60] When the WSF committee discussed the SLP's compromise proposal, Pankhurst warned that it might lose control of the *Workers' Dreadnought* and its offices, and demanded separate negotiations to discuss how its assets could be protected.[61]

On 16 July, while the unity talks were taking place, Pankhurst wrote to Lenin asking for his 'views of action upon the parliamentary field', because she felt 'the question of action on the parliamentary field keeps everything back. The BSP and the SLP still cling to the idea of running parliamentary candidates, and this is repugnant to the revolutionary industrial worker, the WSF and the SWSS'. She dismissed the BSP as believing itself 'to be much advanced than the ILP, but is often little better from a communist outlook. Both these parties think too much of electoral successes and when they have gained such successes they almost invariably betray the workers'.[62] Her article was unsigned and attributed to 'a leading English communist'. Lenin's reply was printed alongside it in the September 1919 issue of the Comintern journal *Communist International*, in

---

59   *The Call*, 21 Aug 1919.
60   Macfarlane 1966, p. 65.
61   WSF Committee minutes, 17 July 1919, IISH.
62   'Socialism in Great Britain', *The Communist International*, Old Series no. 5 (Sept 1919), pp. 50–1.

which he sympathised with her hostility to parliament but said 'I am person-ally convinced that to renounce participation in the parliamentary elections is a mistake on the part of the revolutionary workers of Britain'. Prefiguring his soon-to-be published *Left-Wing Communism: An Infantile Disorder*, he argued that an anti-parliamentarian stance showed 'a lack of revolutionary experi-ence'. He ended by saying that if the issue of parliamentary participation was the only obstacle to a unified communist party in Britain, then 'I should con-sider a good step forward to complete unity the immediate formation of two communist parties' because such a situation 'would most likely be a transition to complete unity'.[63] This exchange appears to have gone unnoticed when it first was published but it would later play in crucial role in the collapse of nego-tiations a few months later.

For the SLP, the unity discussions pitched it into its deepest crisis since the outbreak of World War One. It soon became clear that the SLP leaders in charge of the negotiations – Bell, MacManus, Murphy and Paul – did not have the sup-port of the majority of members.[64] In December the internal dispute poured out onto the pages of *The Socialist*, as letter after letter denounced the negotiat-ors for compromising with the BSP and undermining the SLP's opposition to the Labour Party.[65] In January Tom Bell resigned as editor of *The Socialist*. Shortly after, Arthur MacManus was suspended, and William Paul abruptly withdrew as the party candidate in the Paisley parliamentary by-election, citing the SLP's 'stupid sectarianism' towards the unity negotiations and the 'humiliating spec-tacle the SLP cuts in the eyes of our Russian comrades who are sweeping the armies of imperialism out of their Soviet country'.[66] This decision appears to have been encouraged by the Executive Committee of the Comintern, which was growing impatient with the deadlocked talks and now stressed the urgency of securing the participation of the WSF.[67]

The SLP executive repudiated the actions of its negotiating team and organ-ised a two-part referendum of its members. The first part asked if they were in favour of forming a united communist party, and the second if they sup-ported affiliation to Labour. To no-one's surprise, SLP members voted for a united party and against affiliation. The result, according to an editorial in *The*

63   Lenin, *CW* vol. 29, pp. 561–6.
64   See the debate between the Sheffield and Bridgeton branches in *The Socialist*, 17 and 31 July 1919.
65   See, for example, letters in *The Socialist* throughout Dec 1919 and Jan 1920.
66   *The Worker* [Glasgow], 6 March 1920.
67   MacManus in Transcript of Discussion, Communist International, English Commission (19 June 1923) RGASPI. F. 495. Op. 38. D. 1, Day 2, p. 15.

Socialist, 'demonstrated in no uncertain manner that the SLP, despite much effort to the contrary, still stands firmly on the bed-rock of no compromise with the LP and are determined not to be inveigled into an alliance with such reactionaries'.[68] From that point, the SLP effectively withdrew from the unity negotiations and began to revert to an increasingly desiccated version of its pre-war self, expelling Bell, MacManus and Paul for 'insubordination' and 'disruptive actions'.[69] They and 11 other expelled SLPers formed the Communist Unity Group (CUG) on the basis of opposition to affiliation to the Labour Party and for unity with the BSP and WSF. The CUG held a conference in Nottingham in April 1920, attended by only 22 supporters, who were joined by the SLP's Cardiff branch in May 1920, and its public propaganda was limited to two regular pages in *The Call* that the BSP granted it. It had essentially become the left wing of the BSP.[70]

3   **Britain and the Amsterdam Bureau**

By this time J.T. Murphy had broken with his comrades in the CUG and had become the SLP's major polemicist against unity with the BSP. At the start of February 1920 he and Pankhurst, together with the BSP's Fred Willis and John Hodgson, attended a meeting of the newly established West European Bureau of the Comintern in Amsterdam.[71] The Executive Committee of the Comintern set up the bureau in September 1919, and sent the Dutch revolutionary S.J. Rutgers to Amsterdam to establish a base for propaganda and organise a conference of European and American communists.[72] Rutgers was a leading member of the *Tribune* group which split from the reformist Dutch Social Democratic Workers' Party in March 1909 to create the revolutionary Social Democratic Party. On the far left of the Second International, Rutgers and his comrades were seen as allies by the Bolsheviks before and during World War One, and so the Comintern leadership assumed the new bureau would be in safe hands.

---

68   *The Socialist*, 19 Feb 1920.

69   *The Socialist*, 6 May 1920.

70   22 people signed the CUG's *Manifesto on Communist Unity* issued after its Nottingham conference, a copy of which is in the People's History Museum, CP/CENT/CONG/01/01.

71   According to Gerrit Mannoury's report of his visit to England in January 1920, John Maclean was originally going with Willis 'if they can obtain a passport' for him: Mannoury, *Report of a Visit to England*, RGASPI. F. 497. Op. 1. D. 7, p. 2.

72   For the full story of the Amsterdam Bureau, see Voerman 2007; Yamanouchi 2008; and the *Bulletin of the Provisional Bureau in Amsterdam of the Communist International*, No. 1 (Feb 1920).

Sixteen delegates attended the Amsterdam Bureau's first and only conference in early February. In addition to the four British delegates, it comprised representatives of the Dutch, Swiss and Belgian Communist Parties, as well as the opposition in the German Communist Party (which later that April would break away to form the Kommunistische Arbeiterpartei Deutschlands), the American CP leader Louis Fraina (recently elected chairman of the Communist Party of America at its founding congress), Comintern representative Michael Borodin and non-voting representatives from communist groups in China, the Dutch Indies and Hungary. Delegates from the German, Austrian and Rumanian communist parties and the left-wing of the Spanish Socialist Party arrived after the conference was adjourned when delegates discovered police listening devices in their meeting rooms.[73]

Although it never reconvened, the conference passed a 'Resolution on Unity' stating it was 'necessary that communist groups still in the old reformist and opportunist parties ... should sever their compromising relations' on the basis of 'no compromise with bourgeois or social-patriotic parties, with parties affiliated with the Second International or with the agents of capitalism in the labour movement'.[74] The BSP's Fred Willis did not oppose the resolution because he claimed it was not binding and that the new British party would decide its own tactics towards Labour.[75] Even so, as Louis Fraina implied, the resolution was aimed at the BSP: 'the Communist Party about to be organised in England by unity of British Socialist Party, the Socialist Labour Party, Workers' Socialist Federation and South Wales Socialist Party, must reject affiliation with the Labour Party – the British Socialist Party favours this affiliation, the others are against'.[76] The Bureau later circulated a statement stating 'we strongly appeal to our English friends to unite on the basis of no affiliation to the Labour Party, as we clearly see the catastrophe that will follow the coming into power of a parliamentary Labour government'. It also attacked the BSP's proposal that local branches should decide whether to join Labour: 'a compromise in such a way that local organisations are allowed a policy that is considered objection-

---

73   See Hulse 1964, pp. 152–8. and Draper 1957, pp. 232–6.

74   *Bulletin of the Provisional Bureau in Amsterdam of the Communist International*, No. 2 (March 1920), pp. 7–8, which also contains the full minutes of the meeting. Fraina's account of the meeting is detailed but not strictly accurate in its wording of resolutions, see his 'The International Communist Conference', *The Communist* [Communist Party of America], 1 May 1920.

75   Willis and J.F. Hodgson's Report on the Movement in Great Britain (BSP) is at RGASPI. F. 497. Op. 1. D. 8.

76   'The International Communist Conference', *The Communist* [Communist Party of America], 1 May 1920. *Bulletin of the Provisional Bureau*, No. 2, p. 8.

able as a general method must lead to confusion when accepted by a united communist party'.[77] Murphy himself warned that there was a danger that the Comintern could be 'swamped' by 'muddle-headed leaders of the Second International' and that 'nowhere is there greater danger of this than in Great Britain, where social sentiment gives place so much to clear thinking'.[78]

The Amsterdam delegates also passed other resolutions putting them at odds with the Comintern leadership. It called for 'a struggle against trades unionism', speculated that 'in a period of actual revolution the complete repudiation of parliamentarism may become necessary', and denounced the German Communist Party for its 'hesitation, evasion and compromise' in trade union work.[79] In fact, Rutgers and the Dutch leadership of the Amsterdam Bureau were closer to the ultra-left Kommunistische Arbeiterpartei Deutschlands, who opposed work in existing trade unions, participation in parliamentary elections, and any joint activity whatsoever with parties of the Second International.[80] Two months after the Amsterdam conference, the Executive Committee of the Comintern dissolved the bureau on the grounds that 'on a number of questions (trade unions, parliament), the Dutch bureau has adopted an attitude inconsistent with that of the Executive Committee. The Dutch Bureau did not inform the Executive Committee of its differing point of view before convening the international conference in Amsterdam'.[81]

From a British perspective, the Amsterdam Bureau's opposition to Labour Party affiliation appeared to give Comintern approval to Sylvia Pankhurst. For J.T. Murphy, the strength of the arguments by the Amsterdam delegates against affiliation to Labour convinced him that unity with the BSP would be unprincipled, and he abandoned his support for a united British party. 'There must be no compromise with the BSP. Better a communist party without the BSP than a party including the BSP, trailing with it the spirit of compromise to hamper the party in its revolutionary practice', he wrote in April.[82] The BSP leadership

---

77   'Communist Unity in Britain and the Labour Party', *The Socialist*, 6 May 1920. The BSP's reply to the Amsterdam Bureau is in *The Call*, 13 May 1920.

78   J.T. Murphy, *Report on the Present Conditions of the Political Movements in Britain*, March 1920. RGASPI. F. 497. Op. 1. D. 8. Pankhurst's report to the conference, *Report on the British Movement*, can also be found in the same file.

79   All quotations are from 'The International Communist Conference', *The Communist* [Communist Party of America], 1 May 1920.

80   For a full account of their politics, see Bourrinet 2016, ch. 4.

81   Degras 1956, vol. 1, p. 94. A fuller version of the Comintern decision, 'The Third International and Amsterdam' is in *The Call*, 20 May 1920.

82   'An Open Letter to the Party', *The Socialist*, 6 May 1920. He explains his changed position in *The Socialist*, 29 April 1920. In his autobiography, Murphy disingenuously claims that he

was now worried that Amsterdam had handed the initiative to Pankhurst and its leftist opponents, and *The Call* began to wage all-out war against her and, to a lesser extent, Murphy. In late January Tom Quelch said that Pankhurst's description of the BSP in her letter to Lenin was a 'lie' and that the BSP only wanted to have MPs in parliament 'to secure "points of vantage" from which to assail the capitalist enemy'.[83] At the end of February, Theodore Rothstein's son Andrew weighed in with a two-part article on 'The Labour Party and the Communists' which attacked Pankhurst as 'petty-bourgeois', while J.B. Askew warned 'our foreign friends' to be 'very careful in admitting to their columns such anonymous attacks'.[84]

As Gerrit Mannoury discovered when he visited England on behalf of the Amsterdam Bureau in the first week of 1920, there was a strong personal dislike of Pankhurst in the BSP. Theodore Rothstein told him that 'she was not at all fit for the task [of leading an international conference] in his opinion'.[85] A few weeks later Fred Willis defended the BSP's parliamentary policy against the 'mere bourgeois' Pankhurst, who he claimed was incapable of understanding the BSP's 'distinctively working class' approach to politics, although his allies included Andrew Rothstein, who attended Oxford's Balliol College, and the Old Etonian J.B. Askew. Under pressure, the BSP instinctively resorted to Hyndman-style personal vilification. Murphy, who had been arrested in Germany after the Amsterdam conference, was called a hypocrite for appealing for the BSP's help to free him from prison: 'who is J.T. Murphy, anyhow?' taunted Willis.[86] When the WSF's Harold Burgess was jailed in May for six months for distributing leaflets titled 'Soviets for the British' to soldiers in the Irish Guards' regiment, *The Call* accused him of 'playing at revolution' and complained 'the government only succeeds in making itself look ridiculous' by prosecuting those with a 'comic opera mind'.[87]

The ferocity of the BSP's attacks on Pankhurst and Murphy, together with the response of the WSF, the passivity of the SLP, and Murphy's abrupt political switch, fatally undermine the widespread idea that 'Russian material aid' was

---

tried to maintain unity and that Bell, MacManus and Paul were responsible for the split; see Murphy 1941, p. 180.

83   'Parliamentarism: Lenin and the BSP', *The Call*, 22 Jan 1920. The SLP had printed Pankhurst's letter and Lenin's reply in *The Socialist* a week previously on 15 January.

84   Both articles in *The Call*, 26 Feb 1920.

85   Mannoury, *Report of a Visit to England 4–10 January 1920*, p. 12. RGASPI. F. 497. Op. 1. D. 7.

86   *The Call*, 6 May and 13 May 1920.

87   *The Call*, 27 May 1920. Both of these incidents were gleefully reported in the *Fortnightly Report on Revolutionary Organisations in the UK*, 54, 13 May 1920, TNA CAB/24/105/81.

a crucial factor in the creation of the Communist Party.[88] Substantial amounts of money did flow from Moscow via Theodore Rothstein to the BSP, WSF, SLP and, for short time, George Lansbury's *Daily Herald*.[89] This was well known on the left – 'we would welcome Bolshevik money' admitted *The Call* mischievously in August 1919, while the *Herald* openly asked its readers 'Shall we accept £75,000 of Russian money?' – and also to the British secret service, who estimated in September 1920 that the Comintern had sent around £100,000 to Britain that year alone.[90] In February 1921, Francis Meynell, the then editor of the CPGB weekly *The Communist* boasted in its pages how he had smuggled jewellery supplied by the Comintern into Britain.[91] But this money did not make the slightest difference to the political stance of any of these groups. Wrong or right on the issues facing the working class, none of them steered their politics in pursuit of 'Moscow Gold'. Each believed in its politics regardless of the material consequences, contrary to Walter Kendall's belief that the Comintern unnaturally interfered with the development of homegrown British revolutionary organisations. Their inability to compromise demonstrated that money could not persuade them to abandon their political differences. It was the Comintern and its representatives who sought to show the British groups that their differences could be contained in a single communist party and overcome the proprietorial attitudes that predominated on the British left.

Despite the urging of the Comintern, the unity negotiations disintegrated. On 21 April SLP secretary Tom Mitchell told the BSP's Albert Inkpin that 'no good purpose can be served by further discussion'.[92] Three days later, the BSP, CUG, WSF and SWSS met in London in a final attempt to salvage the unity talks. The meeting also agreed to seat a non-voting representative of the 'Left Wing of the ILP' which had recently been formed by 160 ILPers as an explicitly pro-Third International faction of the ILP.[93] Its representative

---

88 Kendall 1969, p. 256. There is extensive detail on Comintern financial support for the creation of the CPGB in Morgan 2006, pp. 34–59.

89 For more on the *Daily Herald* money, see Richards 1997, pp. 28–30.

90 *The Call*, 7 Aug 1919. *Daily Herald*, 10 Sept 1920. *Fortnightly Report on Revolutionary Organisations in the UK*, no. 78, 23 Sept 1920, TNA CAB/24/111/88. *Report on Sylvia Pankhurst & Rothstein, Theodore* 1 Oct 1920, TNA KV2/1576.

91 *The Communist*, 12 Feb 1921.

92 *The Socialist*, 6 May 1920.

93 WSF minutes, 14 May 1920. The 'Declaration of the Left Wing of the ILP' was published in *The Communist International*, no. 11/12, June–July 1920, cols. 2461–6. According to the *Fortnightly Report*, no. 47, 25 March 1920, the declaration was written and financed by Shapurji Saklatvala, see TNA CAB 24/101/61 and 'The Call of the Third International', *The International*, 25 Sept 1920.

was C.H. Norman, a former SDFer and a leader of the No Conscription Fellowship. Earlier in April the ILP voted to disaffiliate from the Second International but against joining the Third, despite the ILP's Scottish, Welsh and North-West England regional conferences all voting for affiliation to the Comintern.

However, this potential breakthrough in the ILP does not appear to have been discussed at the unity meeting, which saw John Hodgson reiterate the BSP's offer to drop its call for national affiliation to Labour if Communist Party branches could join their local Labour Parties individually.[94] This was rejected in favour of Pankhurst's motion that 'we proceed to the formation of a communist party on the basis of non-affiliation to the Labour Party', which passed by eight votes to the three of the BSP delegates. William Paul of the CUG then proposed a motion in favour of participation in parliamentary elections which was passed by five votes to the WSF's two. The meeting ended with an agreement to call a national convention of all groups on 29 May 'to settle all outstanding issues'.[95]

Unconvinced that the BSP would abide by the decision, Pankhurst invited the SLP to re-join the unity discussions to provide a counter-weight. This, she argued, would allow the opponents of affiliation to debate the issue with the BSP rank and file: 'should the elements best suited to form a communist party come together and agree upon a policy, they might shed the opportunist element and form a party that would do good work and secure the confidence of the mass of the movement'. In response, the SLP reiterated that it saw 'no good purpose' in further meetings but instead suggested the WSF and the SLP should discuss unity with the SWSS, the Irish Communist Party, the British Section International Socialist Labour Party (an earlier minuscule split from the SLP) and the Socialist Party of Great Britain.[96] This was not a serious proposal, and it left Pankhurst and the WSF completely isolated.

Needless to say, when the WSF met with the BSP and CUG again at the end of May another stalemate ensued. The BSP and the CUG insisted that a united communist party should be formed immediately, and that all parties should agree in advance to abide by the decisions of the founding congress. Anticipating they would be in a minority, the WSF stalled for time by claiming they would have to ballot its membership before making a decision, but the BSP and

---

94 The 'local autonomy' option was enthusiastically endorsed by the BSP's conference, see Albert Inkpin, 'British Communists in Conference', *Communist International* (June–July 1920), no. 11–12, pp. 2233–40.

95 *The Call*, 15 May 1920.

96 Pankhurst's letter and the SLP reply are in *The Socialist*, 3 June 1920.

the CUG now had the bit between their teeth. They combined to vote in favour of holding the founding conference of the new communist party in London on 1 August 1920.[97]

In response, the WSF organised its own 'Communist Revolutionary Conference' for 19 June at which it changed its name to the Communist Party (British Section of the Third International). This conference was attended by the WSF and delegates representing unaffiliated communist groups in Aberdeen, Croydon, Holt, Stepney, Gorton, and Manchester, along with the eccentric Edgar Whitehead's one-man Labour Abstentionist Party. The conference passed a motion declaring 'we Revolutionary Communist delegates and individuals pledge ourselves to the Third International, the dictatorship of the proletariat, the soviet system, non-affiliation to the Labour Party, and to abstention from parliamentary action; and decide not to take part in the August 1st Unity Conference, or in the Unity negotiations concerned with it'. Having cleaved to their own path, the delegates scheduled the inaugural congress of their new communist party for Manchester on 22 September.[98]

4   The Fate of John Maclean

Missing from these negotiations was the man most closely associated with Bolshevism in Britain: John Maclean. Still in jail when the war ended, Maclean's imprisonment was raised by Labour Party leader George Barnes in the War Cabinet a fortnight after the Armistice, arguing that his continued imprisonment could have 'bad results on the public mind' now the war was over.[99] The issue was discussed again by the War Cabinet two days later, and on 2 December 1918 Maclean was given a 'free pardon' and released from jail.[100] He arrived by train in Glasgow the following day, to be greeted by as many as 100,000 people cheering his return.[101]

This was Maclean's second period of incarceration during the war. He also spent from April 1916 to June 1917 in prison, when he was freed to placate working-class Glaswegians who had been angered when Lloyd George was made a freeman of the city. On his release he immediately resumed his revolutionary activities. In March 1918 the Secretary for Scotland, Robert Munro,

---

97   *The Call*, 3 June 1920. The conference actually started on 31 July.
98   *Workers' Dreadnought*, 26 June 1920.
99   War Cabinet minutes, 26 Nov 1918, TNA CAB 24/70/82.
100   War Cabinet minutes: 28 Nov 1918, TNA CAB 23/42/10, and 2 Dec 1918, TNA CAB 24/71/101.
101   *The Call*, 5 Dec 1918.

wrote to the War Cabinet urging that 'criminal proceedings' be taken against Maclean because of his anti-war propaganda, which seems to have been provoked by police concerns about his influence among miners in the Fife coalfields.[102] Maclean was arrested once again and sentenced to five years' penal servitude for sedition. It was at this trial that he made his famous speech from the dock of Edinburgh High Court in which he declared 'I am not here, then, as the accused; I am here as the accuser of capitalism dripping with blood from head to foot'.[103]

Maclean paid a heavy price for this defiance. As with many other leftist, pacifist and colonial political prisoners, the British prison authorities subjected Maclean to psychological and physical torture. 'They attempted [to interfere with] my head but failed and then my bronchial tubes and partly succeeded', he wrote to Peter Petroff in July 1917. Just how they tried to interfere with his head was revealed at the BSP's April 1917 conference when delegates were told how 'when Maclean is immersed in study in the evenings, one favourite trick is to lower and higher the gas in his cell in rapid succession. This has the effect of thoroughly unsettling his mind. Afterwards the cell door is suddenly thrown open, and a hollow voice calls out "John, you are wandering"'.[104] He was refused newspapers, restricted to one visitor and one letter in 10 months, and forced to work outdoors. He also claimed that his food was adulterated while in prison.[105] As might be expected, the prison authorities denied there was anything wrong with the food it served Maclean and force-fed him from July to December 1918.[106] The impact that such treatment had on prisoners' mental health was seen by its effect on Maclean's lieutenant James MacDougall and former SLP leader John Muir, whose treatment in Edinburgh's Calton Jail in 1916 led to both suffering nervous breakdowns.

Maclean's reaction to such torture led the Scottish Office to suggest in 1917 that he 'shewed [sic] signs of insanity', the first time that his mental health was questioned.[107] His state of mind would be constantly raised by the British state. This reached its most absurd in January 1920 when a police spy claimed Maclean was insane because of his 'constant references to "spies" being present at public and private meetings' – one of dozens of reports written by

102   Munro to War Cabinet, 7 March 1918, TNA CAB 24/44/38.
103   Milton 1973, pp. 171–4.
104   Maclean to Petroff, 4 July 1917, TNA CAB 306/431/113. J. Townend, 'Impressions of a Delegate', *The Worker* [Huddersfield], 14 April 1917.
105   Rubin 1980.
106   'Demand Maclean's Release', *The Call*, 31 Dec 1918.
107   'Forward copy letter from John Maclean to Prisoner', 6 July 1917, TNA CAB 306/431/113.

actual spies present at Maclean's actual public and private meetings![108] As was often the case with revolutionaries, the accusation of madness was based on Maclean's advocacy of the overthrow of capitalism. He was not the only revolutionary to have his sanity impugned. Just days before the October Revolution, the Russian Provisional Government's new Consul-General in London, Alexander Onou, told a Foreign Office aide 'in confidence that Chicherin was quite mad and in the hands of Jews and German spies'.[109] Less than six months later, Chicherin was the Soviet People's Commissar for Foreign Affairs.

In later years, Maclean's mental health was used to explain his estrangement from the negotiations to form the Communist Party. Both Willie Gallacher and Tom Bell pointed to what Bell called Maclean's 'persecution obsession' about spies as the reason he did not join the CPGB, and in Gallacher's case to justify his own political disagreements with Maclean during the war.[110] Maclean did accuse a number of people of working for the government. One of his targets was the former Liberal MP Colonel Cecil L'Estrange Malone who joined the BSP in November 1919. Previously a member of the anti-communist Reconstruction Society, Malone declined to resign his parliamentary seat and traded on his status as an MP to become a prominent BSP speaker. In late 1920 he was convicted of sedition and sentenced to six months in prison, but to avoid jail, Malone offered the prosecution 'a verbal undertaking to exercise a restraining influence on the communists'.[111] The government turned down his offer to work on their behalf but his actions confirmed Maclean's distrust of him.

In contrast, and contradicting claims he saw police agents everywhere, Maclean supported William Watson, a leader of the London Workers' Committee who wrote for the *Workers' Dreadnought*, when he was accused of spying for the police. Watson admitted passing information to the police but claimed none of it was confidential and that he was trying to mislead the authorities.[112] Maclean accepted Watson's defence, using the case to highlight the dangers

---

108   *Fortnightly Report on Revolutionary Organisations in the UK*, no. 39, 29 Jan 1920, CAB/24/97/24.
109   'Foreign Office memorandum', 25 Oct 1917, TNA CAB 322.428/33.
110   Gallacher 1966, pp. 117–18; Bell 1944, p. 124.
111   His arrest is discussed in *Fortnightly Report on Revolutionary Organisations in the UK*, no. 80, 11 Nov 1920, CAB 24/114, and his offer to collaborate in no. 88, 13 Jan 1921, CAB 24/118/54.
112   That Watson did pass information to Scotland Yard is confirmed in *Fortnightly Report on Revolutionary Organisations in the UK*, no. 33, 10 Feb 1919, TNA CAB 24/75/16. For more, see *Workers' Dreadnought*, 23 Aug, 13 Sept and 13 Dec 1919. J.T. Murphy was also approached by British intelligence in the spring of 1918, see his articles in the *Daily Herald*, 13 and 14 Aug 1919.

of 'contacts with Scotland Yard' and warning militants that the British ruling class would always 'resort to treacherous cunning (spies) as well as brute force (police, army, navy, air force) to maintain their privilege to rob'.[113]

Maclean's most controversial accusation was aimed at Theodore Rothstein. In March 1920 a police agent reported that Maclean's insanity was demonstrated by his public accusation that Rothstein was a government agent.[114] However, it was a fact that Rothstein had been employed by MI7, the propaganda and censorship division of British Military Intelligence. Maclean was not the only one to question his occupation. As a secret service report noted, 'the London labour movement was very uneasy' when it was discovered where Rothstein worked.[115] He began working as a translator in MI7's foreign press unit in 1916 when his employer at the *Daily Review of the Foreign Press* 'lent' him to the War Office.[116] MI7 found that 'his knowledge of languages and of Russian socialist parties was most useful' but he was nevertheless kept under surveillance by MI5 and his mail intercepted.[117] In May 1917 H.M. Hyndman warned the Foreign Office that employing Rothstein was 'entirely opposed to the public interest', but after an investigation by MI5 it was decided to take no action.[118]

The historian John Saville later described Rothstein's duties at MI7 as merely translating and editing, but such activities were not innocent, as translations of articles in *Pravda* and *Novoye Vremya* were used in a dossier justifying George Chicherin's arrest in August 1917, although it is impossible to know if these were Rothstein's work.[119] Eventually, in October 1918 MI5 requested his arrest and deportation 'as an undesirable Bolshevik'. He was interviewed in November by Basil Thomson, then working for Scotland Yard but soon to become the Home Office's Director of Intelligence. He claimed that Rothstein told him 'he was not in favour of the proceedings of the Bolshevists' and concluded 'I think that the decision to allow him to continue his work at the War Office is a wise one'. According to a note in Rothstein's secret service file, he worked for MI7 until August 1919, by which time he was also working closely with Maxim Litvinov,

---

113   'The Attack on W.F. Watson', *The Worker*, 30 Aug 1919.

114   *Fortnightly Report on Revolutionary Organisations in the UK*, no. 46, 18 March 1920, CAB 24/101/2. Gallacher 1966, p. 141.

115   'Precis of Information regarding Theodore Rothstein', 15 Sept 1920, TNA KV2/1575.

116   Unsigned and unaddressed internal letter, 11 Sept 1916, TNA KV2/1575/117143.

117   'Precis of Information regarding Theodore Rothstein', 15 Sept 1920, TNA KV2/1575.

118   Hyndman to R.W. Seton-Watson, 8 May 1917, TNA KV2/1575.

119   'George Tchitcherine', 18 Sept 1917, TNA CAB 322.428/28. John Saville 'Introduction' to Rothstein 1983, p. xii.

the official Soviet representative in Britain.[120] There is, however, no evidence that Rothstein passed information about his political activities to the British authorities.

Maclean's suspicion of Rothstein was fundamentally based on distrust of his politics. Since at least 1915, Rothstein had been an opponent of Maclean. He stood against Maclean's desire to break with Hyndman before 1916, differed in his analysis of the war-time Clydeside strikes, and opposed the Scot's revolutionary opposition to World War One. In June 1918 Rothstein was even invited by Leonard Woolf to become a consultative member of the Labour Party's international advisory committee.[121] For Maclean, the Bolshevik victory in October 1917 had proved him correct and Rothstein wrong. But still trapped in the conventions of pre-war British social democracy, in which socialism was primarily about individual education and moral steadfastness, Maclean was unable to understand how his opponent could now speak on behalf of the Bolsheviks. In Maclean's worldview, Rothstein's rise could only be explained by malicious intent. This also accounts for Maclean's attitude to Willie Gallacher, whom Maclean attacked as a 'government instrument' in 1921.[122] Gallacher too was an opponent of Maclean and Petroff on Clydeside during the war, but following the Second Congress of the Comintern he now had the ear of Lenin.

This inability to break with pre-war conceptions of socialism became the determining factor in Maclean's politics after 1918. His work focused not on building a revolutionary political party but on establishing a Scottish Labour College. This was to be a version of the Central Labour College that had been established in 1909 by the Plebs League. As Maclean outlined in his 1916 pamphlet *A Plea For A Labour College For Scotland*, the college would be a place where workers would learn economics, history, social science and labour law, as well as practical skills such as public speaking, book-keeping and typewriting. So equipped, argued Maclean, militants could take their places in the front line of the class war.[123] The college was modelled on the educational institutions of the German SPD: 'the workers in Germany have already accomplished all that we are anxious to see done for the full training and equipment of our class'. However, as the example of the SPD illustrated, knowledge of Marxist theory

---

120   Note 59 dated August 1920, and 'Precis of Information regarding Theodore Rothstein', 15 Sept 1920, both in TNA KV2/1575.

121   Woolf to Rothstein, 4 June 1918, TNA CAB KV2/1575.

122   *The Socialist*, 13 Jan 1921.

123   John Maclean, *A Plea For A Labour College For Scotland* at https://www.marxists.org/archive/maclean/works/1916-labour.htm, accessed 13 April 2017. See also his articles on the SLC in *The Worker*, 10 and 31 May 1919.

did not necessarily translate into revolutionary politics. Moreover, he sought to finance the college by donations from sympathetic trade unions, hoping that left-wing union leaders such as Bob Smillie would pay the piper but not want to call the tune. Maclean believed that education in itself was sufficient to enlighten workers and make them understand their interests were opposed to those of the capitalists. Left unsaid was the practical question of what would bring capitalist rule to an end.

The problem with this strategy was highlighted during Glasgow's 40-hour strike in January 1919. As events accelerated during the last week of January, Maclean was not in Glasgow but on a speaking tour of mining communities in North West England. On the decisive 'Bloody Friday', he was 130 miles away addressing a meeting near Whitehaven.[124] By the time he returned home, Glasgow was firmly under the control of the authorities. One can only speculate what the impact might have been had Clydeside's unequivocally revolutionary mass working-class leader been present. Earlier in January the Lanarkshire Miners' Reform Committee, a militant group based on *The Miners' Next Step*, had appointed Maclean their official spokesman. His comrade James MacDougall was also a leader of the Fife Miners' Reform Committee. Pits in Lanarkshire and Fife were already striking for their own wage demands and in solidarity with the forty-hours struggle.[125] If Maclean and MacDougall had led a contingent of Lanarkshire and Fife miners into George Square on 30 January, the balance of class forces in Glasgow may possibly have been decisively altered. But Maclean was engaged in propaganda meetings over a hundred miles away from the epicentre of class struggle, and there was no 'Maclean party' of organised revolutionaries to provide a lead to militant Glasgow workers. Constrained by a model of socialism in which capitalism would be ended by the individual enlightenment of the workers, rather than through the organisation of the most class-conscious workers to lead a struggle against the capitalist class, Maclean had little grasp of the importance of creating a communist party.

It was this that stopped him from understanding the importance of the creation of the CPGB and from attending the Second Congress of the Communist International. While many lesser figures on the British left managed to find a legal or illegal way to get to Moscow for the congress, Maclean refused to go because the government would not issue an official passport to him. 'I'm not

---

124   For Maclean's itinerary, see his article 'Maclean in Cumberland' in *The Call*, 4 February 1919.

125   Maclean's role in the Lanarkshire Miners' Reform Committee is in *The Call*, 23 January 1919. MacDougall's own account is 'The Scottish Coalminer' in *The Nineteenth Century and After* (1927), pp. 762–81. More details can be found in Ives 2017, pp. 92–102.

going there underground. I must go openly. Lord Curzon, Foreign Minister, has put the bar on my direct request and on my indirect one through Cook's Touring Agency', he explained.[126] Maclean's restricted political perspective meant that the outstanding revolutionary leader of his class could not confer with his peers from around the world – precisely the outcome that Lloyd George and the British ruling class desired.

---

126   For Maclean's attempts to obtain a passport, see *Vanguard*, July 1920 and Milton 1973, pp. 234, 241 and 243. The quote is taken from his 'Explanation of Election Address' in Maclean 1978, pp. 246–8.

'Long Live the Communist Party!' Building a British Section of the Communist International

Ten British representatives eventually made the perilous journey across northern Europe to the Second Congress of the Communist International: Tom Quelch and William McLaine (BSP), Sylvia Pankhurst (WSF), J.T. Murphy (SLP), Willie Gallacher and John S. Clarke (the Glasgow *Worker*), Dick Beech, Dave Ramsey and Jack Tanner (Shop Stewards and Workers' Committee Movement) and Marjory Newbold of the Young Labour League representing the ILP Left Wing. Her ILP colleague Helen Crawfurd arrived too late to take part.[1] To get there, McLaine, Quelch and the ILPers manoeuvred their way through obstructive government red tape and eventually obtained passports for Russia. J.T. Murphy travelled slowly across Europe after the Amsterdam conference in February, enduring police harassment and arrest along the way. Jack Tanner spent ten weeks criss-crossing Scandinavia to evade the police. Willie Gallacher was refused a passport and stowed away on a ship that took him from Newcastle to Norway, from where he travelled on two further boats which eventually took him to Murmansk. Sylvia Pankhurst arrived in Murmansk on a Norwegian fisherman's boat, and reached the congress as it was in session, 'in spite of the precautions of the Norwegian government to intercept her', as a British Intelligence report rather disappointedly noted.[2]

But whatever challenges or privations they encountered en route were forgotten as soon as they crossed into Soviet Russia. J.T. Murphy arrived at the border on a train full of Russian soldiers belatedly returning home from Estonia, who were greeted by a local commissar:

---

1 Ramsey was also a member of the SLP and Beech was a member of the WSF. For Newbold see *The International*, 31 July 1920. The Young Labour League was a Manchester organisation run by Marjory which, according to her husband J.T. Walton Newbold, 'seemed to exist mainly in her imagination'; see his unpublished manuscript autobiography, ch. 8, p. 8 in the file *Autobiographical Details of Newbold's Political Life*, John Turner Walton Newbold Papers, John Rylands Library, Manchester, ref: GB 133 NEW.

2 McLaine, 'How to Get Abroad', *The Call*, 10 June 1920; Tanner in *Solidarity*, June 1920; Gallacher 1936, pp. 249–51; Pankhurst 1921, pp. 7–9 and *Fortnightly Report*, no. 67, 12 Aug 1920 CAB 24/110/72; *The Autobiography of Helen Crawfurd*, pp. 190–7, unpublished mss, Marx Memorial Library HC/1/3.

Comrades, on behalf of the workers, peasants and soldiers of the republic I welcome you to your homeland ... We have begun to build socialism. Do not misunderstand me. We are having hard times. We are hungry. We are poor. Our country is in ruins from the war, from the invasions of capitalist powers who sought to smash our revolution, from civil war. We have not yet driven all the enemies out of our country. Things are difficult and they will be difficult for a long time to come. But this country is ours now, the country of the workers, soldiers and peasants, to make of it what you will. Welcome, comrades, to your homeland, the republic of socialist soviets ...[3]

His speech movingly expressed both the circumstances in which the Second Congress met and its political outlook.

1   The Second Congress of the Comintern

The Communist International announced on 22 April 1920 that it would be holding its Second Congress that summer.[4] While the founding congress of the Comintern in 1919 was essentially a declaration of intent to build a world revolutionary party, the Second Congress sought to establish the political principles upon which this party and its national sections would be built. The overarching political issue was to complete the political differentiation between the communists and those 'centrists' who sought to occupy a middle ground between revolutionaries and reformists. In order to facilitate this, the Second Congress drew up the famous 'Twenty-One Conditions' for membership of the Third International, which laid down the programmatic basis for the communist parties.

The first condition of membership was that 'day-by-day propaganda and agitation must be genuinely communist in character', and this was immediately followed by the requirement that parties wishing to join the international 'must consistently and systematically dismiss reformists and "centrists" from positions of any responsibility in the working-class movement'.[5] Subsequent conditions included the need to develop parallel legal and illegal forms of organisation, the adoption of a democratic centralist party structure, the carrying

---

3   Murphy 1941, p. 106.
4   It wasn't until 14 June that it was announced that the Congress would convene on 15 July. Even then travel difficulties meant that it did not open until 19 July. See Riddell 1991, p. 6.
5   Lenin, 'The Terms of Admission into the Communist International', *CW* vol. 31, p. 207.

out of revolutionary work in the armed forces, and the necessity to 'ruthlessly expose the colonial machinations of the imperialists of its "own" country, [and] support – in deed, not merely in word – every colonial liberation movement, demand the expulsion of its compatriot imperialists from the colonies, inculcate in the hearts of the workers of its own country an attitude of true brotherhood with the working population of the colonies and the oppressed nations'. To educate delegates in the experiences of the Bolsheviks before and after the October Revolution, every attendee received a copy of Lenin's new pamphlet, *Left-Wing Communism: An Infantile Disorder*, which had been completed on 12 May, and Trotsky's polemic against Kautsky, *Terrorism and Communism*.

The impending congress focused the minds of British communists, and both the BSP and the WSF wanted to be able to report that the task of founding a British communist party was underway. However, the day after the WSF's conference founded its own 'Communist Party (British Section of the Third International)', the BSP seized the initiative and wrote to Lenin asking for his views on affiliation to the Labour Party and participation in parliamentary elections. His reply increased the isolation of the WSF and appeared to boost the BSP's authority:

> I am in complete sympathy with their [BSP] plans for the immediate organisation of a single Communist Party of Britain. I consider erroneous the tactics pursued by Comrade Sylvia Pankhurst and the Workers' Socialist Federation, who refuse to collaborate in the amalgamation of the British Socialist Party, the Socialist Labour Party and others to form a single Communist party. Personally I am in favour of participation in Parliament and of affiliation to the Labour Party, given wholly free and independent communist activities. I shall defend these tactics at the Second Congress of the Third International on July 15, 1920 in Moscow. I consider it most desirable that a single Communist party be speedily organised on the basis of the decisions of the Third International, and that such a party should establish the closest contact with the Industrial Workers of the World and the Shop Stewards' Committees, in order to bring about a complete merger with them in the near future.[6]

Lenin's comments were a component of the wider debate about the relationship between communists and mass reformist parties that would be the focus of the Second Congress. As he pointed out in relation to the Labour Party 'we

---

6   'Reply to a Letter from the Joint Provisional Committee for the Communist Party of Britain' *CW* vol. 31, p. 202. It was reprinted on the front page of *The Call*, 22 July 1920.

may not be fully familiar with the conditions in one party or another, but in this case we are dealing with the principles underlying a Communist Party's tactics'.[7] The Labour Party question was debated initially at the second session of the congress which discussed the role of the Communist Party in the proletarian revolution. Early in the debate William MacLaine attempted to press home the BSP's apparent agreement with Lenin by arguing that

> The Labour Party is not socialist but ... it has the press at its disposal and has its representatives in parliament and on the town councils, and it would be suicide to exclude the possibility of propagandising in the trades union movement and everywhere through this big apparatus. The group I represent does not want to commit suicide in this way. ... The fact that, under pressure from the masses, the right-wing [Labour] leaders and their organisations are gradually disappearing is one more reason for remaining affiliated to this organisation.[8]

Paul Levi of the German Communist Party also spoke in support of affiliation to the Labour Party because it would provide 'a connection with the masses'. David Wijnkoop of the Dutch Communist Party suggested postponing a decision on affiliation because it would disrupt attempts to create a united British party.[9] Lenin ignored MacLaine's claim that the Labour Party was shedding its right wing and argued that:

> we must say openly that the Communist Party can be affiliated to the Labour Party if it is free to criticise and to conduct its own policies. ... The BSP can openly say that Henderson is a traitor and still remain in the Labour Party. This is the collaboration of the vanguard of the working class with the backward workers, the rear-guard. This is so important for the whole movement that we absolutely insist that the British Communists must form a link between the [communist] party, that is the minority of the working class, and the remaining masses of the workers.[10]

However, it was not the case that Lenin agreed with the BSP. When the delegates read their copies of *Left-Wing Communism* they would have realised that

---

7   Riddell 1991, p. 738.
8   Quoted in Riddell 1991, p. 157.
9   Riddell 1991, pp. 164–6.
10   Riddell 1991, pp. 169–70.

Lenin's attitude to the Labour Party differed in its fundamentals from the BSP. While Lenin agreed that communists should vote for Labour at the next general election, this was only to undermine its influence among the millions of workers who believed it would act in their interests. For the BSP, affiliating to and voting for the Labour Party was a principle, but for Lenin these were merely tactical questions. His goal was not to take over the party or push it to the left but to expose its pro-capitalist nature: 'with my vote, I want to support Henderson in the same way as the rope supports a hanged man', he stated, going on to argue 'that the impending establishment of a government of the Hendersons will prove that I am right, will bring the masses over to my side, and will hasten the political death of the Hendersons and the Snowdens'. Although the pamphlet took no position on affiliation to the Labour Party – 'I have too little material at my disposal on this question', Lenin admitted when he was writing it – the affiliation issue became the central debate about Britain at the congress.[11]

The syndicalist shop stewards Dave Ramsey and Jack Tanner argued that it was a mistake to affiliate to the Labour Party and that the existence of the Shop Stewards' Movement meant that there was no need for a revolutionary party. Tanner told the congress that the Russian experience 'must not be set up as a model for all other countries' because many militant workers in Britain believed that working in a political party was a waste of time, and that bourgeois politics 'strives to divert workers away from direct action, making out that parliament is the key factor'. Later, during the discussion on trade unions, Tanner threatened to walk out in support of the American delegation's opposition both to Radek's theses on the trade unions and the creation of an international trade union federation supporting the Comintern.[12] In response, Lenin told Ramsey and Tanner that if they agreed that 'the conscious communist minority of the working class can lead the proletariat ... the only difference between us is that they avoid the word "party" because among the British comrades there is a kind of prejudice against the political party'.

The congress discussed the Labour Party again two weeks later. Responding to MacLaine's claim that 'first of all the Labour Party is the political expression of the workers organised in the trades unions and must be conceived of as a political organisation, and secondly that within the Labour Party the sup-

---

11   V.I. Lenin, 'Left-Wing Communism: An Infantile Disorder', CW vol. 31, pp. 88–9.
12   Riddell 1991, pp. 159–70. At the Congress Tom Mann was made a vice-president and J.T. Murphy appointed to the organising committee of the International Trade Union Council, which would become the Red International of Labour Unions in July 1921; see Tosstorff 2016, pp. 147–53.

porters of another party retain their complete freedom of movement and of criticism', Lenin pointed out that the BSP's analysis of the Labour Party was incorrect:

> I have met the same view several times in the paper of the British Socialist Party. It is erroneous, and is partly the cause of the opposition, fully justified in some measure, coming from the British revolutionary workers. Indeed, the concepts 'political department of the trade unions' or 'political expression' of the trade union movement, are erroneous. Of course, most of the Labour Party's members are workingmen. However, whether or not a party is really a political party of the workers does not depend solely upon a membership of workers but also upon the men that lead it, and the content of its actions and its political tactics. Only this latter determines whether we really have before us a political party of the proletariat. Regarded from this, the only correct, point of view, the Labour Party is a thoroughly bourgeois party, because, although made up of workers, it is led by reactionaries, and the worst kind of reactionaries at that, who act quite in the spirit of the bourgeoisie. It is an organisation of the bourgeoisie, which exists to systematically dupe the workers with the aid of the British Noskes and Scheidemanns.[13]

Drawing on Engels, Lenin had previously summed up this analysis of Labourism by characterising the Labour Party as a 'bourgeois labour party'.[14] Some historians such as Raymond Challinor have argued that Lenin's position on the early CPGB and the Labour Party was flawed because he 'did not possess either a detailed knowledge of British politics or feel for the working-class movement'.[15] While it is undoubtedly true that Lenin lacked precise information about the situation in Britain – and may have been influenced by Joe Fineberg's analysis – his attitude to the Labour Party was based on an understanding that world politics had been fundamentally changed by the October Revolution.

In Britain, this was manifested by a huge and rapid advance in working-class consciousness. Labour received 2.1 million votes at the 1918 General Election, up from 400,000 in 1910, a rising curve that grew to more than four million in 1922. This electoral earthquake was reflected at the local level, where Labour Party members began to flood on to city and town councils. Trade union mem-

---

13   McLaine's speech is in Riddell 1991, pp. 736, and Lenin's response on p. 739.
14   Lenin 1916b, pp. 114–16.
15   See chapter 10 of Challinor 1977, pp. 218.

bership accelerated at an even greater pace, rising from 5.5 million in 1917, to 6.5 million in 1918, and eight million a year later. This leftward shift was echoed in the rhetoric of Labour's leaders. Throughout 1919 and 1920, Labour leaders on the left and the right denounced allied intervention in Soviet Russia. On the very day Lenin made this speech, the Labour Party issued a manifesto signed by Henderson, Bevin and other prominent leaders which denounced Lloyd George's support for Poland against the Red Army, stating that 'Labour in this country will not co-operate in a war as allies of Poland' and warning that 'we think the workers will be thoroughly justified in refusing to render labour services in the event of war'.[16]

The very fact that Ramsay MacDonald himself had been forced to discuss affiliation to the Communist International at the recent Labour Party conference, Lenin argued, demonstrated that it was 'the duty' of communists to join Labour and take part in the debate.[17] The party now had the allegiance of almost all class-conscious working people who, to a greater or lesser extent, believed its leaders' expressions of socialism. Moreover, the rapidly rising tide of electoral support for Labour across Britain allowed its leaders to argue there was no need for revolutionary politics because there would soon be a Labour government which would implement socialist measures. 'A parliamentary election will give us all the power that Lenin had to get by a revolution, and such a majority can proceed to effect the transition from capitalism to socialism with the co-operation of the people, and not merely by edict', MacDonald argued.[18] For Lenin, such rhetoric offered revolutionaries the opportunity to expose the contradiction between Labour's socialist words and the reality of its deeds. In contrast to the BSP's strategy of working permanently inside the Labour Party to push it leftwards, Lenin's conception of affiliation to Labour was a contingent tactic: 'if the British Communist Party starts by acting in a revolutionary manner in the Labour Party, and if the Hendersons are obliged to expel this Party, that will be a great victory for the communist and revolutionary working class movement in Britain'.[19]

The affiliation question also seems to have been discussed at an informal 'Commission on English Affairs' which met in the Tsar's former bedroom in the Kremlin between the formal congress sessions. The attendees included Bukharin, Radek, Zinoviev, Paul Levi, David Wijnkoop of the Dutch CP, and un-named 'Italians and Austrians', according to Pankhurst, although differ-

---

16   'To the Nation', *Daily Herald*, 7 Aug 1920.
17   *Daily Herald*, 26 June 1920. The motion to join was lost by 2,940,000 votes to 225,000.
18   MacDonald 1919, p. 92.
19   Riddell 1991, pp. 744.

ing reports suggest that it was chaired either by Lenin or Alfred Rosmer, the former revolutionary syndicalist who was representing the French Committee for the Third International.[20] Presentations were made in favour of affiliation by William McLaine and Joe Fineberg, who was not a delegate to the congress, while Pankhurst and Gallacher spoke in opposition. No minutes of the meeting appears to exist, and it is not recorded in any congress transcripts, but according to McLaine, it voted by 11 to 4 for the British communists to affiliate to the Labour Party.[21]

Tellingly, the debate in Moscow was the first time that all sides of the Labour Party question had been fully debated in public by British Marxists. From the congress floor Sylvia Pankhurst spoke against electoral support or affiliation to the Labour Party on the grounds that 'if one were to say to the parties that they should join the Labour Party and allow themselves to be tied by a common discipline and action one would thus give the fate of the English proletarian revolution into the hands of the old trades unions'. She also suggested that Lenin was wrong to warn against 'extremism': 'Although I am a socialist I have fought for a long time in the suffragette movement and I have seen how important it is to be extreme and to have the courage to defend one's ideas'.[22] Her contribution, commented Rosmer, 'was suitable for a public meeting rather than a congress; it was an agitator's speech'.[23] She was supported by Willie Gallacher, representing the Scottish Workers' Committees, who earlier in the congress claimed 'the Communist International too is on the road to becoming opportunist'. He argued the experience of the Scottish Workers' Committee in Glasgow demonstrated that revolutionaries did not need the 'diversion' of joining the Labour Party to have contact with the masses: 'what matters is to bring the masses to an understanding of the present moment through agitation and through action. One should call forth the indignation of the proletariat, bring the masses to action by all ways and means, and not choose such diversions, [because] such means could divert them from their revolutionary struggle'.[24] The debate ended with delegates voting 58 to 24 (with 2 abstaining) for affiliation to the Labour Party.

---

20   Pankhurst 1921, pp. 42–4. Murphy 1941, p. 149, says Lenin was the chair, but in contrast
       Rosmer 1971, p. 76, implies he presided.
21   *The Communist*, 23 Sept 1920. Pankhurst says nothing about the commission's discussions.
       No record of these discussions appears to have survived in the Comintern section of the
       Russian State Archives.
22   Pankhurst's speech is in Riddell 1991, pp. 733–5.
23   Rosmer 1971, p. 76.
24   Gallacher's speech is in Riddell 1991, pp. 737–8.

What was not discussed, and was absent from almost every discussion on the affiliation question, was what communists would do once they joined the Labour Party. It was this ambiguity on the practical implications of the policy that allowed the former BSPers to claim agreement with Lenin. But the policy of the BSP inside of the Labour Party could hardly be described as revolutionary. For example, in the March 1919 London County Council (LCC) elections, it declared its goal was 'to capture the greatest municipal body in the world for Labour and Socialism'. What this meant in practice was illustrated by Alf Watts, BSP treasurer and member of the Provisional Executive committee of the CPGB, who after his election as a councillor was invariably referred to by *The Call* as 'A.A. Watts LCC'. Discussing Britain's acute post-war housing shortage, Watts argued against land being confiscated and built upon because 'at present, it is not practicable to seize the land. It will have to be paid for. If we could seize it, the country would be ripe for revolution; but we want to begin at once'.[25] In 1923 Watts would call the police on unemployed demonstrators protesting against cuts being made by the Poplar Board of Guardians.[26] When the CPGB's application to the Labour Party was turned down later in 1920, the *Daily Herald* revealingly expressed surprise because the BSP 'which, everyone knows, forms a very large proportion of the Communist Party, was affiliated to the Labour Party without any great trouble or difficulty being raised about it'.[27] The BSP was essentially a parliamentary party without a parliamentary presence.

According to Alfred Rosmer, William McLaine told Lenin that the BSP was in full agreement with his positions. 'No, it is not that easy, or if you believe it is, it is because you are still imbued with that socialist jabbering that was prevalent in the Second International but which always halted before revolutionary action', Lenin told MacLaine.[28] While tangential tactical agreement on the Labour Party affiliation partially obscured these differences, the gulf that separated the BSP from Lenin became clear when the congress discussed the struggle against British imperialism. Tom Quelch, author of *The Call*'s racist articles on black workers in 1917, complained that 'ordinary British workers' would see support to colonial uprisings against the British Empire as 'treason'. Karl Radek tore into the BSP's failure to raise the flag of anti-imperialism, pointing out that not a single BSP delegate to the recent Labour Party conference had

---

25   Both quotes from *The Call*, 2 Jan 1919.
26   *Workers' Dreadnought*, 6 Oct 1923.
27   *Daily Herald*, 14 Sept 1920.
28   Rosmer 1971, pp. 60–1.

stood up to tell the Conference that the MacDonalds [*sic*] support the British bourgeoisie fooling British workers when they talk about the independence of India, Ireland and Egypt. ... We greatly regret that our party comrades who are in the Labour Party did not tear the mask off these swindlers' faces. The International will not judge the British comrades by the articles that they write in *The Call* and the *Workers' Dreadnought*, but by the number of comrades who are thrown into gaol for agitating in the colonial countries.[29]

This point had also been made by Lenin in the conclusion to *Left-Wing Communism*: 'in Great Britain, further, the work of propaganda, agitation and organisation among the armed forces and among the oppressed and underprivileged nationalities in their "own" state (Ireland, the colonies) must also be tackled in a new fashion (one that is not socialist, but communist; not reformist, but revolutionary)'. For the BSP, which just a few weeks earlier denounced the WSF's agitation among British troops as a 'comic opera', such a position was almost beyond its comprehension.

As the presence of the ILP's Newbold and Crawfurd in Moscow highlighted, there was also another dimension to the debate on Labour Party affiliation. In April a 'British Labour Delegation' organised by the Labour Party and the TUC had arrived in Russia on a fact-finding mission. Accompanying the official party were ILP leaders Clifford Allen and Robert Wallhead, who had been delegated by the ILP's April conference to visit Russia to ascertain 'whether the Third International has any formal constitution to which parties desiring affiliation are expected to subscribe' and to present a list of twelve questions concerning, among others, parliament, soviets, the dictatorship of the proletariat, and the Labour Party. The ILP leadership had allied itself to the Swiss Socialist Party's call for an 'all inclusive international' and its approach to the Comintern was part of an attempt to bring together the Second and Third internationals. This failed and led to the short-lived International Working Union of Socialist Parties, otherwise known as the Two-and-a-Half International, positioned between the two internationals but which itself quickly collapsed. While in Moscow, Allen and Wallhead also met with Lenin, Radek and Bukharin on their trip but neither side gained much satisfaction.[30]

---

29   Riddell 1991, p. 127.
30   Details of the visit are in *Report of the 29th Annual Conference of the ILP, 27–29 March 1921* (London: ILP, 1921) and it is discussed in White 1994. For the ILP Left Wing's assessment of the delegation, see 'Our Official Approach to the Communist International', *The*

However, the ILP's questions did prompt an extensive reply from the Executive Committee of the Communist International (ECCI) in the journal *Communist International*, which was published as *The Communist Party Answers the ILP*.[31] Although the CPGB would later claim that the reply was drafted by Lenin, stylistic and circumstantial evidence suggests it was written by Radek, who was not only secretary of the ECCI but was also familiar with British politics, having written about the Labour Party as early as 1909.[32] While the debate about the Labour Party at the Second Congress was focused on the need to unite British communists in a single party and to agree on tactics towards Labour, Radek's reply to the ILP took a more strategic perspective. 'Affiliation with the Labour Party [is] admissible in so far as it represents a bloc of organisations free to carry on propaganda according to their own programmes', he stated, but warned that 'affiliation should not mean a mechanical utilisation of the party for the purpose of keeping in touch with the masses, gathered under the roof of the Labour Party, but a striving to free the masses from the influences of the opportunist leaders of the Labour Party'. It also highlighted that its leadership was now transforming the party's previous loose organisational structure into:

> a real party with local organisations and a programme. They aim to create a large opportunist party which is to retard the revolutionary development of the masses. Were this tendency to succeed, the Labour Party would never afford the socialist organisations which form part of it the right to an individual communist policy, nor to the propagation of the revolutionary struggle.

If this happened, 'it would then become necessary after a most energetic struggle against this tendency to leave the Labour Party and endeavour to keep in touch with the working masses by means of increasing the communist activity in the trade unions, by detaching these trade unions from the Labour opportunist parties to go over directly to communism'.[33] Radek then went on to criticise the ILP for its refusal to oppose the Labour Party during World War

---

International, 17 July 1920. See also Lazitch and Drachkovich 1972, pp. 284–7, and 2013a, pp. 116–23.

31   The letter and the reply are printed in *The Communist International*, no. 11/12, June–July 1920, cols. 2473–94.

32   This is the view of E.H. Carr; see Carr 1966, p. 191. The CPGB's 1932 reprint claimed on its cover it was 'drafted by Lenin'.

33   All quotes are from *The Communist International*, no. 11/12.

One, and ended his reply with an appeal to communists in the ILP to join the struggle to build a united communist party.

His purpose was less to reply to Allen and Wallhead than to provide ideological ammunition to the ILP Left Wing and, if they chose to look, to the revolutionary opponents of the BSP. The ILP Left Wing rushed it out as a pamphlet, *Moscow's Reply to the ILP*, in July 1920, which by the end of August had almost sold out, and the *Daily Herald* published an article on it shortly after it was published in *Communist International*.[34] Yet despite widespread circulation across the ILP and its periphery, the document was never published nor, as far as can be ascertained, discussed by any of the organisations to the left of the ILP. Only John Maclean's *Vanguard* commented on it, arguing 'this pamphlet must play a greater part in the moulding of British thought than even Marx and Engels' Communist Manifesto did in the past. Out of it we who claim to be communists must get the basis of communist unity in Britain'.[35] But this appears to have been the only reference to the pamphlet by Maclean or other leftists.

However, the ILP Left Wing, like the BSP, interpreted the Comintern's tactical support for affiliation to the Labour Party and participation in parliamentary elections as an endorsement of its own programme. Thus Marjory Newbold triumphantly telegrammed the ILP Left Wing with the message 'parliamentary action carried' when the Second Congress made its decision.[36] The politics of the ILP Left Wing were a jumble of ideas that at times resembled a lukewarm version of syndicalism: 'the best means of effecting a social revolution is for the organised workers to prepare themselves to take over the industrial machine' it wrote. This co-existed with a residual attachment to parliament which, it believed, had to provide 'the formal endorsement of the measures put forward by the workers' organisations for the destruction of capitalism and the demolition of the capitalist state'.[37] The pages of its fortnightly newspaper, *The International*, were full of abstract discussions about the need for socialism, yet there was almost nothing about the class struggle that was raging around them. Not even the 'Hands Off Russia' campaign and the formation of the Council of Action in August 1920 warranted any serious discussion in its pages.

For communist parties across the world, the Second Congress played the decisive role in defining their political programme. But although it brought unity between the British communist groups, British delegates seemed to have understood little about its political implications for the British left. Only

---

34 *Daily Herald*, 16 July 1920. *The International*, 31 July and 28 Aug 1920.
35 *Vanguard*, Aug 1920.
36 The telegram is in *The International*, 28 Aug 1920.
37 'The Programme of the ILP Left Wing', published in *Workers' Dreadnought*, 11 Dec 1920.

J.T. Murphy and Willie Gallacher appear to have drawn any significant political lessons from the discussions and debates in which they participated. Gallacher began the conference sceptical both of the affiliation tactic and the need for a united party but at a meeting after the congress, he told Lenin that he had been convinced of both positions and would campaign for them when he returned home. Murphy too was now committed to the policies of the Comintern.[38] The BSP took Lenin's tactical support for affiliation to the Labour Party as an endorsement of its own principles, while Sylvia Pankhurst essentially repeated her positions and did not engage with the congress debates. This failure to understand what the Comintern was trying to build was not confined to the British. Looking back at the Second Congress in his memoirs, Victor Serge noted that many delegates were 'at an infinite distance from the Bolshevik mentality. The bulk of these men were symptomatic of obsolete movements which had been quite outrun by events, combining an abundance of good intentions with a scarcity of talent', a description that was particularly apt for the BSP.[39] But even those to its left were shocked when they came face-to-face with Bolshevism at the Second Congress. John S. Clarke, the former SLP leader and now editor of the Glasgow *Worker*, overcame his considerable cynicism to contrast the British left with the communists he met in Russia, describing how the latter

> constantly visualise a classless world, not a mere classless Russia. Their vision of revolutionary activity is boundless. Because the International to them 'shall unite the human race', they devote their lives to its realisation. They think, speak, and act only in terms of the universal application of communism. They preach and work for the World Revolution. They are not Slavonic, Tartar, Kalmuck or Mongolian; not Indo-European nor Ural-Altaic; not Aryan nor Semitic. ... They are simply proletarians who have won through, and with that true communistic spirit which prompted the utterance of their favourite slogan, 'Workers of the World Unite', they are working for the emancipation of mankind.[40]

Although Clarke and some of the other British delegates could recognise what had made the Bolsheviks successful, building a similar party in Britain would prove to be much more difficult.

---

38   Gallacher 1936, p. 254. Murphy 1941, pp. 129–31.
39   Serge 1967, p. 104.
40   'Second Congress of the Third International and the British Movement', *The Worker*, 18 Sept 1920.

2   The Birth of the Communist Party of Great Britain

While the Second Congress was taking place in Moscow, 152 delegates assembled on Saturday 31 July in the Pillar Hall of Cannon Street Hotel in the heart of the City of London. Ninety-five of them represented 54 BSP branches, 25 came from the Communist Unity Group, 24 from local independent groups, and eight were from three small organisations, the Land Colonisation and Industrial League, the Guild Communist Group and the teetotallers of the Socialist Prohibition Fellowship. Ten Scottish and seven Welsh branches were represented. Seventeen of the delegates were women. The conference claimed to represent 5,125 members, although no evidence was provided to support this.[41] Walter Kendall later estimated this figure comprised 3,336 former BSPers, 779 for the CUG and 1,260 from other groups. Even so, it was the largest gathering of communists that had ever assembled in Britain.

Welcoming the delegates to the 'Unity Convention' of the Communist Party of Great Britain, chair Arthur MacManus regretted the 'sad experience' that 'it had taken three years of Russia in revolution, and two years of actual negotiating and deliberating, to bring into being a conference of this description'. However, he hoped that the meeting 'would turn out to be the most profitable weekend that the revolutionary movement had ever had in this country'.[42] Both he and Albert Inkpin, who gave the secretary's report, spent considerable time recounting the protracted unity talks of the previous two years, yet neither made any mention of the accelerating campaign to stop the British threat of war against Soviet Russia, the escalating war in Ireland, or any political issue other than Labour Party affiliation and parliament. Nor did any other speaker at the convention mention the political convulsions taking place in Britain or anywhere else. Perhaps the most egregious example of the tenor of the conference came when the Furniture Workers' union leader, and future president of the TUC, Alf Purcell moved the motion to establish the Communist Party. William Mellor pointed out from the floor that it did not mention the Communist International, and asked MacManus 'to use his influence' to persuade the convention's standing orders committee to add the new party's 'adhesion to the Third International' to the motion.[43] Despite its aims, the convention differed little from the routinist and often abstract discussions of BSP confer-

---

41   *Communist Unity Convention, Official Report* (London: CPGB, 1920), p. 21. For a participant's account of the convention, see Stewart 1967, pp. 87–91. Kendall 1969, p. 304.

42   *Communist Unity Convention, Official Report*, p. 4.

43   *Communist Unity Convention, Official Report*, p. 8.

ences. When the party's new paper *The Communist* was published for the first time four days later it was merely a retitled version of the BSP's *Call*. The 'BSP Special Notices' column did not even change its name until issue 14. It would be hard to deny that the new CPGB was anything other than an enlarged BSP.

The debate on parliamentary elections was opened by the CUG's Tom Bell, who proposed a resolution which read:

> The Communist Party repudiates the reformist view that a social revolution can be achieved by the ordinary methods of parliamentary democracy, but regards parliamentary and electoral action generally as providing a means of propaganda and agitation towards the revolution. The tactics to be employed by the representatives of the party elected to parliament or local bodies must be laid down by the party itself, according to national or local circumstances. In all cases such representatives must be considered as holding a mandate from the party, and not from the particular constituency for which they happen to sit.[44]

The discussion demonstrated the political distance between the Communist International and many convention delegates. William Mellor opposed the idea that Communist MPs or councillors should be under the control of the party, because it 'gave the executive an awful amount of authority'. An amendment from Alf Purcell to make communist MPs answerable to their parliamentary constituencies as well as the party gained 52 votes, but was lost due 102 opposing it.[45] That MPs or parliamentary deputies were direct representatives of the Communist Party and subject to its discipline was point eleven of the Comintern's 'Twenty-One Conditions', whereas the belief that an MP had a higher or equal duty to that of fighting for the party's revolutionary programme was, in contrast, a throwback to the parliamentary practices of the Second International. The underlying divisions over the role of parliamentary representatives emerged when the Birkenhead ex-SLPer John Fitton proposed an amendment to Bell's motion stating that:

> in the event of any representative violating the decisions of the party as embodied in the mandate which he or she had accepted or been instruc-

---

44   *The Communist*, 5 Aug 1920.

45   Mellor on p. 23 and Purcell on p. 27 of the *Communist Unity Convention, Official Report*. A somewhat sketchy secret service report on the convention is in the *Fortnightly Report*, no. 66, of 5 Aug 1920, CAB 24/110/43. Some details, including Williams's motion, are in the SLP's report of the conference in *The Socialist*, 12 Aug 1920.

ted upon, he or she shall be called upon to resign his or her membership of parliament or municipality, and also of the party.[46]

Despite this compromise of merely asking for the resignation of the MP from the party rather than expelling them, the motion only passed by a relatively narrow 85 to 54 votes.

The next day saw the convention discuss affiliation to the Labour Party. John Hodgson of the BSP proposed the motion in favour, while the CUG's William Paul argued against it. Lasting over four hours and with 30 speakers, the discussion ended with the motion to affiliate to Labour passing by an unexpectedly narrow 100 votes to 85. The vote made it clear that if the WSF or SLP had taken part in the congress there would have a been a majority in the new party opposed to affiliation. As Tom Bell noted in the first issue of *The Communist*, the success of the pro-affiliationists was 'the responsibility of those elements who were so self-opinionated as to keep away from the convention, while making a virtue of non-affiliation'. Arthur MacManus's assessment of the debate was more appropriate for a football match: 'the battle was fought with healthy vigour and clear frankness, which augurs well for the Communist Party. We demonstrated that we are all capable of disagreeing, and that to my mind was not the least important manifestation of the Convention. The victorious side were generous to a defeated foe, while my own erstwhile colleagues at least demonstrated how they could take a defeat'.[47] Highlighting the unwillingness of the British left to wage a struggle for a political position, Alec Geddes, a delegate from the Greenock Workers' Social Committee and a regular contributor to the Glasgow *Worker*, disagreed with the decision to affiliate to Labour and simply walked away from the CPGB to create another communist party that would oppose affiliation.[48] The SLP's jaundiced report in *The Socialist* drew no conclusions from the closeness of the vote, while the *Workers' Dreadnought* felt that the almost victorious minority should leave the CPGB and join the WSF's communist party.[49]

Having voted to affiliate to the Labour Party, MacManus and Inkpin were delegated to write to Labour's National Executive Committee to request affiliation. In the CPGB's first major political act, a letter was sent to the Labour Party on 9 August which read:

---

46   *Communist Unity Convention, Official Report*, p. 29.
47   Bell and MacManus in *The Communist*, 5 Aug 1920.
48   'An Appeal to Scots' Communists', *The Worker*, 21 Aug 1920.
49   *Workers' Dreadnought*, 7 Aug 1920. *The Socialist*, 12 Aug 1920.

Dear Sir

At a National Convention [on] Sunday, 31 July and 1 August the Communist Party of Great Britain was established; the resolutions adopted by the convention defining the objects, methods and policy of the Communist Party:

(a) The Communists in conference assembled declare for the Soviet (or Workers' Council) system as a means whereby the working class shall achieve power and take control of the forces of production; declare for the dictatorship of the proletariat as a necessary means for combating the counter-revolution during the transition period between capitalism and communism, and stand for the adoption of these means as steps towards the establishment of complete communism wherein all the means of production shall be communally owned and controlled. The conference therefore established itself the Communist Party on the foregoing basis and declares its adherence to Third International.

(b) The Communist Party repudiates the reformist view that a social revolution can be achieved by the ordinary methods of parliamentary democracy, but regards parliamentary and electoral action generally as providing a means of propaganda and agitation towards the revolution. The tactics to be employed by the representatives of the party elected to parliament or local bodies must be laid down by the party itself according to national or local circumstances. In all cases representatives must be considered as holding a mandate from the party and not from the particular constituency for which they happen to sit. In the event of any representative violating the decision of the party as embodied in the mandate which he or she has accepted, the resignation follows of his or her membership of parliament or municipality and also of the party.

(c) That the Communist Party shall be affiliated to the Labour Party. At a meeting of the Provisional Executive Committee held on Sunday last we were directed to send you the foregoing resolutions and to make application for the affiliation of the Communist Party to the Labour Party.

Yours faithfully, Arthur MacManus, Albert Inkpin.[50]

The day before the letter was sent, hundreds of thousands of people across Britain had demonstrated against war with Soviet Russia. On the very day it was

---

50   Reprinted in Bell 1937, pp. 63–4.

sent, the Labour Party and the TUC set up the Council of Action, pledging that 'the whole industrial power of the organised workers will be used to defeat this war'. Yet the leaders of the CPGB did not perceive this as an opportunity to propose common activity that could expose the gap between the rhetoric and the reality of Labour's politics. Unable to transcend the abstract propaganda for socialism that was the hallmark of the pre-war British left, the CPGB was incapable of challenging the Labour Party's politics on the war threat, Ireland, the impeding industrial clashes or any of the other issues facing the working class. Instead, all it could offer was a passive-aggressive invitation to the Labour Party to reject it.

Arthur Henderson replied to the CPGB on 11 September, stating that 'the basis of affiliation to the Labour Party is the acceptance of its constitution, principles and programme, with the which the objects of the Communist Party do not appear to be in accord' and rejected its application for affiliation.[51] The response from Inkpin and MacManus revealed that behind their revolutionary roar lay a timid mouse. 'Does the Labour Party executive rule that acceptance of communism is contrary to the constitution, principles and programme and the Labour Party? ... Does the Labour Party executive decisively and categorically reject the soviet system and the dictatorship of the proletariat?' they asked, seemingly deaf to the obvious answers. 'The past history of the Labour Party, particularly during the war and since peace', they pleaded, demonstrated that Labour was 'so catholic in its composition and constitution that it could admit to its ranks all sections of the working-class movement'. Like a spurned lover, the letter demanded to know 'since when has the practice of the Labour Party changed?' and ended with a plaintive 'they are questions we are entitled to submit and feel justified in seeking a reply'.[52] As Tom Bell later commented, 'whatever illusions we might have, the Labour Party executive certainly had none'.[53]

This reply to Henderson set the tone for the CPGB's attempts to affiliate to the Labour Party in the early 1920s. It adopted the stance of a confused but sincere friend of the party, seeking to demonstrate that its programme was merely a more consistent and unwavering version of Labour's own politics. In doing so, the CPGB allowed the Labour leadership to dictate the terms of the debate, putting itself on the defensive and having to demonstrate that its politics were compatible with those of Labour, sometimes in contradiction to its stated goals.

---

51   Bell 1937, p. 65.
52   Inkpin and MacManus to Henderson, 23 Sept 1920, *The Communist*, 30 Sept 1920.
53   Bell 1937, p. 67.

This was seen most clearly the following year when Labour's national executive met with CPGB representatives to discuss affiliation. In response to Sidney
Webb's question about the CPGB's relationship to Comintern decisions, Mac-
Manus told him 'we adopt them as a general guide, not necessarily as part
of our constitution' and that 'it is a general mistake up and down the country that whatever the Third International issues becomes the property of the
Communist Party. Nothing of the sort', which was not merely disingenuous
but flatly untrue.[54] When Webb and George Lansbury asked if communists
'accepted the parliamentary method' and 'the full and complete use of the parliamentary and municipal machine right up to the end', MacManus replied 'yes,
they do. All the difference is that our crime is that we are so suspicious of the
capitalist class in this country that we cannot see them yielding to what may
become a legal enactment. What we have done is that we have tried to frame
a point of view that will be prepared to force it'. Willie Gallacher rushed to
defend himself from Arthur Henderson's assertion that the CPGB was 'fundamentally opposed' to the Labour Party: 'Fundamentally, we are in agreement
with it. ... What the Labour Party and members of the Labour Party are fighting for and subscribing to is the overthrow of capitalism and the institution
of socialism. That is what the Communist Party is fighting for'. The meeting
ended with MacManus requesting that the Labour Party send a questionnaire
to the CPGB so that they could give specific answers to questions about its politics.

   This was not a case of dissembling before authority in order to achieve organisational goals. The CPGB leadership not only denied its own politics in order to
convince right-wing Labour leaders such as Henderson and Webb, but it also
prettified the politics of Labour, suggesting, in Gallacher's words, that 'what
the Labour Party and members of the Labour Party are fighting for and subscribing to is the overthrow of capitalism and the institution of socialism'. It
was almost as if MacManus and Gallacher still believed that affiliation to the
Labour Party was a right-wing opportunist tactic, and therefore they now had to
behave as right-wing opportunists. So, in response to Henderson's initial letter
refusing affiliation, *The Communist* wrote that 'we conceived the Labour Party
as something different from this; as something that was striving to express politically the half-formed aspirations and ideas of the surging mass of organised
workers in this country. In such a party we conceived we held a place. Perhaps
we were mistaken. We prefer to think that the executive of the Labour Party is

---

54   All quotes in this paragraph are from *Report of interview with Communist Party*, 29 Decem-
      ber 1921, in Harrison 1974.

mistaken'.[55] The idea that the Communist Party was merely a more consistently socialist version of the Labour Party, rather than being a revolutionary alternative to Labour's pro-capitalist politics, ran deep in the instincts of the CPGB's leadership and would, with the exception of the ultra-left Third Period politics of 1928 to 1934, always underpin its politics.

But the public manoeuvring over Labour Party affiliation was not quite the full story. Although not mentioned at the time, the CPGB's decision to affiliate was based on a trade-off between the BSP and CUG that allowed the party to be created. This compromise, as Willie Gallacher described it to the Comintern's 1923 British Commission, 'took the form of putting in an application for affiliation to the Labour Party in such a way as to ensure rejection by the Labour Party'.[56] In exchange the ex-CUGers agreed not to fight against affiliation to the Labour Party, and consequently raised no objection to the work of the ex-BSPers who continued their daily work in the Labour Party. In Gallacher's words, the new party was an uneasy alliance between what he called the 'MacManus faction' of ex-CUGers and the 'Rothstein faction' of ex-BSPers, of whom Theodore's son Andrew was now a leader. According to MacManus himself, the main axis of this division was a split between the 'Ultra-Labour Party' affiliationists of the BSP and the 'impossibilists' of the former SLPers.[57]

Moreover, a pre-unity agreement that all full-time employees of the BSP and the CUG would continue in their jobs after unification meant that there was a material basis for ex-BSP leaders to maintain the division. The British revolutionary left had a suspicion of paid officials, and so the SLP traditionally had no full-time officers. The three leaders of the CUG – Bell, MacManus and Paul – were funded via Comintern money but the BSP had its own minor bureaucracy with a head office staff and around a dozen paid regional organisers, all of whom were employed by the new CPGB.[58] This mentality could also be seen when the ILP Left Wing discussed joining the party in 1921. J.T. Walton Newbold and Shapurji Saklatvala assured their supporters who were ILP employees that they would retain their jobs in the new party.[59] Such horse-trading became one more factor in the political and organisational paralysis of the new party.

55   'Ourselves and the Labour Party', *The Communist*, 9 Sept 1920.
56   Transcript of Discussion, Communist International, English Commission (19 June 1923) RGASPI. F. 495. Op. 38. D. 1, Day 2, pp. 2–3.
57   MacManus assessment in Transcript of Discussion, Communist International, English Commission (19 June 1923) RGASPI. F. 495. Op. 38. D. 1, Day 2, p. 18.
58   See Gallacher's report to the 1923 English Commission, above, and *Fortnightly Report*, 3 Feb 1921, TNA CAB 24/119/42 for the amounts paid to officials.
59   Page 8 of chapter 11 of *Autobiographical Details of Newbold's Political Life*, John Turner Walton Newbold Papers, John Rylands Library, Manchester, ref: GB 133 NEW.

3   The Unification Conference

Now that the CPGB had been created, the Comintern pressed it to unify with
those supporters of the Third International who remained outside of the party.
As Gallacher later recalled, at a meeting shortly before he returned home Lenin
asked him three questions: if he now agreed with participation in parliament
and affiliating to the Labour Party; if he would join the CPGB; and if he would
do his best to persuade his Scottish comrades to join it too. He answered in
the affirmative to all three and immediately made it his goal to bring Scottish
revolutionaries into the CPGB.[60] To underline the urgency of the matter, on
10 August – three days after the end of the congress – the ECCI passed a resolution which insisted:

> In Britain, a single Communist Party must be organised on the basis of
> the decisions of the Second World Congress of the Communist Interna-
> tional. To achieve this in the space of four months a general congress
> of all the communist groups and organisations of all Britain and Ireland
> must be summoned. In this congress there must participate (1) the United
> Communist Party, (2) the Communist Party, (3) the Shop Stewards, (4)
> the Scottish Communist Group, (5) the Welsh Groups, (6) the Irish Com-
> munists (on a federal basis), (7) The Socialist Labour Party, (8) The left
> wing of the Independent Labour Party. For the summoning of this gen-
> eral congress, and to pave the way for unity, a general committee of action
> is appointed, into which there enters one representative of each group,
> under the presidency of a representative of the Executive Committee.[61]

On 11 September a provisional organising committee was set up in Glasgow
to set a date to establish a communist party in Scotland. This resulted in
the founding congress of the Communist Labour Party being held at Glasgow's Central Hall on 2 October.[62] Its core comprised militants associated with
The Worker, but of the 21 local organisations represented, three were Scottish
branches of the SLP and one was the Anderston branch of the ILP in Glasgow.
Tom Mitchell, who had replaced Tom Bell as the secretary of the SLP, also attended the conference as an observer but simply told the delegates that as their

---

60   Gallacher 1936, p. 215.

61   'Communist Unity Convention, Report of the Communist Unity Organisation Committee',
        15 Nov 1920, PHM CP/CENT/CONG/01/02. A further resolution was passed on 20 August lay-
        ing down the basis for the election of delegates.

62   *The Worker*, 18 Sept 1920.

constitution and programme was similar to that of the SLP, there was no point in creating a new party. The main discussion took place over the question of participation in parliament, in response to a motion from two of the particip- ating SLP branches that the new party should boycott all parliamentary activity. Gallacher argued that to support such a motion would put them outside of the Comintern, following the decision of the Second Congress, and the con- ference voted 41–9 in favour of parliamentary activity.[63] A ten-strong executive was elected, with former IWWer Jack Leckie elected chair, Alec Geddes treas- urer, and the Bridgeton-based organiser of the Parkhead Communist Group John Mclean as secretary. Gallacher, despite playing a central role in the confer- ence, took no position in the new party.[64] By early December, it was claiming 22 branches and 'close to' 2,000 members.[65]

Almost entirely absent from these developments was John Maclean him- self. Frustrated and alienated by the BSP's political passivity, in May 1920 he relaunched his war-time revolutionary newspaper *Vanguard*, 'in the hope that we may concentrate the minds of the workers on the revolution to be gone through in this country as well as on the one gone through already in Russia'.[66] However, it did not seek to intervene in the debates which led to the formation of the CPGB, portraying them as nothing more than 'discussing whether Lenin can wink as well with the right eye as with the left'.[67] Maclean also claimed that Ernie Cant had refused to accept his delegate credentials to the found- ing CPGB congress and so did not attend.[68] Most importantly, his refusal to go to the Second Congress of the Comintern handed political authority to those who did make the trip, and when Gallacher returned from Moscow at the end of September Maclean found himself marginalised in the communist unity negotiations in Scotland. In December, as a riposte to the formation of the Communist Labour Party – whom he accused of deliberately sowing confusion by appointing the similarly-named John McLean as secretary – the *Vanguard* published an appeal to 'all in Scotland who favour the gist of the "Twenty-One Points" to attend in person or by delegate a conference to form a Scottish Com-

---

63   A report of the conference is in *The Worker*, 16 Oct 1920 and a typescript report 'Com-
       munist Labour Party' is at PHM CP/CENT/COMM/10/03. For an overview, see McKay 1994,
       pp. 84–97.
64   Gallacher claimed he only joined the CLP a few weeks after its formation; 'A Straight Talk
       on Unity', *The Worker*, 13 Nov 1920. For the Bridgeton John Mclean, see *The Socialist*, 7 Oct
       1920.
65   *The Worker*, 4 Dec 1920.
66   *Vanguard*, May 1920.
67   *Vanguard*, June 1920.
68   Maclean's account is in *Vanguard*, Nov 1920.

munist Party to represent the Marxian communism in Scotland, or a definite series of groups who will co-operate or amalgamate with the most definitely Marxian organisation in Scotland, the Socialist Labour Party'.[69]

The conference took place on Christmas Day but was not successful. The SLP attended but showed no interest in any regroupment of Scottish revolutionaries, suggesting only that attendees should join the SLP. The event was better remembered for the confrontation between Maclean and Gallacher. The latter had written to the SLP accusing its chairman James Clunie of taking advantage of Maclean who, claimed Gallacher, suffered from hallucinations. When Gallacher turned up at the conference, Maclean read out the letter as an example of Gallacher's unscrupulousness. The two almost came to blows, which was gleefully reported by the *Daily Record* and the *Sunday Mail*, and ended any possibility that Maclean would play any role in a British communist party.[70]

But by this time, Maclean had abandoned the idea of a Britain-wide party and was calling for a separate communist party for Scotland. Although this reflected his growing belief that Scotland's relationship with England was analogous to that of Ireland and that the Scottish nation should be independent (which led to the *Vanguard* publishing articles by Scottish nationalists Liam Mac Gille Iosa and the aristocrat Erskine of Mar) it was also a response to the right-wing leadership of the CPGB. Pointing out that the CPGB was promoting Colonel Malone as one of its public leaders, Maclean declared 'if England is to be led by Malone, then let us Marxians in Scotland forge ahead on entirely independent lines'. 'We in Scotland must not let ourselves play second fiddle to any organisation with headquarters in London, no more than we would ask Dublin to bend to the will of London', he argued.[71] Accordingly, after his relationship with the SLP soured, he and a small group of supporters set up the Scottish Workers' Republican Party, committed to a Scottish workers' republic. His commitment to the liberation of the working class never wavered, but he increasingly found himself on the fringe of working-class politics. In October 1921 he was yet again jailed for sedition and force-fed while in prison. His health wrecked by the treatment he had suffered at the hands of the prison authorities over the course of the previous eight years, John Maclean died on 30 November 1923, steadfast until his last breath in his commitment to the liberation of the working class.

69   For Mclean, see his reply in *The Worker*, 20 Nov 1920. For the appeal see *Vanguard*, Dec 1920.
70   For reports of the conference, see *The Socialist*, 30 Dec 1920, *The Worker*, 8 Jan 1920 and the *Daily Record*, 27 Dec 1920.
71   'A Scottish Communist Party', *Vanguard*, Dec 1920.

Like Gallacher, Sylvia Pankhurst also discussed with Lenin the urgency of uniting British communists during her time in Moscow and she too pledged herself to creating a unified party on her return home. She still did not agree with the Second Congress's decisions on parliamentarism or Labour party affiliation, but was reassured from her meeting with Lenin that 'he considers that they are not questions of principle at all, but of tactics, which may be employed advantageously in some phases of the changing situation and discarded with advantage in others. Neither question, in his opinion, is important enough to cause a split in the Communist ranks'.[72] Shortly after she arrived back in London in September, her Communist Party (BSTI) held its inaugural conference, at which it decided to support the ECCI's directive to form a united communist party within four months, with the intention of acting as a left-wing faction within the CPGB.[73]

Although it had grown from around 150 to 430 members since its formation, the CP(BSTI) was no more coherent in its politics than the CPGB, and Pankhurst's imperious control of the party was questioned by many of its new members.[74] Edgar Whitehead, who was appointed national secretary in June, was at this stage of his political career essentially a radical Christian socialist, much taken with his belief that 'the essence of our Bolshevik theory lies in the fact that man is a spiritual being' which was taking humanity to a 'glorious Canaan'. He also had rather inchoate objections to the Third International's trade union policy and objected to the party distributing Zinoviev's pamphlet *The Communist Party and Industrial Unionism*.[75] Moreover, he clearly saw himself as rival to Pankhurst's leadership of the party. In September, he complained at the founding conference of the Communist Party of South Wales, the successor to the South Wales Socialist Society, that Pankhurst treated the *Workers' Dreadnought* as her personal property, pointing out she did not consult with the party when she appointed an editor of the paper during her trip to Russia for the Second Congress.[76] In December, the Altrincham and Manchester branches of CP(BSTI) declared that they would not join a unified communist party because of the Comintern's position on parliament, and at the start of

---

72 Pankhurst 1921, p. 45.

73 *Workers' Dreadnought*, 2 Oct 1920.

74 Membership figures in Macfarlane 1966, p. 65. See also 'CP(BSTI) Progress Report (Dec 1920) at RGAPI 495/100/12.

75 'The Spiritual Purposes Behind the Communist', *Workers' Dreadnought*, 11 Sept 1920 and *Workers' Dreadnought*, 2 Oct 1920. Whitehead would subsequently join the Labour Party, move to the British Union of Fascists and end up offering to spy for Nazi Germany; see McIlroy and Campbell 2020a, p. 17.

76 *The Communist*, 30 Sept 1920.

January four branches resigned in opposition to the unity talks. Even Sylvia's loyal lieutenant Norah Smyth publicly called for a referendum of party members to decide whether to join the united party.[77]

The party's difficulties were exacerbated when Pankhurst was arrested on 19 October after the police raided the *Dreadnought* offices and seized copies of the newspaper. She was charged with sedition under Regulation 42 of the Defence of the Realm Act on the basis of four articles in the 16 October 1920 issue of the *Dreadnought*. The articles – on discontent in the navy, opposition to racism on the London docks, the preparation for a national miners' strike, and the betrayals of the Labour Party – revealed more about the current concerns of Lloyd George's government than anything unknown about Pankhurst's politics. However, as the most prominent personality involved in the moves towards a united communist party, her arrest and subsequent jailing sent a strong message to militants that harassment and imprisonment would be a permanent feature of their lives. In late November, two rank and file members of Pankhurst's party had been jailed in Birmingham for making seditious speeches.[78] The following month Colonel Malone l'Estrange was also jailed for six months for sedition. But unlike the Colonel, who secretly offered to work for 'restraint' if the government did not jail him, Pankhurst gave an uncompromising defence of her revolutionary principles from the dock: 'Although I have been a socialist all my life', she told the judge,

> I have tried to palliate the capitalist system. ... But all my experience showed that it was useless trying to palliate an impossible system. This is a wrong system and has got to be smashed. I would give my life to smash it. You cannot frighten me with any sentence you may impose. The only thing that distresses me is that if I am sentenced I shall have to stop work for a while. But ... my friends and I have definitely made up our minds that the capitalist system is an iniquitous one, and it must go. I have just returned from Soviet Russia. There the children are not left to starve. The charge is that I have taught revolution in this country, and I shall continue to teach it.[79]

A month after Pankhurst's incarceration, representatives of her CP(BSTI), the CPGB, the Communist Labour Party, and the National Shop Stewards and Work-

---

77   For Manchester, Altrincham and Smyth, see *Workers' Dreadnought*, 18 Dec 1920. For resignations see *Workers' Dreadnought*, 8 Jan 1921.
78   *Workers' Dreadnought*, 4 Dec 1920.
79   *Workers' Dreadnought*, 6 Nov 1920.

ers' Committee held an informal meeting in London to map out a plan for the unification conference to take place in January. On 11 and 12 December the leaders of those groups, along with observers from the ILP Left Wing, met in Manchester to issue a manifesto on communist unity and agree that the unity conference would be held in Leeds at the end of January. Its goal was the

> clearing away for all time those differences of opinion which have served to keep us apart in the past, thereby preventing the consolidation of the revolutionary forces in this country. It is not our purpose either to explain or justify those differences, but simply to record the fact that our task has been much simplified by the decisions of the recent Congress of the Third International. Those decisions prescribe for the world movement the basis upon which such efforts as ours should he founded, and constitute a clear and definite demand that a united Communist Party shall be established in Britain.[80]

However, those past differences were not so easily overcome. Shortly after her arrest, Pankhurst wrote to Lenin saying that the CPGB leadership was opposed to unity with the other groups, and that she would find it difficult to persuade her supporters that unity was desirable because of the 'parliamentarism and the tameness of the BSP crowd'.[81] A fortnight before the unity congress Pankhurst published a letter in *Workers' Dreadnought* stating she would immediately form a 'left faction' when the new party was created and that the merger with the CPGB meant that 'the conditions under which I placed the *Workers' Dreadnought* at the disposal of the party as its organ will have ceased to operate' and that it would therefore become 'an independent organ, giving an independent support to the Communist Party from the Left Wing standpoint'. This was opposed by Edgar Whitehead but 'A.T.' supported her, arguing that the paper was 'an independent organ, lent to the CP(BSTI). The party has never made itself responsible for any part of the burden of maintaining it'.[82] On 16 January, the CP(BSTI) executive somewhat ambiguously endorsed her action, declaring that

---

80   *Workers' Dreadnought*, 18 Dec 1920.
81   This letter was seized by the police before it reached Russia and published by *The Times*, 27 Oct 1920. Like his father, Andrew Rothstein disliked Pankhurst and opposed merging with the CP(BSTI), see his letter to the ECCI, 20 Oct 1920, at RGASPI, 495/100/10/112.
82   *Workers' Dreadnought*, 15 Jan 1921. Whitehead's opposition is expressed in his letter of 16 Jan 1921, in the Sylvia Pankhurst Papers. It is notable that CP(BSTI) suggested a resolution to the January unity congress that insisted that editors should be appointed rather than elected. See 'Resolutions passed unanimously for incorporation in the agenda of the Leeds Convention', CP/CENT/CONG/01/02.

the paper 'would no longer be the official organ of the party' and repeating her statement that it would instead give 'independent support to the party from the left-wing standpoint'.[83] The rationale for this decision was disingenuous to say the least. When the paper was launched as the *Woman's Dreadnought* in March 1914 its masthead stated that it was 'published by the East London Federation of the Suffragettes' rather than Pankhurst herself, and there had never previously been any indications it was not a party publication. The new publishing arrangement replicated Hyndman's method of putting the SDF's *Justice* outside the control of the party by vesting its ownership in a company he personally controlled. Nor was it any less factionally motivated. Pankhurst's decision could carry no other message than that her support for a united party was in bad faith.

Nevertheless, on 14 January representatives of the CPGB, CLP and CP(BSTI) issued an official call for a conference to found a united communist party, and on Saturday 29 January, under the name of the 'National Fruiterers' Association', over 150 delegates from almost all of Britain's communist organisations met at the Victory Hotel in the centre of Leeds.[84] One hundred and three delegates came from the CPGB, 31 from Scotland's Communist Labour Party, 13 from Pankhurst's CP(BSTI), two each from the Shop Stewards Movement and the ILP Left Wing, and one each from six local organisations. A federal executive committee was created to include representatives from the South of England, the North, Scotland and Wales, who would sit alongside three members nominated by the CPGB and two each from the Scottish and Pankhurst organisations. Arthur MacManus comfortably defeated Willie Gallacher in the election for national chairman, while Albert Inkpin was unopposed as national secretary. The conference did not decide any programmatic issues nor discuss the class struggle in Britain or elsewhere. Its focus was entirely on forging a united party, as the only substantive motion on the agenda made clear:

> This joint convention of the Communist Party of Great Britain, the Communist Labour Party, the Communist Party (BSTI), and independent Communist groups declares its adhesion to the statutes, theses, and conditions of affiliation of the Communist International. Accepting the instructions of the Central Executive Committee regarding the establishment of one Communist Party for Britain on the basis of the Theses of

---

83   *Workers' Dreadnought*, 22 Jan 1921. This has been interpreted as a boycott of the *Dreadnought* by the party, but the executive's statement insisted that 'this formal change in no way affects the policy or financial position of the paper'.

84   'A United Communist Party' at PHM, CP/CENT/CONG/01/02.

the Communist International, the convention hereby merges the above-mentioned organisations in one united Communist Party.[85]

It achieved its goal. As Arthur MacManus told his assembled comrades: 'Today is different from yesterday, or any other day. We are no longer servants of a section, but of a united movement. The communist parties are dead. Long live the Communist Party!'[86]

4   A Stillborn Party?

Two days before MacManus made his speech, Lloyd George's cabinet had met to discuss the coal industry. It decided that control of the mines, which had been ceded to the government during the war, should revert back to the owners on 31 March.[87] The long-anticipated clash between the owners and the miners was now only a matter of time.

The decision was a reflection of, and a response to, Britain's rapidly declining economic position. From the summer of 1920, the post-war boom had come screeching to a halt and quickly went into reverse. Export markets for coal, cotton and shipbuilding evaporated, causing unemployment to shoot up, doubling in the four months from December 1920 to March 1921. The government slashed spending, raised interest rates, and embarked on a policy of increasing productivity and cutting wages. Crucially, it also sought to turn its victories over the trade unions during the previous eighteen months into a decisive defeat of the labour movement and fundamentally shift the balance of power in British politics. Lloyd George's long-held desire to put an end finally to the 'Long 1914' of labour unrest was coming to fruition.

To achieve that victory, Britain's 1.19 million miners had to be defeated. As soon as the government announced it was withdrawing from the coal industry, the mine owners declared they would scrap national wage agreements and slash wages by up to fifty per cent. As everyone expected, the Miners' Federation would not negotiate on such terms, and on 1 April the employers locked out all miners until they agreed to wage cuts and local bargaining. As tensions rose, the government mobilised troops and invoked the Emergency Powers Act.

---

85   'Communist Unity Convention Agenda' at PHM, CP/CENT/CONG/01/02.

86   The official report of the Leeds conference is covered in *Workers' Dreadnought*, *The Worker*, and *The Communist*, all 5 Feb 1921, and in a detailed secret service report, *Fortnightly Report*, 3 Feb 1921, TNA CAB 24/119/42.

87   'Position of the Coal Industry', 27 Jan 1921, TNA CAB 24/118/92.

A week after the lock-out began, the Triple Alliance announced it would take strike action on 12 April in support of the miners unless the owners agreed to negotiations. This was postponed until 15 April after Lloyd George met the miners on 11 April, but still the employers refused to budge. The night before the Triple Alliance was due to strike, Miners' Federation secretary Frank Hodges met with MPs and allegedly told them vaguely he would be prepared to discuss better terms with the employers. Through this narrow crack the leaders of the Triple Alliance, desperate to avoid confrontation with the government, drove a coach and horses, declaring that now Hodges had agreed to talks there was no need for a strike. Although Hodges and the Federation denied this was case, the Triple Alliance called off the strike – and Friday 15 April 1920 would forever be remembered as 'Black Friday'. Isolated and facing a determined enemy, the miners were eventually forced back to work on 1 July. The government and the employers now held the whip hand.

Throughout the dispute, the new CPGB warned that the right-wing Triple Alliance leaders might sell out the miners. The week before Black Friday *The Communist* wrote 'our reformist leaders may yet be compelled to call for action. If they give the signal – good. But if they fail to give the signal? If they fail, you must not fail. Out of the hands of the reformists must power be taken, and into the hands of those who see straight and clearly must power go'.[88] One of those it thought saw 'straight and clearly' was Transport Workers' Federation secretary and CPGB member Robert Williams who, along with the NUR's J.H. Thomas, was a central leader of the Triple Alliance. Williams was as implicated as Thomas in Black Friday, and *The Communist* publicly criticised him shortly before the betrayal for 'consistently assisting negotiations towards a climb-down'.[89] The following week MacManus wrote a letter to Williams on behalf of the CPGB asking him to explain his conduct during the crisis, which ended, without sarcasm, 'trusting you are somewhat recovered from the strain. Yours fraternally, Arthur MacManus'.[90] Williams does not appear to have replied and was expelled from the CPGB at its Third Congress at the end of April. Although Williams's membership clearly had little political significance for him and he was not integrated into the party, his role in the betrayal indicated how the CPGB struggled to differentiate itself from the 'official' left-wing leadership of the labour movement. During the lock-out, its propaganda focused on the danger that Thomas would betray the miners, something of which even Lloyd George was certain, but said nothing about the left-wing union leaders.

---

88   *The Communist*, 9 April 1921.
89   *The Communist*, 16 April 1921.
90   *The Communist*, 23 April 1921.

When the CPGB drew up a balance sheet of the events at its third congress in April, it merely repeated the pre-war analysis of the syndicalists and the SLP, with a belated criticism of the left-wing union leaders: 'We repeat, Watch Your Leaders! Watch even the left wingers, for their own sakes as well as yours. Being a leader is very unhealthy work. One is cut off from the influence of the rank and file, and is plunged into the artificial life of hotels, conferences and the political maelstrom. The most vigorous left-winger is apt to wilt and fade under these circumstances. Watch them!'[91] The belief that the left-wing labour and trade union leaders were well-intentioned but prone to go astray – a mark of the CPGB's politics for almost its entire life – meant the party was unable to present a coherent alternative programme to the lefts. As was the case during its discussions with the Labour Party leadership about affiliation, it presented itself as nothing more than the most steadfast supporter of the same political programme as the Labour left. To some extent this reflected its pre-war roots, when Williams and Robert Smillie had been elected to lead their unions on a tide of working-class militancy. But the events of the post-war years, especially during 1919, had demonstrated that workplace militancy and an abstract belief in socialism were not enough when faced with the question of state power. Williams and Smillie failed that challenge, not because they had been 'softened' by office but because they did not have a political perspective of fighting for working-class state power. This was the crucial difference between the Communist International and all other tendencies in the labour movement internationally, yet it was not a distinction understood by the CPGB.

The weaknesses of the CPGB were laid bare in June 1921 when the Third Congress of the Comintern convened. In his report on tactics and strategy, Karl Radek criticised the party's work during the miners' strike, saying it had no slogans and no policy for the strike, and failed to organise its activities systematically. *The Communist* at this time was edited by Francis Maynell, an upper-class intellectual who remained a Christian throughout his editorship.[92] Radek singled out *The Communist* for particular criticism, saying 'it is significant that the paper does not carry any reports of what the party is doing in the mining districts'.[93] In response, Joe Vaughan, the CPGB's Labour mayor of Bethnal Green in London's East End, claimed the party was 'blameless', arguing that 'it would be simple idiocy for the CP to have attempted to influence or give advice to the miners, who have one and a quarter million members in their union'.[94]

91   *The Communist*, 30 April 1920.
92   Postgate 1994, pp. 113–14.
93   Radek, 'Report on Tactics and Strategy' in Riddell 2015, p. 415.
94   Riddell 2015, p. 477.

Quite what the purpose of the party therefore was, he did not explain. Tom Bell also defended the party's failure to recruit new members by claiming that 'there has never been a large political party in Britain ... for this reason, the British workers' organisations cannot be measured by European standards. ... It will probably never be possible to organise a big political party in Britain'.[95] Although Bell claimed the party had 10,000 members, the number of seriously active, politically engaged, and, not unimportantly, dues-paying members was probably less than 2,000.[96] Exasperated, Radek replied to the British by telling them 'When we say "to the masses", you reply, "Lloyd George also has a small party". That is not the way to respond when we say go to the masses'.[97]

The burden of overcoming the shortcomings of the CPGB fell to the Communist International. The party's failure to campaign against British imperialism, especially in relation to Ireland and India, was first addressed by Lenin and Radek in 1920, and was raised again by Zinoviev at the Third Enlarged Plenum of the Executive Committee of the Comintern in June 1923, when he observed that the party's 'greatest political weakness, in my opinion, is found on the national question, where it is paying an excessive tribute to the traditions of the Second International'.[98] At the Fourth Congress of the Comintern, Clara Zetkin also pointed out that 'in Britain, party bodies for the necessary and systematic activity among the female proletariat are almost completely absent' and attacked the party for its 'abstention' from work among women workers.[99] Far from being a malign influence in the formative era of the CPGB, as historians such as Walter Kendall have claimed, the Comintern sought to pull the party away from the national and chauvinist pressures exerted on it by British society.

The CPGB's inability to intervene in the 1921 miners' strike demonstrated that it was a very sickly infant. Sylvia Pankhurst's supporters played little role in it, and the now independent *Workers' Dreadnought* grew increasingly detached from the CPGB. In July the *Dreadnought* attacked the Labour-controlled Poplar Council for a ten per cent cut in 'outdoor relief' payments to the unemployed, and pointed out that CPGB councillors Edgar and Minnie Lansbury had suppor-

---

95   Riddell 2015, p. 533.
96   The 1922 party commission found that the CPGB had one paid official for every 33 dues-paying members; as it had 55 officials on the party payroll, this meant it had 1,815 paid-up members: Thorpe 2000, p. 50.
97   Riddell 2015, p. 585.
98   Zinoviev report to the Third Enlarged Plenum of the ECCI, in Taber and Riddell, 2019, p. 409.
99   Zetkin speech in Riddell 2012, pp. 841–2.

ted the cuts. The Bow branch of the CPGB then attacked Pankhurst, who had been released from prison in May, for violating 'party discipline' and demanded approval of any article that might 'cause injury to the party or to prejudice the communist reputation of any other member'.[100] Shortly after, Pankhurst was asked by a sub-committee of the CPGB executive to hand control of the *Dreadnought* over to the party. She refused and was summoned to appear before the executive on 10 September. Once again, she declined to relinquish control of the paper and was expelled from the party.[101] Her close supporters such as Norah Smyth did not fight the decision but simply gave up and resigned from the party.[102] Pankhurst subsequently aligned herself with the ultra-left German Communist Workers' Party and its call for a new communist international but she became an increasingly isolated figure on the left and, less than three years later, the *Dreadnought* and her organisation ceased to exist.[103]

It wasn't just Pankhurst and her supporters who faded out of communist politics. The old BSP leadership which led the founding of the CPGB also disappeared from the scene. Apart from Albert Inkpin, who began his career as a party secretary under Hyndman in 1913 and finished under Harry Pollitt in 1929, all five BSP members elected to the CPGB central committee at its founding congress had left by the fifth congress in late 1922. The central committee's only link with the historic leadership of the BSP would then be Tom Quelch, and he too would be gone at the next congress. But although the BSP's leading personnel largely left the scene, its politics did not.

The accretion to the CPGB of the 'Guild Communists' of the National Guilds' League and the ILP Left Wing, which joined in March 1921 after the ILP voted decisively against joining the Comintern, provided the party with a group of highly-educated middle-class radicals who would constitute its intellectual core during the inter-war years. The Guild Communists grew out of the Guild Socialist movement, which emerged in the mid-1900s as a peculiarly British concoction of syndicalist ideas and romantic notions of medieval craft guilds,

---

100   *Workers' Dreadnought*, 30 July 1921. See the 2 and 16 July issues for the debate on Poplar council.

101   Pankhurst's extensive account of her expulsion is in *Workers' Dreadnought*, 17 Sept 1921. Robin Page Arnot later claimed that her expulsion was at least in part motivated by Arthur MacManus's animus towards her; see Robin Page Arnott papers, 'Transcript of Interview – 1920–21 Miscellany', UDAR 2/2/23, Hull History Centre. I am grateful to Robert Styles for his comments on this section.

102   See Smyth's letter of resignation from the Bow branch of the CPGB in *Workers' Dreadnought*, 24 Sept 1921.

103   For the subsequent history of the 'WSF tradition', see Shipway 1988; Hayes 2005; Bullock 2014.

similar to Robert Blatchford's nationalist conceptions of socialism reviving 'Merrie England'. Guild Socialism gained some traction before the war as a drawing room version of syndicalism which saw 'guilds' of workers taking control of each industry and thus overcoming capitalism. It captured the imagination of a layer of Oxford University Fabian Society students around G.D.H. Cole and William Mellor, and in 1912 they became the founding cadre of Sydney and Beatrice Webb's Fabian Research Department, better known later as the Labour Research Department. In 1915, Cole and his allies formed the National Guilds' League, which by the end of the war had branches in most major cities in Britain. Its journal *The Guildsman* boasted an eclectic range of high-profile contributors, including Bertrand Russell, R.H. Tawney and Hilaire Belloc. Inevitably the organisation began to splinter over support for the October Revolution and at its 1920 conference the 'Guild Communist' faction, which included Robin Page Arnot, Norman and Monica Ewer, William Mellor and Ellen Wilkinson, won a majority to support the 'Soviet System'.[104] It sent five delegates to the CPGB's founding congress, and by the end of 1921 it had been fully integrated into the party, leaving a non-communist rump to limp on until the summer of 1923.[105]

One of those who joined the CPGB from the National Guilds' League was Rajani Palme Dutt, who would become the dominant intellectual figure of the party.[106] Dutt, born in Cambridge to a Bengali father and Swedish mother, had apparently swapped his membership of the ILP Left Wing to the National Guilds' League so that he could attend the CPGB's founding congress.[107] The rest of his ILP comrades joined him in the CPGB in April 1921 following the ILP conference's rejection of the Comintern. The ILP split was neither as large nor as significant as had been hoped – Kendall estimates that it numbered between 500 and one thousand – but it did bring in a number of people who would become significant CPGB cadre, such as Emile Burns, Helen Crawfurd, Shapurji Saklatvala, Ernie Brown, and, for a short time, the future Communist MP J.T. Walton Newbold.[108] With the exception of Brown and Crawfurd, the

---

104   'The Annual Conference of 1920', *The Guildsman*, June 1920, pp. 4–5.

105   For the National Guilds League, see Macintyre 1980, pp. 180–4; Kendall 1969, pp. 278–83; *Autobiographical Details of Newbold's Political Life*, John Turner Walton Newbold Papers, John Rylands Library, Manchester, ref: GB 133 NEW, chapter 2, page 3; *The Call*, 22 July 1920.

106   Dutt had written an article in support of the dictatorship of the proletariat in the October 1919 edition of *The Guildsman*.

107   Callaghan 1993, p. 24. Dutt is not listed as a delegate to the congress, see the *Official Report*, p. 72.

108   See the 'Manifesto of the ILP Left Wing', in *The Communist*, 26 March 1921.

leaders of both the ILP Left Wing and the Guild Communists were young intellectuals with little experience of the class struggle, whose politics were shaped by their proximity to the Labour Party. Saklatvala's resignation letter from the ILP merely complained that the party was 'seeking municipal and parliamentary advantages at the sacrifice of the spirit of true socialism' and made no mention of the huge political questions facing the working class at that time.[109] With the former SLP leaders such as Bell and MacManus essentially embracing the position of the BSP on Labour Party affiliation, this meant that there was no internal counter-weight to what was effectively the continuation of the BSP policy by the CPGB.

This inability to deal with the legacy of the BSP's politics was not helped by Comintern chairman Gregory Zinoviev's shifting position on the Labour Party which moved away from Lenin's definition of it as a 'bourgeois labour party'. At the Third Congress of the Comintern in April 1921, Zinoviev called on the CPGB to 'take part in the mass organisation that embraces hundreds of thousands and millions of proletarians, to organise our forces there, form cells, and in this way influence it', implying that Labour was not political party with its own programme but an organisation that could be taken over, a position not unlike that of the BSP or even Kautsky in 1908.[110] In December this stance was reinforced in the 'Theses on the United Front' which characterised Labour as 'a kind of general workers' association for the whole country', and a few months later he described it as 'a curious phenomenon, half trade union and half party'.[111] In contrast, Radek at the Fourth Congress of the Comintern rebuked the CPGB for its failure to differentiate itself from the Labour left, quoting a Bible story to describe its stance as being 'wherever Naomi is, there too am I, Ruth'.[112]

Despite confusion over the Labour Party question, it was the Third Congress of the Comintern in April 1921 which systematically sought to correct the post-partum problems of the CPGB. Spurred by the ECCI's decision to set up a commission to look into the state of the party, the CPGB voted at its March 1922 congress to establish a committee of Harry Pollitt, Rajani Palme Dutt and Harry Inkpin (Albert Inkpin's brother) to develop proposals that would reorganise the party on the principles laid out in the *Guidelines on the Organizational Struc-*

---

109   Saklatvala's letter is printed in Squires 1990, pp. 31–2.

110   Riddell 2015, p. 179.

111   Taber and Riddell 2019, pp. 99 and 258.

112   Riddell 2012, p. 473. After attending the 1924 CPGB Congress, the KPD's Ruth Fischer had reported that 'It seems to me that the [CPGB] member belongs to the Labour Party on weekdays, and on Sundays, by way of rest and recreation, plays a little with the communists', quoted in Carr 1972, pp. 133–4.

ture of Communist Parties which had been passed at the Third Congress.[113] Yet, its heritage meant that the CPGB instinctively took positions to the right of the Comintern leadership, even after the Stalin faction had consolidated its control of the international by 1924. Rather than being pulled to the right by Stalin leadership, as Brian Pearce and Michael Woodhouse argued, the British party's attitude to the left-wing leadership of the labour movement throughout the early 1920s prefigured the Comintern's later soft-pedalling of political differences in the Anglo-Russian Trade Union Committee and during the General Strike.[114]

If not quite stillborn, the CPGB suffered severe congenital weakness from birth. Its political genes were inherited from the Rothstein/Fineberg wing of the BSP and these traits were replicated by the cadres who joined it from the Guild Socialists and the ILP Left Wing, not to mention Theodore Rothstein's son Andrew, who became a central leader of the party. The historians John McIlroy and Alan Campbell have also shown in their biographical analyses of the CPGB's early leadership that former SLP members 'maintained near parity' with the ex-BSPers in the allocation of senior party roles throughout the 1920s.[115] Despite this potential fractious situation, the CPGB did not undergo any serious factional disputes before the Comintern's 'Third Period' of the late 1920s, unlike almost every other communist party in the world. When the old divisions did occasionally resurface it was over personal issues, such as Mac-Manus's leadership style. As was seen during the CPGB's attempts to affiliate to the Labour Party, the former SLP leaders also essentially adopted the framework of the BSP's politics.

Those who rejected the political compromises of the former SLPers in the CPGB offered no serious alternatives. John Maclean and Sylvia Pankhurst, the two most capable and charismatic leaders on the Marxist left, were incapable of working collectively with others or subordinating their personalities to the needs of fighting for revolutionary politics. The SLP itself sought to shut the door on the new world of the 1920s and quickly slipped into irrelevance, with *The Socialist* ceasing publication in December 1922. Whatever its weaknesses, the CPGB stood alone as a revolutionary organisation that survived the maelstrom of post-war Britain, albeit frail, confused, and forever weakened by its inheritance from its BSP parents.

---

113   The background and the outcomes of the commission are best described in Macfarlane 1966, pp. 74–82.
114   This argument is also made in Hinton and Hyman 1975.
115   McIlroy and Campbell 2020b, p. 647.

Conclusion

The defeat of Black Friday of April 1921 marked a decisive shift in the balance of class forces in British society. The working-class combativity which challenged the status quo from 1910 now started to recede. In the first half of 1922 engineering workers, the most militant and strongest section of the working class during World War One, suffered a major defeat when they were locked out and forced to accept deep wage cuts. Economic depression, rising unemployment levels which hit two million people in 1922, and the employers' renewed confidence meant that the working class found itself on the defensive. These defeats were not merely due to the aggressive stance of the employers. As Black Friday demonstrated, the leadership of the trade unions, right and left, did not want to confront the government and sought to compromise with, rather than challenge, the employers.

This change in class relations was symbolised by the fall of Lloyd George in October 1922. Now that the explosive tensions of the previous decade were being defused, there was no need for the flamboyant charisma of the would-be Welsh Bonaparte.[1] He was replaced briefly by the industrialist and pre-war Conservative Party leader Bonar Law, who symbolically represented a return to the *status quo ante bellum*, and then by the staid and sober Stanley Baldwin, who like Bonar Law was an iron manufacturer, a section of the British capitalist class that was keenly aware of its declining position in world trade and acutely conscious of class conflict in industry and society. Together with Labour's Ramsay MacDonald, Baldwin established the template for British politics in the interwar years, and the two alternated as prime minister for the next 14 years. Lloyd George's personal ambition had destroyed his own Liberal Party as a serious force, and the electoral rise of the Labour Party in the early 1920s – MacDonald would become the first Labour Prime Minister in January 1924 – set the stage for the British two-party system for the rest of the twentieth century. The power of the organised working class and the fear of another great labour unrest resulted in capitalism granting reforms to alleviate working-class living conditions, and in return the Labour Party and trade union leaders sought to prevent workers' militancy from challenging capitalism.

This recasting of British politics was ultimately made possible by the defeat of the General Strike in May 1926. Despite the demoralisation caused by Black

---

1   For an assessment of Lloyd George's career, see Karl Radek, 'Lloyd George's Resignation', *International Press Correspondence*, Vol. 2, No. 95 (3 Nov 1922), pp. 729–31.

Friday and its consequences, militancy was not extinguished, and in the coal-fields dissatisfaction with falling wages and increasing hours was widespread. Nor had the mine-owners yet taken the full pound of flesh they craved. When they announced further wage reductions in June 1925, pressure from the TUC led to a government-inspired compromise that postponed the cuts and, as in 1919, a royal commission was established to look into the state of the industry. When Herbert Samuel's commission reported back in March 1926, it suppor-ted the wage cuts. Six weeks of negotiations resulted in deadlock and on 1 May the miners were locked out. When Baldwin abruptly broke off discussions with the TUC aimed at finding a compromise, the TUC General Council found itself with no alternative but to call the general strike it had threatened but never expected to deliver.

However, unlike 1919, there was never any serious fear that the situation could escalate to threaten the state. The government had spent the previous year making meticulous plans, and both the right and the left of the TUC were desperate to reach an agreement with the government, even at the expense of the miners. Nevertheless, the General Strike captured the imagination of signi-ficant sections of the working class, to the extent that there were more people on strike the day after the TUC called it off than there had been on the day before. The miners were left to starve and were eventually forced back to work by the end of the year. The final act of the 'Long 1914' was complete, carried out by a ruling class that now felt itself to be firmly in the saddle, aided by a Labour Party and trade union leadership content with its place in the prevailing order. And so British politics were defined for almost the rest of the twentieth century.

1   In Praise of Learning

By the time of the General Strike, the membership of the CPGB had grown from probably less than 2,000 in 1921 to 6,000. *Workers' Weekly*, the newspaper that had replaced the widely criticised *The Communist* in February 1923 would claim, probably without too much exaggeration, that it was selling 60,000 cop-ies in early 1926. By the end of the year, the party declared that it had over 300 factory-based branches.[2] Throughout this period, the CPGB broadly continued the policy of the BSP rendered into the language of the Comintern. Thus its slogan of 'All Power to the General Council' was an extension of the call for a 'general staff' of the labour movement that the BSP had first raised in 1917.

---

2 Macfarlane 1966, p. 302.

The CPGB's attitude to the left-wing leaders of the Labour Party and the trade unions, such as Alf Purcell, Alonso Swales and George Hicks, was, like that of the BSP, based on a belief that they were merely inconsistent socialists whose resolution needed stiffening. These tendencies were encouraged by Zinoviev's equivocal stance towards the Labour Party. By presenting itself as essentially a more resolute and consistent version of Labour's left-wing, the CPGB disarmed itself against the Labour leadership's argument that there was no need for a revolutionary party because the Labour Party would deliver socialism through parliament.

The shock and disorientation felt by the CPGB leadership at the betrayal of the General Strike by the left-wing trade union leaders underlined its inflated expectations of the Labourite left. The collapse of this perspective, combined with its loyalty to the political vicissitudes of Stalin's leadership of the Comintern, meant that the party leaders had little difficulty falling in behind the Comintern's 1928 view that world capitalism had entered a 'Third Period' of economic collapse in which the labour and social democratic parties were being transformed into 'social fascist' organisations. Thus it went from Willie Gallacher stating it was 'fundamentally' in agreement with the Labour Party in 1921 to J.T. Murphy in 1930 describing the 'evolution of the Labour Party into a Social-Fascist party and the rapid growth of Social-Fascism in the trade unions' while denouncing the 'left social-fascism' of the ILP.[3] Such statements were at best a product of frustration at the failure of its previous conciliatory perspectives rather than any serious analysis of the Labour Party or, indeed, the CPGB's past politics.

However, by this time, the CPGB was a very different party to that born of the tortuous unity discussions 1919 and 1920. Few of those involved in that process still played any role in the party. Even Tom Bell and Arthur MacManus (who died in 1927) would be relegated to the sidelines after the re-organisation of the party that began in March 1922, and although he had been active in revolutionary politics before the war, the talented Harry Pollitt was not previously a significant figure on left. Why did so few of the revolutionaries of the pre-war and war-time period become part of the Communist Party or continue as revolutionaries? Of course, some of this can be explained by generational shift and the physical and mental toll of being a revolutionary in Britain. The threat of prison was ever-present in the daily lives of working-class militants, not to mention the likelihood of being sacked or victimised for political activit-

---

3   J.T. Murphy, 'The Growth of Social-Fascism in Britain', *Communist Review*, vol. 2, no. 1 (Jan 1930). For a sympathetic view of the Third Period in Britain, see Worley 2001.

ies. During the 1921 miners' dispute, MacManus told the Executive Committee of the Comintern, 130 members of the CPGB had been jailed, along with party secretary Albert Inkpin.[4]

But the full explanation lies in the political sphere. The certainties of pre-war revolutionary politics no longer applied. The belief that the working class could take over industry and force the capitalists to surrender, which in various forms had been the common view of syndicalists and the SLP, or that raising the educational level of the workers would lead to the scales falling from their eyes and lead to a massive parliamentary majority for socialism, as was believed by John Maclean and the left of the BSP, were demonstrated to be inadequate in the immediate post-war period. The experience of the 1919–20 period in Britain, and the rest of Europe since 1917, highlighted the centrality of the question of state power to the establishment of working-class rule. As Lloyd George made clear in his famous discussion with Robert Smillie in February 1919, it was not enough for the workers to take over an industry; they would still be confronted by the force of the capitalist state. For many of those who had spent their lives fighting against capitalism with pre-war revolutionary politics, having to leave behind their old ideas was too big a leap to make.

The eclipse of a generation of revolutionaries was not a new phenomenon. The defeat of the Chartists ended revolutionary politics in Britain for over a generation. Physical exhaustion and death played a role but political disorientation took the heaviest toll, as former revolutionaries despaired of working-class action and instead sought democratic reforms through the Liberal Party. Although not entirely analogous, the waves of electoral successes of the Labour Party in the post-World War One years seemed for many veterans of the Great Labour Unrest and war-time militancy to offer a compelling alternative to revolutionary socialism. It did not. The Labour Party sought to curb working-class struggle when in opposition and acted no differently to Lloyd George and his Conservative successors when it came to power in 1924. But the collapse of the pre-war revolutionary left meant that the CPGB essentially had to be built from scratch following the Third Congress of the Comintern. With the partial exception of Pollitt, no central CPGB leader had played any significant role in the working-class movement before 1919.

Does the failure of the CPGB to build a mass revolutionary party in the 1920s mean that the revolutionaries who fought to liberate the working class since the 1889 London dockers' strike had failed? Although it is currently fashion-

---

4   MacManus, 'Report on Britain' in Zinoviev report to the Third Enlarged Plenum of the ECCI, in Taber and Riddell 2019, p. 80.

able to believe that the men and women who fought for workers' revolution were at best mistaken or at worst delusional, the reality is that whatever mistakes they made, they left a crucial legacy. Whether through the bravery of their struggle or the heroism of their sacrifices, they provided a beacon for the future. Without the example of Eleanor Marx, John Maclean or the thousands of others who fought against capitalism, war and oppression – and sought to build a communist party in the best way they knew – the fight for the liberation of humanity today would be weaker. Most importantly, their political struggles allow those who possess the benefit of hindsight to examine the political lessons of the past, and turn them into a political programme that will free the working class and all the oppressed from the chains that reduce them to wage slaves and crush the human spirit. As the great German communist poet Bertolt Brecht wrote:

> Learn the elementary things!
> For those whose time has come
> It is never too late!
> Learn the ABC. It won't be enough,
> But learn it! Don't be dismayed by it.
> Begin! You must know everything.
> You must lake over the leadership.[5]

5   Willett 1990, p. 110.

Timeline

1864	International Workingmen's Association ('First International') founded.
1871	Paris Commune takes power from 18 March to 28 May.
1881	Democratic Federation founded by H.M. Hyndman.
1883	Karl Marx dies on 14 March.
1884	Democratic Federation changes name to Social Democratic Federation. On 27 December, Eleanor Marx and William Morris lead a split from the SDF and found the Socialist League.
1887	'Bloody Sunday' in London when police attack a demonstration against unemployment and repression in Ireland.
1888	Women workers strike at Bryant & May's match factory East London in July.
1889	London dockers' strike begins in August.
1889	Second International founded in Paris.
1893	Independent Labour Party founded in Bradford.
1893	Two miners shot dead in Featherstone by troops during a national mining lock out.
1895	Death of Friedrich Engels on 5 August.
1897	National engineering lock out.
1898	Death of Eleanor Marx on 31 March.
1899–1902	Anglo-South African 'Boer' War.
1900	Labour Representation Committee founded.
1900	Second International congress in Paris debates 'Millerandism'.
1901	Taff Vale court judgement threatens unions with bankruptcy.
1903	Socialist Labour Party formed in June.
1903	Russian Social Democratic and Labour Party splits into Bolsheviks and Mensheviks at London congress in August.
1903	Women's Social and Political Union founded in October.
1904	Socialist Party of Great Britain founded in June.
1904	Second International congress in Amsterdam calls for unity of socialist parties in each country.
1906	LRC changes name to the Labour Party and gains 29 MPs at General Election.
1907	Belfast dockers' strike.
1908	SDF changes its name to the Social Democratic Party.

1908	SLP forms the 'Advocates of Industrial Unionism', renamed the Industrial Workers of Great Britain in 1909.
1909	Ruskin College strike leads to the formation of the Plebs League and the Central Labour College.
1910	Cambrian Combine miners strike in South Wales. Start of 'Great Labour Unrest'.
1910	Tom Mann forms Industrial Syndicalist Education League in November.
1911	Major strike at Singer's Sewing Machine factory strike in Glasgow in March.
1911	Two protestors shot dead by troops during Liverpool transport strike in August.
1911	National railway strike ended after Lloyd George warns union leaders they are damaging the national interest during the Agadir Crisis.
1911	British Socialist Party founded in September.
1912	National coal miners strike begins in February.
1912	Tom Mann jailed for sedition in May for publishing 'Don't Shoot!' leaflet. *The Miners' Next Step* pamphlet is published.
1913	Dublin dockers locked out for almost five months from August. In November the Irish Citizen Army is founded.
1914	Sylvia Pankhurst is expelled from WSPU in February, launches *The Woman's Dreadnought* in March.
1914	Britain enters World War One on 4 August.
1915	Labour Party joins Asquith's government in May.
1915	Glasgow Rent strike begins in May. John Maclean begins publishing *Vanguard* in September.
1915	Zimmerwald conference of anti-war socialists held in Switzerland in September.
1916	Clyde Workers Committee begins publishing *The Worker* in January.
1916	Anti-war faction of BSP begins publishing *The Call* in February.
1916	John Maclean, Willie Gallacher and John Muir jailed, and five shop stewards are deported from Glasgow.
1916	Kienthal conference of the left wing of anti-war socialists held in April in Switzerland.
1916	Hyndman leads his supporters out of the BSP in April to form the National Socialist Party.
1916	Easter Rising in Dublin.
1917	Russian Revolution begins in Petrograd in January.

1917	In March Alice Wheeldon is sentenced to 10 years penal servitude on trumped-up charges.
1917	In May the Leeds Convention meets. Lloyd George sets up Commission of Enquiry into Industrial Unrest.
1917	October Revolution takes place.
1918	Labour Party adopts new constitution which include Clause Four in February and becomes a membership party.
1918	World War One ends on 11 November. General Election held on 14 December.
1919	Soldiers' strikes break out in the British Army in January, as do engineering strikes in Belfast and Glasgow. On 31 January 'Bloody Friday' takes place in Glasgow.
1919	'Hands Off Russia' campaign founded in 18 January.
1919	Dáil Éireann established in Dublin on 21 January, Irish independence declared, and War of Independence breaks out.
1919	In February the national miners' strike is postponed as union leaders accept Lloyd George's offer of places on the Sankey Commission enquiry.
1919	On 2 March the Communist International is founded in Moscow.
1919	Amritsar massacre takes place on 13 April.
1919	National rail strike called off in October after Lloyd George compromises.
1920	In February the West European Bureau of the Comintern meets in Amsterdam discusses unity of British revolutionary groups.
1920	On 10 May London dockers refuse to load 'Jolly George' with armaments for Polish war against Soviet Russia.
1919	On 9 August Labour Party and the TUC set up a Council of Action to oppose war with Soviet Russia.
1920	On 19 June the WSF forms the Communist Party (British Section of the Third International).
1920	On 19 July the Second Congress of the Communist International opens in Moscow.
1920	On 31 July Communist Party of Great Britain formed by the BSP and the Communist Unity Group, along with smaller revolutionary organisations.
1920	Communist Labour Party formed in Glasgow on 2 October.
1921	On 29 January 'Communist Unity' congress is held in Leeds, and unites CPGB, CP(BSTI), CLP, the ILP Left Wing, the Shop Stewards Movement and six other groups in a united Communist Party.

Figures

FIGURE 1   The SLP's *Socialist* (June 1915) opposes World War One.

THE CALL

An Organ of International Socialism

No. 84	THURSDAY, NOVEMBER 15, 1917	ONE PENNY

The Second Russian Revolution

The expected has happened, Kerensky and the Provisional Council has been overthrown, and the Soviet has taken control in Petrograd. Would that the Soviet had never surrendered its power at the beginning of the Revolution, Russia would have been in a far stronger position than she is now. As it is this second revolution may still have been brought about in time. The reactionaries are hoping for civil war. How affairs will shape in the event of an armed conflict, we cannot at the time of writing predict. We know that Maximalist opinion has rapidly spread throughout Russia. The workmen, peasants, and soldiers have remained faithful to the Revolution. Even if the reactionaries are able to muster a force to oppose the new Government, there are, nevertheless, strong hopes that the Revolution will be saved. It is not difficult to trace the events that led up to, and made necessary the deposing of Kerensky and the Provisional Government. From the first moment that he began to compromise with the middle-class parties he has steadily drifted towards the Right. He became an easy tool in the hands of the reactionaries. He sanctioned the disastrous offensive. He sought the suppression of the Army Committees that protected the Army from its reactionary Generals. It is established now that he was closely implicated in the Korniloff rising. Its object at first was to suppress the Soviet and establish a triple dictatorship, including himself. That he was not the leader of the Korniloff rising instead of its apparent suppressor was simply the result of a misunderstanding. Since then his opposition to the Soviet took another form. The recent Coalition Government and Provisional Council was designed to remove all powers from the Soviet. This it would have done but for the action of the Maximalists. It was becoming noticeable, too, that the Government was reverting to the Imperialist policy of Tsarism. Kerensky, from leader of the Revolution, became the leader of the counter-revolution.

The programme of the new revolutionary Government brings the immediate objects of the Revolution back to what it was at the commencement: Immediate democratic peace, the granting of land to the peasants, and the convocation of the Constituent Assembly. Russia must have peace now, there is no question about that. Kerensky admitted that she is worn out. Russia once again holds out the offer of a general democratic peace, which, if the peoples of Europe desired it, can be secured now. If, however, a deaf ear is once again turned to her entreaties, what is she to do? Revolutionary Russia does not desire a separate peace. The Revolution prevented the Tsar from making a separate peace. The Soviet prevented Miliukoff from doing the same. It is the reactionary Minister of War, Vertchovsky, who proposes a separate peace to Kerensky. But if Russia is compelled through sheer exhaustion to make a separate peace the responsibility will rest on the Governments and people of the Entente. Their treatment of the Revolution has been shameful. A conference on war aims was promised for months, it has now been abandoned. Lloyd George's contemptible trick on the occasion of the Stockholm discussion did not enhance the respect for the honour of British statesmanship in Russia. Added to this is the flood of abuse and invective that daily pours from the press that is supposed to represent the ideas of "Liberal" England. Russia has a right to say that she has been betrayed by her Allies.

Once again the democracy of Russia stretches out its hand to the people of Europe. Surely the eyes of the people have by now been opened to the real character of this war. Are they to continue to allow the Imperialist Governments to drag the world to its ruin? Or will they respond to this further appeal from Russia to end this horrible carnage, and establish the reign of peace and freedom?

Notes and Comments

THE OPEN DOOR IN CHINA.

When the struggle to gain supremacy in China's markets is resumed, the other exporting nations will probably find that the economic agreement just signed by the United States and Japan, constitutes a formidable barrier to the acquisition of riches at the expense of the people of the Chinese Republic. By her treaty with Great Britain, Japan is pledged to preserve the territorial integrity of China, but our eastern Ally has not failed to reap advantages in Asia because of Britain's heavy obligations in other parts of the globe. Japanese statesmen proceed on the principle that economic conquest need not be *preceded* by military victory. Hence Mr. Lansing, the United States Foreign Secretary, in his letter to Viscount Ishii, points out that while the new understanding preserves Chinese territory intact, territorial propinquity creates special relations between countries. The prohibition of the export of steel by America to Japan provided the Japanese diplomatists with a ground for demanding some compensating concession. The Government at Washington has for long regarded Japanese movements in China with considerable misgiving, but Japan is now in a position to enforce her demands and so bring to an end what Mr. Lansing described as an increasingly critical situation. We are given to understand that the terms of the conversations between the United States Government and the Japanese Mission cannot now be made public. But in case there should be doubt and suspicion in the minds of the capitalist traders of other nations, looking forward to their share of Chinese favours to come, we are informed from Washington that the pact was really made in order to defeat German machinations, intended to alienate Japan from her

Allies in the war. Thus does statesmanship acting in agreement with the interests of finance and trade turn patriotism into gold. Apparently the United States Government, despite its preference for Republicanism, did not consult the victim—China.

SUPPRESSING THE HOUSE OF COMMONS

The most interesting part of the sittings of the House of Commons is question time. Not because of the variety of matters dealt with, but because of the remarkable skill exhibited by the various heads of departments concerned in juggling with the questions put to them. Mr. Balfour and Mr. Bonar Law, however, are complete masters of what one might call the art of evasion. They can reply to a whole string of questions and supplementary questions without telling the questioners anything. It is a great accomplishment, and marks them out as statesmen of the front rank. But to be continuously called upon to exhibit one's cleverness becomes tiring, and so the Government has decided to place restrictions on the kind of questions to be put to Ministers. Any questions that are likely to injure the national interest will be suppressed in future. The Government will, of course, decide whether the questions are safe or not. Naturally any question that is likely to injure the Government would injure the national interest. It is an effective way of breaking criticism. The House of Commons does not seem to mind this interference with its rights. It takes it lying down, as it has taken a good many other things. The House of Commons is reduced to the same level of the Reichstag. If anything the advantage lies with the Reichstag. At least, it was responsible for the fall of two Chancellors, and will judge the third. The House of Commons has had nothing to do with the change in the British Government since the war. It has accepted the Government imposed on it by the camarilla that controls this country outside of Parliament. This

war, we are told, is for the purpose of democratising Germany. We are wondering whether this is not intended as a kind of punishment for the German people, considering the readiness with which this country is surrendering its own democratic institutions.

UNDER WHICH FLAG?

Recently there was a change at the Ministry of Munitions which resulted in Sir John Hunter, of Sir William Arrol and Co. and other concerns, standing down from the post of Director of Steel Production. His place was taken by Colonel J. R. Wright, chairman of that very go-ahead firm of iron and steel masters, Baldwins, Ltd., of South Wales and the Midlands. It might have been expected that this gentleman would have resigned his directorships for the period during which he was at the Ministry. But at the annual meeting of the company, held the other day, he appears to have spoken as chairman, and to have had something to say about the prospects of the Oxfordshire Ironstone Co., of which his concern and Alfred Hickman, Ltd., are the owners. A railway has been constructed from the main line at Banbury to tap their iron properties, and arrangements are in hand to develop the mines, with a view to increasing the output of ironstone for steel production. This has been done by order of the Ministry of Munitions, and apparently at the expense of the nation. After the war the arrangement is that the railway and properties shall revert to the company. What with their chairman at the Ministry of Munitions and their connection with the propaganda and efforts of the Federation of British Industries and the National Alliance of Employers and Employed, Baldwins, Ltd., would appear to be most active in the service of their country and in the effort to make the world safe for democracy.

THE PEACE DEBATE.

While British statesmen denounce the German conception of a peace based on the war map, it is quite clear from the speech of Mr. Balfour during the peace debate in the House of Commons last week that the attitude of the British Government is not different from the German. It still clings to the motto, "No peace without victory." Mr. Balfour refused to be bound by a peace formula consistent with the aims for which the millions of the workers of the country imagined they were going to fight for. It is doubtful whether the Government has any clear idea of the manner in which it proposes to re-draw the map of Europe. Apparently that is to be thought out after the Germans are beaten. It claims to stand by the reply to President Wilson's Note. But since that reply was given, great changes have occurred which seriously affect it through Russia's rejection of all Imperialist aims. Is the Allies' conception of peace still guided by the ambitions of Tsarism? Mr. Balfour's denial of any agreement with France over the Saar Valley only complicates matters. That such an agreement existed between France and Russia cannot be denied. Does it suggest that under the cloak of a common ideal of establishing world-freedom, each member of the Entente is playing for its own hand? If so, a clue to the present military situation may be discovered. We know that Mr. J. R. Macdonald is an excellent debater, but we think he is mistaken in basing his pleading with the Government on the assumption that its war aims are dictated by any principles of abstract justice. They are dictated solely by Imperialist considerations, and for that reason it cannot or will not disclose its terms. When will the people awake and save themselves from those who are encompassing their destruction?

☞ NOW READY ☜

Trade Unionism ⁂ Cross Roads

By W. McLAINE (A.S.E.)

I. **ESSAYS IN SOCIALISM AND WAR.** By John Bryan.
II. **THE POLITICS OF CAPITALISM.** By J. T. Walton Newbold, M.A.
III. **THE ECONOMICS OF WAR.** By E. C. Fairchild.

One Penny Each; post free, three half-pence. Usual terms for quantities.

BRITISH SOCIALIST PARTY, 21a Maiden Lane, Strand, London, W.C.2

FIGURE 2   The BSP's *Call* (15 November 1917) welcomes the October Revolution.

Workers' Dreadnought

FOR INTERNATIONAL SOCIALISM.

| VOL. VI.—No. 45. | SATURDAY, JANUARY 31st, 1920. | PRICE TWOPENCE. |

SOCIALISM AND THE NEGRO.

Chiefly through the efforts of Dr. Dubois, author of "The Souls of Black Folk," there came into being in the United States, some ten years ago, the National Association for the Advancement of Coloured People. In the main, the organisation strove to combat the wide and insidious influence of Booker-Washington who, making light of the social and political status of his race, had put into practice, for its material benefit, the principle of work advocated by the latter-day Carlyle. A group of wealthy and, socially and politically, influential bourgeois of the North, helped to launch the movement and became its directing spirit.

In it were men and women representative of the old conservative and Quaker aristocracy of New England and Pennsylvania, and the liberal capitalists. It comprised intellectual and commercial Jews, and its finest spirit was Oswald Garrison Villard, editor of the American Nation and grandson of the great Abolitionist, who, vilified and denounced by the hide-bound capitalist press, stands out as the solitary and only consistent representative of the American bourgeoisie, counselling peace and moderation between aggressive Capitalism and its government, and Militant Labour and Socialism, and all the forces of passion struggling in America to-day. This group, palpably ignorant of the fact that the Negro question is primarily an economic problem, evidently thought it might be solved by admitting Negroes who have won to wealth and intellectual and other attainments into white society on equal terms, and by protesting and pleading to the political and aristocratic South to remove the notorious laws limiting the political and social status of coloured folk. So far as I am able to judge, it has done good work on the technically legal and educational side. It developed race-consciousness in the Negro and made him restive; but on the political side it has flirted with different parties and its work is quite ineffective.

Further, it has taken a firm stand against segregation, which is a moot and delicate question. While all Negroes are agreed that the social barriers must be removed, there is much difference in regard to education and some institutions like hospitals and churches. The growing numbers of cultured Negro men and women find it extremely difficult to obtain employment that is in keeping with their education under the capitalist system of government. For one instance, had a scholar like Dr. Dubois been white he would certainly have secured a chair at Harvard, Yale or Columbia University, for which he is eminently fitted. Many Negroes have obtained a sound education at great sacrifice, only to be forced, upon completion of their studies, into menial or uncongenial toil. In the black belt of New York City, where there is an estimated population of 100,000 Negroes, the Police Force, hospital, library, and elementary schools—patronised chiefly by coloured people—are entirely manned by white staffs. It would be impossible for such conditions to exist under a soviet system of Government.

Just about the beginning of the late War the Socialists and I.W.W. realising that the Negro population offered a fertile field for propaganda, began working in earnest among them. With the aid of the Messenger Magazine, edited by two ardent, young Negro university men, and The Liberator, they have done real constructive work that is now bearing fine fruit. The rank-and-file Negroes of America have been very responsive to the new truths. Some of them have been lured away by the siren call

THE ENTENTE AND RUSSIA

of the American Federation of Labour to enter its ranks. For years this reactionary association held out against Negro membership, but recently the capitalist class, alarmed over the growth of revolutionary thought among the blacks, used its creature, Gompers, to put through a resolution admitting Negroes to membership at the last conference. It has, however, had no effect on the lily-white and inconsequential trade unions of the South.

A splendid result of the revolutionary propaganda work among the blacks was the Conference of the National Brotherhood of Workers of America (entirely Negro) which was held at Washington, D.C., in September of last year. Its platform is as revolutionary in principle as that of the I.W.W. Over 100 delegates were in attendance and the majority came from the South. As always, the coloured workers are ready and willing to meet the white workers half way in order that they might unite in the fight against capitalism; but, owing to the seeds of hatred that have been sown for long years by the master class among both sections, the whites are still reluctant to take the step that would win the South over to Socialism. The black workers hold the key to the situation, but while they and the whites remain divided the reactionary South need not fear. The great task is to get both groups together. Coloured men from the North cannot be sent into the South for propaganda purposes, for they will be lynched. White men from the North will be beaten and, if they don't leave, they will also be lynched. A like fate awaits coloured women. But the South is boastful of its spirit of chivalry. It

sage of Socialism to both white and black workers. There are many of them in the movement who should be eager to go. During the period of Reconstruction a goodly number went from New England to educate the freed men, and, although they were socially ostracised by the Southerners, they stood to their guns. To-day they are needed more than ever. The call is louder and the cause is greater. Among the blacks they will be safe, respected and honoured. Will they rise to their duty?

Strangely, it is the professional class of Negroes that is chiefly opposed to Socialism, although it is the class that suffers and complains most bitterly. Dr. Dubois has flirted with the Socialist idea from a narrow, opportunist-racial standpoint; but he is in spirit opposed to it. If our Negro professionals are not blindly ignorant they should realise that there will never be any hope—no sound material place in the economic life of the world—for them until the Negro masses are industrially independent. Many coloured doctors, lawyers, journalists, teachers and preachers literally starve and are driven to the wall because the black working class does not earn enough to give them adequate support. Naturally, the white workers will hardly turn from their kind to coloured aspirants to the professions, even though the latter should possess exceptional ability. And even when they are capable they are often up against the prejudice of their own people who have been subtly taught by the white ruling class to despise the talented of their race and sneer at their accomplishments.

During the War, Marcus Garvey, a West Indian Negro, went to New York and

believes that it is the divinely-appointed guardian of sacred white womanhood, and it professes to disfranchise, outrage and lynch Negro men and women solely for the protection of white women.

It seems then that the only solution to the problem is to get lovely and refined white women volunteers to carry the mes-

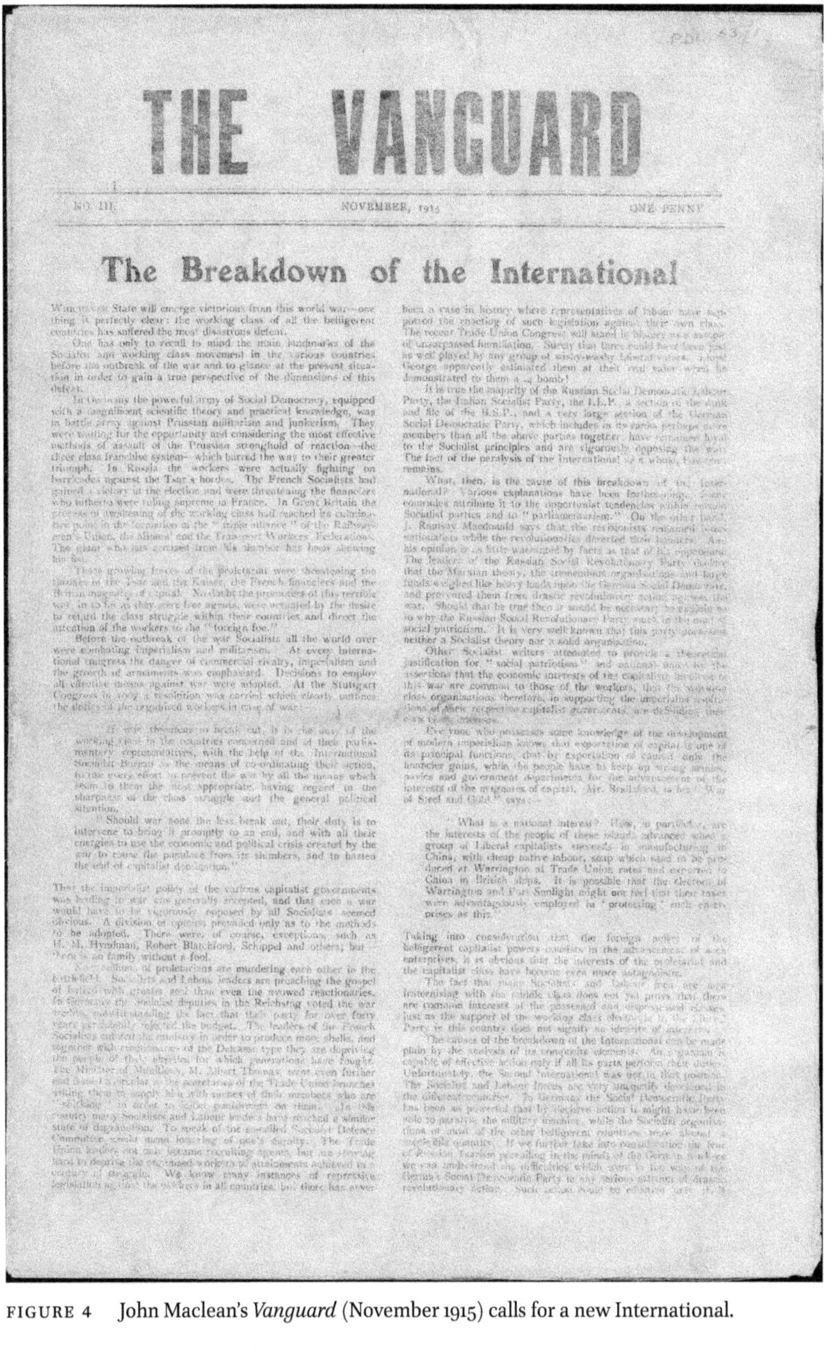

THE VANGUARD

NO. III. NOVEMBER, 1915 ONE PENNY

The Breakdown of the International

FIGURE 4   John Maclean's *Vanguard* (November 1915) calls for a new International.

THE

TRANSPORT WORKER.

CIRCULATION
20,000.

NON
POLITICAL.

Edited by TOM MANN.

SPECIAL STRIKE EDITION.

Vol. I. No. 1.   AUGUST, 1911.   Monthly.—One Penny.

TOM MANN.

Contents.

POLICE BUTCHERY OF WORKERS

RAILWAY STRIKE; LATEST EXCLUSIVE NEWS.

CARTERS' GRIEVANCES.

HISTORICAL CARTOON—RED SUNDAY.

RAILWAYMEN'S POSITION.

MANCHESTER RAILWAY STRIKE.

UNORGANIZED WORKERS OF LIVERPOOL.

LIVERPOOL NAVVIES.

WAREHOUSE & MILLWORKERS' TROUBLES.

NORTH-END DOCKERS.

SAILORS AND FIREMEN.

DEATH OF Bro. D. J. ENNY.

FIGURE 5   Tom Mann
THE TRANSPORT WORKER, AUGUST 1911

FIGURE 6   Peter Petroff
COTTON FACTORY TIMES, 9 NOVEMBER 1917

FIGURE 7   Arthur MacManus
GEORGE GRANTHAM BAIN COLLECTION, THE LIBRARY OF CONGRESS

FIGURE 8   Eleanor Marx, Wilhelm Liebknecht (left) & Edward Aveling (right)
            THE COMRADE, JANUARY 1905

FIGURE 9
Georgy Chicherin
BUNDESARCHIV, BILD 102–12859A / CC-BY-SA 3.0,
CC BY-SA 3.0 DE

FIGURE 10
Theodore Rothstein
PUBLIC DOMAIN, HTTPS://
COMMONS.WIKIMEDIA
.ORG/W/INDEX.PHP?CURID
=8045929

FIGURE 11   CPGB founding central committee 1920. MacManus in front centre, flanked by
Arthur Inkpin (left) and Willie Gallacher (right)
COMMUNIST UNITY CONVENTION OFFICIAL REPORT, 1920

FIGURE 12   J.T. Murphy
TOPICAL PHOTOS 1925

FIGURE 13   John Maclean

FIGURE 14   Sylvia Pankhurst
GETTY IMAGES

FIGURE 15   Henry Hyndman
            PUBLIC DOMAIN

FIGURE 16   SLP Offices at Renfrew Street in Glasgow
THE SOCIALIST, NOVEMBER 1917

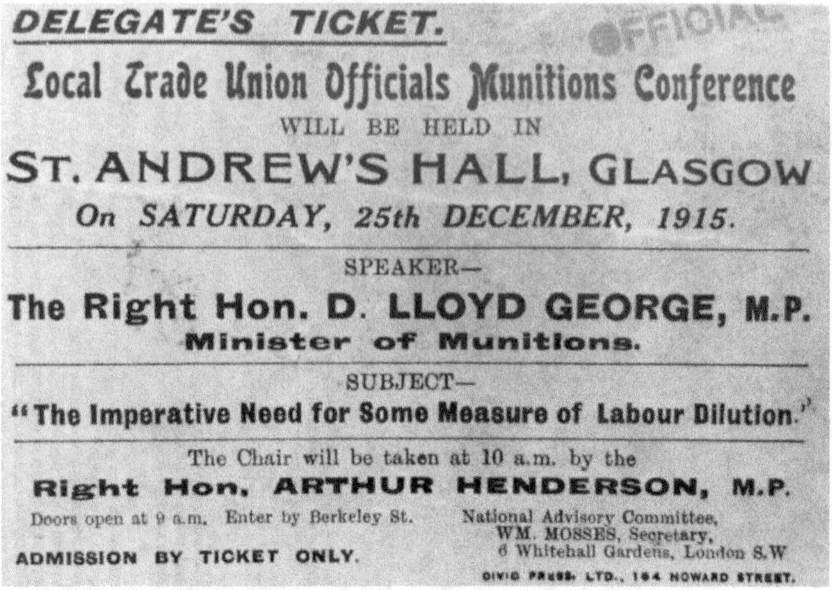

DELEGATE'S TICKET.

Local Trade Union Officials Munitions Conference

WILL BE HELD IN

St. ANDREW'S HALL, GLASGOW

On SATURDAY, 25th DECEMBER, 1915.

SPEAKER—

The Right Hon. D. LLOYD GEORGE, M.P.

Minister of Munitions.

SUBJECT—

"The Imperative Need for Some Measure of Labour Dilution."

The Chair will be taken at 10 a.m. by the

Right Hon. ARTHUR HENDERSON, M.P.

Doors open at 9 a.m.   Enter by Berkeley St.   National Advisory Committee,
                                                    WM. MOSSES, Secretary,
ADMISSION BY TICKET ONLY.   6 Whitehall Gardens, London S.W

CIVIC PRESS, LTD., 154 HOWARD STREET.

FIGURE 17   Delegate ticket to Glasgow shop stewards' meeting with Lloyd George 1915
CLYDEBANK DISTRICT LIBRARY

FIGURE 18   Alice Wheeldon and family on trial
SUNDAY PICTORIAL, 4 FEBRUARY 1917

FIGURE 19   London dockers' meeting addressed by unnamed woman
                LEEDS MERCURY, 12 AUGUST 1911

FIGURE 20   The ELFS's People's Army weapons training 1914
              INTERNATIONAL INSTITUTE FOR SOCIAL HISTORY

FIGURE 21   Melvina Walker addresses an ELFS street meeting in 1913
             INTERNATIONAL INSTITUTE FOR SOCIAL HISTORY

FIGURE 22   Martial law in Glasgow 1919
            ILLUSTRATED LONDON NEWS, 8 FEBRUARY 1919

FIGURE 23   Troops with fixed bayonets march by Liverpool strike meeting 1911
THE SPHERE, AUGUST 1911

FIGURE 24   Women pickets at the Singer's Strike 1911
            GLASGOW HERALD, MARCH 1911

Bibliography

Archives

British Library, London
Heritage Quay, University of Huddersfield
Hull History Centre, University of Hull
International Institute of Social History, Amsterdam
John Rylands Library, University of Manchester
London School of Economics
Marx Memorial Library, London
Modern Records Centre, University of Warwick
National Library of Scotland
People's History Museum, Manchester
Russian Centre for the Preservation and Study of Contemporary Historical Documents, Moscow
The National Archives, London
Working-Class Movement Library, Manchester

Newspapers and Periodicals

All Power
British Socialist
The Call
Commonweal
Communist [Communist Party of America]
Communist [Communist Party of Great Britain]
Communist International
Communist Review
Cotton Factory Times
Daily Herald
Daily Record
Derby Daily Telegraph
Die Neue Zeit
Dundee Courier
Economist
Evening Times [Glasgow]
Forward [Glasgow]

The Globe
Guardian [Manchester]
Guildsman
ILP News
Industrial Syndicalist
The International
Irish Worker
Justice
Kommunist
Labour Leader
Leicester Daily Post
London Gazette
Manchester Evening News
Nashe Slovo
Pioneer [Merthyr]
Plebs
Police and Prison Officers' Magazine
Portsmouth Evening News
Revolutionary History
Rhondda Socialist
SDP News
Social Democrat
Socialist
Socialist Review
Solidarity
Syndicalist
The Times
Tit-Bits
Transport Worker
Vanguard
Vorwärts
Woman's Dreadnought/Workers' Dreadnought
Worker [Glasgow]
Worker [Huddersfield]
Workers' Record
Workers' Republic
Workers' Weekly
Yorkshire Post

Books and Articles

Allen, Barbara 2015, *Alexander Shlyapnikov, 1885–1937. Life of an Old Bolshevik*, Leiden: Brill.

Allen, Barbara 2018, *Leaflets of the Russian Revolution*, Chicago: Haymarket.

Allen, V.L. 1958, 'The National Union of Police and Prison Officers', *Economic History Review*, 11, 1: 133–43.

Anonymous n.d., *Glasgow 1919: The Story of the Forty Hours' Strike*, Kirkintilloch: Molendinar Press.

Anonymous 1912, *The Miners' Next Step*, Tonypandy: Unofficial Reform Committee.

Archer, Robert (ed. and trans.) 1977 [1920], *Second Congress of the Communist International: Minutes of Proceedings*, London: New Park.

Arthey, Vin 2015, *Abel: The True Story of the Spy They Traded for Gary Powers*, London: Biteback.

Auerbach, Sasha 2009, *Race, Law, and 'The Chinese Puzzle' in Imperial Britain*, London: Palgrave Macmillan.

Backer, Thomas B. 1978, *The Mutualists: The Heirs of Proudhon in the First International, 1865–1878*, Cincinnati: University of Cincinnati Press.

Baillie, Myra 2002, *The Women of Red Clydeside: Women Munitions Workers in the West of Scotland during the First World War*, Unpublished PhD thesis, McMaster University.

Balbirnie, Steven 2016, '"A Bad Business": British Responses to Mutinies Among Local Forces in Northern Russia', *Revolutionary Russia*, 29, 2: 129–48.

Bantman, Constance 2014, 'The Franco-British Syndicalist Connection and the Great Labour Unrest 1880s–1914', *Labour History Review*, 79, 1: 83–96.

Barltrop, Robert 1975, *The Monument: The Story of the SPGB*, London: Pluto.

Beckett, Francis 1995, *The Enemy Within: Rise and Fall of the British Communist Party*, London: John Murray.

Beer, Max 1920, *A History of British Socialism*, London: G. Bell & Sons.

Béliard, Yann 2014, 'Revisiting the Great Labour Unrest, 1911–1914', *Labour History Review*, 79, 1: 1–17.

Bell, Geoffrey 2016, *Hesitant Comrades: The Irish Revolution and the British Labour Movement*, London: Pluto.

Bell, Tom 1937, *The British Communist Party: A Short History*, London: Lawrence & Wishart.

Bell, Tom 1941, *Pioneering Days*, London: Lawrence & Wishart.

Bell, Tom 1944, *John Maclean. A Fighter for Freedom*, Glasgow: CPGB Scottish Committee.

Berger, Stefan 1995, *The British Labour Party and the German Social Democrats 1900–1931*, Oxford: Oxford University Press.

Bernstein, Eduard 1921, *My Years of Exile*, New York: Harcourt, Brace and Howe.

Bevan, Aneurin 1952, *In Place of Fear*, London: Heinemann.

Bevir, Mark 1991, 'H.M. Hyndman: A Rereading and Reassessment', *History of Political Thought*, 12, 1: 125–46.

Bevir, Mark 2011, *The Making of British Socialism*, Princeton: Princeton University Press.

Blackledge, Paul 2019, *Friedrich Engels and Modern Social and Political Theory*, Albany: State University of New York Press.

Board of Trade 1896, *Report of the Chief Labour Correspondent on the Strikes and Lock-outs of 1896*, London: HMSO, 1896.

Boos, Florence (ed.) 1985, *William Morris's Socialist Diary*, Nottingham: Journeymen Press.

Bourrinet, Philippe 2016, *The Dutch and German Communist Left (1900–68)*, Leiden: Brill.

Braunthal, Julius 1967, *History of the International 1864–1914*, New York: Praeger.

Brockway, Fenner 1942, *Inside the Left*, London: Allen & Unwin.

Brooke, Stephen 2012, *Sexual Politics: Sexuality, Family Planning, and the British Left from the 1880s to the Present Day*, Oxford: Oxford University Press.

Brooker, Keith 1979, *The 1911 Strikes in Hull*, Hull: East Yorkshire Local History Society.

Brotherstone, Terry 1969, 'The Suppression of the "Forward"', *Journal of the Scottish Labour History Society*, 1: 5–23.

Bruce Lockhart, R.H. 1932, *Memoirs of a British Agent*, London: Putnam.

Bullock, Alan 1969, *The Life and Times of Ernest Bevin. Volume 1, Trade Union Leader 1881–1940*, London: Heinemann.

Bullock, Ian 2014, 'The Original British Ultra-Left, 1917–24', *Socialist History*, 44: 1–20.

Burke, Catherine 1983, *Working-class Politics in Sheffield, 1900–1920: A Regional Study in the Origins and Early Growth of the Labour Party*, Unpublished PhD thesis, Sheffield Hallam University.

Burke, David 1997, *Theodore Rothstein and Russian Political Emigre Influence on the British Labour Movement 1884–1920*, Unpublished PhD thesis, University of Greenwich.

Burke, David 2008, *The Spy Who Came in from the Co-op*, Suffolk: Boydell & Brewer.

Burke, David 2018, *Russia and the British Left: From the 1848 Revolutions to the General Strike*, London: I.B. Taurus.

Burke, David and Lindop, Fred 1999, 'Theodore Rothstein and the origins of the British Communist Party', *Socialist History*, 15: 45–65.

Burns, John 1889, 'The Paris International Congress', *Labour Elector*, 3 August.

Butler, William 2019, '"The British Soldier is no Bolshevik": The British Army, Discipline, and the Demobilization Strikes of 1919', *Twentieth Century British History*, 30, 3: 321–46.

Callaghan, John 1993, *Rajani Palme Dutt: A Study in British Stalinism*, London: Lawrence & Wishart.

Campbell, Calum 1986, *The Making a Clydeside Working Class*, London: Our History.

Campbell, Peter 2014, '"Black Horror on the Rhine": Idealism, Pacifism, and Racism in Feminism and the Left in the Aftermath of the First World War', *Histoire sociale/ Social History*, 47, 94: 471–93.

Carr, E.H. 1966, *The Bolshevik Revolution 1917–1923*, vol. 3, Harmondsworth: Pelican.

Carr, E.H. 1972, *Socialism in One Country*, vol. 3, Harmondsworth: Pelican.

Carsten, Francis 1982, *War Against War: British and German Radical Movements in the First World War*, London: Batsford Academic.

Challinor, Raymond 1977, *The Origins of British Bolshevism*, London: Croom Helm.

Clark, David 1985, *Victor Grayson: Labour's Lost Leader*, London: Quartet Books.

Coates, Ken (ed.) 1974, *British Labour and the Russian Revolution: The Leeds Convention*, Nottingham: Spokesman.

Coates, W.P. and Coates, Z.K. 1935, *Armed Intervention in Russia*, London: Gollancz.

Cole, Margaret (ed.) 1952, *Beatrice Webb's Diaries, 1912–24*, London: Longmans.

Collar, Peter 2012, *The Propaganda War in the Rhineland: Weimar Germany, Race and Occupation After World War One*, London: I.B. Taurus.

Collins, Henry and Abramsky, Chimen 1965, *Karl Marx and the British Labour Movement: Years of the First International*, London: Macmillan.

Collins, Henry 1971, 'The Marxism of the Social Democratic Federation', in A. Briggs and J. Saville (eds), *Essays in Labour History 1886–1923*, London: Macmillan.

Collins, Jodie 2016, *Clear out the Reds! Anti-Communism and the Conservative Right: The Case of Oliver Locker-Lampson, 1926–1933*, Unpublished MA thesis, University of Leeds.

Collins, Tony 2006, *Rugby League in Twentieth Century Britain*, Abingdon: Routledge.

Communist International 1988 [1921], *Guidelines on the Organizational Structure of Communist Parties, on the Methods and Content of Their Work*, New York: Prometheus Research Library.

Communist Party Historians Group 1957, *Some Dilemmas for Marxists, 1900–14*, London: Our History.

Communist Party of Great Britain 1920, *Communist Unity Convention, Official Report*, London: CPGB.

Connolly, James, 1903, 'The Socialist Labor Party of America and the London SDF', *The Socialist*, June.

Connelly, Katherine 2013, *Sylvia Pankhurst: Suffragette, Socialist and Scourge of Empire*, London: Pluto.

Cook, A.J. 1926, 'A.J. Cook Tells His Own Story', *Tit-Bits*, 15 May.

Cowley, John 1992, *The Victorian Encounter with Marx: A Study of Ernest Belfort Bax*, London: British Academic Press.

Crick, Martin 1991, 'A Collection of Oddities: The Bradford Branch of the Social-Democratic Federation', *The Bradford Antiquary*, 5: 24–40.

Crick, Martin 1994, *The History of the Social Democratic Federation*, Keele: Ryburn Publishing.

Czerwinska-Schupp, Ewa 2017, *Otto Bauer (1881–1938): Thinker and Politician*, Leiden: Brill.

Dallas, Gloden and Gill, Douglas 1975, 'Mutiny at Etaples Base, 1917', *Past and Present*, 69: 88–112.

Dallas, Gloden and Gill, Douglas 1985, *The Unknown Army: Mutinies in the British Army in World War 1*, London: Verso.

Dangerfield, George 2015 [1935], *The Strange Death of Liberal England*, London: Serif edition.

Darlington, Ralph 1998, *The Political Trajectory of J.T. Murphy*, Liverpool: Liverpool University Press.

Darlington, Ralph 2008, *Syndicalism and the Transition to Communism: An International Comparative Analysis*, Aldershot: Ashgate.

Darlington, Ralph 2012, 'Re-evaluating Syndicalist Opposition to the First World War', *Labor History*, 53, 4: 517–39.

Darlington, Ralph 2013, *Radical Unionism: The Rise and Fall of Revolutionary Syndicalism*, Chicago: Haymarket.

Darlington, Ralph 2016, 'British Labour Movement Solidarity in the 1913–14 Dublin Lockout', *Labor History*, 57, 4: 504–25.

David, Wayne 2016, *Remaining True. A Biography of Ness Edwards*, Caerphilly: Caerphilly Local History Society.

Davis, Jonathan 2005, 'Left Out in the Cold: British Labour Witnesses the Russian Revolution', *Revolutionary Russia*, 18, 1: 71–87.

Davis, Mary 1999, *Sylvia Pankhurst: A Life in Radical Politics*, London: Pluto.

Davis, Sam and Noon, Ron 2014, 'The rank-and-file in the 1911 Liverpool General Transport Strike', *Labour History Review*, 79, 1: 55–81.

Day, Richard B. and Gaido, Daniel 2011, *Discovering Imperialism: Social Democracy to World War 1*, Leiden: Brill.

Debo, Richard K. 1964, *George Chicherin: Soviet Russia's Second Foreign Commissar*, Unpublished PhD thesis, University of Nebraska.

Degras, Jane, (ed.) 1956, *The Communist International 1919–1943 Documents, volume one*, Oxford: Oxford University Press.

Desmarais, Ralph 1975, 'Lloyd George and the Development of the British Government's Strikebreaking Organisation', *International Review of Social History*, 20: 1–15.

Deutscher, Isaac 1954, *The Prophet Armed*, Oxford: Oxford University Press.

Dewar, Hugo 1976, *Communist Politics in Britain*, London: Pluto.

Draper, Hal 2014 [1953], *The Myth of Lenin's 'Revolutionary Defeatism'*, Alameda, CA: Center for Socialist History.

Draper, Theodore 1957, *The Roots of American Communism*, New York: Viking Press.

Durham, Martin 1982, *The Origins and Early Years of British Communism, 1914–1924*, Unpublished PhD thesis, University of Birmingham.

Eaden, James and Renton, David 2002, *The Communist Party of Great Britain since 1920*, Basingstoke: Palgrave.

Egan, David 1978, 'The Unofficial Reform Committee and the Miners' Next Step', *Llafur*, 2, 3: 64–80.

Egan, David 1986, 'Noah Ablett 1883–1935', *Llafur*, 4, 3: 19–32.

Emsley, Clive 2000, 'The Policeman as Worker: A Comparative Survey c. 1800–1940', *International Review of Social History*, 45: 89–110.

Engels, Friedrich 1871, 'On the Political Action of the Working Class', *Karl Marx Frederick Engels Collected Works*, vol. 22, Moscow: Progress Publishers.

Engels, Friedrich 1885, 'England in 1845 and 1885', *Karl Marx Frederick Engels Collected Works*, vol. 26, Moscow: Progress Publishers.

Engels, Friedrich 1890, 'May 4 in London', *Karl Marx Frederick Engels Collected Works*, vol. 27, Moscow: Progress Publishers.

Evans, Neil 1980, 'The South Wales Race Riots of 1919', *Llafur*, 3, 3: 5–29.

Fishman, Nina 2004, 'CPGB History at the Centre of Contemporary British History', *Labour History Review*, 69, 3: 381–3.

Fishman, Nina 2010, *Arthur Horner, A Political Biography*, London: Lawrence & Wishart.

Fishman, William J. 2004, *East End Jewish Radicals 1875–1914*, Nottingham: Five Leaves.

Flaherty, Seamus 2020, *Marx, Engels and Modern British Socialism: The Social and Political Thought of H.M. Hyndman, E.B. Bax and William Morris*, London: Palgrave Macmillan.

Fletcher, Ian 1996, '"Prosecutions … are Always Risky Business": Labor, Liberals, and the 1912 "Don't Shoot" Prosecutions', *Albion*, 28, 2: 251–78.

Foster, George 1985, 'British Communism Aborted: The Far Left, 1900–1920', *Spartacist*, 36/37, Winter.

Foster, John 1974, *Class Struggle and the Industrial Revolution*, London: Weidenfeld & Nicolson.

Foster, John 1990, 'Strike Action and Working-Class Politics on Clydeside 1914–1919', *International Review of Social History*, 35: 33–70.

Foster, John 1992, 'Red Clyde, Red Scotland', in Ian Donachie and Christopher Whatley (eds), *The Manufacture of Scottish History*, Edinburgh: Polygon.

Foster, John 2010, 'The Aristocracy of Labour and Working-Class Consciousness Revisited', *Labour History Review*, 75, 3: 245–62.

Fox, R.M. 1938, *Smoky Crusade*, London: Hogarth Press.

Fryer, Peter 1984, *Staying Power. The History of Black People in Britain*, London: Pluto.

Futtrell, Michael 1963, *Northern Underground. Episodes of Russian Revolutionary Transport and Communications through Scandinavia and Finland 1863–1917*, London: Faber.

Gallacher, William 1936, *Revolt on the Clyde*, London: Lawrence & Wishart.

Gallacher, William 1966, *The Last Memoirs of William Gallacher*, London: Lawrence & Wishart.

Gallacher, William and J. Paton 1917, *Towards Industrial Democracy: A Memorandum on Workers' Control*, Glasgow: Paisley Trades and Labour Council.

Gankin, Olga Hess and H.H. Fisher (eds) 1940, *The Bolsheviks and World War*, Stanford: Stanford University Press.

Gawore, Norbert 1975, 'From Blockade to Trade: Allied Economic Warfare Against Soviet Russia, June 1919 to January 1920', *Jahrbücher für Geschichte Osteuropas Neue Folge*, 23, 1: 39–69.

Gitlow, Benjamin 1939, *I Confess: The Truth About American Communism*, New York: E.P. Dutton.

Glasgow Labour History Workshop 1992, 'Roots of Red Clydeside: The Labour Unrest in West Scotland, 1910–14', in Robert Duncan and Arthur McIvor (eds), *Militant Workers: Labour and Class Conflict on the Clyde 1900–50*, Edinburgh: John Donald.

Goldman, Lawrence 1995, *Dons and Workers: Oxford and Adult Education Since 1850*, Oxford: Clarendon Press.

Grant, Ron 1984, *British Radicals and Socialists and their Attitudes to Russia, c. 1890–1917*, Unpublished PhD thesis, University of Glasgow.

Grant, Ron 1984, 'G.V. Chicherin and the Russian Revolutionary Cause in Great Britain', in John Slatter (ed.), *From the Other Shore: Russian Political Emigrants in Britain: 1880–1917*, London: Cass.

Graubard, S.R. 1956, *British Labour and the Russian Revolution 1917–24*, Cambridge, MA: Harvard University Press.

Gray, Robert 1981, *The Aristocracy of Labour in Nineteenth Century Britain*, London: Macmillan.

Greenslade, William 2000, 'Revisiting Edward Aveling', in John Stokes (ed.), *Eleanor Marx (1855–1898): Life. Work. Contacts*, Aldershot: Ashgate.

Groves, Reg 1975, *The Strange Case of Victor Grayson*, London: Pluto Press.

Halévy, Elie 1952, *A History of the English People in the Nineteenth Century, vol. 6. The Rule of Democracy 1905–1914*, London: Ernest Benn.

Hannam, June 1992, 'Women and the ILP, 1890–1914', in T. James, T. Jowitt and K. Laybourn (eds), *The Centennial History of the Independent Labour Party*, Halifax: Ryburn.

Hannington, Wal 1940, *Industrial History in Wartime, including a record of the shop stewards' movement*, London: Lawrence & Wishart.

Hardie, Kier 1910, *Karl Marx: The Man and His Message*, Manchester: National Labour Press.

Harrison, Royden 1974, 'Documents. Communist Party Affiliation to the Labour Party', *Bulletin of the Society for the Study of Labour History*, 29: 16–34.

Hasegawa, Tsuyoshi 1981, *The February Revolution, Petrograd, 1917*, Seattle: University of Washington Press.

Haupt, Georges 1972, *Socialism and the Great War: The Collapse of the Second International*, Oxford: Oxford University Press.

Haupt, Georges and Jean-Jacques Marie (eds) 1974, *Makers of the Russian Revolution*, London: Allen & Unwin.

Hayes, Mark 2005, *The British Communist Left: A Contribution to the History of the Revolutionary Movement 1914–1945*, London: International Communist Current.

Henderson, Arthur 1918, *The Aims of Labour*, London: Headley.

Henderson, Fred 1911, *The Labour Unrest, what it is and what it portends*, London: Jerrold & Sons.

Henderson, Robert 2020, *The Spark That Lit the Revolution*, London: I.B. Tauris.

Hessel, Bertil (ed.) 1980, *Theses, Resolutions and Manifestos of the First Four Congresses of the Third International*, London: Ink Links.

Hiley, Nicholas 1986, 'Internal Security in Wartime: The Rise and Fall of P.M.S.2, 1915–1917', *Intelligence and National Security*, 1, 3: 395–415.

Hill, Jeffrey 1969, *Working-Class Politics in Lancashire: A Regional Study in the Origins of the Labour Party*, Unpublished PhD thesis, Keele University.

Hinton, James 1983, *Labour and Socialism: A History of the British Labour Movement 1867–1974*, Amherst: University of Massachusetts Press.

Hinton, James 1973, *The First Shop Stewards Movement*, London: Allen & Unwin.

Hobsbawm, Eric 1964, 'Hyndman and the SDF', in his *Labouring Men: Studies in the History of Labour*, London: Weidenfeld & Nicolson.

Hobsbawm, Eric 1964, 'The Labour Aristocracy in Nineteenth Century Britain', in *Labouring Men*, London: Weidenfeld and Nicolson.

Hobsbawm, Eric 1983 [1973], 'Karl Marx and the British Labour Movement', in *Revolutionaries*, London: Abacus.

Hochschild, Adam 1999, *King Leopold's Ghost: A Story of Greed, Terror, and Heroism in Colonial Africa*, Boston: Houghton Mifflin.

Hochschild, Adam 2011, *To End All Wars: A Story of Protest and Patriotism in the First World War*, London: Picador.

Holmes, Rachel 2014, *Eleanor Marx*, London: Bloomsbury.

Holmes, Rachel 2020, *Sylvia Pankhurst: Natural Born Rebel*, London: Bloomsbury.

Holton, Bob 1976, *British Syndicalism 1900–1914*, London: Pluto.

Hopkin, Deian 1983, 'The Llanelli Riots, 1911', *Welsh History Review*, 11, 4: 488–515.

Horner, Arthur 1960, *Incorrigible Rebel*, London: McGibbon & Kee.

Howell, David 1983, *British Workers and the Independent Labour Party 1888–1906*, Manchester: Manchester University Press.

Hulse, James W. 1964, *The Forming of the Communist International*, Stanford: Stanford University Press.

Hunt, Karen 1996, *Equivocal Feminists: The Social Democratic Federation and the Woman Question 1884–1911*, Cambridge: Cambridge University Press.

Hyndman, H.M. 1881, *England for All*, London: Gilbert & Rivington.

Hyndman, H.M. 1883, *The Historical Basis of Socialism in England*, London: Kegan Paul.

Hyndman, H.M. 1884, *The Coming Revolution in England*, London: Reeves.

Hyndman, H.M. 1887, 'The English Workers as They Are', *Contemporary Review*, 52, July: 121–36.

Hyndman, H.M. 1889, 'The International Congress of Workers', *International Review*, August: 33–44.

Hyndman, H.M. 1911, *The Record of an Adventurous Life*, London: Macmillan.

Hyndman, H.M. 1912, *Further Reminiscences*, London: MacMillan.

Institute of Marxism-Leninism of the CC, CPSU 1964, *Documents of the First International*, vol. 1, Moscow: Progress Publishers.

Ives, Martyn 2017, *Reform, Revolution and Direct Action Among British Miners*, Chicago: Haymarket.

Jacobs, Dan N. 1981, *Borodin: Stalin's Man in China*, Cambridge, MA: Harvard University Press.

James, David, Tony Jowitt and Keith Laybourn (eds) 1992, *The Centennial History of the ILP*, Ryburn: Keele University Press.

Jeffrey, Keith, and Peter Hennessy 1983, *States of Emergency: British Governments and Strikebreaking since 1919*, London: RKP.

Jenkinson, Jacqueline 2008, 'Black Sailors on Red Clydeside: Rioting, Reactionary Trade Unionism and Conflicting Notions of "Britishness" following the First World War', *Twentieth Century British History*, 19, 1: 29–60.

Jenkinson, Jacqueline 2009, *Black 1919: Riots, Racism and Resistance in Imperial Britain*, Liverpool: Liverpool University Press.

Johnson, Graham 1988, *Social Democratic Politics in Britain 1881–1911: The Marxism of the SDF*, Unpublished PhD thesis, University of Hull.

Johnstone, Monty 1967, 'The Communist Party in the 1920s', *New Left Review*, 41: 47–63.

Joll, James 1956, *The Second International 1889–1914*, New York: Praeger.

Jones, Douglas 2010, *The Communist Party of Great Britain and the National Question in Wales, 1920–1991*, Unpublished PhD thesis, University of Wales.

Kaddish, Sharman 1992, *Bolsheviks and British Jews*, London: Frank Cass.

Kapp, Yvonne 2018 [1976], *Eleanor Marx*, London: Verso.

Kendall, Walter 1963, 'Russian Emigration and British Marxist Socialism', *International Review of Social History*, 8, 3: 351–78.

Kendall, Walter 1969, *The Revolutionary Movement in Britain 1900–21: The Origins of British Communism*, London: Weidenfeld and Nicolson.

Kenefick, William 2007, *Red Scotland! The Rise and Fall of the Radical Left, c. 1872–1932*, Edinburgh: Edinburgh University Press.

Kettle, Michael 1992, *Churchill and the Archangel Fiasco, November 1918–July 1919*, London: Routledge.

Kidd, Matthew 2020, *The Renewal of Radicalism. Politics, Identity and Ideology in England, 1867–1924*, Manchester: Manchester University Press.

Kinvig, Clifford 2006, *Churchill's Crusade: The British Invasion of Russia 1918–20*, London: Hambledon Continuum.

Kirby, David 1982, 'International Socialism and the Question of Peace: The Stockholm Conference of 1917', *Historical Journal*, 25, 3: 709–16.

Kirk, Willis 1977, 'The Introduction and Critical Reception of Marxist Thought in Britain, 1850–1900', *Historical Journal*, 20, 2: 417–59.

Kirkwood, David 1935, *My Life of Revolt*, London: Harrap.

Kissin, S.F. 1988, *War and the Marxists. Socialist Theory and Practice in Capitalist War, vol. 1 1848–1918*, London: Andre Deutsch.

Klugmann, James 1968, *History of the Communist Party of Great Britain. Formation and Early Years, Volume 1: 1919–24*, London: Lawrence & Wishart.

Knee, Fred 1950 [1910], 'The Revolt of Labour', *The Social Democrat*, 15 November 1910, reprinted in *Labour Monthly*, June.

Kochan, Lionel 1970, 'Lenin in London', *History Today*, 20, 4: 19–26.

Krupskaya, Nadezhda 1970 [1930], *Memories of Lenin*, London: Panther.

Lamb, Dave n.d., *Mutinies: 1917–20*, Oxford: Solidarity.

Lavin, Deborah 2011, *Bradlaugh contra Marx: Radicalism versus Socialism in the First International*, London: Socialist History Society.

Laybourn, K. and J. Reynolds 1975, 'The Emergence of the Independent Labour Party in Bradford', *International Review of Social History*, 20: 313–46.

Laybourn, Keith and Dylan Murphy 1999, *Under the Red Flag: The History of Communism in Britain*, Stroud: Sutton.

Lazitch, B. and M.M. Drachkovich 1972, *Lenin and the Comintern*, Stanford: Hoover Institution Press.

Lee, H.W. 1935, *Social Democracy in Britain. Fifty Years of the Socialist Movement*, London: SDF.

Leeworthy, Daryl 2018, *Labour Country*, Swansea: Parthian.

Lenin, V.I. 1902, 'What is to be Done?', in *Collected Works*, vol. 5, Moscow: Progress Publishers.

Lenin, V.I. 1908, 'Meeting of the International Socialist Bureau', in *Collected Works*, vol. 15, Moscow: Progress Publishers.

Lenin, V.I. 1914, 'The Position and Tasks of the Socialist International', in *Collected Works*, vol. 21, Moscow: Progress Publishers.

Lenin, V.I. 1915a, 'The Slogan of Civil War Illustrated', in *Collected Works*, vol. 21, Moscow: Progress Publishers.

Lenin, V.I. 1915b, 'The Conference of the RSDLP Groups Abroad', in *Collected Works*, vol. 21, Moscow: Progress Publishers.

Lenin, V.I. 1916a, 'Split or Decay', in *Collected Works*, vol. 22, Moscow: Progress Publishers.

Lenin, V.I. 1916b, 'Imperialism and the Split in Socialism', in *Collected Works*, vol. 23, Moscow: Progress Publishers.

Lenin, V.I. 1917a, 'The Stockholm Conference', in *Collected Works*, vol. 25, Moscow: Progress Publishers.

Lenin, V.I. 1917b, 'Kamenev's Speech in the CEC', in *Collected Works*, vol. 25, Moscow: Progress Publishers.

Lenin, V.I. 1920a, 'Left-Wing Communism: An Infantile Disorder', in *Collected Works*, vol. 31, Moscow: Progress Publishers.

Lenin, V.I. 1920b, 'The Terms of Admission into the Communist International', in *Collected Works*, vol. 31, Moscow: Progress Publishers.

Lewis, Richard 1976, 'The South Wales Miners and the Ruskin College Strike of 1909', *Llafur*, 2, 1: 57–72.

Lincoln, W. Bruce 1990, *Red Victory, A History of the Russian Civil War*, London: Simon & Schuster.

Lockley, Antony 2003, 'Propaganda and the First Cold War in North Russia, 1918–19', *History Today*, September: 46–53.

Lusk, Kirsty and Willy Maley (eds) 2016, *Scotland and the Easter Rising: Fresh Perspectives on 1916*, Edinburgh: Luath.

MacDonald, J. Ramsay 1919, *Parliament and Revolution*, Manchester: National Labour Press.

Macfarlane, L.J. 1967, *The British Communist Party: Its Origin and Development until 1929*, London: MacGibbon and McKee.

Macfarlane, L.J. 1967, 'Hands Off Russia: British Labour and the Russo-Polish War, 1920', *Past and Present*, 38: 126–52.

MacIntyre, Stuart 1980, *Little Moscows: Communism and Working-Class Militancy in Inter-War Britain*, London: Croom Helm.

MacIntyre, Stuart 1986, *A Proletarian Science: Marxism in Britain, 1917–33*, New Jersey: Humanities Press.

MacKinlay, Alan and R.J. Morris (eds) 1992, *The ILP on Clydeside, 1893–1932: From Foundation to Disintegration*, Manchester: Manchester University Press.

Maclean, Iain 1999, *The Legend of Red Clydeside*, Edinburgh: John Donald.

Maclean, John 1978, *In the Rapids of Revolution*, London: Allison & Busby.

Maclean, John n.d., *The Irish Tragedy: Scotland's Disgrace*, Glasgow: The John Maclean Society.

MacShane, Harry 1978, *No Mean Fighter*, London: Pluto.

Madiera, Victor 2016, *Britannia and the Bear: The Anglo-Russian Intelligence Wars, 1917–1929*, Woodbridge: Boydell.

Maisky, Ivan 1962, *Journey into the Past*, London: Hutchinson.

Marks, Sally 1983, 'Black Watch on the Rhine: A Study in Propaganda, Prejudice and Prurience', *European Studies Review*, 13: 297–333.

Marley, Laurence (ed.) 2015, *The British Labour Party and Twentieth-Century Ireland*, Manchester: Manchester University Press.

Marquand, David 1977, *Ramsay Macdonald*, London: Cape.

Marson, Dave 1973, *Children's Strikes in 1911*, London: History Workshop.

Martin, Roderick 1969, *Communism and the British Trade Unions 1924–1933*, Oxford: Oxford University Press.

Marx, Eleanor 1890, 'The Liverpool Congress', *Time*, October: 1088–97.

Marx, Karl 1864, 'Provisional Rules of the Association', in *Karl Marx Frederick Engels Collected Works*, vol. 20, Moscow: Progress Publishers.

Marx, Karl 1875, 'Critique of the Gotha Programme', in *Karl Marx Frederick Engels Collected Works*, vol. 24, Moscow: Progress Publishers.

Mates, Lewis 2013, 'The Limits and Potential of Syndicalist Influence in the Durham Coalfield before the Great War', *Labor History*, 54, 1: 42–63.

Mates, Lewis 2016, *The Great Labour Unrest: Rank and File Movements and Political Change in the Durham Coalfield*, Manchester: Manchester University Press.

Matthew, H.C.G., R.I. McKibbin, and J.A. Kay 1976, 'The Franchise Factor in the Rise of the Labour Party', *English Historical Review*, 91: 723–52.

McGuire, Charlie 2011, *Sean McLoughlin. Ireland's Forgotten Revolutionary*, Pontypool: Merlin.

McGuire, Charlie 2018, ' "They'll Never Understand Why I'm Here": British Marxism and the Irish Revolution, 1916–1923', *Contemporary British History*, 32, 2: 147–68.

McGuire, Charlie and B.J. Ripley 1985, 'Russian Political Internees in First World War Britain: The Cases of George Chicherin and Peter Petroff', *Historical Journal*, 28, 3: 727–38.

McHugh, John 2000, 'Peter Petroff: The View from the Home Office File', *Scottish Labour History*, 35: 25–32.

McIlroy, John, and Alan Campbell 2003, 'Histories of the British Communist Party: A User's Guide', *Labour History Review*, 68, 1: 33–59.

McIlroy, John, and Alan Campbell 2020a, 'The Early British Communist leaders, 1920–1923: A Prosopographical Exploration', *Labor History*, 61, 5–6: 423–65.

McIlroy, John, and Alan Campbell 2020b, 'The Socialist Labour Party and the Leadership of Early British Communism', *Critique*, 48, 4: 609–59.

McKay, Claude 1985, *A Long Way from Home*, London: Pluto.

McKay, John 1994, 'Communist Unity and Division 1920: Gallacher, MacLean and the "Unholy Scotch Current"', *Scottish Labour History Society Journal*, 29: 84–97.

McKibbin, Ross 1978, 'Arthur Henderson as Labour Leader', *International Review of Social History*, 23, 1: 79–101.

McKibbin, Ross 1984, *The Evolution of the Labour Party*, *1910–24*, Oxford: Oxford University Press.

McKibbin, Ross 1990, 'Why Was There No Marxism in Great Britain?', in his *The Ideologies of Class*, Oxford: Oxford University Press.

McKinlay, Alan, and R.J. Morris (eds) 1991, *The ILP on Clydeside, 1893–1932: From Foundation to Disintegration*, Manchester: Manchester University Press.

McNeilly, Edward 2009, 'Labour and the Politics of Internationalism, 1906–1914', *Twentieth Century British History*, 20, 4: 431–53.

Meacham, Standish 1972, 'The Sense of an Impending Clash. English Working Class Unrest before the First World War', *American Historical Review*, 77, 2: 1343–64.

Meynell, Hildamarie 1960, 'The Stockholm Conference of 1917', *International Review of Social History*, 5, 2: 1–25.

Miles, Andy 1984, 'Workers Education: The Communist Party and the Plebs League in the 1920s', *History Workshop*, 18: 102–14.

Miliband, Ralph 1961, *Parliamentary Socialism*, London: Allen & Unwin.

Millar, J.P.M. n.d., *The Labour College Movement*, London: National Council of Labour Colleges.

Millman, Brock 2000, *Managing Domestic Dissent in First World War Britain*, London: Frank Cass.

Milotte, Mike 1984, *Communism in Modern Ireland: The Pursuit of the Workers' Republic Since 1916*, Dublin: Gill and Macmillan.

Milton, Giles 2015, *When Churchill Slaughtered Sheep*, London: John Murray.

Milton, Nan 1973, *John Maclean*, London: Pluto Press.

Moore, Bill 1960, *Sheffield Shop Stewards 1916–18*, London: Our History.

Morgan, Kevin 2002, 'Labour with Knobs On: The Recent Historiography of the British Communist Party', in Stefan Berger (ed.), *Labour and Social History in Great Britain: Historiographical Reviews and Agendas, Mitteilungsblatt des Instituts fur soziale Bewegungen*, 27: 69–84.

Morgan, Kevin (ed.) 2005, *Communists and British Society 1920–1991: People of a Special Mould*, London: Rivers Oram Press.

Morgan, Kevin 2006, *Labour Legends and Russian Gold*, London: Lawrence & Wishart.

Morgan, Kevin 2013a, *Bolshevism, Syndicalism and the General Strike: The Lost Internationalist World of A.A. Purcell*, London: Lawrence & Wishart.

Morgan, Kevin 2013b, 'In and Out of the Swamp: The Unpublished Autobiography of Peter Petroff', *Scottish Labour History*, 48: 23–45.

Morris, Marcus 2014, 'From Anti-colonialism to Anti-imperialism: The Evolution of H.M. Hyndman's Critique of Empire, c. 1875–1905', *Historical Research*, 87: 293–314.

Morris, Marcus 2018, 'The General Strike as a Weapon of Peace: British Socialists, the Labour Movement, and Debating the Means to Avoid War before 1914', *Labour History Review*, 83, 1: 29–53.

Morton, Vivien, and Stuart Macintyre 1979, *T.A. Jackson, A Centenary Appreciation*, London: Our History.

Mulholland, Marc 2015, 'Marxists of Strict Observance? The Second International, National Defence, and the Question of War', *Historical Journal*, 58, 2: 615–40.

Munck, Ronald 1985, 'Class and Religion in Belfast: A Historical Perspective', *Journal of Contemporary History*, 20, 2: 241–59.

Murphy, J.T. 1917, *The Workers' Committee*, Sheffield: Sheffield Workers' Committee.

Murphy, J.T. 1934, *Preparing for Power: A Critical Study of the History of the British Working-Class Movement*, London: Jonathan Cape.

Murphy, J.T. 1941, *New Horizons*, London: Bodley Head.

Mustill, Edd 2016, *The Sheffield Workers' Committee*, Nottingham: Spokesman.

Nettl, Peter 1965, 'The German Social Democratic Party 1890–1914 as a Political Model', *Past and Present*, 30: 65–95.

Neville, Robert G. 1976, 'The Yorkshire Miners and the 1893 Lockout: The Featherstone "Massacre"', *International Review of Social History*, 21, 3: 337–57.

Nevin, Donal 2006, *James Connolly, A Full Life*, Dublin: Gill and Macmillan.

Nevin, Donal (ed.) 2007, *Between Comrades. James Connolly, Letter and Correspondence 1889–1916*, Dublin: Gill & Macmillan.

Newsinger, John 1983, 'James Connolly and the Easter Rising', *Science and Society*, 47, 2: 152–77.

Newsinger, John 2004, *Rebel City: Larkin, Connolly and the Dublin Labour Movement*, London: Merlin Press.

Newsinger, John 2006, 'Recent Controversies in the History of British Communism', *Journal of Contemporary History*, 41, 3: 557–72.

Nottingham, Christopher 1984, *The State and Revolution in Britain 1916–1926*, Unpublished PhD thesis, University of Sheffield.

O'Brien, Mark 2012, 'The Liverpool Transport Strike of 1911: "Overcomings", Transformations, and the "New Mentalities" of the Liverpool Working Class', *Historical Studies in Industrial Relations*, 33: 39–60.

O'Casey, Sean 1980 [1919], *The Story of the Irish Citizen Army*, London: Journeyman Press.

O'Connor, Emmet 1992, *A Labour History of Ireland*, Dublin: Gill & Macmillan.

O'Connor, Emmet 2004, *Reds and the Green: Ireland, Russia and the Communist Internationals, 1919–43*, Dublin: UCD Press.

O'Connor, Emmet 2014, 'Old Wine in New Bottles? Syndicalism and "Fakirism" in the Great Labour Unrest, 1911–1914', *Labour History Review*, 79, 1: 19–36.

O'Riordan, Manus 1988, 'Connolly Socialism and the Jewish Worker', *Saothar: Journal of the Irish Labour History Society*, 13: 120–30.

Occleshaw, Michael 2006, *Dances in Deep Shadows: Britain's Clandestine War in Russia 1917–20*, London: Constable.

Owen, James 2008, 'Dissident Missionaries? Re-Narrating the Political Strategy of the Social-Democratic Federation, 1884–1887', *Labour History Review*, 73, 2: 157–77.

Owen, Nicholas 2007, *The British Left and India: Metropolitan Anti-imperialism, 1885–1947*, Oxford: Oxford University Press.

Page Arnot, Robin 1967, *The Impact of the Russian Revolution in Britain*, London: Lawrence & Wishart.

Palmer, Bryan D. 2007, *James P. Cannon and the Origins of the American Revolutionary Left, 1890–1928*, Champaign: University of Illinois Press.

Pankhurst, Sylvia 1921, *Russia As I Saw It*, London: Dreadnought Publishers.

Pankhurst, Sylvia 1932, *The Home Front*, London: Hutchinson.

Pankhurst, Sylvia 1977 [1931], *The Suffragette Movement*, London: Virago.

Paul, William 1918, *Scientific Socialism: Its Revolutionary Aims and Methods*, Glasgow: Socialist Labour Press.

Paul, William n.d, *The State: Its Origin and Function*, Glasgow: Socialist Labour Press.

Pearce, Brian [as Joseph Redman] 1958, 'The Early Years of the Communist Party of Great Britain', *Labour Review*, 3, 1: 11–22.

Pearce, Brian [as Joseph Redman] 1961, 'Lenin and Trotsky on Pacifism and Defeatism', *Labour Review*, 6, 1: 29–40.

Pearce, Brian [as Joseph Redman] and Michael Woodhouse 1975, *Essays on the History of Communism in Britain*, London: New Park.

Pearce, Cyril 2001, *Comrades in Conscience*, London: Francis Boutle.

Pelling, Henry 1958a, 'The Early History of the Communist Party of Great Britain, 1920–29', *Transactions of the Royal Historical Society*, 8: 41–57.

Pelling, Henry 1958b, *The British Communist Party: A Historical Profile*, London: A & C Black.

Pelling, Henry 1965, *The Origins of the Labour Party 1880–1900*, Oxford: Clarendon.

Pelling, Henry 1979, 'The Labour Unrest, 1911–14', in his *Popular Politics and Society in Late Victorian Britain*, London: Macmillan.

Pelling, Henry 1992, *A History of British Trade Unionism*, London: Palgrave Macmillan.

Pennell, Catriona 2012, *A Kingdom United. Popular Responses to the Outbreak of the First World War in Britain and Ireland*, Oxford: Oxford University Press.

Perrett, Bryan, and Anthony Lord 1981, *The Czar's British Squadron*, London: Kimber.

Perry, Matt 2015, *'Red Ellen' Wilkinson*, Manchester: Manchester University Press.

Phillips, Hugh D. 1992, *Between Revolution and the West: A Political Biography of Maxim Litvinov*, Boulder: Westview Press.

Pierson, Stanley 1973, *Marxism and the Origins of British Socialism: The Struggle for a New Consciousness*, Ithaca: Cornell University Press.

Pipes, Richard 1998, *The Unknown Lenin*, New Haven: Yale University Press.

Pitt, Robert 1989, 'Educator and Agitator: Charlie Gibbons, 1888–1967', *Llafur*, 5, 2: 72–83.

Pollitt, Harry 1940, *Serving My Time*, London: Lawrence & Wishart.

Pollitt, Harry 1947, *Looking Ahead*, London: CPGB.

Pollock, Sam 1969, *Mutiny for the Cause: The Story of the Revolt of Ireland's 'Devil's Own' in British India*, London: Leo Cooper.

Pope, Arthur Upham 1943, *Maxim Litvinov*, London: Secker & Warburg.

Postgate, John and Mary 1994, *A Stomach for Dissent. The Life of Raymond Postgate: 1896–1971*, Keele: Keele University Press.

Pribićević, Branko 1959, *The Shop Stewards' Movement and Workers' Control 1910–1922*, Oxford: Blackwell.

Pugh, Martin 2010, *Speak for Britain: A New History of the Labour Party*, London: Bodley Head.

Putkowski, Julian 1998, *British Army Mutineers 1914–1922*, London: Francis Boutle.

Quail, John 2014, *The Slow Burning Fuse: The Lost History of the British Anarchists*, London: Freedom Press.

Rabinovitch, Victor 1977, *British Marxist Socialism and Trade Unionism: The Attitudes, Experiences and Activities of the SDF 1884–1901*, Unpublished PhD thesis, University of Sussex.

Rabinowitch, Alexander 2007, *The Bolsheviks in Power*, Bloomington: Indiana University Press.

Radice, Giles and Lisanne 1974, *Will Thorne: Constructive Militant*, London: Allen & Unwin.

Ransome, Arthur 1919, *Russia in 1919*, New York: Huebsch.

Rappaport, Helen 2010, *Conspirator: Lenin in Exile*, New York: Perseus.

Raw, Louise 2011, *Striking a Light: The Bryant and May Matchwomen and their Place in History*, London: Continuum.

Redfern, Neil 2005, *Class or Nation? Communists, Imperialism and Two World Wars*, London: I.B. Tauris.

Reeve, Carl 1972, *The Life and Times of Daniel De Leon*, New York: Humanities Press.

Reid, Carole 1981, *The Origins and Development of the ILP in Manchester and Salford, 1890–1914*, Unpublished PhD thesis, University of Hull.

Reid, Fred 1971, 'Keir Hardie's Conversion to Socialism', in Asa Briggs and John Saville (eds), *Essays in Labour History 1886–1923*, London: Macmillan.

Reinders, Robert C. 1968, 'Racialism on the Left: E.D. Morel and the "Black Horror on the Rhine"', *International Review of Social History*, 13, 1: 1–28.

Richards, Huw 1997, *The Bloody Circus: The Daily Herald and the Left*, London: Pluto.

Riddell, John (ed.) 1984, *Lenin's Struggle for a Revolutionary International*, New York: Monad.

Riddell, John (ed.) 1986, *The German Revolution and the Debate on Soviet Power*, New York: Pathfinder.

Riddell, John (ed.) 1987, *Founding the Communist International*, New York: Pathfinder.

Riddell, John (ed.) 1991, *Workers of the World and Oppressed Peoples Unite: Proceedings and Documents of the Second Congress 1920*, New York: Pathfinder.

Riddell, John (ed.) 2012, *Toward the United Front: Proceedings of the Fourth Congress of the Communist International 1922*, Chicago: Haymarket.

Riddell, John (ed.) 2015, *To the Masses: Proceedings of the Third Congress of the Communist International, 1921*, Chicago: Haymarket.

Ripley, B.J., and J. McHugh 1989, *John Maclean*, Manchester: Manchester University Press.

Rippon, Nicola 2009, *The Plot to Kill Lloyd George: The Story of Alice Wheeldon and the Peartree Conspiracy*, London: Wharncliffe.

Rogers, Murdoch, and James J. Smith 1984, 'Peter Petroff', in William Knox (ed.), *Scottish Labour Leaders*, Edinburgh: Mainstream.

Rose, Jonathan 2001, *The Intellectual Life of the British Working Classes*, New Haven: Yale University Press.

Rosmer, Alfred 1959, *Le mouvement ouvrier pendant la première guerre mondiale*, Paris: Mouton.

Rosmer, Alfred 1971, *Lenin's Moscow*, London: Pluto.

Rothschild, Joseph 1959, *The Communist Party of Bulgaria*, New York: Columbia University Press.

Rothstein, Andrew 1970, *Lenin in Britain*, London: CPGB.

Rothstein, Andrew 1985, *The Soldiers' Strikes of 1919*, London: Journeyman Press.

Rothstein, Theodore 1973 [1929], *From Chartism to Labourism*, London: Lawrence and Wishart.

Rowbotham, Sheila 1982, *The Daughters of Karl Marx: Family Correspondence 1866–1898*, New York, Harcourt Brace.

Rowbotham, Sheila 1986, *Friends of Alice Wheeldon*, London: Pluto.

Rubenstein, David 1986, *Before the Suffragettes: Woman's Emancipation the 1890s*, Brighton: Harvester.

Rubin, G. 1980, 'A Note on the Scottish Office Reaction to John Maclean's Drugging Allegations', *Scottish Labour History Society Journal*, 14: 40–5.

Runciman, W.G. 1972, *Relative Deprivation and Social Justice*, Harmondsworth: Penguin.

Saklatvala, Sehri 1991, *The Fifth Commandment: A Biography of Sharpurji Saklatvala*, Salford: Miranda Press.

Salvatori, Massimo 1979, *Karl Kautsky and the Socialist Revolution*, London: New Left Books.

Sanders, W. Stephen 1927, *Early Socialist Days*, London: Hogarth Press.

Saunders, David 1985, 'Tyneside and the Making of the Russian Revolution', *Northern History*, 21, 1: 259–84.

Saunders, David 2004, 'A Russian Bebel Revisited: The individuality of Heinrich Matthaus Fischer (1871–1935)', *Slavonic and East European Review*, 82, 3: 625–54.

Saunders, David 2005, 'The 1905 Revolution on Tyneside', in Anthony Heywood and

Jonathan Smele (eds), *The Russian Revolution of 1905: Centenary Perspectives*, Abingdon: Routledge.

Saville, John 1960, 'Trade Unions and Free Labour: The Background to The Taff Vale Decision', in Asa Briggs and John Saville (eds), *Essays in Labour History*, London: Macmillan.

Saville, John 1973, 'Introduction', to Theodore Rothstein, *From Chartism to Labourism*, London: Lawrence & Wishart.

Schlesinger, Rudolf 1965, 'Lenin as a Member of the International Socialist Bureau', *Soviet Studies*, 16, 4: 448–58.

Seretan, L. Glen 1979, *Daniel De Leon: The Odyssey of an American Marxist*, Cambridge, MA: Harvard University Press.

Serge, Victor 1967, *Memoirs of a Revolutionary*, Oxford: Oxford University Press.

Service, Robert 2010, 'Russian Marxism and its London Colony before October 1917 Revolution', *Slavonic and East European Review*, 88, 1–2: 359–76.

Seymour, Joseph 1978, 'The Organisational Question in Classical Marxism', in *Young Spartacus*, November and December.

Shepherd, John 2002, *George Lansbury: At the Heart of Old Labour*, Oxford: Oxford University Press.

Shipman, Charles 1993, *It Had To Be Revolution: Memoirs of an American Radical*, Ithaca: Cornell University Press.

Shipway, Mark 1988, *Anti-Parliamentary Communism: The Movement for Workers' Councils in Britain, 1917–45*, London: Palgrave Macmillan.

Shlyapnikov, Alexander 1982, *On the Eve of 1917. Reminiscences of the Revolutionary Underground*, London: Allison & Busby.

Silbey, David 2005, *The British Working Class and Enthusiasm for War, 1914–1916*, London: Cass.

Simkins, Peter 1988, *Kitchener's Army*, Manchester: Manchester University Press.

Sires, R.V. 1955, 'Labour Unrest in England, 1910–14', *Journal of Economic History*, 11: 246–66.

Slatter, John (ed.) 1984, *The Other Shore: Russian Political Emigrants in Britain: 1880–1917*, London: Cass.

Slatter, John (ed.) (trans.) 1988, 'Observations and Reminiscences of a Petersburg Worker: G.M. Fisher in Newcastle Upon Tyne', *North East Labour History*, 22: 29–34.

Slaughter, Cliff 1967, 'Lenin and the Imperialist War of 1914–1918', *Fourth International*, 4, 3: 81–8.

Smillie, Robert 1924, *My Life for Labour*, London: Mills & Boon.

Smith, Dai 1980, 'Tonypandy 1910: Definitions of Community', *Past and Present*, 87, 1: 158–84.

Squires, Mike 1990, *Saklatvala: A Political Biography*, London: Lawrence & Wishart.

Stack, David 2000, 'The First Darwinian Left: Radical and Socialist Responses to Darwin, 1859–1914', *History of Political Thought*, 21, 4: 697–701.

Stedman Jones, Gareth 1971, *Outcast London*, Oxford: Clarendon Press.

Stevenson, James A. 1980, 'Daniel De Leon and European Socialism 1890–1914', *Science & Society*, 44, 2: 199–223.

Stewart, Bob 1967, *Breaking the Fetters: The Memoirs of Bob Stewart*, London: Lawrence & Wishart.

Swartz, Marvin 1971, *The Union of Democratic Control in British Politics during the First World War*, Oxford: Clarendon.

Swift, David 2017, *For Class and Country: The Patriotic Left and the First World War*, Liverpool: Liverpool University Press.

Taber, Mike, and John Riddell (eds) 2019, *The Communist Movement at a Crossroads: Plenums of the Communist International's Executive Committee 1922–1923*, Chicago: Haymarket.

Tanner, Duncan 1990, *Political Change and the Labour Party 1900–1918*, Cambridge: Cambridge University Press.

Tanner, Frank 2014, *British Socialism in the Early 1900s*, London: SHS Occasional Publication.

Taplin, Eric 1994, *Near to Revolution. The Liverpool General Transport Strike of 1911*, Liverpool: Bluecoat Press.

Terrett, J.J. n.d., *H.H. Asquith and the Featherstone Massacre*, London: Twentieth Century Press.

Thatcher, A.R. (ed.) 1971, *British Labour Statistics: Historical Abstract 1886–1968*, London: HMSO.

Thatcher, Ian D. 1999, 'Representations of Scotland in Nashe Slovo during World War One: A Brief Note', *Scottish Historical Review*, 78: 243–52.

Thompson, E.P. 1955, *William Morris: Romantic to Revolutionary*, London: Lawrence & Wishart.

Thompson, E.P. 1960, 'Homage to Tom Maguire', in Asa Briggs and John Saville, *Essays in Labour History*, London: Macmillan.

Thompson, E.P. 1968 [1963], *The Making of the English Working Class*, Harmondsworth: Pelican.

Thompson, E.P. 1994, *Persons and Polemics, Historical Essays*, London: Merlin Press.

Thompson, J. 2014, 'The Great Labour Unrest and Political Thought in Britain', *Labour History Review*, 79, 1: 37–54.

Thompson, Paul 1967, *Socialists, Liberals and Labour: The Struggle for London 1885–1914*, London: RKP.

Thompson, Willie 1992, *The Good Old Cause*, London: Pluto.

Thomson, Basil 1922 *Queer People*, London: Hodder & Stoughton.

Thonnessen, Werner 1973, *The Emancipation of Women: The Rise and Decline of the Women's Movement in German Social Democracy 1863–1933*, London: Pluto.

Thorpe, Andrew 1998, 'Comintern "Control" of the Communist Party of Great Britain, 1920–43', *English Historical Review*, 113: 637–62.

Thorpe, Andrew 2000, *The British Communist Party and Moscow 1920–43*, Manchester: Manchester University Press.

Thorpe, Andrew 2015, *A History of the British Labour Party*, London: Palgrave.

Thorpe, Wayne 2001, 'The European Syndicalists and War, 1914–1918', *Contemporary European History*, 10, 1: 1–24.

Thorpe, Wayne 2010, 'Internationalist Syndicalists in Europe 1914–18', *Socialist History*, 37: 23–47.

Tillett, Ben 1931, *Memories and Reflections*, London: J. Long.

Tosstorff, Reiner 2016, *The Red International of Labour Unions (RILU) 1920–1937*, Leiden: Brill.

Townshend, Charles 1979, 'The Irish Railway Strike of 1920: Industrial Action and Civil Resistance in the Struggle for Independence', *Irish Historical Studies*, 21, 83: 265–82.

Tressell, Robert 2005 [1914], *The Ragged Trousered Philanthropists*, Oxford: Oxford World's Classics.

Trotsky, Leon 1926, *Where Is Britain Going?* London: CPGB.

Trotsky, Leon 1968 [1948], *Stalin: An Appraisal of the Man and His Influence, volume one*, London: Panther.

Trotsky, Leon 1974a, *The First Five Years of the Communist International*, London: New Park.

Trotsky, Leon 1974b, *Trotsky's Writings on Britain*, London: New Park.

Trotsky, Leon 1975 [1930], *My Life*, Harmondsworth: Penguin.

Trotsky, Leon 1983 [1904], *Our Political Tasks*, London: New Park.

Tsuzuki, Chushichi 1956, 'The "Impossibilist Revolt" in Britain', *International Review of Social History*, 1, 3: 377–97.

Tsuzuki, Chushichi 1961, *H.M. Hyndman and British Socialism*, Oxford: Oxford University Press.

Tsuzuki, Chushichi 1983, 'Anglo-Marxism and Working Class Education', in J. Winter (ed.), *The Working Class in Modern British History*, Cambridge: Cambridge University Press.

Tsuzuki, Chushichi 1991, *Tom Mann, 1856–1941*, Oxford: Clarendon Press.

Turnbull, Robert 2017, *Climbing Mount Sinai. Noah Ablett 1883–1935*, London: Socialist History Society.

Ugolini, Laura 2002, 'We Must Stand By Our Own Bairns: ILP Men and Suffrage Militancy, 1905–1914', *Labour History Review*, 67, 2: 149–69.

Ullman, Richard H. 1961, *Anglo-Soviet Relations 1917–21: Intervention and the War*, Princeton: Princeton University Press.

Ullman, Richard H. 1968, *Britain and the Russian Civil War*, Princeton: Princeton University Press.

Valtin, Jan 1941, *Out of the Night*, London: Heinemann.

Veitch, Colin 1985, '"Play Up! Play Up! and Win the War!" Football, the Nation and the First World War 1914–15', *Journal of Contemporary History*, 20, 3: 363–78.

Vellacott, Jo 2007, *Pacifists, Patriots and the Vote: The Erosion of Democratic Suffragism in Britain During the First World War*, London: Palgrave.

Voerman, Gerrit 2007, 'Proletarian Competition: The Amsterdam Bureau and Its German Counterpart 1919–1920', *Jahrbuch für historische Kommunismusforschung*, Berlin: Aufbau.

Wade, Rex A. 1967, 'Argonauts of Peace: The Soviet Delegation to Western Europe in the Summer of 1917', *Slavic Review*, 26, 3: 453–67.

Walling, William 1915, *The Socialists and the War: A Documentary Statement of the Position of the Socialists of All Countries*, New York: Henry Holt.

Watt, Richard M. 1973, *The Kings Depart: The German Revolution and the Treaty of Versailles 1918–19*, Harmondsworth: Pelican.

Webb, Sydney and Beatrice 1920, *The History of Trade Unionism*, London: Longmans, Green & Co.

West, Nigel 2005, *Mask: MI5's Penetration of the Communist Party of Great Britain*, London: Routledge.

White, James D. 2004, 'Vincas Kapsukas and the Scottish Lithuanians', *Revolutionary Russia*, 12, 2: 67–89.

White, Joe 1982, '1910–1914 Reconsidered', in James E. Cronin and Jonathan Schneer (eds), *Social Conflict and the Political Order in Modern Britain*, London: Croom Helm.

White, Joe 1974a, 'Labour's Council of Action, 1920', *Journal of Contemporary History*, 9, 4: 99–122.

White, Joe 1974b, 'Soviets in Britain: The Leeds Convention of 1917', *International Review of Social History*, 19, 2: 165–93.

White, Joe 1979, *Britain and the Bolshevik Revolution: A Study in the Politics of Diplomacy, 1920–24*, New York: Holmes & Meier.

White, Joe 1994, 'British Labour in Soviet Russia, 1920', *English Historical Review*, 109: 621–40.

Whitfield, Roy 1988, *Frederick Engels in Manchester*, Manchester: Working-Class Movement Library.

Wicks, Harry 1992, *Keeping My Head*, London: Socialist Platform.

Wigger, Iris 2010, '"Black Shame": The Campaign Against "Racial Degeneration" and Female Degradation in Interwar Europe', *Race & Class*, 51, 3: 33–46.

Wilkins, M.S. 1959, 'The Non-Socialist Origins of England's First Important Socialist Organisation', *International Review of Social History*, 4, 2: 199–207.

Willett, John (ed.) 1990, *Bertolt Brecht: Poems and Songs from the Plays*, London: Methuen.

Williams, Stephen, and Tony Chandler 2020, '"Tussy's Great Delusion" – Eleanor Marx's Death Revisited', *Socialist History*, 58: 7–31.

Winslow, Barbara 1996, *Sylvia Pankhurst: Sexual Politics and Political Activism*, London: UCL.

Winter, J.M. 1972, 'Arthur Henderson, the Russian Revolution, and the Reconstruction of the Labour Party', *Historical Journal*, 15, 4: 753–73.

Winter, J.M. 1974, *Socialism and the Challenge of War: Ideas and Politics in Britain 1912–18*, London: RKP.

Winter, J.M. 1988, *The Experience of World War One*, Oxford: Macmillan.

Wintringham, Tom 1936, *Mutiny: Being a Survey of Mutinies from Spartacus to Invergordon*, London: Stanley Nott.

Wood-Simons, May 1910, *Report of Socialist Party Delegation and Proceedings of the International Socialist Congress at Copenhagen, 1910*, Chicago: H.G. Adair.

Worley, Matthew 2002, *Class Against Class: The Communist Party in Britain between the Wars*, London: I.B. Taurus.

Wrigley, Chris 1976, *David Lloyd George and the British Labour Movement*, Brighton: Harvester.

Wrigley, Chris 1990, *Lloyd George and the Challenge of Labour*, Brighton: Harvester.

Wrigley, Chris 1992, 'The ILP and the Second International: The Early Years, 1893–1905', in T. James, T. Jowitt, and K. Laybourn (eds), *The Centennial History of the Independent Labour Party*, Halifax: Ryburn.

Wrigley, Chris (ed.) 1993, *Challenges of Labour: Central and Western Europe 1917–1920*, London: Routledge.

Yamanouchi, Akito 1989, 'Internationalized Bolshevism: The Bolsheviks and the International, 1914–1917', *Acta Slavica Iaponica*, 7: 17–32.

Yamanouchi, Akito 2008, 'The Early Comintern in Amsterdam, New York and Mexico City', *The Shien or the Journal of History (Faculty of Humanities, Kyushu University)*, 145: 99–139.

Young, David M. 2005, 'Social Democratic Federation Membership in London', *Historical Research*, 78: 354–76.

Young, James D. 1985, 'Militancy, English Socialism and the Ragged Trousered Philanthropists', *Journal of Contemporary History*, 20, 2: 283–303.

Zamyatin, Yevgeny 1984, *Islanders*, Edinburgh: Salamander.

Zelnik, Reginald E. (ed.) 1986, *A Radical Worker in Tsarist Russia: The Autobiography of S.I. Kanatchikov*, Stanford: Stanford University Press.

Zumoff, Jacob A. 2014, *The Communist International and US Communism, 1919–1929*, Leiden: Brill.

Index

Abdullah, Mahommed 153
Ablett, Noah 59–60, 122, 148
Adamson, William 135
Addison, Christopher 95, 127
Adler, Victor 40
Advocates of Industrial Unionism 56
Alexander, Harry 122, 169, 174
Allen, Clifford 199, 201
Allen, E.J.B. 56, 59
Amalgamated Society of Engineers 24, 69, 114
Amalgamated Society of Railway Servants 34, 43
Amalgamated Stevedores Union 7
American Federation of Labor 26
Amsterdam Bureau of the Communist International 177–180
  See also Communist International
Anderson, Will 50, 121, 122–123
Anglo-Russian Trade Union Committee 224
Arnot, Robin Page 222
Askew, J.B. 180
Asquith, Herbert 48, 63, 72, 80, 92, 114, 158
Associated Society of Locomotive Engineers and Firemen 43
Aveling, Edward 18–20, 23, 27, 64
Avramov, Roman 39

Bakunin, Mikhael 11
Baldwin, Stanley 225
Barbour, Mary 93
Barnes, George 116, 119, 168, 183
Beard, John 151
Bebel, August 13, 18, 70
  Women and Socialism 65
Beech, Dick 190
Beer, Max 37–38, 39, 40
Belfast Dock Strike (1907) 43, 88
Belfast Engineers' Strike (1919) 134–135
Belfort Bax, Ernest 64, 87
Bell, Tom 54, 76, 185, 220, 223, 227
  at founding of CPGB 204, 205
  Communist Unity Group 177
  on affiliation to Labour Party 207
Bell, Walter 95, 99

Benn, William Wedgwood 127
Bernstein, Eduard 17, 37
Bevan, Aneurin 113, 140
Bevin, Ernest 68, 121, 145, 165, 196
Bismark, Otto von 13
'Black Friday' (1921) 218, 225
Blatchford, Robert 25
'Bloody Sunday' (1887) 19
Bloomsbury Socialist Society 20, 27
Bolshevik Party 3, 33–34, 37, 54, 84, 103
Bonar Law, Andrew 135, 136, 225
Bondfield, Margaret 155
Booth, Herbert 85
Borgbjerg, Frederik 124
Borodin, Michael 178
Brecht, Bertolt 229
Bridges, Robert 94
Bridges-Adams, Mary 112
British Labour Delegation to Soviet Russia (1920) 199
British Socialist Party 49, 104, 203, 204
  1914 conference 53
  1918 General Election 169
  atitude to Ireland 101, 158
  attitude to Triple Alliance 146–147
  colonial policy 156
  debates joining Comintern 174
  debate on Labour Party 51
  discussions with Lenin 192–193
  Glasgow branch 90
  Glasgow 'Bloody Friday' 138
  internal opposition to War 75–76
  Labour party affiliation 174–177
  Labour Party councillors 198
  relations with Amsterdam Bureau 178–179
  Russian Revolution 128–129
  splits over war (1916) 82, 106–107
  support for police strikes 143–144
  supports Sankey Commission 141
  unity talks 167
  World War One 73–74
  See also Social Democratic Federation
Brockway, Fenner 72
Bromley, John 164
Brouse, Paul 17, 29

Brown, Ernie   222
Buchanan, George   161
Bukharin, Nikolai   196
Bulgarian Social Democratic Workers' Party
    (Narrow Socialists)   70
Burgess, Harold   180
Burke, David   3
Burns, Emile   222
Burns, John   12, 15, 21

Cachin, Marcel   124
Campbell, Alan   224
Cant, Ernie   75, 211
Carlyle, Thomas   14
Carson, Edward   67
Casement, Roger   85
Central Labour College   59, 187
Challinor, Raymond   3, 195
Chandler, A.E.   61
Chartism   8–9
Chicherin, George   3, 89, 100, 111, 153, 163
    accused of insanity   185
    attitude to war   107, 109
    opposes racism   151–152
    World War One activity   106–107
Childs, Wyndham   139
Chkheidze, Nikolai   128
Churchill, Winston   44, 132, 162, 164
Clarke, John S.   65, 190, 202
Clemanceau, Georges   132
Clunie, James   212
Clyde Workers' Committee   94, 96
    'Should the Workers Arm?'   98–99
    opposes racism   153
    The Worker banned   95
    The Worker newspaper   96–97
Clynes, J.R.   46, 157
Cole, G.D.H.   222
Colne Valley Socialist League   48
Committee of Delegates of the Russian
    Socialist Groups   111
Communist International   2
    1920 'Commission on English Affairs'
        196–197
    1923 'English Commission'   3, 203
    debate on Labour Party affiliation   192–
        194, 197
    ECCI demands a unified communist party
        210

First Congress (1919)   172–173
Fourth Congress (1922)   220
Second Congress (1920)   188, 190–199
The Communist International Answers the
    ILP   200–201
Third Congress (1921)   223–224
Western European Bureau (Amsterdam
    Bureau)   177–179
Communist Labour Party (Scotland)   210–
    211, 214, 216
Communist Party (British Section of the
    Third International)   183, 216
    founding conference   213
    fuses with CPGB   214
    internal disputes   215–216
    See also Workers' Socialist Federation
Communist Party of Great Britain   148, 155,
    198
    1920 Unity Convention   203–205
    1921 Leeds conference   216–217
    applies to affiliate to Labour Party   206–
        207
    'Black Friday'   218
    criticised at Third Comintern Congress
        219–220
    discusses affiliation to Labour Party
        205–206
    debated at Fourth Comintern Congress
        220
    in 1926 General Strike   226–227
    participation in parliament   204–205
    unity with communist groups   214, 216
Communist Unity Group   177, 182, 183, 203,
    209
    See also Socialist Labour Party (Britain)
Connolly, James   3, 61, 65, 102, 1030
    and Millerandism   29
    break with Sean O'Casey   87
    execution   101, 103
    ILP   27, 28
    opposes racism   153
    opposition to anti-semitism   26
    relations with De Leon   25–26, 3
    SDF membership   25–6
    World War One   85–87, 109
Conscientious objectors   83–84
Cook, A.J.   61
Crawfurd, Helen   93, 190, 199, 222
Crick, Martin   2, 21

Crump, Charlie   164
Curran, Pete   21, 22

Daly, James   138
Dangerfield, George   48
Defence of the Realm Act (1914)   92, 95, 98,
      135
De Leon, Daniel   3, 25, 30, 54, 58, 59,
      118
   See also Socialist Labour Party (United
      States)
Democratic Federation   12, 21
   See Social Democratic Federation
Denikin, Anton   162
Despard, Charlotte   64
Deutscher Fichte-Bund   155
Dock strike (London 1889)   7–8, 12
Dock, Wharf, Riverside and General Labour-
      ers Union   12
Dollan, Patrick   112
Doull, J.P.   26
Doyle, W.G.   71
Dublin Lock Out (1913)   45
Duggan, James   24
Dutt, Rajani Palme   4, 222, 223

Easter Rising (1916)   101–102
East London Federation of Suffragettes   63–
      67
   changes name to Women's Suffrage Feder-
      ation   81
   discusses World War One   79–80
   People's Army   66
   supports Easter Rising   102–103
   Woman's Dreadnought launched   66
   See also Workers' Socialist Federation
Ebury, George   144
Engels, Friedrich   2
   1889 London Dock strike   8
   attitude to ILP   27
   attitude to Keir Hardie   37
   Chartism   9
   SDF   13, 15, 18
Erskine of Mar   212
Étaples mutiny   84
Ewer, Monica   222
Ewer, Norman   222
Ewington, John   36

Fabian Society   35, 64, 124, 167, 222
Fairchild, Edwin   73, 82, 112, 121, 122, 168, 169,
      170, 174
Featherstone   24
February Revolution (1917)   111
Fenwick, Charles   17
Fife Miners' Reform Committee   189
Fineberg, Joe   53, 75, 82, 112, 122, 148, 169,
      170
   at First Comintern Congress   173
   at Second Comintern Congress   197
First International (International Working-
      men's Association)   2, 10–11
Fischer, M.A.   33
Fischer, Willie (Rudolf Abel)   33
Fisher, Victor   50, 98
Fitten, John   204
Fitzgerald, Jack   29
Fox, Albert   43
Fraina, Louis   178
Frankford, Philip   75

Gallacher, William   49, 99, 122, 136, 152, 187,
      216
   1916 legal defence   100
   accuses Maclean of insanity   185, 212
   agreement with Lenin   210
   and Clyde Workers' Committee   96–99
   arrested and jailed in 1916   95–96, 99
   at Second Comintern Congress   190, 197,
      202
   Communist Labour Party   210–211
   discussions with Labour Party   208
   expels Maclean from meeting   97
   Towards Industrial Democracy   118
Galliffet, Marquis de   28
Geddes, Alec   205, 211
Geddes, Eric   132
General Strike (1926)   224, 225
Gibbs, James   24
Glading, Percy   75
Glasgow Rent Strike (1915)   81, 93–94
Glasgow 40 Hour Week Strike (1919)   135–
      136
Glasgow 'Bloody Friday' (1919)   136
Glasier, John Bruce   21, 27, 44, 63, 101
Govan Trades Council   94
Gray, Jack   83
Grayson, Victor   39, 43, 44, 48, 49, 88

Guesde, Jules 37
Guild Communist Group 203, 221–222

Haig, Douglas 138, 145
Hall, Leonard 53
'Hands Off Russia' campaign 138, 164–167
Hardie, Keir 27, 35, 37, 44, 69, 72, 78
Hargreaves, Leonard 114
Harney, Julian 9
Hassan, Kathryn 76
Hay, Will 62
Henderson, Arthur 42, 46, 69, 72, 78, 85, 94, 101, 103, 114, 116, 196
    1918 Labour Party constitution 126–127
    'Hands Off Russia' 165
    Labour Party and revolution 125–126
    replies to CPGB on affiliation 207, 208
    visit to Petrograd (1917) 124–125
Hicks, George 227
Hill, John 164
Hinton, James 2
Hobsbawm, Eric 23
Hodge, John 170
Hodges, Frank 218
Hodgson, John 182, 205
Holliday, William 92
Holton, Jim 2
Horner, Arthur 102
Hull dock strike (1893) 24
Hunt, Karen 2
Huysmans, Camille 50
Hyndman, Henry M. 12–15, 18, 39, 156, 186
    and Possibilists 17
    anti-semitism 18
    attacks Peter Petroff 98
    calls for citizen army 49
    Millerandism 28
    supports Labour Party 51
    splits from BSP 82, 105
    support for Royal Navy 16–17
    World War One 73

Impossibilists 29
Independent Labour Party 21–23, 27–28
    1920 delegation to Russia 199
    and Labour Representation Committee 35
    attitude to suffragettes 63

Easter Rising 101
    fall in membership 48
    former SDF members 21
    Forward banned 95
    Glasgow branch 93
    leaves Second International 182
    Leeds Convention 120–122
    The Communist International Answers the ILP 200–201
    'Two and a Half International' 199
    unity talks 167, 171
    World War One 72, 73, 123–124
Independent Labour Party Left Wing 181–182, 201, 221, 222
    discusses officials' jobs after unity 209
    publishes *The Communist International Answers the ILP* 201
    unity with CPGB 215
Industrial Workers of Great Britain 56
Industrial Workers of the World 26, 55
Industrial Syndicalist Education League 59–60
Inkpin, Albert 73, 75, 104, 181, 203, 206, 216, 221, 228
Inkpin, Harry 223
International Conference of Socialist Women (1910) 64
International Socialist Bureau (see Second International)
International Socialist Labour Party 182
International Working Union of Socialist Parties ('Two-and-a-Half International') 199
Irish Citizen Army 61, 66, 86, 101, 102
Irish Republican Army 157
Irish Socialist Republican Party 25
Irish Transport and General Workers Union 43, 86
Irish War of Independence 157–158
Ironside, Edmund 161
Irving, Dan 36, 53

Jackson, T.A. 16
Jackson, Harold 100
Jaures, Jean 37
John, Jack 45
Jolly George 165
Jones, Ernest 9
Jowett, Fred 122, 125

Kaclerović, Triša 70
Kahan, Zelda 105–106
　criticises Bolsheviks 129
　on Labour Party 52
　opposes Hyndman 51
Kamanev, Lev 166
Kapp, Yvonne 2
Kautsky, Karl 28, 105, 107, 192, 223
　and Labour Party 38–39, 40–41
　Sekte oder Klassenpartei 51–52
Kavanagh, Matt 163
Kendall, Walter 2, 5, 181, 203, 220, 222
Kerensky, Alexander 80, 128, 161
Khozetsky, Alexander 33
Kiel Mutiny 133
Kirkwood, David 94, 96, 136, 168
　deported in 1916 95, 99
Klugmann, James 3
Knee, Fred 22, 47
Knox, Alfred 161
Kollontai, Alexandra 32, 64
Kommunistische Arbeiterpartei Deutsch-
　lands 178, 221
Kornilov, Lavr 161
Krassin, Leonard 166
Kropotkin, Pyotr 32

Labour Intelligence Division 95
Labour Party 168
　1918 General Election 195
　admitted to Second International 38
　attitude to Russian Revolution 124–125
　changes name to Labour Party 36
　Clause Four 126
　'Hands Off Russia' campaign 165–166
　International Advisory Committee 187
　Labour Representation Committee 28
　Litvinov adresses 1918 conference 133–
　　134
　origins 34–36
　policy on Ireland 101, 158
　pre-1918 structure 41
　World War One 72
Labour Research Department 222
Lafargue, Laura 8
Laird, Mary 93
Lanarkshire Miners' Reform Committee
　188
Lanchester, Edith 64

Land Colonisation and Industrial League
　203
Lansbury, Edgar 220–221
Lansbury, George 63, 69, 101, 150, 154
Lansbury, Minnie 220–221
Lapčević, Dragiša 70
Larkin, James 43, 45, 46, 61, 65
Lasalle, Ferdinand 13
Leckie, John 211
Lee, H.W. 2
Leeds Convention (1917) 120–123
Lenin, V. I. 3, 32, 34, 70, 81, 147, 163, 187, 197
　debates Labour Party joining Second
　　International 38
　discussions with BSP 192
　*Left-Wing Communism: An Infantile Dis-
　　order* 192, 194, 199
　Labour Party affiliation 192–194
　nature of Labour Party 195
　on British imperialism 199, 220
　revolutionary defeatism 109
Levi, Paul 193, 196
Liberal Party 9, 10
Liebknecht, Karl 34, 70, 79, 81, 163, 172
Liebknecht, Wilhelm 19
Lincoln, W. Bruce 162
Linnell, Alfred 20
Litvinov, Maxim 33, 78–79, 89, 133–134, 162,
　186
Liverpool Transport Workers strike (1910)
　44–45
Lloyd George, David 5, 35, 45, 46, 67–68, 85,
　92–93, 94–95, 114, 116, 124, 132, 134, 135,
　139–140, 142–144, 189, 217, 225, 228
　challenges Robert Smillie 140–141
　defeats the Triple Alliance 145
Locker-Lampson, Oliver 161
Lockhart, Robert Bruce 124
London Trades Council 22
London Workers' Committee 116
Luxemburg, Rosa 70, 172
Lynch, Patrica 103, 159
Lyne, J.T. 163

Macassey, Lynden 98
MacDonald, James Ramsay 21, 34, 35, 42,
　44, 45, 46, 72, 78, 121, 122, 125, 225
　debates Labour joining the Comintern
　　196

denounces Lenin 126
Labour Party 1918 constitution 126–127
MacDougall, James 87–88, 90, 97, 184, 189
   arrested in 1916 95
Macfarlane, L.J. 2
Mac Gille Iosa, Liam 212
Maclean, John 3, 76, 85, 96, 102, 122, 143, 147, 149, 168, 169, 170, 172, 224, 228
   1916 legal defence 100
   accused of insanity 185, 212
   and 'Bloody Friday' 188
   arrest in 1915 92, 94
   arrest in 1916 95–96
   calls for split in BSP 105
   criticises Gallacher 97
   differences with Gallacher 187
   differences with Theodore Rothstein 187
   early life 88
   on Ireland 159–160
   opposes Sankey Commission 141
   Peter Petroff 89–90
   prison sentences 183
   refuses to join CPGB 211–212
   Scottish Labour College 187–188
   Scottish Workers' Republican Party 212
   The Communist International Answers the ILP 201
   tortured in prison 184–185
   Vanguard banned 95
   Vanguard launched 90
   World War One 87, 90–91
Maclean, John (Parkhead Comunist Group) 211
Maclean, Neil (Barr & Stroud director) 100
Maclean, Neil (Labour MP) 137
MacManus, Arthur 76, 96, 102, 115–116, 117, 148, 170, 206, 216, 217, 218, 223, 227
   at founding of CPGB 203, 205
   Communist Unity Group 177
   deported in 1916 95, 99
   discussions with Labour Party 208
   on 'Bloody Friday' 137
MacShane, Harry 84, 97, 99, 102
Maguire, Tom 21
Maisky, Ivan 33
Mallon, James 115
Malone, Cecil L'Estrange 169, 185, 212, 214

Mann, Tom 12, 21, 22, 44, 59, 60, 61, 164
   defends suffragettes 65
   'Don't Shoot' leaflet 45
   resignation from SDF 57
   The Industrial Syndicalist 58
   World War One 77
Manningham Mills strike (1891) 22
Mannoury, Gerrit 180
Martov, Julius 32, 89
   Nashe Slovo 106–108
Matheson, Jane 65
Marx, Eleanor 18–20, 64
Marx, Jenny 13
Marx, Karl 2, 62
   attitude to Hyndman 13
   Chartism 9
   correspondence about Hyndman 38
Marx, Laura 19
Maxton, James 95
McEntee, Val 75
McIlroy, John 224
McKay, Claude 154–155, 167
   Socialism and the Negro 154
McKibbin, Ross 1, 23
McLaine, William 147, 174, 190
   at Second Comintern Congress 193, 197, 198
McLoughlin, Sean 158
Mellor, William 203, 204, 222
Menshevik Party 3, 34, 37, 89, 106, 124, 128, 129
Meynell, Francis 181, 219
Millerand, Alexander 28–29
Milner, Alfred 98
Miners' Federation of Great Britain 45, 164
   1919 miners' strikes 139–140
   and Ireland 157
   'Black Friday' 217–218
   'Hands Off Russia' campaign 164, 165
Mitchell, Tom 181, 210
Monatte, Pierre 57
Montifiore, Dora 64, 121
Morel, E.D. 148, 154–155
Morgan, Kevin 4
Morris, William 18–19, 21
'Moscow Gold' 5, 181
Muir, John 74, 76, 77, 94, 95–96, 97, 99, 100, 184
Munitions of War Act (1915) 92, 93

Munro, Robert   135
Murby, Millicent   64
Murphy, J.T.   114, 117, 160, 171, 227
   1919 *Manifesto*   170–171
   and Amsterdam Bureau   179–180
   at Second Comintern Congress   190, 202
   joins SLP   119
   on police strikes   144
   The Workers' Committee   117–118
   World War One   118–119, 120
mutinies in British armed forces   133, 134,
   137

National Guilds League   222
National Sailors' and Firemen's Union   125,
   152
National Socialist Party   82
National Transport Workers' Federation   69,
   112, 218
National Union of Police and Prison Officers
   142–144
National Union of Railwaymen   67, 141–142,
   143, 145–146, 157, 163, 165, 218
National Union of Ships' Stewards, Cooks,
   Butchers and Bakers   152
Nevinson, Henry   112
Newbold, J.T. Walton   209, 222
Newbold, Marjory   190, 199, 201
No Conscription Fellowship   118, 182
Norman, C.H.   182
Norwood, Melita   34

O'Brien, William   121
O'Casey, Sean   87
O'Grady, James   21, 124

Paddock Socialist Club (Huddersfield)   69
Palmer, Brian   5
Pankhurst, Christabel   63, 66, 80
Pankhurst, Emmeline   63, 80, 85
Pankhurst, Sylvia   63, 65, 76, 80, 102, 112, 117,
   122, 130, 131, 146, 148, 155, 168, 179, 220,
   224
   1920 arrest   214
   anti-parliamentarism   168–169
   attends Second Comintern Congress
   190, 196, 197, 202
   attitude to affiliation to Labour Party
   182

BSP antipathy towards   180
   control of *The Workers' Dreadnought*
   215–216
   discussions with Lenin   175, 192, 213
   expulsion from CPGB   221
   on Ireland   158, 159
   personal bravery   65
   World War One   79–80
Paris Commune   11, 28
Parkhead Comunist Group (Glasgow)   211
Paul, William   58, 153, 170, 177, 182, 205
Peak, Frean & Co. strike   7
Pearce, Brian   4, 224
Peet, George   117, 120
Pelling, Henry   2
People's Paper   9
People's Russian Information Bureau   162–
   163
Petrograd Soviet   123–124
Petrov, Peter   3, 97, 104, 184
   and Hyndman   89–90
   arrested   95, 98
   criticises Willie Gallacher   97
   denounced by *Justice*   98
   differences with Lenin   108–109, 110
   influence on John Maclean   88–89
   opposes affiliation to Labour Party   53
   on women's rights   65
Phillips, Marion   64
Plebs League   59, 187
Plekhanov, George   32
Police strikes   142–144
Pollitt, Harry   4, 44, 127, 143, 163, 164, 167, 221,
   223, 227
Pollitt, Mary   44
Ponsonby, Arthur   127
Poole, Frederick   161
Poplar Board of Guardians   198
Poplar Council   220
Possibilists   17
Prendergast, Michael   44
Princip, Gavrilo   68
Proudhon, Pierre   10
Purcell, Alf   203, 204, 227

Quelch, Harry   18, 22, 27, 29, 33, 34, 39, 47–
   48, 49
Quelch, Tom   122, 150–151, 180, 190, 198–199,
   221

Radek, Karl   40, 108–109, 148, 194, 196, 198, 223
  on CPGB and 'Black Friday'   219–220
  The Communist International Answers the ILP   200–201
Ragged Trousered Philanthropists, The   16, 58
Railworkers' strike (1919)   145
Ramsey, Dave   116, 190, 194
Reagan, Willie   99
Redmond, John   87
Reform Act (1867)   10
Rhondda Socialist Society   60
Rickard, William   85
Riddell, George   145
Rose, Frank   69
Rosmer, Alfred   57, 197, 198
Rothstein, Andrew   180, 187, 209, 224
Rothstein, Theodore   3, 15–16, 34, 38, 103–104, 181
  analysis of Russian Revolution   128
  attitude to Labour Party   51–52
  calls for BSP unity   105, 107
  criticised by Lenin   107
  dislike of Sylvia Pankhurst   180
  early life   31–2
  relations with RSDLP   32
  work with British Intelligence   186
Ruskin College strike (1909)   59
Russian Political Prisoners' and Exiles' Relief Committee   106
Russian Social Democratic and Labour Party   32, 37
  congresses in London   34
  See also Bolshevik Party, Menshevik Party
Rylance, Mark   33

Saklatvala, Shapurji   209, 222
Samms, Adolfo   92
Sanders, William   124
Samuel Commission (1925)   226
Sankey Commission (1919)   141–142
Scheidemann, Philipp   129
Scott, William   163
Scottish Labour College   187
Scottish Socialist Federation   25
Scottish Workers Parliamentary Committee   29
Scottish Workers' Republican Party   212

Second International
  1900 Paris congress   28–29
  1904 Amsterdam congress   36–37, 156
  1907 Stuttgart congress   70
  1912 Basel congress   70
  accepts Labour Party ias member   38
  'Allied' Socialist Conference 1915   78–79
  calls for unity of British left   50–51
  debate on Millerandism   28–29
  founding   17
  ILP resigns from   182
  Womens' Conference (1910)   64
Sembat, Marcel   78
Sexton, James   147
Shaw, Fred   122, 170
Shinwell, Manny   135, 136, 152
Shlyapnikov, Alexander   33
Shop Stewards and Workers' Committee Movement   116, 117, 119, 144, 157, 214
Sifleet, Arthur   156
Singer Sewing Machine factory strike (1910)   56–7, 88
Sinn Fein   134
Sirtis, Alexander   33–4
Smart, Russell   49, 53
Smillie, Robert   63, 112, 140–141, 146, 147, 188, 219, 228
Smith, F.E.   85
Smyth, Nora   79, 81, 169, 213, 221
Snell, Henry   21
Snowden, Philip   42, 44, 121, 122
Social Democratic Federation
  1902 conference debates   29–30
  and 1889 dock strike   11
  attitude to Labour Party   50
  birth   11–12
  formation of Labour Representation Committee   34–35
  forms British Socialist Party   49
  growth in 1890s   25
  origins as Democratic Federation   12, 21
  relations with ILP   27, 29
  Russian emigres   30–31
  splits   18
  support for Royal Navy   16
  trade union policy   14–15, 23
  See also British Socialist Party
Socialist Labour Party (Britain)   2, 3, 210, 211, 224

1918 General Election manifesto   170
attitude to Ireland   101–102, 158–159
attitude to police strikes   144
arrests of members   92
and John Maclean   149, 212
Communist Unity Group split   177
Communist unity talks   171, 176–177,
  180–182
comparison with Bolsheviks   54–55
dismisses formation of CPGB   205
foundation   30
ideology   53–54
industrial unionism   56–57
Labour party affiliation   174–177
on Triple Alliance   148–149
opposes racism   151, 153
printing press destroyed   95
representation in CPGB   224
support for Bolshevik Party   130
World War One   73–77
Zimmerwald conference   109
Socialist Labor Party (United States)   3, 25–
  6, 29–30
Socialist League   18–20, 21
Socialist National Defence Committee   105
Socialist Party of Great Britain   30–31, 55,
  78, 182
Socialist Prohibition Fellowship   203
Socialist Trade and Labor Alliance   26, 55
Society of Friends of Russian Freedom   32
Sorge, Friedrich   20, 37
South Wales Socialist Society   60, 174, 213
Sozialdemokratische Partei Deutschlands
  10, 13, 17–18, 28, 105–106, 172, 187
Stalin, J.V.   224, 227
Stephenson, J.J.   38, 43
Stockholm Peace Conference (1917)   124
Stoker, W.R.   76
Sullivan, James   64
Sutcliffe, John   44
Swales, Alonzo   227
Syme, John   144

Taff Vale Judgement   24, 36
Tanner, Frank   51
Tanner, Jack   57, 190, 194
Taylor, G.R.S.   48
Thiel, Thomas   142
Thomas, J.H.   141–142, 145, 157, 166, 218

Thompson, E.P.   2, 6
Thomson, Basil   157, 165, 186
Thorne, Will   21, 39, 124
Thorpe, Andrew   4
Tillett, Ben   44, 46
Trades Union Congress   35, 146–147
Trades Disputes Act (1906)   36
Tressell, Robert (Robert Noonan)   16
Trevelyan, Charles   127
Triple Alliance   67, 69, 145, 146, 157, 218
Trotsky, Leon   32, 33, 62, 84, 110, 159, 163
  founding of Comintern, 172–173
  Nashe Slovo   106–108
  Terrorism and Communism   192
Tsuzuki, Chushichi   2
Tukhachevsky, Mikhail   165
Tupper, Edward   121
Turner, Ben   21

Ulster Volunteer Force   67
Union for Democratic Control   82, 150
United Socialist Council   50, 120–121, 167
Unofficial Reform Committee (South Wales)
  60, 174
  The Miners' Next Step   60–61

Vaillant, Edouard   78
Vane, Francis   103
Vaughan, Joe   219
Vollmar, Georg von   70
Vandervelde, Emile   28, 50, 78

Waldeck-Rousseau, Pierre   28
Walden, George   144
Walker, Melvina   78, 80, 169
Wallhead, Robert   199, 201
Walsh, Stephen   170
Ward, Albert   83
Watson, William   116, 120, 163, 167, 185
Watts, A.A.   198
Watts, Hunter   51, 98
Webb, Beatrice   21, 37, 49, 50, 222
Webb, Sydney   21, 37, 126–127, 208, 222
Wedgwood, Ethel   150
Weir, William   93
West India Dock (London)   7
Weygand, Maxime   166
Wharf, Riverside and General Workers Union
  165

Wheatley, John   96, 99
Wheeldon, Alice   85
White, Jack   61
Whitehead, Edgar   183, 213, 215
Whitley, J.H.   170
Wijnkoop, David   193, 196
Wilkinson, Ellen   222
Wilkinson, Lily Gair   65
Williams, Jack   143
Williams, Robert   112, 121, 146, 148, 218, 219
Willis, Fred   169, 178, 180
Wilson, Havelock   125, 152
Wilson, Henry   132
Woodhouse, Michael   224
Woolf, Leonard   187
Workers' Socialist Federation   167, 169
   attitude to racism   150, 154–55
   criticises left-wing union leaders   146
   debates Labour party affiliation   174–177
   forms Communist Party (British Section
      of the Third International)   183
   opposes Sankey Commission   141, 148
   position on Ireland   159
   rejects unity with BSP   168
   support for Bolshevik Party   130–131

withdraws from Labour Party   169
See also East London Federation of Suf-
   fragettes, Communist Party (British
   Section of the Third International)
Workers' Union   119, 151
Women's International League for Peace and
   Freedom   155
Women's Labour League   64
Women's Social and Political Union   63, 80
Women's Suffrage Federation (see East Lon-
   don Federation of Suffragettes)
Worsell, Leonard   45
Wrigley, Chris   46

Yates, Arnold   163
Yates, George   29, 30

Zamyatin, Yevgeny   33
Zasulich, Vera   32
Zetkin, Clara   64, 163, 220
Zilliacus, Konni   33
Zimmerwald conference (1915)   82, 108–110
Zinoviev, Grigory   196, 213, 220, 223, 227
Zollner, John   142
Zumoff, Jacob   5